JOSEPH CONRAD
LIFE AND LETTERS

JOSEPH CONRAD

LIFE AND LETTERS

by

G. JEAN-AUBRY

Volume I

Published by

DOUBLEDAY, PAGE & CO.

GARDEN CITY

NEW YORK

1927

TO EDWARD GARNETT AND ROBERT CUNNINGHAME GRAHAM

To you I dedicate this book: not only because you are likely to be among those most interested in it, but because you two were the first friends Conrad's writings won for him, and because your friendship, which he valued greatly, lasted till the day he died. Better than others you know with what engaging and simple sincerity he used to talk about his childhood and his youth; but though his talk about himself was free from pose and mystification, that past was so unusual that none of us could feel sure that our knowledge of it was either accurate or complete.

Naturally, in these days, when curiosity is keener than the desire for truth, the picturesqueness of such a career bred many rumours, the inaccuracy of which merely amused Conrad himself, who was quite indifferent to notoriety. Nevertheless, it should be possible—and it is most desirable—to trace every step in that strange career, and this is what I have tried to do, trusting that the narration of plain facts would reveal most clearly his greatness as a man. And more than that, my plan of following minutely the events of his life will show how immense was the transmuting power of his imagination and that nothing happened to him in vain.

It would have been easy for me, who have lived in some intimacy both with Conrad and his books, to introduce my own sentiments and opinions in the course of it, but I have carefully, even regretfully, abstained; perhaps some day I shall write from a more personal point of view.

Long before Conrad died and left us our unfading memories, I began to collect material for this biography, little thinking, however, that I should be so suddenly entrusted with the melancholy task of tracing the path through life of one of the rarest spirits of our times. I cannot flatter myself that I have unravelled every puzzle; some incidents still remain obscure: but you will find nothing conjectural in this book, nothing unsupported by documentary evidence. If others, more fortunate, should some day discover facts unknown to me, I can at least feel sure that their discoveries will not discredit what is here recorded. The Bibliography at the end will show that my authorities have been diverse and many.

v

It was thought best that Conrad's Letters should be bound up with his biography, and the selection has devolved upon me. I have done my best to choose among not less than two thousand of his letters, English, French, and Polish. Some of the latter have been translated and included, but those written in French are so many and so individual in style that it has been decided to publish them, later, in a book for a French-reading public. The English letters are, of course, much the most numerous: so numerous, indeed, that it was impossible to include them all, though many of those which had to be omitted are nearly as worthy of publication.

I must thank you both for the personal recollections which you have put at my disposal, for your good advice, and for the letters you have entrusted to my discretion.[1]

I should like also to take this opportunity of thanking others who have contributed to the making of this book. First, Mrs. Conrad and Miss Angèle Zagórska, the cousin of our friend: both of them have helped me immensely by allowing me to draw upon those memories of Conrad which they treasure. I must thank, too, His Excellency Mr. Skirmunt, Polish Minister in Great Britain, Miss Cecile Podoska and Mr. F. B. Czarnowski of the Polish Legation in London: M. and Mme C. Godebski, Mme Luniewska, née Rakowska, who have helped me with Polish documents; Sir Sidney Colvin, Sir Edmund Gosse, Sir Hugh Clifford, Messrs. Richard Curle, John Galsworthy, Spiridion Kliszczewski, Desmond MacCarthy, Eric Pinker, E. L. Sanderson, and H. G. Wells. I also wish to thank the manager of the "Société Anonyme Belge pour le Commerce du Haut-Congo"; M. Berthet, Maritime Administrator at Havre; M. Nègre, Maritime Administrator at Marseilles; M. Joseph Colmain, clerk of the Maritime Registry at Marseilles; Captain Nicholson, secretary to the Ship Masters' Association, and Mr. Basil Lubbock: also Mr. Henry James, nephew of the distinguished novelist, and, lastly, Mr. T. J. Wise, who has generously lent me some of the treasures of his valuable Conrad library.

I have endeavoured, in writing this life, to do service to the memory of one who is equally dear to us; nor do I forget that it is to the devotion which we share that I also owe the kindness you have shown me and the right to sign myself now

Your affectionate and grateful friend,

G. JEAN-AUBRY.

[1] Some of Joseph Conrad's letters to Edward Garnett have been included. The whole of this correspondence will be published shortly in a separate volume.

CONTENTS

VOLUME I

NOTE

Throughout these two volumes, where references to pages in the books of Joseph Conrad are made, the page numbers given are those of the Uniform Edition of the Works of Joseph Conrad (J. M. Dent & Sons, Ltd., London) and the Concord Edition of the Works of Joseph Conrad (Doubleday, Page & Co., Garden City, New York).

LIST OF ILLUSTRATIONS

JOSEPH CONRAD LIFE AND LETTERS

CHAPTER I

POLISH YEARS

(1857–1874)

My young days, the days when one's habits and character are formed, have been rather familiar with long silences.

("A PERSONAL RECORD," A FAMILIAR PREFACE)

TOWARD the middle of the last century, at the time of the Crimean War, there lived at Oratow, in Podolia—one of the southern provinces of Poland under Russian rule—a family of landowners, Bobrowski by name. Ten years before, they had been a large family, but by 1855 the father, Joseph Bobrowski, and the two eldest sons were already dead, as also one daughter Teofila, who had died suddenly at the age of eighteen.[1] Mme Bobrowska remained on the land which had belonged to her husband's family for several generations. She lived there with her four remaining sons, Stanislas, Thaddeus, Casimir, and Stefan, and one daughter, Evelina.

On April 28, 1856, Evelina Bobrowska married Apollo Nalecz Korzeniowski at the village church of Oratow. The

---

[1] The sources of information concerning Joseph Conrad's family are: the *Memoirs* of his uncle Thaddeus Bobrowski, published posthumously in 1900; a manuscript document by the same and called, "For the information of my dear nephew Conrad Korzeniowski," which we will henceforth call the "Bobrowski Document," and another also by him called "Information which may be useful to you" (both these documents were found amongst the novelist's papers, together with photographs and family papers which I have also used): letters from Apollo Korzeniowski to his friend Casimir Kaszewski (now in the Jagellon Library at Cracow); a book by Michael Rolle, *In Illo Tempore*, published at Lwów in 1914, and finally, two volumes by Conrad himself: *A Personal Record* and *Notes on Life and Letters*.

young man was thirty-six,[1] the bride twenty-five. Had it depended on the lovers they would have been united several years earlier; but the girl's father had consistently opposed their union. There was no fault to find with the young man on the score of either birth or morals, but he was ardent and changeable. He had no settled position, and, in addition, he betrayed literary inclinations which were naturally disquieting to a family of provincial nobles as deeply rooted in the soil as the Bobrowskis. Although the young man came from a good family on his father's side, and very good Lithuanian stock, the Dyakewicz, on his mother's side, he had no money of his own. Teodor Korzeniowski, his father, after having served as a lieutenant in the Napoleonic armies in 1807, and later as a captain in the Polish Army during the first insurrection in 1831, had lost, through unfortunate speculation, the greater part of the modest property he once possessed at Pienkowa, in the Winnica district of Podolia. According to Thaddeus Bobrowski, Apollo Korzeniowski's father was the best fellow in the world, but a very excitable and moody man. The Korzeniowskis had the reputation of being extremely talented and great talkers, with rather malicious tongues.[2]

Apollo Korzeniowski began his school education at Niemirow and continued his studies at Winnica. At the High School at Jitomir in Volhynia he made the acquaintance of his future brother-in-law, Thaddeus Bobrowski, who was considerably younger than himself. The effect of a haphazard education upon such a character was what might have been

[1] "Your father was born in 1820" (Bobrowski Document); "He was born at Janow, February 21st, 1820." (Michael Rolle, *In Illo Tempore*, p. 30.)

[2] There were at that time several families in Poland by the name of Korzeniowski who were not related to one another. Another of these families also became illustrious through an author, Joseph Korzeniowski (born 1797, died 1863), a novelist and dramatist of merit. Before 1826, he had written dramas under the influence of Shakespeare and Schiller, and poems after Byron. Later, he wrote novels and comedies in which life in Warsaw and the Polish Provinces is shrewdly depicted.

If Conrad did not use his real name of Korzeniowski when he began to write, it was probably because, even as a sailor, the difficulties he had encountered in the writing and pronouncing of his name had led him to adopt his more simple Christian name of Conrad; but the existence of the other Polish novelist, called Korzeniowski, whose work Conrad knew, would have been enough in itself to deter him from using his surname as an author.

expected: he finished his studies without distinction. But he already shone as a talker in the salons at Jitomir. Toward 1840, he went to St. Petersburg when he took up, rather lazily, Oriental languages; these he abandoned for the Faculty of Arts, a subject more suited to his tastes and gifts. Though he neglected his regular studies, he read indefatigably, more particularly French literature, for which he had a strong taste. It was only later that he learnt English sufficiently well to read it. Without profound culture, he possessed quick intuition and a natural taste for good literature. At an early age he showed a poetic gift which, together with the studied elegance of his dress, made him remarkable among the squires with whom he lived.

In 1847 he met Mlle Bobrowska at Koryna near Lipowiec, and almost immediately fell in love with her. She was very beautiful; her education was superior to that of most women of her time: she was eager-minded and seemed to expect much from life. But, even then, her health was not very robust, and an agitating and absorbing love affair certainly did not help to improve it. Apollo Korzeniowski was ardent, and although he was not generally considered handsome, he was not lacking in charm. His mind was active, and though he was thoroughly good-hearted he could be sarcastic in repartee; his vivacious eyes and his whole personality radiated a kind of flame capable of kindling more than one heart.

Evelina Bobrowska had fought against her feelings for a long time in obedience to her father who, although he liked Apollo Korzeniowski, did not fancy him as a son-in-law notwithstanding that he was the spoilt darling of society, where he dominated people of maturer age by the charm of his light conversation and his caustic wit, while at the same time conciliating them by that old-fashioned Polish courtesy of manner which was natural to him. His own generation were attracted by his animation, generosity, and malicious sarcasm.

When her father died, Evelina Bobrowska did not wish to seem disrespectful to his memory, or indifferent to his views, but she remained deeply in love with Apollo Korzeniowski. For several years she was so tortured by scruples and contradictory impulses that her health suffered greatly.[1] Her relations were concerned about her. Mme Bobrowska could not bear the thought of losing her only remaining daughter through continuing to oppose her—besides, the young man himself pleased her, and he was a great friend of her own sons, who adored their sister. The marriage took place.

The dowry of the young woman was modest: eight thousand roubles, some silver, a trousseau, a few pieces of furniture. Apollo Korzeniowski, who had found something to do in order to marry Evelina Bobrowska, was now managing Mme Melanie Sobanska's property, an estate in the area of Luczyniec, in Podolia, and there the young couple spent the first year of their married life, while waiting for the marriage settlement to be paid out of the sale of her father's estate.

The following year, the dowry having been paid, Apollo Korzeniowski rented the Derebczynka property in the jurisdiction of Mohilow, and on December 3, 1857, at Berdiczew, their only child was born. He was christened Teodor Josef Konrad Korzeniowski.[2]

The family lived almost continuously from 1857 to the end of 1859 on the Derebczynka property; but the failure of this undertaking, which in three years drained their resources and in part those of Mme Bobrowska, who had taken a third share in the lease, decided Apollo Korzeniowski to seek fortune in other ways. Husband, wife, and child moved to Jitomir, a short distance off.

---

[1] See *A Personal Record*, p. 28. The words which Conrad puts in the mouth of his uncle Thaddeus Bobrowski about his mother are an almost literal translation of a passage from *Memoirs*, by Thaddeus Bobrowski, Vol. I, p. 362.

[2] Although other dates have been given—even during Joseph Conrad's lifetime—as the date of his birth, December 3, 1857, can be taken as certain. It was confirmed on two occasions by Thaddeus Bobrowski: "You were born at Berdiczew on November 21st" (Bobrowski Document); "You came into the world in 1857, at Berdiczew, on November 21st (Information which may be useful to you)." Which, with the twelve days between the Gregorian and the Russian calendars, makes December 3, 1857. This date, December 3, 1857, is also carried on the Standard Life Insurance Society's certificate in Joseph Conrad's policy of January 21, 1901. Finally, Conrad himself writes in 1897, "Thanks many times for the book. I see you put the date 3rd of Dec. Did you know that on that day I went over the rise of forty to travel downwards, and a little more lonely than before?" (Letter to Edward Garnett, December 7, 1897.)

Apollo Korzeniowski, who had many connections there, hoped to turn his literary gifts to some profit. He had a genuine poetic gift, and as a critic he was lively and just. He was then extremely interested in French and English literature, and his translations are still held in high estimation by Polish men of letters. A letter to his friend Casimir Kaszewski, written soon after his arrival at Jitomir, shows that, as a translator, he did not confine himself to easy subjects.[1]

Could not my translation of "Le Sacre de la Femme" [he writes], the first legend in the *Légende des Siècles,* be printed? Even though, in my opinion, it was perhaps harder to translate than to write, I do not ask to be paid, for I know that the Warsaw Library is not rolling in money.[2]

The young couple remained about two years at Jitomir. Count Alexandre Wielopolski's policy had just succeeded in obtaining mitigation of Russian tyranny in Poland, and hope began to rise again in those who, for three generations, had not ceased to dream of regaining national independence. The younger Poles were impatient. They had small sympathy with Wielopolski's discreet half measures, or with the hesitations of those who had seen the failure of the insurrection in 1831.

Apollo Korzeniowski had many friends in both political groups. They urged him to come to Warsaw, and he yielded the more readily since he had just quarrelled with the committee of a publishing firm of which he was member and secretary. He arrived at Warsaw in the spring of 1862 with the intention of starting a literary paper of the *Revue des Deux-Mondes* type, to be called the *Fortnightly Review.*

[1] Casimir Kaszewski (1813–1890) critic and translator. He produced remarkable Polish translations of the ancient classics and had a profound knowledge of the Eighteenth and Nineteenth Century philosophers. He was then living in Warsaw.

[2] The letters of Apollo Korzeniowski to Casimir Kaszewski are filed in the library of the Cracow University. It is to these letters that Conrad alluded when he wrote in *First News:* "Next day the Librarian of the University invited me to come and have a look at the library. . . . 'There is a bundle of correspondence that will appeal to you personally. Those are letters written by your father to an intimate friend in whose papers they were found. They contain many references to yourself, though you couldn't have been more than four years old at the time. Your father seems to have been extremely interested in his son.'" (*Notes on Life and Letters,* p. 175. See also, *A Personal Record,* Author's Note, p. xi.)

Before his departure, the little Conrad, who had only been privately baptized, was officially baptized at the Roman Catholic Church at Jitomir;[1] and as Apollo Korzeniowski did not wish to be separated for long from his wife and child, they joined him in Warsaw in the beginning of the autumn.[2] The intimate tenderness between them, and the intensity of their patriotic sentiments—possibly even more concentrated in her—lead us to infer that she knew the real reasons that had drawn her husband to Warsaw. Perhaps she even suggested his going herself.

Under cover of literary activities—real, nevertheless—Apollo Korzeniowski was, in fact, about to help in organizing the secret National Committee. Its object was to encourage moral resistance to Russian oppression and ultimately to win back independence.[3] This movement culminated in the unfortunate insurrection which broke out in Warsaw on January 22, 1863, in which Apollo Korzeniowski was not fated to take a part. The Russian authorities, informed by their spies, already knew of the clandestine meetings in the white and scarlet salon of Apollo Korzeniowski's house. Little Conrad sometimes saw people with grave faces enter and disappear, among them his mother, always dressed in black as a sign of national mourning, though this was forbidden by the Russian police. These were the first meetings of the National Committee. At the end of October, 1862, Apollo Korzeniowski was arrested and imprisoned in the citadel. Mme Jozefowa Bobrowska immediately hurried to Warsaw to support her daughter and to try what her influence could do, but all was in vain. Convicted of conspiracy against the Imperial government, after a hasty trial, the Polish patriot was condemned to exile.

He was judged by a committee presided over by a Colonel

[1] Extract from the certificate of baptism obtained May 10, 1872, on the request of Th. Bobrowski.

[2] The portraits given here of Joseph Conrad's father and mother date from this year (1862), as well as that of Conrad himself as a child with a whip in his hand, on the back of which was written: "To my dear Alexander, in remembrance, 1862. Apollo Korzeniowski." These three photographs bear the following inscription on the back: "Zaklad Fotograficzny.—Karola Beyera.—W. Warszawie."

[3] See *A Personal Record*, Author's Note p. xi.

Roznow, who had been his brother-in-law Stanislas's comrade in the Grodno Hussars. This connection accounts for the "relatively light" sentence passed by the military court. Apollo Korzeniowski was to be deported to a distant part of Russia but not to Siberia. He had asked to be sent to Perm.[1] He had hoped that the Governor Laszkarew, being one of his old university comrades, might relax a little from the regimen of political convicts in his favour: but Laszkarew ignored an acquaintance which might have compromised him. His young wife requested to be allowed to accompany her husband, and permission was granted on condition that she herself be subjected to the same discipline. She was now thirty, and though physically frail, she was spirited and inflexible. She accepted that condition.

Meeting with calm fortitude the cruel trials of a life reflecting all the national and social misfortunes of the community, she realized the highest conceptions of duty as a wife, a mother and a patriot, sharing the exile of her husband and representing nobly the ideal of Polish womanhood.[2]

While they were on their way to Perm, orders arrived to send the prisoner to Vologda in northern Russia, and during the last stage of the journey toward Moscow, the little Conrad fell seriously ill. The escort peremptorily refused to allow them to break the journey. Fortunately, a traveller who overtook them on the road offered to ride on to Moscow and fetch a doctor. Korzeniowski remembered that he had an old friend who was a professor of medicine in Moscow University, who arrived in time to save the child, and succeeded in inducing the escort to wait until it should be better. A little later, Mme Korzeniowska herself became so ill that the escort were obliged to carry her. An officer who met them on the outskirts of Nijni Novgorod was so shocked by the brutality and insolence with which the prisoners were treated that he galloped to the town and lodged a complaint with the police.

---

[1] Perm is situated in the most eastern part of European Russia, on the Volga, not far from the Ural Mountains.

[2] *A Personal Record*, p. 29. These words, which Conrad puts in the mouth of his uncle, are taken from the latter's *Memoirs*.

He obtained from official headquarters permission for the young wife to rest in an inn for a few days.

The convoy reached Vologda in the first fortnight of February. The Governor, Treminski, who had been a Maréchal de la Noblesse, was a humane man, treating with a certain measure of kindness the small colony of deported Poles, who numbered about twenty-one, under his charge. The climate, however, was extremely severe, especially for people used to more southern regions. Nearly all the Poles suffered from scurvy, and although the Korzeniowskis escaped that, their vital strength diminished to an extent which was soon to prove fatal.

Of their exile to Vologda we possess a touching souvenir, a photograph of little Conrad, aged five, on the back of which he has written: "To my dear grandmother who helped me to send cakes to my poor father in prison—Pole Catholic, gentleman. July 6th, 1863. Konrad." [1]

To the severity of the climate were added the miseries of defeated patriotism and family bereavement. The insurrection had completely failed; the repression which followed was harsher than ever. Apollo's two brothers, Robert and Hilary, were among the victims. Robert had been killed fighting (he was fifty years of age), and Hilary had been sent to Siberia, where he died ten years later. Mme Korzeniowska had lost the youngest and most brilliant of her brothers, Stefan, who had been one of the moving spirits of the Polish insurrection and a member of the brief national revolutionary government of 1862. He was killed in a duel shortly before the rising.

The Korzeniowskis' privations in exile were great. They had practically no money, and they were kept alive by Casimir Bobrowski who, unknown to the rest of the family, sent his brother-in-law what little money he had—one or two thousand roubles.

From the moment Apollo Korzeniowski arrived at Vologda, he became the leader and inspirer of the little band of exiles,

---

[1] This inscription reminds us of the words that Conrad puts into the mouth of J. M. K. Blunt, one of the characters in the *Arrow of Gold:* "American, Catholic and gentleman."

supporting their courage and keeping alive in them a patriotic spirit that enabled them to bear their sufferings with dignity. It seems that, thanks to his influence and that of his wife, the Polish exiles not only won respect from the Russians, but, in many cases, affection. The Governor and the colonel of the gendarmes often came to see the Korzeniowskis.

During the summer of 1863 they were permitted, in consideration of Mme Korzeniowska's state of health, to leave Vologda for Tchernikow, which was farther south and nearer their own province and the government of Kiev. And thanks to their having some interest among influential Petersburg people, Mme Korzeniowska obtained the unusual grace of three months' leave. Taking her little boy with her, she left for Nowofastow, where her brother Thaddeus had recently bought an estate. Her relations and friends came from far and near to show their devotion to one who had confessed "her faith in national salvation by suffering exile." [1] Her health was shattered by what she had undergone, and many knew that they were probably seeing her for the last time. Her only chance of recovery would have been to stay longer in a warm climate and among those who loved her, but permission was refused. A fortnight before she was due to leave, she was suddenly taken ill, so ill that she seemed utterly unfit for the journey, but even a fortnight's grace was denied her. The head of the district police came one evening asking to speak to Thaddeus Bobrowski and handed him the official order.

"There. Pray read this. I have no business to show this paper to you. It is wrong of me. But I can't either eat or sleep with such a job hanging over me."

That police captain, a native of Great Russia, had been for many years serving in the district. My uncle unfolded and read the document. It was a service order issued from the Governor General's Secretariat, dealing with the matter of the petition and directing the police captain to disregard all remonstrances and explanations in regard to that illness either from medical men or others. "And if she has not left her brother's house," it went on to say, "on the morning of the day specified on her

[1] *A Personal Record*, p. 63.

permit, you are to dispatch her at once under escort, *direct* to the prison hospital in Kiev, where she will be treated as her case demands."

"For God's sake, Mr. Bobrowski, see that your sister goes away punctually on that day. Don't give me this work to do with a woman,—and one of your family too. I simply cannot bear to think of it." He was absolutely wringing his hands. My uncle looked at him in silence.

"Thank you for this warning. I assure you that even if she were dying, she would be carried out to the carriage." "Yes—indeed—and what difference would it make—to travel to Kiev or back to her husband? For she would have to go—death or no death. And mind, Mr. Bobrowski, I will be here on the day, not that I doubt your promise, but because I must. I have got to. Duty. All the same, my trade is not fit for a dog since some of you Poles will persist in rebelling, and all of you have got to suffer for it." [1]

Conrad, a child of six, was, of course, unaware of all this, nor did he understand that the doctors had given his mother up. At Nowofastow, in his uncle's house, he met his little cousin Josephine, "a delightful and vivacious little girl a few months younger than he." [2] He also saw something of the neighbours' children. This was the first time that he had lived with children of his own age, and the happy interval lasted only three months. Though he could not understand the full significance of what was happening, the tragic sadness of that day when he and his mother were forced to tear themselves away from their relations and take again the road to Russia remained graven in his memory. Forty-five years later, he described that scene with the perfect and noble restraint of which he was a master.

The elongated, bizarre, shabby travelling carriage with four post horses, standing before the long front of the house with its eight columns, four on each side of the broad flight of stairs. On the steps, groups of servants, a few relations, one or two friends from the nearest neighbourhood, a perfect silence, on all the faces an air of sober concentration; my grandmother all in black gazing stoically, my uncle giving his arm to my mother down to the carriage in which I had been placed already; at

[1] *A Personal Record*, pp. 66–67.
[2] Thaddeus Bobrowski lost his wife in 1858 when his daughter Josephine was born.

Apollo Nalecz Korzeniowski, Joseph Conrad's father (1862)

the top of the flight my little cousin in a short skirt of a tartan pattern with a deal of red in it, and like a small princess attended by the women of her own household: the head *gouvernante,* our dear corpulent friend Francesca (who had been for thirty years in the service of the Bobrowski family), the former nurse, now outdoor attendant, a handsome peasant face wearing a compassionate expression, and the good, ugly Mademoiselle Durand, the governess, with her black eyebrows meeting over a short thick nose, and a complexion like pale brown paper. Of all the eyes turned towards the carriage, her good-natured eyes only were dropping tears, and it was her sobbing voice alone that broke the silence with an appeal to me: *"N'oublie pas ton français, mon chéri."* In three months, simply by playing with us, she had taught me not only to speak French, but to read it as well. She was indeed an excellent playmate. In the distance, halfway down to the great gates, a light, open trap, harnessed with three horses in Russian fashion, stood drawn up on one side with the police captain of the district sitting in it, the visor of his flat cap with a red band pulled down over his eyes.[1]

The Governor General of Kiev had not only refused Bobrowski's petition, he had written in the margin of the order: "To be carried out to the letter." He had taken no count of the fact that Mme Korzeniowska was a voluntary exile, or that a dying woman and a small child were not likely to be politically dangerous. History has preserved his name; he was called Bezak. At Tchernikow, Mme Korzeniowska's health became rapidly worse. In 1864 her frightened mother came to see her and to help her to look after little Conrad, and in the midst of these troubles Apollo Korzeniowski received the news of the sudden death of his father. In the New Year of 1865, Thaddeus Bobrowski went to see the exiles, taking with him a doctor who held out small hope of saving his sister. In February he returned again to see her. She was now far gone in consumption and the doctor told him that she was lost. A letter from Apollo Korzeniowski, dated February 26th, to his friend Casimir Kaszewski shows that he himself had no illusions about her condition.

My poor wife has been dying, for several years, of homesickness and from the repeated blows which have fallen on our family. During the last few months she has been cruelly and gravely ill. The lack of every-

[1] *A Personal Record,* pp. 64–65.

thing here to support body and soul—the lack of doctors and medical necessaries have brought her to this condition. I myself have been obliged to do everything in the house, to be both master and servant. I do not complain, or rather, only of the fact that I cannot satisfy or comfort her. Our little Conrad is inevitably neglected in the midst of all this.[1]

Two days later he again pours out his sorrows and despair to his friend:

Homesickness, like a rust, has slowly eaten away my poor wife's strength. A year and a half ago she attributed her condition to nerves. In my anxiety—I could never have done it for myself—I begged and prayed that we might be moved from this place. My petition having been repeatedly refused I have lost all hope. Since many months she has been suffering from fever, tuberculosis and an internal tumour, the result of bad circulation, which calls for an operation. . . . Her mind alone remains unshaken. I ask myself, is this courage or does she not know how ill she really is? Who could read the answer in her eyes, if I, to whom they have ever been an open book, cannot see what is written there? And yet, I cannot read her eyes. Only, sometimes, a stronger pressure of her hand in mine, or in little Conrad's, betrays her courage. We are wretched and unhappy indeed, but we thank God that we have been allowed at least to bear it all together.[2]

Her mother, Mme Bobrowska, and her brother, Thaddeus, were called to her side at the beginning of March, and they remained with her until she died on April 6, 1865. She was thirty-four years old. She is buried at Tchernikow.

When she died Apollo Korzeniowski lost not only the only person he cared for, but his hold on life. The hopes that had so long sustained him were withering in the shadow of the Russian Empire, a "shadow lowering with the darkness of a new-born national hatred fostered by the Moscow school of journalists against the Poles." [3] His patriotic hopes had turned to ashes. His eyes were now constantly fixed upon his own death, which religious faith enabled him to contemplate without fear. It approached less rapidly than he expected. He lingered on for another four years, devoting what strength

[1] Letters now in the library of the Cracow University.
[2] Letter to Casimir Kaszewski, February 28, 1865.
[3] A Personal Record, p. 24.

he had to work which could bring him neither profit nor glory. He had never been personally ambitious, and now he had lost all that was dear to him, such aims were meaningless to him. The day after his wife died he already thought of placing his little son in safer hands than his own. To Casimir Kaszewski he writes:

Do you remember saying to me at the sad moment of our parting, while you were looking at our little Conrad, "If you do not come back soon, send him to me and I will look after him as my own son"? Now that she will never return and I maybe will not come back, and little Conrad will probably have to grow up without me, fulfil your promise. He is all that remains of her on this earth and I want him to be a worthy witness to what she was. Who, better than you, could bring him up to be worthy of her? Her heart and soul were so set upon this child that I cannot leave him, I cannot separate myself from him, unless I feel certain that he will fulfil her hopes; and to take no steps to that end would be, it seems to me, to be false to my poor wife. I have arranged that Conrad should have a little patrimony sufficient for his education and something more. I have made all the necessary sacrifices to secure his future.[1] He may add to your cares but, at least, he will not be an expense to you. Tell me, dear friend, if you will do this for me, so that I may know what instructions I ought to give those into whose hands, when the time comes, the little orphaned Conrad will fall.

Thus, deprived of his mother and in the company of a father already ill and more often than not sunk in gloomy silence, exiled among men whom he could regard only as enemies, Conrad spent his early childhood. He had no companions, no child to play with; and the tension in the atmosphere which had surrounded him from birth now approached its height. His surroundings brought home to him ideas which seldom come close to men in childhood, death, faith, and liberty. Unconsciously he was being trained in a secret and inflexible fidelity to ideals disassociated from hope. There was only one door open to him leading from the world

---

[1] Apollo Korzeniowski's health and his exile prevented him from earning a living. He was forced to depend on his brother-in-law Thaddeus Bobrowski to support the child, and he received from him an income of 400 roubles himself. In 1866 Conrad's great uncle Nicholas Bobrowski died and left him a small legacy which afterward formed the greater part of the small capital which his uncle Thaddeus put aside to provide an allowance for Conrad.

in which he lived, one escape for his lively imagination—
reading. His father was a man of fifty and physically tired,
but among the ruins of his hopes he kept a love of all literature which bore the stamp of deep and human thought. His
child, too, took refuge in reading omnivorously and haphaz-
ardly, often books far too serious for his age. He read for
many hours on end with his elbows on his knees and his fore-
head in his hands, day after day, in their small silent house
on the outskirts of Tchernikow. He revelled in books which
described countries where it was possible to breathe and act
freely, to fight openly, if necessary, and to speak thoughts
above a whisper. A longing was born in him to fly to those
strange distant countries where one could be free. Sometimes
these were Polish books, but more often they were French,
for French literature often escaped the supervision of the
Russian authorities. His father's library was not a large one,
and so, for lack of new books, in the absence, too, of games
and amusements, the child often went back to the same page,
to dream over it and live in it, as though the characters and
landscapes described there were real. He was born with a
strong imagination, and his sensitiveness had been intensified
by the sight of the sufferings of those he loved. Living in close
companionship with a father to whom death was a familiar
thought, and for whom life had no longer any attraction,
the child was driven to live in a world only created by his
own imagination.

Apollo Korzeniowski's vitality diminished day by day. He
spent his time in writing and translating the works he admired. He wrote his Memoirs, which began with the preparations for the insurrection, but these he decided to destroy
before his death. Sometimes little Conrad would enter softly
the room in which his father was writing. One day his father
found him there kneeling in his chair, head on elbows, absorbed in the translation of *Two Gentlemen of Verona*, upon
which Korzeniowski was at work. This was Conrad's first
taste of English literature. A month before, Apollo Korzeniowski being ill in bed, the child had read aloud to him the
proofs of his translation of Victor Hugo's *Travailleurs de la
Mer*. It had made an immediate, deep, and durable impression

upon him. It was the first book that directed his imagination toward the sea.

His father divined that such surroundings in which feelings were suppressed for fear they might undermine self-control were likely to develop in a child a serious melancholy and a stoical despair. He set about educating him as best he could. On September 18, 1865, he writes to his friend:

How can I thank you for all your kindness to my poor little orphan. What you have promised him was our dream in the days of our deepest distress and it has helped us through trying times. Your promise to send me school books and directions for study fills me with joy. I await its fulfilment with impatience. Sell my writing table to buy these books. It was her favourite piece of furniture but she will never see me sitting at it again. The poor child does not know what it is to have a companion of his own age. He sees the sadness of my old age, and who knows, perhaps that sight may freeze and wither his own young heart; that is one of the chief reasons which makes me wish to send him away from me.[1]

Nevertheless, he found it very difficult to reconcile himself to separation from his son, the only visible link with the past and the future, with the woman he had lost and with the country from which he had been exiled. A little later he wrote again to his friend, and his words this time seem to suggest that he already divined the deep nature of his child and noticed in him characteristics which he had inherited from both parents.

I remind you again of your promise to send school books and outlines of study for my little Conrad. I want to prepare him on sound lines. Since autumn my health has not a little declined and my little one has had to take care of me. We are alone here. For his heart I have no fear, for it is his mother's, and as far as his intellectual gifts are concerned (though these are hardly enviable) he has inherited mine.[2]

A letter written in the same year to his cousin Jan Zagórski, shows more clearly his own character, the religious resignation habitual to him:

[1] Kaszewski Letters, Cracow University Library.
[2] Apollo Korzeniowski's letter, October 31, 1865.

I have passed through heavy and even terrible days of brooding on God's blessings and, if I survive, it will not be thanks to my own, but God's strength. I know I have not suffered and never could suffer like our Saviour, but then I am only a human being. I have kept my eyes fixed on the Cross and by that means fortified my fainting soul and reeling brain. The sacred days of agony have passed, and I resume my ordinary life, a little more broken but with breath still in me, still alive. But the little orphan is always at my side, and I never forget my anxiety for him. And so, my friends, I am still alive, and still love what is left me, and still love as fervently as ever, though I can no longer give anything to the object of my affections. Whatever remains for me to do in life, I cannot either sacrifice or give anything, for I have nothing to sacrifice or offer up. It is sad indeed for a man to see the two doors through which alone he can approach the presence of God shut against him, but such is the will of Providence. When my bitterness chokes me, I read your second dear letter and the pride of despair changes into divine sadness. My tears flow, but their fount is reason. Then, my composure recovered, I take up my life again, which is entirely centred upon my little Conrad. I teach him what I know, but that, unfortunately, is little. I shield him from the atmosphere of this place, and he grows up as though in a monastic cell. For the *memento mori* we have the grave of our dear one, and every letter which reaches us is the equivalent of a day of fasting, a hair shirt or a discipline. We shiver with cold, we die of hunger. We are overwhelmed by the destitution of our fellowmen, our brothers, but prayer remains to us, and in our prayers I call God to witness there is scarce a word about ourselves. Should I describe this place I would say that on one side it is bounded by locked doors behind which the being dearest to me breathed her last, without my being able to wipe even the death sweat from her brow, while on the other, though there the doors are open, I may not cross the threshold, and I see, what Dante did *not* describe, for his soul, appalled through it was with terror, was too Christian to harbour inhuman visions. Such is our life.

During the May of this year, Apollo Korzeniowski at last made up his mind to part from his son, and till the following September Conrad was sent to his uncle at Nowofastow in Polish Ukraine, to improve his health and in order that he might lead the normal life of a child of nine with companions of his own age. At the end of the same month Mme Bobrowska brought him back to his father, but he grew sickly and his grandmother was obliged to take him to doctors at Kiev, where he remained during the early winter months. The first weeks of 1867 he spent as a convalescent at his uncle's house at Nowofastow.

His father's regret at having to part from him is easy to understand; but the child too, on his side, seems to have been homesick for that atmosphere of sad exaltation to which he had been so long accustomed. Such a feeling in the child seems to indicate an affinity between the natures of father and son, and to forecast that profound nostalgia which lies behind Conrad's genius, and of which we find such abundant evidence in his works.

The manner in which strong feeling is concealed beneath surface irony in the following letter written by Apollo Korzeniowski is not uncharacteristic of Conrad himself:

Conrad has gone to his uncle in the country. We are both of us unhappy. The child is silly enough to be troubled about my solitude and to regret a life in which my gloomy face and his lessons have been his only distractions. He pines for me in spite of the country and games with a cousin of his own age. Even under the wing of his grandmother's tender care and in spite of the indulgencies of his uncle who spoils him and has transferred to him all the love he had for his mother, the boy pines for me. As his uncle always thought the unforgotten dead a wonderful human being, he lavishes on the little boy a sort of tender respect. He languishes because he is a little fool. I am afraid he will always be one. He has grown, his face has changed; he begins to resemble his mother. May God bless him, for I, alas, cannot and never shall be able to do anything for him.[1]

While Conrad was at Nowofastow, Prince Roman Sanguszko came to see his uncle. Conrad has described this hero accurately in his story "Prince Roman." [2]

Conrad spent the spring and summer of 1867 with his uncle at Nowofastow, and this was the last visit he was des-

[1] Letter to Casimir Kaszewski, November 22, 1866.

[2] *Tales of Hearsay*, pp. 97 *et seq.* The prince was an old comrade in arms of his grandfather Korzeniowski, during the insurrection of 1831. He was sentenced to Siberia for life and survived service in the Siberian mines. Later he was allowed to serve as a common soldier in the Caucasus. He returned to Poland fourteen years later completely deaf, and he devoted the remainder of his strength and fortune to helping his compatriots who had returned from exile. It is probable that Conrad's childish recollection of him was revived on reading the passages about him in his uncle's *Memoirs*, Vol. I, pp. 372–73.

tined to make to Ukraine for nearly twenty-five years. In the autumn he went to stay with his grandmother at Jitomir.

His father's health continued its downward course. Indeed, his energies were now so obviously on the wane that the Russian authorities no longer feared him. In the beginning of December, 1867, thanks to the intervention of Mme Bobrowska, the Minister of the Interior signed a passport available for one year "to nobleman Apollo Korzeniowski, accompanied by his son Conrad, ten years old, to go to Algiers and Madeira." It reached the exiles in January of the next year. Apollo Korzeniowski was not well enough to travel so far. After spending some weeks with his people in Ukraine, he took up his residence in Lemberg in Galicia, where Conrad was sent to the Polish High School, although neither the system of teaching nor the accent of the Polish taught there was to his father's taste.

Since 1866, the persecution of Poles by the Prussian and Russian governments had redoubled, but the Austrian government, after its defeat at Sadowa, had adopted the policy of conciliating the Poles within its frontiers. Shortly after Apollo Korzeniowski's arrival in Galicia, that province obtained a relative autonomy. Galician Poles were allowed to speak their own language, and the comparative liberty which they enjoyed awoke in Korzeniowski a new desire for life. He wrote to his friend, Kaszewski:

I am absorbed in looking after my own health and also Conrad's. I am deep in the mountains at Topolnica and my time is so taken up with drinking sheep's milk that when the Imperial and Royal police came to ask how I spent my time in Galicia, I was able conscientiously to answer "drinking sheep's milk." My boy's complaint has come back and causes him painful cramps in the stomach. It is difficult to teach him anything while he is unwell: he is already eleven and two years have passed since he learnt anything. He is a dear fellow.

When term began in October, Conrad was still too unwell to go to school and his father decided that he should stay at home and study under his supervision. Another reason for this decision was that the Polish spoken at Lemberg was exceedingly bad. He constantly returns to this subject in his

Evelina Korzeniowska, *née* Bobrowska, Joseph Conrad's mother
(1862)

letters. On Christmas Eve he writes that the child is much better, though he is of a very nervous temperament. Korzeniowski meant to devote himself to journalistic work, but he had not the strength for it. After the autumn his health begins to decline again. At last he cannot leave his room and he is obliged to abandon even teaching his little boy: "I only watch," he writes, "to see that during his lessons Polish is not changed into the Galician language." [1]

At the beginning of February, 1869, father and son went to live at Cracow, at 136 Poselska Street. Conrad was then sent to a preparatory school of which he recalled some dim memories many years later:

At 8 o'clock of every morning that God made, sleet or shine, I walked up Florian Street. But of that, my first school, I remember very little . . . But I did not suffer much from the various imperfections of my first school. I was rather indifferent to school troubles. I had a private gnawing worm of my own. This was the time of my father's last illness. Every evening at seven, turning my back on the Florian Gate, I walked all the way to the big old house in a quiet, narrow street a good distance beyond the Great Square. There, in a large drawing room, panelled and bare, with heavy cornices and a lofty ceiling, in a little oasis of light made by two candles in a desert of dusk, I sat at a little table to worry and ink myself all over till the task of my preparation was done. The table of my toil faced a tall white door, which was kept closed; now and then it would come ajar and a nun in a white coif would squeeze herself through the crack, glide across the room, and disappear. There were two of these noiseless nursing nuns. Their voices were seldom heard. For, indeed, what could they have had to say? When they did speak to me it was with their lips hardly moving, in a cloistral clear whisper. Our domestic matters were ordered by the elderly housekeeper of our neighbour on the second floor, a Canon of the Cathedral, lent for the emergency. She, too, spoke but seldom. She wore a black dress with a cross hanging by a chain on her ample bosom. And though when she spoke she moved her lips more than the nuns, she never let her voice rise above a peacefully murmuring note. The air around me was all piety, resignation and silence.

I don't know what would have become of me if I had not been a reading boy. My prep finished I would have had nothing to do but sit and watch the awful stillness of the sick room flow out through the

[1] Letter, December 24, 1868.

closed door and coldly enfold my scared heart. I suppose that in a futile, childish way I would have gone crazy. But I was a reading boy. There were many books about, lying on consoles, on tables, and even on the floor, for we had not had time to settle down. I read! What did I not read! Sometimes the elder nun, gliding up and casting a mistrustful look on the open pages, would lay her hand lightly on my head and suggest in a doubtful whisper, "Perhaps it is not very good for you to read these books." I would raise my eyes to her face mutely, and with a vague gesture of giving it up she would glide away.

Later in the evening, but not always, I would be permitted to tiptoe into the sick room to say good-night to the figure prone on the bed, which often could not acknowledge my presence but by a slow movement of the eyes, put my lips dutifully to the nerveless hand lying on the coverlet, and tiptoe out again. Then I would go to bed, in a room at the end of the corridor, and often, not always, cry myself into a good sound sleep.[1]

One evening in May, Apollo Korzeniowski, seated in his armchair and propped up with cushions, supervised the burning of all his recent manuscripts.[2] Through the open door little Conrad, silent and dismayed, watched this last act of renouncement on the part of one who was not only "desperately ill, mortally weary but a vanquished man." [3] Afterward he took to his bed, and fifteen days later, on May 23, 1869, at three o'clock in the afternoon, the Polish patriot breathed his last, a victim, among others, of the Russian oppression.

Although he had been only a short time at Cracow and few had seen him, what he had done for his people and the Polish cause was widely known. His funeral was the occasion of a silent respectful demonstration in which all classes of society took part.

The long procession moved out of the narrow street, down a long street, passed the Gothic front of St. Mary's under its unequal towers towards the Florian Gate. . . .
Half the population had turned out on that fine May afternoon. They

[1] *Notes on Life and Letters,* "Poland Revisited," pp. 167–168.
[2] He had previously handed his friend Stefan Buszczynski some of his manuscripts.
[3] *A Personal Record,* Author's Note, p. x.

had not come to honour a great achievement, or even some splendid failure. The dead and they were victims alike of an unrelenting destiny which cut them off from every path of merit and glory. They had come only to render homage to the ardent fidelity of the man whose life had been a fearless confession in word and deed of a creed which the simplest heart in that crowd could feel and understand.[1]

Apollo Korzeniowski's literary work, though it never reached the general public, was recognized by a few critics, and it has not entirely died with him. In the opinion of Thaddeus Bobrowski, he was one of the best of the authors who came under Krasinski's influence, and he praises the style of two of his dramas. He was an incomparable translator of Victor Hugo and of Heine, with whose lyrical bitterness he profoundly sympathized. It is clear, then, that, on one side of Joseph Conrad's descent, there was marked literary talent and that he was brought up in an atmosphere of letters. From Thaddeus Bobrowski's *Memoirs* we can complete the portrait of Apollo Korzeniowski.

Unpractical in daily life, he was invariably spontaneous and sincere in his feeling. Exceptionally harsh and uncompromising in his writing, he was often too indulgent to those around him. In his judgment of the powerful he was severe, and toward the weak he was very benevolent. He selected as victims of his mockery either those who had personally offended him or struck him as unduly proud of their social position. He called himself an ardent democrat and he was sometimes taken for a Socialist; but, as I told him many times, his carriage and behaviour were much more aristocratic than mine and no one attributed to me democratic sentiments.[2]

Conrad was now eleven years old. After his father's death, Stefan Buszczynski looked after him with affectionate care. According to his father's wish, he was placed *en pension* with M. Georgeon at Cracow and he attended classes at the St. Anne High School. He was backward in Latin and German compared with his schoolfellows, but from a letter written three weeks after his father's death by his maternal grand-

---

[1] *Notes on Life and Letters*, "Poland Revisited." See also *A Personal Record*, Author's Note, pp. x and xi.
[2] Thaddeus Bobrowski's *Memoirs*, Vol. I, pp. 361 *et seq.*

mother we gather that he was working with great assiduity. During the summer she took him to Wartenberg in Bohemia and she decided she would come to live in Cracow when his term began again. A family council decided that he should be placed under the guardianship of his grandmother and Count Ladislas Mniszek. The date of the deed of guardianship is 1870. From that date onward his studies were supervised by a young tutor, Mr. Pulman, a student of the University of Cracow, who looked after him during the next four years. In the summer they used to go together to Krynica in the Tatra Mountains.

Conrad does not seem to have retained a very agreeable recollection of this period of his education. He was, of course, a child with a very lively imagination, and he had not been used to routine and discipline. The subjects which were important in the curriculum were by no means those in which he was most interested. He showed rather a special inclination for geography, and in "Geography and Some Explorers" he complained of the lifeless, unimaginative way he was taught.

. . . A latent devotion to geography . . . interfered with my devotion (such as it was) to my schoolwork.

Unfortunately, the marks awarded for that subject were almost as few as the hours apportioned to it in the school curriculum by persons of no romantic sense for the real, ignorant of the great possibilities of active life; with no desire for struggle, no notion of the wide spaces of the world—mere bored professors, in fact, who were not only middle-aged but looked to me as if they had never been young. And their geography was very much like themselves, a bloodless thing with a dry skin covering a repulsive armature of uninteresting bones.

I would be ashamed of my warmth in digging up a hatchet which has been buried now for nearly fifty years if those fellows had not tried so often to take my scalp at the yearly examinations. There are things that one does not forget. And besides, the geography which I had discovered for myself was the geography of open spaces and wide horizons built up on men's devoted work in the open air, the geography still militant but already conscious of its approaching end with the death of the last great explorer. The antagonism was radical.[1]

[1] See *Last Essays*, p. 12.

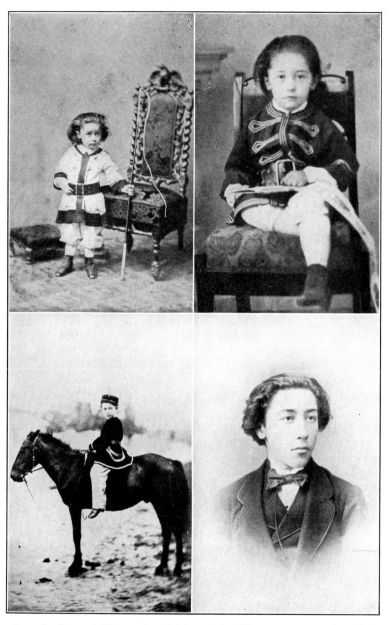

Joseph Conrad Korzeniowski in 1862 (Warsaw): in 1863 (Vologda): in 1865 (Tchernikov) and in 1873 (Cracow).

To honour the memory of his father, on December 28, 1872, the Municipal Council of Cracow gave to the young Korzeniowski the freedom of the city, exempt from tax. This favour should have entailed his being naturalized as an Austrian subject, and proceedings to that end were begun, but they were not concluded; probably because there was some understanding between Austria and Russia that they should abstain from absorbing each other's Poles. This is the first of a series of attempts on his part to get himself naturalized. Since he could not be legally what he was in fact, a Pole, anything was better than being a Russian. His relations seem to have accepted this idea in deciding that he should continue to remain at Cracow without once setting foot on Russian territory.

The same year that he received the freedom of the city, he confided to his uncle a longing which he had privately nourished for two or three years: he wanted to be a sailor. It seemed a most surprising wish to his relations, whose traditions were exclusively military or literary and those of an inland race. Thaddeus Bobrowski at first treated it as a childish whim. From his point of view, the Korzeniowskis had always been eccentric, but this was a new form for their eccentricity to take. He journeyed all the way from the Ukraine to discover what was at the bottom of his nephew's fancy. He thought it wiser not to meet him with a peremptory refusal, but to coax him tactfully away from the idea, and to point out the importance of his first completing his studies, at any rate. At the end of term Conrad was found to have done well, and Mr. Pulman, his tutor, to whom Conrad was much attached, was instructed to discourage as much as possible this new, strange project.

In May, 1873, on doctor's advice, Conrad was sent with his tutor for a trip of about six weeks to Germany and Switzerland, a journey which was prolonged to nearly three months owing to an outbreak of cholera in Cracow. They first visited Vienna and Munich, and from there they proceeded to Schaffhausen. After visiting the Swiss lakes, they made their way through the valley of the Reuss by way of Andermatt and

Hospenthal. The St. Gothard tunnel was then in process of being excavated, and they crossed the Furka Pass. It was between Hospenthal and the Furka Pass that the discussion with his tutor took place—which Conrad reports in *A Personal Record*—that decided once and for all his choice of a career. They reached Milan and finally Venice, where Joseph Conrad from the Lido for the first time saw the sea.

By the end of July they were back again at Cracow, and Mme Bobrowska, his grandmother, being obliged to live at Warsaw, Conrad was placed in the care of one of his relations, Antoine Syroczynski, with whom he spent September at Lemberg. The remonstrances of his tutor, the advice of his uncle, the entreaties of his grandmother, and the astonished indignation of his relations and friends had failed to shake his determination to go to sea. It was all the stronger since it was not born of reflection but sprang from an impulse deep within him.

Later on he was to write in *A Personal Record:*

> I don't mean to say that a whole country has been convulsed by my desire to go to sea. But for a boy between fifteen and sixteen, sensitive enough in all conscience, the commotion of his little world had seemed a very considerable thing indeed. So considerable that, absurdly enough, the echoes of it linger to this day. I catch myself in hours of solitude and retrospect meeting arguments and charges made thirty-five years ago by voices now for ever still; finding things to say that an assailed boy could not have found, simply because of the mysteriousness of his impulses to himself. I understood no more than the people who called upon me to explain myself.

It is possible, however, that sentimental reasons may have played a part in strengthening his determination. In a young, exalted nature, the disappointments of first love are likely to prompt a desire for flight at all costs. Twice, later in life, Conrad himself lifted a corner of the veil. Once in his Author's Note to *Nostromo:*

> If anything could induce me to revisit Sulaco (I should hate to see all these changes) it would be Antonia—and the true reason for that— why not be frank about it?—the true reason is that I have modelled her

on my first love. How we, a band of tallish schoolboys, the chums of her
two brothers, how we used to look up to that girl just out of the schoolroom herself, as the standard-bearer of a faith to which we were all
born, but which she alone knew how to hold aloft, with an unflinching
hope! She had perhaps more glow and less serenity in her soul than Antonia, but she was an uncompromising Puritan of patriotism with no
taint of the slightest worldliness in her thoughts. I was not the only one
in love with her; but it was I who had to hear oftenest her scathing
criticism of my levities—very much like poor Decoud—or stand the
brunt of her austere, unanswerable invective. She did not quite understand—but never mind. That afternoon when I came in, a shrinking yet
defiant sinner, to say the final good-bye, I received a hand-squeeze that
made my heart leap and saw a tear that took my breath away. She was
softened at the last as though she had suddenly perceived (we were such
children still!) that I was really going away for good, going very far
away—even as far as Sulaco, lying unknown, hidden from our eyes, in
the darkness of the Placid Gulf.

The second time he does so in a cancelled passage in a
manuscript; it gives us a deeper glimpse into the earliest
phases of the story of his heart:

A great austerity of feeling and conviction is not a very common
phenomenon in youth. But that young girl seems to have been an uncom-
mon personality, the moral centre of a group of young people on the
threshold of life. Her own education appears to have been not finished at
the time. But she had the power of an exalted character.

Of that time he reminds her at great length. And no wonder. He was
in love with her. But he never betrayed this sentiment to her, to anybody.
He rather affected resistance to her influence. He even tried to cheat his
own self in that respect.

The secret of this resistance is that she was not his first love. That
experience had come to him the year before in the late summer of his last
school holiday. . . . From the nature of things first love can never be a
wholly happy experience. But this man seems to have been exceptionally
unlucky. His conviction is that, in colloquial phrase, he had struck something particularly wicked and even devilish. He holds that belief after
thirty-five years, and positively shudders at the mere recollection. If she
was really devilish, then she may count it for an amazing success. My
opinion, however, is that the girl was simply very ordinarily stupid.
Stupid people are very prone to turn a genuine display of sentiment into
ridicule—and, women, of course, have special opportunities in this way.

I imagine that at first he amused her, then he bored her (perhaps was in the way of some more serious flirtation), and discovering that she could make him suffer she let herself go to her heart's content. She amused herself again by tormenting him privately and publicly with great zest and method and finally "executed" him in circumstances of peculiar atrocity—which don't matter here.

Perhaps he was unduly sensitive. At any rate, he came out of it seamed, scarred, almost flayed and with a complete mistrust of himself, an abiding fear. He still thought her a superior being, but not yet a devil. That opinion came later. But he said to himself: if that's it then never, never again.

In common parlance: once bit—twice shy. But there was something more there. He had been bitten all over as it were, enough to make him shy of expressing himself for ever.

In the case of the other young girl (the one he is writing to after all these years) she obviously awed him a little. And yet it was she who at the last put some heart into him. It was very little that she had done. A mere pressure of the hand. But he had remembered it for five and thirty years of separation and silence! [1]

Such emotions as these perhaps intensified a longing to leave for distant lands which had the glamour of the unknown.

Such, then, were the circumstances in which Conrad spent his childhood. When one remembers that he inherited an ardent temperament and that, as far as he could see, being a Pole, all doors were closed to him, it is not surprising that a boy of sixteen, who had caught from those nearest him a spirit of adventure and felt from his first years the oppressive weight of tyranny, should thus desire to escape, cost what it

[1] This passage is in the first draft of *The Arrow of Gold,* entitled *The Laugh,* to-day in the collection of Mr. T. J. Wise. This first draft is composed of 94 manuscript pages, and they are the same text as *The Arrow of Gold* with the exception of the first five pages, which were left out in the book, and from which the above passage is drawn. The autobiographical character of *The Arrow of Gold* cannot be doubted—it will be seen in the second chapter of this *Life of Conrad.* The passage quoted above clearly refers to one of his two heroines, namely, to the friend of his childhood who became Antonia Avellanos in *Nostromo.* It is, therefore, more than probable that he is in the above passage also evoking scenes from his own life at Cracow, in 1873. Another allusion to such memories can be detected in a sentence written much later: ". . . you must squash him yourself. Women know how to do that thing almost from babyhood. I remember the squashings." (Letter to Miss Catherine Willard, April 30, 1917.)

might, into a freer world. It was not so much the sea—he had only once caught a glimpse of it—that was drawing him; it was life in the open that he longed for with all the eagerness of a youth who had hitherto been physically and spiritually cramped and suffocated.

However unreasonable he might appear in the eyes of his relatives, his obstinacy got the better of their arguments. He spent September, 1874, with his cousins Antoine and Léon Syroczynski [1] at Lemberg; his grandmother and his uncle arrived in October to accompany him to Cracow, and there, on the 14th, [2] they said farewell with tears and blessings.

Joseph Conrad Korzeniowski travelled light; he took little with him on that journey to Marseilles, save a few introductions and the promise of a small monthly allowance. No doubt, the day he left, he did not know his "Polish days" were over; indeed, full sixteen years were to pass before he set foot again upon his native soil and moved among scenes associated with the fierce despair of his people, his own sorrows, and his early hopes and dreams.

[1] Léon Syroczynski died at the age of seventy-nine in July, 1925. Some days before his death, he visited Warsaw, where he met Conrad's cousin, Angela Zagórska, to whom he spoke of Conrad's last holidays before the departure for Marseilles. He also told her that, when Conrad was eleven or twelve years old, he used to write comedies and act them with the Syroczynski girls. (Letter from Mlle Angela Zagórska, July 19, 1925.)

[2] The precise date of his departure from Cracow is given by a letter from Thaddeus Bobrowski written two years later and dated October 14th. "Two years ago to-day your grandmother and I let you have your heart's desire and watched you wing away." It is confirmed, too, by a passage in the "Bobrowski Document" which records Uncle Thaddeus's presence at Lemberg and Cracow to see Conrad off, and mentions the repayment of MM. Antoine and Léon Syroczynski for expenses incurred on Conrad's behalf during his holidays. The ticket to Marseilles cost 137.75 gulden, and the receipt is dated October 15, 1874, which confirms the date of his departure as the 14th.

CHAPTER II

FRENCH DAYS

(1874–1878)

"In Marseilles I did begin life. . . . It's the place where the puppy opened his eyes."

(LETTER TO JOHN GALSWORTHY, MAY 8, 1905.)

IT was natural that a Polish boy who had set his heart on going to sea should first turn his eyes toward France, for to take service even in the Mercantile Marine of Russia or Germany was out of the question. The national sentiments of a Pole toward those two countries precluded it. On the other hand, Conrad could easily have entered the Austrian Navy, and, at that time, Poles were actually rising to high posts in the dual monarchy. His family were thinking of sending him to the Naval School at Pola, where his career would not have suffered through his nationality, but Conrad himself had never entertained that idea. Indeed, up till now he had not thought about having a "career" at all. To him the important thing was to escape, at whatever cost, from a certain atmosphere, and to win liberty in life and action. This liberty was symbolized by the sea.

Now, the easiest and most direct way to the sea lay through France. Poland and France had been bound together by ties of sympathy for several centuries; indeed, from 1831–1863 the real capital of Poland may be said to have been Paris, and among good Polish families there were hardly any which had not one or two members established or even naturalized in France. In France, too, it would be easier for those at home to keep an eye upon the boy, and in addition Conrad had spoken fluent French since he was a child.[1]

---

[1] Conrad's knowledge of French was perfect. He not only spoke correctly, with a good accent and with great fluency, but he showed later, as a literary

28

His relations in Cracow and Lwów got into touch with the people they knew in France, and the most useful person proved to be one Victor Chodzko, a Pole of good family who had himself entered the French marine service.

Conrad reached Marseilles by way of Vienna, Geneva, and Lyons on October 17, 1874. Victor Chodzko was absent from Marseilles when he arrived, but he had recommended Conrad to a very good fellow called Baptistin Solary, who had promised "to put *le jeune homme* in the way of getting a decent ship for his first start if he really wanted a taste of *ce métier de chien*." [1] Solary began to look after him the moment he arrived.

Conrad has recorded his first impressions on waking up at Marseilles:

This Solary (Baptistin), when I beheld him in the flesh, turned out a quite young man, very good-looking, with a fine black, short beard, a fresh complexion, and soft, merry black eyes. He was as jovial and good-natured as any boy could desire. I was still asleep in my room in a modest hotel near the quays of the old port, after the fatigues of the journey via Vienna, Zurich, Lyons, when he burst in, flinging the shutters open to the sun of Provence and chiding me boisterously for lying abed. How pleasantly he startled me by his noisy objurgations to be up and off instantly for a "three years' campaign in the South Seas." O magic words! *"Une campagne de trois ans dans les mers du sud"*—that is the French for a three years' deep-water voyage.

He gave me a delightful waking, and his friendliness was unwearied; but I fear he did not enter upon the quest for a ship for me in a very solemn spirit. [2]

Baptistin had, himself, given up following the sea as soon as he had seen a chance to make a better livelihood with less risk on land, and, consequently, he eyed young Conrad's enthusiasm with a certain benevolent irony, but he was not too

man, a nice feeling for French style and a knowledge of the precise meanings of words which many Frenchmen might have envied. In 1907 he enjoyed revising, himself, a French translation of his story "Karain," and during the last years of his life he revised with me my translations of five or six of his books. In this work he showed most delicate discrimination in choosing the French word which conveyed the precise shade of meaning.

[1] *A Personal Record*, p. 122.
[2] *Ibid.*

old to understand such youthful ardour and to find it sympathetic. If he was not very active in finding a ship for him, he at least introduced Conrad to his own circle, which was a large one and amongst whom were shipbrokers, master stevedores, caulkers, and shipwrights.

Southern Frenchmen are hospitable people, and Conrad, on his side, had a full share of that natural democratic friendliness which is characteristic of Poles even when they are proud of their birth and manners. Naturally, he saw by choice those who could best help him to get in touch with a seafaring life, namely, the pilots. At the Lido he had caught his first glimpse of the sea, but at Marseilles for the first time he began to know it.

The very first whole day I ever spent on salt water was by invitation, in a big half-decked pilot-boat, cruising under close reefs on the look-out, in misty, blowing weather, for the sails of ships and the smoke of steamers rising out there, beyond the slim and tall Planier lighthouse cutting the line of the wind-swept horizon with a white perpendicular stroke. They were hospitable souls, those sturdy Provençal seamen. Under the general designation of *le petit ami de Baptistin* I was made the guest of the Corporation of Pilots, and had the freedom of their boats night or day. And many a day and a night too did I spend cruising with these rough, kindly men, under whose auspices my intimacy with the sea began. Many a time "the little friend of Baptistin" had the hooded cloak of the Mediterranean sailor thrown over him by their honest hands while dodging at night under the lee of Château d'If on the watch for the lights of ships. Their sea-tanned faces, whiskered or shaved, lean or full, with the intent wrinkled sea-eyes of the pilot-breed, and here and there a thin gold loop at the lobe of a hairy ear, bent over my sea-infancy. The first operation of seamanship I had an opportunity of observing was the boarding of ships at sea, at all times, in all states of the weather. They gave it to me to the full. And I have been invited to sit in more than one tall, dark house of the old town at their hospitable board, had the *bouillabaisse* ladled out into a thick plate by their high-voiced, broad-browed wives, talked to their daughters—thick-set girls, with pure profiles, glorious masses of black hair arranged with complicated art, dark eyes, and dazzlingly white teeth.[1]

[1] *A Personal Record*, p. 123. See also last chapter for Conrad's relations with the pilots of Marseilles. In spite of my search among the Marseilles newspapers of 1874-1875, I could find no trace of the steamer *James Westoll*, which Conrad mentions in the last pages of *A Personal Record*,

From what he wrote years later, it is clear that he retained
a grateful and vivid recollection of friends he made among
those who spent their lives round Le Vieux-Port; but pilots,
seafaring folk, and their families were not the only people
with whom young Korzeniowski associated. He also moved in
a very different kind of society, if not with the same pleasure,
at least with the same ease.

His uncle had opened a small banking account for him,
sufficient to provide for his modest needs, and the banker
himself belonged to the Conservative party who were known
as *les légitimistes*. Republican rule in France was of recent
date in 1875 and still rather shaky. It would not have taken
much to overturn it, and the hopes of the Royalist party were
far from being mere visions. Those who belonged to elegant
society in Marseilles could very well aim at reëstablishing the
old order without any misgivings that such an aim was
ridiculous and anachronistic. This was the opinion of the
banker with whom Conrad had been given credit. M. Delestang was also a shipowner [1] and, by conviction, an ardent
Royalist—"such a frozen mummified Royalist that he used
in current conversation terms of speech contemporary with
the good Henry IV." According to Conrad, he had even retained the habit of counting in écus instead of francs, as though
he were living in the reign of Louis XIV. His wife was known
as *"la belle Mme Delestang."* She was a woman with an imposing presence and a manner languidly haughty, and she reminded
Conrad of the famous Lady Dedlock in Dickens's *Bleak House.*
However, her aristocratic carriage relaxed sufficiently to show
now and then some sympathy for the young man—at least,
to the extent of occasionally asking him a question, speaking
a kind word or two, or even offering him a ride in her carriage and inviting him to one of those afternoon receptions
where the legitimist cause was discussed over teacups and
cakes.

In the intervals between the voyages he made from Mar-

---

[1] The offices of Messrs. Delestang & Sons were at 3 rue d'Arcole. The
house still exists and is adjacent to that occupied to-day by the British Consul
General at Marseilles. Conrad gives a short description of it in the last chapter
but one of *A Personal Record.*

seilles, it is clear that Conrad preferred the society of his friends at the Vieux-Port to that of his friends in the rue d'Arcole, though he had from time to time to go there to get his allowance and to attend Mme Delestang's receptions. Nevertheless, it was to the rue d'Arcole that he owed his early voyages, and it was in Mme Delestang's salon that he formed those connections which first launched him on his romantic adventures.

Messrs. Delestang & Sons owned at that time two sailing ships, a very old one, the *Mont-Blanc*,[1] and a new one, the *Saint-Antoine*. Conrad was successively a member of the crew of each of these ships.

The French period of his life is the only one which, in spite of close research, has remained shrouded in some mystery, not as regards the facts themselves but as regards their exact dates.

One passage in the *Mirror of the Sea* suggests that Conrad had begun his sea career before Christmas, 1874, that is to say, very shortly after he arrived at Marseilles.

The very first Christmas night I ever spent away from land was em-ployed in running before a Gulf of Lyons gale, which made the old ship groan in every timber as she skipped before it over the short seas until we brought her to, battered and out of breath, under the lee of Majorca, where the smooth water was torn by fierce cat's-paws under a very stormy sky. We,—or rather, they, for I had hardly had two glimpses of salt water in my life till then,—kept her standing off and on all that day, while I listened for the first time with the curiosity of my tender years to the song of the wind in a ship's rigging. . . . The thing (I will not call her a ship twice in the same half-hour) leaked. She leaked fully, generously, overflowingly, all over,—like a basket. I took an enthusiastic part in the excitement caused by that last infirmity of noble ships, with-out concerning myself much with the why and the wherefore.[2]

Conrad had either confused the date or is alluding to an-other ship, for the *Mont-Blanc* had left Marseilles for Mar-

---

[1] The *Mont-Blanc* was a three-masted vessel of 394 tons, built at Saint-Brieuc in 1853. The schooner *Saint-Antoine* was built in 1870.
[2] *Mirror of the Sea*, "The Nursery of the Craft," p. 153.

tinique on December 11, 1874, and could not have arrived in
the Gulf of Lyons by Christmas.[1]

There is no doubt about the journey he made in 1875 on
board the *Mont-Blanc*. The ship with Captain Duteil as master left Marseilles on June 25, 1875, arrived at St. Pierre
(Martinique) on July 31st, remained there two months,
touched at St. Thomas on September 27th, and proceeded the
same day to Cap-Haitien, where the ship arrived on October
2d to take up a cargo of logwood destined for Le Havre.[2]
Leaving Cap-Haitien on October 2d, Conrad landed at Le
Havre on Christmas Eve, after a voyage of six months, which,
though it had given him a sight of the West Indies, had not
been a pleasure trip. The voyage had been a particularly rough
one during the last month of its course, and the ship returned
to Le Havre rather gravely damaged, according to the captain's report.[3]

Thus Conrad, besides becoming familiar as an apprentice
with his work, had learnt also what a storm felt like. At home,
they had hoped that one such experience would be enough
to quench his youthful passion for the sea, but young Korzeniowski showed no signs of being discouraged.

The *Mont-Blanc* was obliged to remain in Le Havre for
repairs and Conrad returned by train to Marseilles. He broke
his journey for a few days in Paris,[4] and when he arrived at
Marseilles, during the first days of January, the *Saint-
Antoine* was in Martinique, whence she returned at the end of

[1] It must remain uncertain whether, or not, he did make his first journey
in the *Mont-Blanc* in 1874, for his name does not figure on the crew's roll
for that year. If, however, he really did so, he would have left Marseilles
on December 11th and arrived at St. Pierre, Martinique, on February 16,
1875, remained there until March 30, and returned to Marseilles on May
23, 1875.

I think I remember him telling me that he made only one journey on board
the *Mont-Blanc,* and at any rate his name does not figure in the list of the
crew in 1874.

[2] On his voyage the crew's list includes "Korrcuiwski [sic] Conrad, born
December 3, 1857, at Jitomir (Russia), son of Apollo and Eva Bobrowska
(foreigners), embarked at Marseilles June 25, 1875, as apprentice. Landed
at Havre December 23, 1875. Thus, the voyage took 5 months, 29 days. (Extracts supplied by the Marine Registry of Le Havre.)

[3] *Journal du Havre,* September 23, 1875.

[4] I had this detail from Conrad himself.

May, 1876. He had decided to wait for the boat, so he remained at Marseilles from the beginning of January to July 10, 1876. What he did during these six months we do not know precisely, but one document throws light on his life and suggests that the young man was sowing his wild oats.

In 1876 a letter dated April 5th from Mr. Victor Chodzko informed me that after having drawn out the whole of your allowance for eight months (1200 fcs.) you lent this money (or perhaps you lost it) and that you found yourself in great embarrassment. Later in May you wrote to me and apologized without giving any explanation. On May 21st you wired asking me to send you 700 fcs. which I did, and on July 2d on receipt of another telegram, I dispatched a further 400 fcs. On your departure from Marseilles you asked me to pay 165 fcs. to M. Bonnard, a friend who had lent you this sum. This I also did. Therefore in three months you have spent 1265 fcs. Since each one of us should pay for his own follies, and especially for those which affect his own pocket, and as I have no superfluous money to meet the superfluous expenses of my nephew, I met the demand by making use of 500 florins which belonged to you.[1]

Uncle Thaddeus was a punctilious, economical, and rather timid man, who, watching from the Ukraine, far away, probably concluded that his nephew was indulging in the wildest extravagances and that it was high time a Bobrowski sense of proportion should curb the impulsive irregularities of a Korzeniowski. In any case, it is clear that Conrad had what is called "a good time," and certainly all his life he retained a most particular affection for Marseilles. He was fond of alluding afterward to his evenings in the company of pilots, on the roadsteads or among their families, and to those he spent at the Théâtre de Marseilles, listening to the operas of Rossini, Verdi, or Meyerbeer, or to the operettas of Offenbach, which were then all the rage. Many hours slipped by in

[1] Bobrowski Document. "For the information of my dear nephew Conrad Korzeniowski." It is probable that the beginning of the year 1876 is the date of an adventure which may be found "arranged" in the form of a story called "Ashes" in *From the Four Winds* by John Sinjohn, the first book by John Galsworthy. This is a story of an evening spent at Monte Carlo in the company of some cleaned-out gamblers who, being unable to pay for their dinner, sent young Conrad, who had never gambled in his life, to stake their last five francs. He brought back, it appears, more than enough money to pay the bill.

the company of young people of all classes and in the discussion of every conceivable subject in the cafés, which were more numerous then than they are to-day on either side of the Cannebière; or, in a café of the rue Saint-Ferréol, the name of which Conrad, even toward the end of his life, still pronounced with some emotion: the Café Bodoul where, small as it was, an excellent dinner might be ordered.[1] It was patronized by clients who mostly belonged to the legitimist party.

It is possible to identify only one of the young men Conrad used to meet in one or other of these cafés, namely Clovis Hughes,[2] who later on made something of a name for himself in literature and French politics, as a poet and a deputy of advanced opinions.

After having let himself go during these six months, Conrad embarked again on July 10, 1876, on board the *Saint-Antoine,* commanded by Captain Escarras. The crew was composed of four officers and thirteen men,[3] and Conrad's position, though not exactly that of an apprentice, placed him halfway between the officers and sailors. Among the officers was a man destined to play a considerable part in Conrad's life; indeed, perhaps, the most important part. His name was

[1] The Café Bodoul at that time was at 18 rue Saint. Ferréol where a bodega stands to-day. Conrad alludes to it in Chap. I of *The Arrow of Gold,* when he writes, "I was the one to speak first, proposing that my companions should sup with me, not across the way, which would be riotous with more than one 'infernal' supper, but in another much more select establishment in a side street away from the Cannebière. It flattered my vanity a little to be able to say that I had a corner always reserved in the Salon des Palmiers, otherwise Salon Blanc, where the atmosphere was legitimist and extremely decorous."

There is another allusion to the Café Bodoul in *The Arrow of Gold* (Part IV, Chap. I): "For lunch I had the choice of two places, one Bohemian, the other select, even aristocratic, where I had still my reserved table in the *petit salon* up the white staircase.

[2] "A young gentleman who had arrived furnished with proper credentials and who apparently was doing his best to waste his life in an eccentric fashion with a Bohemian set (one poet, at least, emerged out of it later)." (*The Arrow of Gold,* First Note.)

[3] On the *Saint-Antoine's* crew list and opposite to Conrad's name is written "steward": monthly wages: 35 francs. There were three apprentices on board of whom one was a César Cervoni, the nephew of that Dominic of whom much is said in *The Mirror of the Sea.* This youth was about the same age as Conrad, having been born at Luri (Corsica) on January 18, 1858. The second lieutenant of the *Saint-Antoine* was a certain Pierre Defaucompré, probably a relation of the well-known translator of Walter Scott and Fenimore Cooper.

Dominic Cervoni. He was a man of forty. He had already seen twenty-five years' service at sea, partly in the mercantile marine, partly in the navy, and his character was already set.[1] Conrad has drawn a portrait of him in *The Mirror of the Sea:*

His thick black moustache, curled every morning with hot tongs by the barber at the corner of the quay, seemed to hide a perpetual smile. But nobody, I believe, had ever seen the true shape of his lips. From the slow, imperturbable gravity of that broad-chested man you would think he had never smiled in his life. In his eyes lurked a look of perfectly remorseless irony, as though he had been provided with an extremely experienced soul; and the slightest distention of his nostrils would give to his bronzed face a look of extraordinary boldness. This was the only play of feature of which he seemed capable, being a Southerner of a concentrated, deliberate type. His ebony hair curled slightly on the temples. He may have been forty years old, and he was a great voyager on the inland sea. . . .

For want of more exalted adversaries Dominic turned his audacity, fertile in impious stratagems, against the powers of the earth, as represented by the institution of Custom-houses and every mortal belonging thereto—scribes, officers, and guardacostas afloat and ashore.[2]

He figures also in *The Arrow of Gold* and Dominic's personality crops up constantly in Conrad's work under different names. He was Conrad's true initiator into the life of the sea. His long experience, the concentrated steadiness of his character and his quick judgment, awoke in Conrad an admiration and affection which time never effaced. Dominic's influence was not limited to what concerned ships and the sea; he was a humane man, yet without illusions, and he talked to Conrad freely of people and things. Dominic was the mentor of this young Telemachus; a mentor of a rather unusual kind, with a contempt for law, an ardent, romantic scepticism and a love of adventure which found an echo in the restless heart of his pupil. In him Conrad found a man who sympathized with the heady impulses of youth but who, on occasion, was prepared to use his influence to curb them.

[1] Cervoni, Dominic, André, born May 22, 1834, at Luri (Corsica); son of Charles and Flore Cervoni Registered at Rogliano (Corsica). (Extract from the Maritime Registry of Bastia.)

[2] *The Mirror of the Sea*, p. 163.

It is scarcely surprising that afterward, when Conrad became a writer, he should not only have delighted to pay a personal tribute to Dominic Cervoni in *The Mirror of the Sea* and in *The Arrow of Gold,* where he followed fairly closely his own life at Marseilles, but that he should have given to creations otherwise so diverse as Tom Lingard, Nostromo, and Peyrol the soul and moral outlook of Dominic himself. *Suspense,* which was left unfinished at his death, reflects accurately also the part which Dominic Cervoni had played in his life.[1]

After a voyage of thirty-nine days, Conrad, on August 18, 1876, was once more at St. Pierre, where he remained till September 23d, when he left for St. Thomas, where he was four days later. Fifteen days later, he reached Port-au-Prince, whence, laden with logwood and sugar, the *Saint-Antoine* continued her route, arriving at Marseilles on February 15, 1877.[2]

Such was the outline of the *Saint-Antoine's* voyage, but it had another aspect: it was also bound on the ticklish and illegal mission of carrying arms and munitions for a political party in one of the Central American republics. We do not know at what point in the Gulf of Mexico a landing was made, but several passages in Conrad's work showed traces of this contraband adventure and of a visit to the North Coast of South America.

In *Victory* the Author's Note upon the sinister Ricardo runs thus:

[1] As regards Nostromo, we have Conrad's admission in his Author's Note: "Nostromo is what he is because I received the inspiration for him in my early days from a Mediterranean sailor. Those who have read certain pages of mine will see at once what I mean when I say that Dominic, the padrone of the *Tremolino,* might under given circumstances have been a Nostromo. At any rate, Dominic would have understood the younger man perfectly—if scornfully." In *The Rover* Jean Peyrol is undoubtedly an old Dominic. In the case of Tom Lingard, the transposition is more subtle, and as for Attilio, in *Suspense,* the correspondence cannot be doubted by any reader. The scene of action in *Suspense* is the Mediterranean, the subject is a political plot with a sea atmosphere, and the analogy of age and nationality between Attilio and Cosmo Latham in that story, holds good of Dominic and Conrad in 1876.

[2] Information taken from the record of the *Saint-Antoine,* No. 143, year 1877. (Archives of the Maritime Registry of Marseilles.)

It so happened that the very same year Ricardo,—the physical Ricardo,—was a fellow passenger of mine on board an extremely small and extremely dirty little schooner, during a four days' passage between two places in the Gulf of Mexico whose names don't matter.[1]

A clearer allusion to this expedition is also made in *The Arrow of Gold:*

I had just returned from my second West Indies voyage. My eyes were still full of tropical splendour, my memory of my experiences, lawful and lawless, which had their charm and their thrill: for they had startled me a little and had amused me considerably.[2]

Conrad's correspondence unfortunately gives only one indication, but it is more precise:

. . . Puerto Cabello where I was ashore about twelve hours. In La Guayra as I went up the hill and had a distant view of Caracas, I must have been two and a half to three days. It's such a long time ago! And there were a few hours in a few other places on that dreary coast of Venezuela.[3]

From this expedition Conrad carried away with him a story about a particularly daring robbery of silver bullion which had taken place in those latitudes some time before. This story later furnished the substance of the plot of *Nostromo.*[4]

In the course of this voyage to the West Indies, Conrad received from his uncle Thaddeus Bobrowski the first of those letters which have been preserved, of those he wrote to him continuously for nearly twenty years.[5] Already, in this first letter, Uncle Thaddeus draws the distinction, which he was fond of stressing again and again, between the two strains in Conrad's inheritance, from the Bobrowskis on the one hand

---

[1] *Victory,* Author's Note.

[2] *The Arrow of Gold,* Part I, Chap. I.

[3] Letter to Richard Curle, July 22, 1923.

[4] "As a matter of fact in 1875 or '6 when very young, in the West Indies or rather in the Gulf of Mexico, for my contacts with land were short, few, and fleeting, I heard the story of some man who was supposed to have stolen single-handed a whole lighter-full of silver somewhere on the Tierra Firme seaboard during the troubles of a revolution." (*Nostromo,* Author's Note.)

[5] Seventy-one letters from Thaddeus Bobrowski to his nephew have been preserved. One is dated September 20, 1869, the others range from September 27, 1876, to July 13, 1893.

Certificate of discharge delivered to Joseph Conrad Korzeniowski by the Marseilles shipowners.

and the Korzeniowskis on the other. Throughout this correspondence, whenever his nephew portrays a leaning to wildness, or to what appeared as such in his uncle's eyes, the blame is put upon the Korzeniowski blood; when he acts prudently, credit is given to the Bobrowski strain in him.

You are always restive and careless. You remind me much more of the Korzeniowskis than of my dear sister, your mother. I note you have lost your trunk and your belongings. Do you need a nurse or suppose that I am one? Now you inform me you have lost your family photographs and your Polish books and you want me to send you others. . . .[1]

His uncle then adds: "I will send you the photographs all the same," and he informs him where he can get the books in Paris and sends him money to buy them.

His subsequent letters often allude to the money the young man is spending, guessing that his nephew's sojourns on land are making a hole in his purse, and he hopes Conrad will stay at Marseilles for as short a time as possible. "If," he writes, "you can do two journeys without expense in 1877, that will be satisfactory. I expect to see you in the autumn of 1877, either in Switzerland or in Cracow, or even in Marseilles."

These plans were never realized, for Conrad did not reëmbark in the *Saint-Antoine* on his return from the Gulf of Mexico, and he quarrelled soon afterward with M. Delestang[2]

---

[1] Letter from Thaddeus Bobrowski,—Kasimierowka (Ukraine), October 9, 1876. In this letter he also draws Conrad's attention to the Librairie du Luxembourg at 16 rue de Tournon, Paris, where Ladislas Miszkiewicz, son of the great Polish poet, was at that time.

[2] "You have probably forgotten the old Polish proverb: 'He who is humble benefits in both ways,' otherwise you would not have had this quarrel with M. Delestang." (Letter from Thaddeus Bobrowski, August 8, 1877.)

Three years later, at the request of his uncle, M. Delestang sent Conrad a certificate in the following terms: "We the undersigned C. Delestang & Son, late shipowners, certify that Conrad de Korzeniowski, native of Poland, entered our service in the month of February, 1874, as midshipman on board our vessel the *Mont-Blanc,* then served as lieutenant on board our ship the *Saint-Antoine* and left this last-named vessel after 3 years constant service in the West Indies and South America trade, on the 14th February, 1877, and that during that time he gave perfect satisfaction to his superior officers by his sobriety, general conduct and strict application in the discharge of his duties. Marseilles, 26th April, 1880. C. Delestang & Son."

The dates here are slightly inexact. In February, 1874, as we have seen, Conrad was still in Poland and the *Saint-Antoine* returned to Marseilles February 15, 1877.

and entered upon an adventure which, in some respects, still remains obscure.

On October 14, 1876, Thaddeus Bobrowski alludes in a letter to Conrad's intention to join the Carlist forces and threatens to stop his allowance. Indeed, it looks as though this resolve on Conrad's part had probably been prompted by angry disappointment and money difficulties. Before Conrad left for the West Indies he had come into contact at Marseilles with people who had strong sympathy for Don Carlos's cause. Legitimist circles in France saw in the Carlist aspirations a parallel to their own. Both parties were founded on the principle of legitimacy, and Marseilles had become an important centre, not only of Carlist sympathy, but a base for helping practically the revolution in Spain with money, provisions, and ammunition.

The adventure in the Gulf of Mexico had delighted Conrad, and he wished for nothing better than to repeat it.

He had met several legitimists in Mme Delestang's salon, lit by the last flickers of romantic politics and of traditions about to disappear. It was very natural that a young man proud of his birth, in love with adventure, who had been inspired from his childhood with the passion of a lost cause, should respond to such ideas.

The Delestang salon was not the only one to revel in the delights of conspiracy. In such circles, young men and young women were not in a minority, and young Conrad mixed a great deal in Royalist society. One day he met an Englishman called Henry C———, a man of good family living in the suburbs of London. A kindred desire for adventure had drawn him into gun-running on behalf of the Carlist movement. When Conrad first met him he had just escaped by swimming to the shore of the Gulf of Gascony, after being under fire from a Spanish man-of-war. In the salons of Marseilles, he was the lion of the moment.[1]

His quiet composure at once attracted Conrad and they became friends.[2] Through him Conrad became acquainted with

[1] See *The Arrow of Gold,* Chap. I.
[2] In *The Arrow of Gold* Conrad gives Henry C——— the name of Mills. His appearance is also modified. Conrad told me that he had given Mills

an elegant young man of fashion, an American of North
Carolina, about thirty years of age, called J. M. K. Blunt.
Blunt's family had been ruined in the War of Secession, and
his sword being his only remaining property, he had placed it
at the service of the Carlist cause. A young man from Marseilles, Roger P. de la S——, cousin of an important leather
merchant, whose wife also had a Carlist salon, was likewise
one of Conrad's intimate companions at this time. The possibility of rousing Catalonia to rebel in the interest of "Rey
Netto" was being animatedly discussed. As a matter of fact,
not one of these four young men really cared about Don Carlos himself or his cause: it was the adventure, the risk, which
attracted them. Meanwhile, the Carlists in Marseilles were
looking for someone who would be ready to ship arms and
munitions across the Mediterranean. Conrad was young, keen,
and he had had a certain amount of experience at sea. No
one doubted his attachment to the Carlist cause. He was of
good family and he had been recommended to some of the
outstanding Legitimist families in Marseilles. His credentials
were thus even better than they need have been. Doubtless,
too, Conrad had talked of his friend, Dominic Cervoni, his
skill as a seaman and his contempt for customs officials. It was
natural that Conrad should seem the very man they needed,
and it only remained to find a ship. Conrad broached the subject to Dominic, and the other four young men formed themselves into a kind of syndicate to buy a small sixty-ton *tar-
tane* which bore the name of *Tremolino*.

Fate had played into the hands of the young Conrad. He
had been thirsty for adventure, and now, though he was
not twenty years old, he was embarking on the last romantic
dynastic enterprise of the Nineteenth Century.

The last days and the death of the *Tremolino* have inspired some of the most beautiful and touching chapters of
The Mirror of the Sea. The accuracy of the facts related there
cannot be doubted,[2] but, so far, no official trace of this little

the physical appearance of his great friend Marwood whom he met thirty
years later in England. For the real portrait of Mills see *The Mirror
of the Sea,* "The *Tremolino*," p. 158.
[1] They are related again in *The Arrow of Gold* (Part V, Chap. III).

vessel has been discovered. She probably sailed under the Italian flag.[1]

Exactly how long she plied between Marseilles and the Spanish coast we do not know. It could not have been more than a few months, but those months brought Conrad moments of keen excitement. It was necessary to evade the watch of the coast guards and to land on a coast often dangerous. They had to give carabineers and customs officers the slip in order to reach the Carlists on land at a given point on a prescribed day. All this was enchanting to a youth who was something of a daredevil, and the kind of navigation necessary was an excellent training for him. Dominic had become the padrone of the *Tremolino,* and continued to educate the *signorino,* as he called Conrad, by his example, his aphorisms, and his comments on life.[2]

The adventure was doomed to failure. It finished disastrously and dangerously when, one fine day, Dominic and the *signorino* were compelled to drive the *Tremolino* against the rocks of the Baie de Rosas in order to escape the Spanish coast guards.[3]

The little vessel, broken and gone like the only toy of a lonely child, the sea itself, which had swallowed it, throwing me on shore after a shipwreck that instead of a fair fight left in me the memory of a suicide. It took away all that there was in me of independent life, but just failed to take me out of the world, which looked then indeed like Another World fit for no one else but unrepentant sinners. Even Dominic failed

[1] The archives of the Mercantile Registry at Marseilles yield nothing. The *Tremolino* had been built in the Savone River and rigged in Corsica.

[2] "All this gun-running was a very dull if dangerous business. As to intrigues, if there were any, I didn't know anything of them. But in truth, the Carlist invasion was a very straightforward adventure conducted with inconceivable stupidity and a foredoomed failure from the first." (Conrad's letter to J. C. Squire, August 21, 1919.)

"Dominic and I were engaged together in a rather absurd adventure, but the absurdity does not matter. It is a real satisfaction to think that in my very young days there must, after all, have been something in me worthy to command that man's half-bitter fidelity, his half-ironic devotion. Many of Nostromo's speeches I have heard first in Dominic's voice. His hand on the tiller and his fearless eyes roaming the horizon from within the monkish hood shadowing his face, he would utter the usual exordium of his remorseless wisdom: *'Vous autres gentilshommes!'* in a caustic tone that hangs on my ear yet." (Author's Note to *Nostromo.*)

[3] See *The Mirror of the Sea,* "The *Tremolino,*" p. 179.

me, his moral entity destroyed by what to him was a most tragic ending of our common enterprise. . . . And one evening, I found myself weary, heartsore, my brain still dazed and with awe in my heart, entering Marseilles by way of the railway station, after many adventures, one more disagreeable than another, involving privations, great exertions, a lot of difficulties with all sorts of people who looked upon me evidently more as a discreditable vagabond deserving the attentions of gendarmes than a respectable (if crazy) young gentleman attended by a guardian angel of his own.[1]

The *Tremolino* adventure also initiated him into emotions of a different kind. It introduced him to his first passion.

Among those who were working in the Carlist interest in Marseilles and helping it with money, was a young woman who, rumour said, had at one time attracted Don Carlos himself. She had been the mistress of a rich painter in Paris who had left her a considerable fortune; among other properties, on his death, he had bequeathed her several houses in Marseilles. She used to retire to one of these houses on the Prado from time to time in order to escape her over-assiduous admirers, some of whom were attracted by her fortune. She was a very charming young woman; the discretion of her manners, the legend of her adventure with the "king," and her habit of hiding herself created an air of mystery around her, and in the Legitimist salons where her social position did not allow her to be received, and she herself showed no eagerness to figure, she was often spoken of in hushed but sympathetic whispers.

There is no doubt that this young woman supported largely the *Tremolino* adventure, and it is she who sat for that bewitching and mysterious character, Rita de Lastaola, in *The Arrow of Gold*. Her real name is not known. The inner history of Carlism remains to be written, but, in all probability, the personages and the atmosphere of *The Arrow of Gold* keep close to facts. If Conrad modified the names and appearance of some of the actors, at least Rita, Thérèsa, Ortega, Mills, J. M. K. Blunt, Henry Allègre, Mme Léonore, the journalist, the housemaid, Mrs. Blunt herself, are all living beings whom Conrad knew at Marseilles, while in the character of Rita he drew the woman who first taught him to feel pas-

[1] *The Arrow of Gold,* Part V, Chap. III.

sionately, and in her he embodied his conception, chivalrous and romantic, of the "woman of all time." From a hint which Conrad once threw out in conversation on the identity of one of the principal characters in *The Arrow of Gold*, Mrs. Blunt, we are able to trace her to the *Souvenirs* of Judith Gautier, which describes her father's connection with this woman some ten years before Conrad knew her:

People came from all parts of the world to Théophile Gautier to ask for encouragement and protection. . . . Amongst the unknown solicitors who came without introduction or recommendation was a certain Madame Key Blunt who was particularly tenacious and pestered us for a long time. She came from America and she had been the wife, so she said, of a President of the United States, who had recently died. He had left her with children and without means; but she had a love and, she believed, a talent for the stage which she expected would help her to restore her fortunes. She was quite a pretty woman of middle height and she always dressed in mourning crêpe: "My husband is still dead," she would reply to those who pointed out to her that the period for mourning had passed.

My father had allowed himself to be touched by this exotic unfortunate one, but he combated, as far as he could, the design of the lovely widow to act in English a great Shakespearean drama. In justice to her talent and in order to obtain fame in America it was necessary, she said, for her to be heard in Paris. To act in English to Parisians was idiotic, but she could not be dissuaded.

In the end my father gave up trying to convince her and, thinking that it was the only way to get rid of her, he considered means of furthering her plan, while reducing it to as modest dimensions as possible.

Taillade, whom Théophile Gautier helped considerably and admired immensely, consented to back the project. It came down to playing one act from "Macbeth" in English, the act of Duncan's murder. Taillade knew very little English but this seemed no drawback to Madame Key Blunt, who undertook to teach the French artist as one teaches a parrot to talk.

The Vaudeville obligingly lent its premises and after innumerable and laborious rehearsals that performance took place, but as had been suspected, it turned out that Madame Key Blunt had exceedingly little talent and that Taillade, even though he was acting in English, had a great deal. He was able to make himself understood by the Parisian public, much bewildered as they were by the unknown words, and he carried away all the laurels himself.

My father, in his criticism, tried to leave a share of glory to the American actress, but it is obvious that he is much more sincere when praising Taillade. . . .

I believe that Madame Key Blunt never forgave my father for Taillade's success.[1]

This incident in Mrs. Blunt's life makes even more plausible the astonishing scene in *The Arrow of Gold* in which she persuades Monsieur George (that is to say Conrad) to give up Rita and induce her to marry J. M. K. Blunt, her own son.

Rita and Conrad were nearly the same age and they were both in a somewhat similar position, being both without any firm roots in the society in which they lived. Conrad's devotion to an enterprise in which his political passions were not involved, but which he pursued, first through a love of adventure, then through his attachment to her, could not fail to touch Rita. She seems to have struggled for a long time against this attraction. Her earlier experiences had made her views of life more worldly and mature than his own, but after the destruction of the *Tremolino,* when young Conrad, emaciated, abandoned even by Dominic, returned, a beaten man, to Marseilles, Rita could hold out no longer against his devotion. He had suffered too much. Their love affair was short, and in all probability the course of it was that which Conrad traced at the end of *The Arrow of Gold.* Its date is the last months of the year 1877.[2]

Conrad had been due to sail in the *Saint-Antoine* on March

---

[1] Judith Gautier, *Le Second Rang du Collier,* end of Chap. III. Mrs. Key Blunt was certainly not the widow of a President of the United States. At the most, she may have been the wife of an important magistrate in one of the states.

[2] The chronology of the *Tremolino* adventure still remains rather obscure. Conrad in *The Mirror of the Sea,* as well as in *The Arrow of Gold,* places it after his voyage in the *Saint-Antoine.* This is probable, since it was on board that vessel he made Dominic's acquaintance, but that would bring the *Tremolino* expedition to a date later than February, 1877, and by that time the Carlist war had ended. Again, an examination of Dominic Cervoni's record of service shows that from June 14, 1875, to October 14, 1877, he was employed without interval as second officer on board the *Saint-Antoine,* but, on the other hand, his record of service from October 14, 1877, to March 1, 1879, shows a blank, which would correspond fairly well with the events relating to the *Tremolino,* though the last half of the year 1877 seems very late for an attempt at contraband gun-running, since, by then, Carlism was a hopeless cause.

31, 1877, but at the last moment he had not embarked.[1] It will be remembered that he had broken with M. Delestang, and letters from Thaddeus Bobrowski give us to understand that in June, 1877, Conrad had informed his uncle that he intended to leave for India, and that, for this purpose, he had asked him to advance his allowance for four years. The uncle's letters also reveal that in the following month Conrad thought of becoming naturalized as a Frenchman.

As for French naturalization, I do not wish it on account of obligatory military service, God knows on behalf of whom and for what. I would rather you thought of Swiss naturalization and I would like you to make inquiries and find out what it would cost. . . . I beg you to take care of your papers, your birth certificate, and your father's passport, so as to avoid difficulties later on. We will decide this question definitely when you return from India.[2]

From another letter, dated September 2, 1877, we gather that Conrad's intentions were becoming more definite. On the other hand, the Bobrowski Document reveals that, toward the end of 1877, Conrad was contemplating a year and a half to a two years' voyage on board the *Saint-Antoine* under Captain Escarras;[3] but it may be doubted whether that intention was a serious one. It was more probably a passing whim, the result of the agitations of a sentimental adventure about which, of course, he did not breathe a word to his uncle:[4]

This emotional adventure fated to end, at it ends in a world not meant for lovers, and between these two beings both outside the organized scheme of society, not because they are *déclassés* in any sense, but because of the origin of one and the deliberate renunciation of the other.[5]

---

[1] On the crew's list, opposite "Korrcuiowski [sic] Conrad, matelot," are written the words "embarquement nul" without any other explanation. It is probable that he went instead to live in the house described in *The Arrow of Gold,* not situated in the rue des Consuls, but probably either in the rue Sylvabelle or in the rue Breteuil.

[2] Letter from Thaddeus Bobrowski, August 8, 1877.

[3] The captain of the *Saint-Antoine.*

[4] Letters from Thaddeus Bobrowski and the Bobrowski Document show also that Conrad did not inform his uncle of the *Tremolino* adventure. One letter mentions the Japanese Consul at Marseilles, with whom Conrad was very friendly.

[5] Letter to Sir Sidney Colvin, August 7, 1919.

At the end of February, 1878, Uncle Thaddeus received a telegram from Marseilles from a friend of Conrad, Richard Fecht, telling him that Conrad had received a bullet wound. This was the first his uncle heard of Conrad's duel with J. M. K. Blunt, with which the Rita love affair ended. The moment she was certain that Conrad was out of danger, Rita disappeared from his life as suddenly as she had entered it, but she never vanished from his memory.

On receiving this telegram, Uncle Thaddeus hurriedly left Kiev for Marseilles. When he arrived, his nephew was already on his legs but in a more embarrassed financial position than ever. His uncle remained at Marseilles a fortnight,[1] and after his departure, Marseilles became intolerable to Conrad. The tragic end of his love affair and the disappearance of Rita decided him to go—it mattered not where.

On April 24, 1878, he left on board an English steamer, the *Mavis,* bound for Constantinople with a cargo of coal. The Russo-Turkish War was just over, the preliminaries of peace having been signed on March 3d, and Conrad was still able to catch sight from afar of the tents of the San Stefano.[2]

The *Mavis* pursued her course from Constantinople to Yeisk at the extremity of the Sea of Azov, where she took up a shipment of linseed destined for Lowestoft.[3] Thus the ship arrived at Lowestoft on the 18th of June, 1878 and thus, after three years of adventurous life at Marseilles and in the West Indies, in his twenty-first year and knowing hardly a word of the language, Conrad first put his foot on English soil.

[1] Information taken from the Bobrowski Document.

[2] See letter to Joseph de Smet, January 23, 1911.

[3] The dates of departure and putting into port of the S.S. *Mavis* have been taken from the *Semaphore* of Marseilles of April 25 and June 6, 1878; that of the arrival at Lowestoft has been given us by Mrs. Kate Durrant, chief librarian, Public Library, Lowestoft, through the courtesy of a relative of the late Captain Munnings, with whom Joseph Conrad had sailed. From the "Arrival Book" in the hands of the Berthing Master (Mr. Geo. Munnings) at Lowestoft Harbour, it is ascertained that a vessel, the S.S. *Mavis,* came into the port on Tuesday, June 18, 1878.

CHAPTER III

YOUTH

(1878–1883)

*O youth! The strength of it, the imagination of it! . . . Oh,
the glamour of youth! . . .*

("YOUTH")

WHEN Conrad stepped off the *Mavis* at Lowestoft, he
found himself alone in the world. During his voyage on board
that small English steamer, he had picked up a few words of
the language, but he knew no one in England, and he had
practically no money. He felt that his uncle was still annoyed
by his Marseilles escapades, and he could not for the present
ask him for help.

At the beginning of July, he received a letter from his uncle,
still irritable in tone, the kind of letter often written by
anxious uncles, bidding him work and live within his means;
threatening also to withdraw his allowance, since he had arrived at an age when many young men support their families
instead of depending upon them. He added that he had not
been able to go this year to Marienbad, through having had
to pay for his nephew's follies.

You wanted to be a sailor, and you must be responsible for the consequences; you have forfeited my confidence. Work now to regain it;
you will win it back if you apply yourself steadily and pull yourself
together.[1]

The same letter shows that Conrad was thinking of joining the French Navy. It is probable that this idea had been
in his mind for some time and that it was only finally dropped
when his circumstances changed.[2]

[1] Thaddeus Bobrowski's letter to Joseph Conrad, July 8, 1878.
[2] It was probably the recollection of Conrad's having entertained this idea
which made Mr. Ford Madox Ford say in his book, *Joseph Conrad: A Personal*

His uncle made no objection to that. If he had written in a threatening tone, he was, none the less, a soft-hearted man who had no wish to see his nephew suffer. But he did continue to scold him.

If you cannot find a ship for the moment, take to something—shop-keeping or anything else, but work. . . . I am writing to M. Richard to send you 600 francs; live as you can on that money, and if at present you cannot pay your premium, enroll yourself as an Able-Bodied Seaman. If you learn what poverty is, that will teach you to value the money given you by others. . . . If you wish to wait before signing on as a sailor in the French Navy, find some occupation while you are waiting, for even if you write to me that you are certain to be a Vice-Admiral one day, you won't otherwise get a penny from me. . . . I do not want to work for a lazy fellow.

In spite of such remonstrances, Thaddeus Bobrowski's goodness of heart was really as great as his nephew's pride. Without further delay, on July 11, 1878, Conrad signed on in a ship bearing the picturesque name of *The Skimmer of the Seas*. She was, as a matter of fact, only a "coaster" plying between Lowestoft and Newcastle, and by September 25th Conrad had already made six voyages between these ports.[1] There are brief references both in his correspondence and his work to his experiences on board this "coaster." In a letter twenty years later to Mr. R. B. Cunninghame Graham, he writes:

A coaster, eh! I've served in a coaster. Also a barquentine, *Skimmer of the Seas*. What a pretty name! But she's gone and took a whole lot of good fellows away with her into the other world. *Comme c'est vieux tout ça!* In that craft I began to learn English from East Coast chaps, each built as though to last for ever, and coloured like a Christmas card. Tan and pink—gold hair and blue eyes—with that Northern straight-away-there look! Twenty-two years. From Lowestoft to Newcastle and back again. Good school for a seaman.

Another reference in a letter to Joseph de Smet, the Belgian author, reads:

Remembrance, that Conrad "entered the French Navy . . . that he remained an indefinite time, leaving with the rank of *Lieutenant de torpilleur de la Marine Militaire Française* [sic]." This is not correct. Conrad would have had to naturalize himself first as a Frenchman, which he did not do.
[1] See General Register and Record Office of Shipping and Seamen.

In May of the same year I landed in Lowestoft (on the East Coast) knowing no one in England. My first English reading was the *Standard* newspaper, and my first acquaintance by the ear with it was in the speech of fishermen, shipwrights and sailors of the East Coast.[1]

Lastly this passage occurs in *Notes on Life and Letters:*

The North Sea had been for some time the schoolroom of my trade. On it, I may safely say, I had learned, too, my first words of English. A wild and stormy abode, sometimes, was that confined, shallow-water academy of seamanship from which I launched myself on the wide oceans. My teachers had been the sailors of the Norfolk shore; coast men, with steady eyes, mighty limbs, and gentle voice; men of very few words, which at least were never bare of meaning. Honest, strong, steady men, sobered by domestic ties, one and all, as far as I can remember.[2]

This brief apprenticeship was just enough to familiarize him with the routine of his profession and to enable him to acquire sufficient knowledge of the language for technical and everyday purposes.

Conrad never dreamt of sticking to coasting; he wanted to see distant countries and take long voyages, but how was he to do so without connections and without support? In a daily paper, probably in the *Standard,* he came across an advertisement of a shipping agent in London which seemed to offer him the chance of employment. He at once wrote a letter, his first composition in English, explaining what he wanted and saying that he would call, himself, a few days later.

Toward the end of September, he left Lowestoft for London by train. He was not bent on pleasure but desperately set upon finding employment, on which might depend not only his future but his present means of livelihood. Many years afterward he recalled that visit to London:

At nineteen years of age,[3] after a period of probation and training I had imposed upon myself as ordinary seaman on board a North Sea coaster, I had come up from Lowestoft—my first long railway journey in England—to "sign on" for an Antipodean voyage in a deep-water ship. Straight from the railway carriage I had walked into the great

[1] January 23, 1911.
[2] *Notes on Life and Letters,* p. 155.
[3] He was really nearly twenty-one.

city with something of the feeling of a traveller penetrating into a vast and unexplored wilderness. No explorer could have been more lonely. I did not know a single soul of all these millions that all around me peopled the mysterious distances of the streets. I cannot say I was free from a little youthful awe, but at that age one's feelings are simple. I was elated. I was pursuing a clear aim, I was carrying out a deliberate plan of making out of myself, in the first place, a seaman worthy of the service, good enough to work by the side of the men with whom I was to live; and, in the second place, I had to justify my existence to myself, to redeem a tacit moral pledge. Both these aims were to be attained by the same effort. How simple seemed problems of life then on that hazy day of early September [1] in the year 1878, when I entered London for the first time.

From that point of view—Youth and a straightforward scheme of conduct—it was certainly a year of grace. All the help I had to get in touch with the world I was invading was a piece of paper, not much bigger than the palm of my hand—in which I held it—torn out of a larger plan of London for the greater facility of reference. It had been the object of careful study for some days past. The fact that I could take a conveyance at the station never occurred to my mind, no, not even when I got out into the street, and stood, taking my anxious bearings, in the midst, so to speak, of twenty thousand hansoms. A strange absence of mind, or unconscious conviction that one cannot approach an important moment of one's life by means of a hired carriage? Yes, it would have been a preposterous proceeding. And indeed, I was to make an Australian voyage and encircle the globe before ever entering a London hansom.

. . . I had vowed to myself not to inquire my way from anyone. Youth is the time of rash pledges. Had I taken a wrong turning I would have been lost; and if faithful to my pledge I might have remained lost for days, for weeks, have left perhaps my bones to be discovered bleaching in some blind alley of the Whitechapel district, as it has happened to lonely travellers lost in the Bush. But I walked on to my destination without hesitation or mistake, showing there, for the first time, some of that faculty to absorb and make my own the imaged topography of a chart, which in later years was to help me in regions of intricate navigation to keep the ships entrusted to me off the ground.[2]

The little office, when he found it, was such a one as Dickens might have described. To Conrad the windows seemed gray with the dust of 1815. Inside, he saw a man with a big

[1] He left the *Skimmer* on the 23d. He must have arrived in London on one of the last days of the month.

[2] *Notes on Life and Letters,* pp. 150–152.

gray beard, a big nose, thick lips, large shoulders, and a head of white curly hair which gave him the look of an apostle in the Baroque Italian style. Astride his nose were a pair of silver-rimmed spectacles, and he was busy upon a chop, which had just been brought from an eating-house near by.

I produced elaborately a series of vocal sounds which must have born sufficient resemblance to the phonetics of English speech, for his face broke into a smile of comprehension almost at once. "Oh, it's you, who wrote a letter to me the other day from Lowestoft about getting a ship." [1]

Without ceasing to eat, the man began to explain the nature of his business, which was to find ships for young men who wished to go to sea as premium-apprentices with a view to becoming officers. This was not at all what Conrad wanted. He had no money with which to pay a premium, however small it might be. "Of course," said the man, "I see you are a gentleman, but your wish is to get a berth before the mast as an able seaman, if possible. Isn't that it?" This was what Conrad did desire, but "on principle" the agent could do nothing to help him: "an Act of Parliament made it a penal offence to procure ships for sailors."

"An Act of Parliament. A Law," he took pains to impress it again and again on my foreign understanding, while I looked at him in consternation. I had not been half an hour in London before I had run my head against an Act of Parliament! What a hopeless adventure!

At the same time, the Baroque apostle, on noticing the evident distress of the young man before him, at once set about circumventing the law. He suggested he should get him a job as ordinary seaman in a sailing ship which made voyages to and from Australia. She was a very fine "wool clipper" called the *Duke of Sutherland*,[2] who, the gray-whiskered second mate was in the habit of declaring, "knew the round to the Antipodes better than her own skipper."

He was successful in his efforts, and Conrad embarked on the 15th of October, 1878, for Sydney, where he must have

---

[1] *Notes on Life and Letters*, p. 153.

[2] Built by Smith and Aberdeen, 1865. Registered 1047. Owner, D. Louttit; Captain, T. Louttit. (Information given by Mr. Basil Lubbock.)

arrived by the end of January, returning to London on board the same ship a year later almost to a day. Of this voyage no record remains except that of a sufficiently disagreeable experience which Conrad describes in *The Mirror of the Sea*.[1]

One wintry, blustering, dark night in July, as I stood sleepily out of the rain under the break of the poop, something resembling an ostrich dashed up the gangway. I say ostrich because the creature, though it ran on two legs, appeared to help its progress by working a pair of short wings; it was a man, however, only his coat, ripped up the back and flapping in two halves above his shoulders, gave him that weird and fowl-like appearance. At least, I suppose it was his coat, for it was impossible to make him out distinctly. How he managed to come so straight upon me, at speed and without a stumble over a strange deck, I cannot imagine. He must have been able to see in the dark better than any cat. He overwhelmed me with panting entreaties to let him take shelter till morning in our forecastle. Following my strict orders, I refused his request, mildly at first, in a sterner tone as he insisted with growing impudence.

"For God's sake let me, matey! Some of 'em are after me—and I've got hold of a ticker here."

"You clear out of this!" I said.

"Don't be hard on a chap, old man!" he whined pitifully.

"Now then, get ashore at once. Do you hear?"

Silence. He appeared to cringe, mute, as if words had failed him through grief; then—bang! came a concussion and a great flash of light in which he vanished, leaving me prone on my back with the most abominable black eye that anybody ever got in the faithful discharge of duty. Shadows! Shadows! I hope he escaped the enemies he was fleeing from to live and flourish to this day. But his fist was uncommonly hard and his aim miraculously true in the dark.

This is the one incident connected with the *Duke of Sutherland* which Conrad ever related.

His voyage in this ship does not seem to have been particularly agreeable. His limited knowledge of English, the fact that he was a sailor before the mast who, up till then, had sailed under less hard conditions, the necessity of drawing upon his solitary pride for the nervous force necessary to resist the fatigue of work, often extremely exhausting for one of his temperament and antecedents, all probably con-

[1] P. 123.

tributed to his depression.[1] Not only did he not reëmbark
in the *Duke of Sutherland,* but a letter from his uncle [2] shows
that after his return to London a craving seized him to return to the Mediterranean. This may have been due simply
to the attraction which that old classic sea had for his imagination, but more probably to a desire to see Dominic again
or to some stirring within him of his love affair, or to a more
general longing for an atmosphere less strange to his temperament. What, however, is certain is that, at this time, Conrad
did not know clearly what it was he really wanted to do. He
certainly entertained the notion of going next year to Odessa
to meet his uncle, but his uncle wrote: "I do not want you to
come to Russia before you have been naturalized as an Englishman." [3] Indeed, during the next seven years, his uncle
never ceased to urge him to naturalize himself, and this letter
shows, too, how impossible it was for Conrad to return to
Russian Poland.

He proposed several times to visit his uncle in the Ukraine,
and his uncle invariably dissuaded him, fearing, with good reason, that, if his nephew set foot on Russian territory, the Imperial Government would not leave the son of a Polish gentleman sentenced ten years before for a political offence, long at
liberty. Turn and turn about, Thaddeus Bobrowski tried to
persuade his nephew to be naturalized, either as an Austrian,
English, or Swiss citizen. Conrad, for his part, had often
thought at Marseilles of becoming a Frenchman. Being a
Pole, it was important for him to get rid as soon as possible
of the Russian citizenship which the unhappy state of Poland
had imposed upon him. There is no doubt that he often bitterly resented the fact that he could not return to his father-
land without risk. This fact, in addition to the persecution to
which his own family had been subjected by the Russian au-

---

[1] A nigger called James Wait was a member of the crew, whose name
Conrad borrowed afterward and bestowed upon the nigger in *The Nigger
of the "Narcissus."* It was during his stay at Sydney that he made the acquaintance of the French sailor without hands who sold tobacco in George Street and
who occurs as a character in *Because of the Dollars* (see Conrad's letter in
the *Sydney Bulletin,* March 23, 1916).

[2] Th. B., October 26, 1876. In this letter his uncle writes in favour of British
naturalization, as it does not entail military service.

[3] Letter of October 26, 1879.

thorities, induced in him, maybe, that permanent Russophobia which the generosity of his nature never succeeded in overcoming, and which was in him not merely a matter of sentiment or family feeling, but a passionate hostility which reflection in maturity confirmed.

Without having decided yet to naturalize himself as a British subject, he proposed, in any case, to make use of his service in the French Mercantile Marine in the hope of improving his position in the English service. At the end of 1879, he asked his uncle to intervene on his behalf with M. Delestang in order to obtain a testimonial of his services as a seaman at Marseilles.[1] Meanwhile, without waiting any longer, he found a berth on the *Europa,* a London steamship bound for Mediterranean ports. He embarked on the 12th of December, and touched at Genoa, Leghorn, Naples, Patras, Cephalonia, Messina, Palermo, returning to London on the 30th of January. His voyage in this steamer brought him no satisfaction, so far as we can guess from his uncle's answers to his letters. Conrad seems to have come across a captain particularly difficult to work under, and this experience did not diminish the distaste he already had for steamships. His uncle writes:

I did not receive your letter from Patras. I was becoming uneasy about you when your letter of February 2d reached me and disturbed me again. Your unpleasant experiences on the *Europa* do not make me very uneasy, although they may have given you some pain. Such things appear quite normal when you know human nature. They hurt you because they are undeserved and because you consider yourself exploited.[2]

Conrad returned to London more or less ill, with a fever on him and with a cough. He was absolutely without money, and his uncle, who was himself in difficulties at that time, could not come to the rescue,[3] but it was not his nature to remain long discouraged or to rely on others and pity himself without taking action. The predictions of relations and friends in Poland that he was a feckless fellow who would never come to any good were constantly before his mind. His knowledge

[1] Letter of Th. B., November 7, 1879: "I have written to M. Delestang an urgent letter asking him to send you a testimonial. Write to him yourself, now."
[2] Th. B., February 12, 1880.
[3] Th. B., May 13, 1881.

of English and his professional proficiency had increased with
such astonishing rapidity that he was already thinking of passing his examination as second mate, although it was scarcely
eighteen months since he had first set foot in England.

During his stay in London on returning from his voyage
in the *Europa,* he had written, one after the other, several
letters to his uncle, and his uncle's answers indicate Conrad's
worried state of mind. It is clear from these letters that he
had thought for a time of leaving the sea and becoming secretary to a Canadian interested in railways and politics.

I thoroughly sympathize with your mishap in connection with that
madman of a Captain Monroe, but if he is mad his commission ought to
be taken from him; on the other hand, if he cannot legally be considered
insane, his commission is valid. I do not understand the way the English
reason, but one cannot change them and one must adapt one's self to
them. I suppose the *Europa* is now in port and that you have the certificate from your First Mate who has become a captain and that you have
passed your exam or that you will pass it. Never doubt that I wish you
every kind of good, and that you have my blessing. Françoise prays for
you night and morning.

What I had to say about your naturalization I have already said in
my last letter. It is impossible to live for ever like a bird on a branch, one
must have, sooner or later, a legal standing, and it is better to do it when
you are free than under pressure of circumstances. You would not be a
"Nalecz," my dear boy, if you did not change your plans. I say that because you have told me of Mr. Lascalle's offer to make you his secretary
and to engage you to help him with his railway business. As for me I
should not be your uncle nor the man I am if I did not say straight out
that it is hopeless to throw yourself from one profession to another.
Changes of that kind make men into those kinds of wasters who, as we
say at home, have no fireside and achieve nothing for themselves. . . .
Think over the matter for yourself. Is it sensible to link your fate to a
man—however great he may be—who is a business man or a politician?
It is far more dignified and sensible to stick to a profession which one
gets to understand more and more by working at it. You have chosen to
be a sailor, you can enlarge your career through trading, and I am sure
that you will succeed without constantly changing your occupation. That
is my advice, but act in your own way, for in everything that concerns
your career I leave you complete freedom, being ignorant of the circumstances in which you live. I have never been anything of an adventurer

myself, and it is that fact which makes me wish regular employment for you.[1]

But Conrad was not tempted for long to give up the sea; his vocation always remained stronger than such temptations. At the beginning of June, 1880, he passed successfully his examination as third mate. What he felt at this time is faithfully reflected in a passage in *Chance* where, thirty years later, Conrad has transferred to the young Powell his own experience of the past.[2]

They agreed that the happiest time in their lives was as youngsters in good ships with no care in the world but not to lose a watch below when at sea and not a moment's time in going ashore after work hours when in harbour. They agreed also as to the proudest moment they had known in that calling which is never embraced on rational and practical grounds, because of the glamour of its romantic associations. It was the moment when they had passed successfully their first examination and left the seamanship examiner with the little precious slip of blue paper in their hands.

"That day I wouldn't have called the Queen my cousin," declared our new acquaintance enthusiastically.

At that time the Marine Board examinations took place at the St. Katherine's Dock House on Tower Hill, and he informed us that he had a special affection for the view of that historic locality, with the Gardens to the left, the front of the Mint to the right, the miserable tumble-down little houses farther away, a cab-stand, bootblacks squatting on the edge of the pavement and a pair of big policemen gazing with an air of superiority at the doors of the Black Horse public house across the road. This was the part of the world, he said, his eyes first took notice of, on the finest day of his life. He had emerged from the main entrance of St. Katherine's Dock House a full-fledged second mate after the hottest time of his life with Captain R——,[3] the most dreaded of the three seamanship examiners who at the time were responsible for the merchant service officers qualifying in the port of London.

"We all who were preparing to pass," he said, "used to shake in our shoes at the idea of going before him. He kept me for an hour and a half in the torture chamber and behaved as though he hated me. He kept his eyes shaded with one of his hands. Suddenly he let it drop saying, 'You

---

[1] Th. B., May 30, 1880.

[2] See also *A Personal Record*, pp. 112 *et seq.*

[3] Captain Rankin. See also the scene in *A Personal Record.*

will do!' Before I realized what he meant he was pushing the blue slip across the table. I jumped up as if my chair had caught fire.

" 'Thank you, sir,' says I, grabbing the paper.

" 'Good morning, good luck to you,' he growled at me. . . .

"I found myself downstairs without being aware of the steps as if I had floated down the staircase. The finest day in my life. The day you get your first command is nothing to it. For one thing, a man is not so young then, and for another, with us, you know, there is nothing much more to expect. Yes, the finest day of one's life, no doubt, but then it is just a day and no more. What comes after is about the most unpleasant time for a youngster, the trying to get an officer's berth with nothing much to show but a brand-new certificate. It is surprising how useless you find that piece of ass's skin that you have been putting yourself in such a state about. It didn't strike me at the time that a Board of Trade certificate does not make an officer, not by a long, long way. But the skippers of the ships I was haunting with demands for a job knew that very well. I don't wonder at them now, and I don't blame them either. But this 'trying to get a ship' is pretty hard on a youngster all the same. . . ."

He went on then to tell us how tired he was and how discouraged by this lesson of disillusion following swiftly upon the finest day of his life. He told us how he went the round of all the shipowners' offices in the City where some junior clerk would furnish him with printed forms of application which he took home to fill up in the evening. He used to run out just before midnight to post them in the nearest pillar box. And that was all that ever came of it. In his own words: he might just as well have dropped them all properly addressed and stamped into the sewer grating.[1]

As a matter of fact, his own natural impatience made the time he had to wait for a job as third mate seem longer than it was, for it was only three months later that he found a berth, this time as an officer. Before that date, he had already received a delighted letter from Poland.

MY DEAR BOY AND LIEUTENANT:

Two days ago I received your two letters telling me of the happy result of your examination. You have filled me with joy. The sheet of paper on which the "Messieurs du Board Office" have written such terrible threats in event of your not fulfilling your duties, has been my recompense, and I owe it to you. I sympathize entirely with your joy, which comes from two sources: (1) you have proved to your uncle and

[1] *Chance*, Part I, Chap. I, pp. 4 *et seq.*

to the whole world that you have not eaten unearned bread during these four years; (2) that you have been able to overcome the drawbacks of being a foreigner without backing. You are also indebted to Captain Wyndham, to Professor Newton [1] and to all your comrades who rejoice over your success.

There are honest folk everywhere—think of Solary and Richard—only one must find them. From the very start you have met them on your path and you are bound to love them and to help others when they need it. You see, there are many more honest folk than bad ones. I congratulate you, *Monsieur l'officier de second rang de la Marine de la Grande-Bretagne!*

Being an officer, the first step is taken. You need only now work and persevere. You are nearly twenty-four. You have one year in front of you to secure a position in which you would be independent of your uncle. Your uncle will not on that account cease to watch your progress with love and interest, but you will no longer have any claim upon his purse, for there are others who are growing up, your young cousins. I am very grateful to you for having shared your projects and interests with me, and—I repeat it again—do what you like, for I cannot judge from here how you are situated. You know much better than I what you ought to do. I give you a free hand, even to the point of becoming a Yankee if you choose. I told you in my last letter that it would be wiser, in my opinion, to remain a sailor than to become an American politician. Nevertheless, I shall have nothing to say if you do otherwise, but on two conditions: that you always keep in mind that you have to take the consequences of your own acts, and that you never forget in the stormy confusion of American life, what you owe to the nobility of the race and family to which you belong. . . . I embrace you and bless you.[2]

By the end of June Conrad had finally abandoned all idea of leaving the Merchant Service to become the secretary of a Canadian business man. His uncle was one of the first to hail the new resolution with joy, and, as usual, he attributed Conrad's perseverance to the Bobrowski strain in him.

I see with pleasure that the "Nalecz" in you has been modified by the influence of the "Bobruszczuki," as your incomparable mother used to call her own family before she flew away to the nest of the "Nalecz."

---

[1] The author of a small handbook on seamanship, much used at that date. He was Conrad's first coach in navigation and seamanship. He was not a seaman himself. (Letter from Conrad's secretary, Miss Hallowes, to F. G. Cooper, October 12, 1921.)

[2] Th. B., June 17, 1880.

This time I rejoice over the influence of my family, not, however, without recognizing in the "Nalecz" a spirit of initiative and enterprise superior to that which runs in our veins. From the blend of these two famous races should emerge a character so steadfast and so energetic that the whole world will be astonished at it.[1]

His uncle's letters no longer betray the least lack of confidence in Conrad's mind and will power. Those years at Marseilles, that long year's voyage between England and Australia, the peremptory and exacting education provided by his profession, not to speak of his birthright of natural energy, had ripened him prematurely into a man.

From this time onward, neither disappointment nor poor pay deflected him from a life which appealed to his imagination as a perpetual struggle between a crew and the treachery of the sea. His sense of human solidarity in the face of an enemy intensified day by day, and with his increasing responsibilities his love of independence grew stronger. After a childhood weighed down by oppression, how excellent and moving it was to be free from social conventions and political tyranny, alone, and face to face with the wide spaces of the sea! The sea might be an enemy, but it was no ignoble one. This feeling, together with a sense of the romance of a handful of men, sternly commanded and united by ties of simple human loyalty, became the inspiration of his work, an inspiration strangely begotten by resolution out of despair.

On the 21st of August, 1880, he embarked at London for Sydney on the *Loch Etive*, a ship of 1,200 tons, belonging to the well-known Loch Line of Glasgow. William Stuart of Peterhead was the captain, who, for more than fifteen years since 1863, had made his reputation as commander of the *Tweed*, one of the fastest clippers known.[2]

Conrad wrote later in *Chance:* "It is a fact that with us mer-

[1] Th. B., June 28, 1880. "Bobruszczuki" is a play upon the family name and the Polish word for a beaver, *bobrusz,* suggesting a claim to the patient industry of that animal.

[2] The *Loch Etive* (registered 1235 tons, 226.9 feet in length, was launched in November, 1877. Captain Stuart commanded her for her first voyage, January, 1878, to the time of his death on board her, September 21, 1894. Her voyages, outward or homeward bound, averaged ninety days. "The *Loch Etive,*" by Basil Lubbock. *The Blue Peter,* October, 1925.)

chant sailors the first voyage as officers is the real start in life," and a reflection of his feelings at the moment when he first stepped into his position on board the *Loch Etive* can be found in the passage in the same book:

"After I had bundled in my things somehow I struck a match and had a dazzling glimpse of my berth; then I pitched the roll of my bedding into the bunk, but took no trouble to spread it out. I wasn't sleepy now, neither was I tired. And the thought that I was done with the earth for many many months to come made me feel very quiet and self-contained, as it were. Sailors will understand what I mean."

Marlow nodded. "It is a strictly professional feeling," he commented. "But other professions or trades know nothing of it. It is only this calling whose primary appeal lies in the suggestion of restless adventure which holds out that deep sensation to those who embrace it. It is difficult to define, I admit."

—"I should call it the peace of the sea," said Mr. Charles Powell. . . .

—"A very good name," said Marlow looking at him approvingly. "A sailor finds a deep feeling of security in the exercise of his calling. The exacting life of the sea has this advantage over the life of the earth, that its claims are simple and cannot be evaded." [1]

We know from the chapter, "Cobwebs and Gossamer," in *The Mirror of the Sea*, where he alludes to the *Loch Etive* and its captain without naming either, that Conrad was the youngest officer on board. It was a pretty severe but a profitable education in initiative and responsibility to work for the first time under such an officer as Captain William Stuart, who had made himself "a great name for sailorlike qualities—the sort of name that compelled a youthful admiration," and with a second officer such as Mr. P——, who had "the name of being the very devil of a fellow for carrying on sail on a ship." Captain Stuart was then about fifty years old, and it may be deduced from *The Mirror of the Sea* that his temper was not very equable.

It generally happened in this way: Night clouds racing overhead, wind howling, royals set, and the ship rushing on in the dark, an immense white sheet of foam level with the lee rail. Mr. P., in charge of

[1] *Chance*, Part I, Chap. I, p. 31.

the deck, hooked on to the windward mizzen rigging in a state of perfect serenity; myself, the third mate, also hooked on somewhere to windward of the slanting poop, in a state of the utmost preparedness to jump at the very first hint of some sort of order, but otherwise in a perfectly acquiescent state of mind. Suddenly, out of the companion would appear a tall dark figure, bareheaded, with a short white beard of a perpendicular cut, very visible in the dark—Captain S., disturbed in his reading below by the frightful bounding and lurching of the ship. Leaning very much against the precipitous incline of the deck, he would take a turn or two, perfectly silent, hang on by the compass for a while, take another couple of turns, and suddenly burst out:

"What are you trying to do with the ship?"

And Mr. P., who was not good at catching what was shouted in the wind, would say interrogatively:

"Yes, sir?"

Then in the increasing gale of the sea there would be a little private ship's storm going on in which you could detect strong language, pronounced in a tone of passion, and exculpatory protestations uttered with every possible inflection of injured innocence.

"By Heavens, Mr. P.! I used to carry on sail in my time, but . . ." and the rest would be lost to me in a stormy gust of wind.

Then, in a lull, P.'s protesting innocence would become audible:

"She seems to stand it very well."

And then another burst of an indignant voice:

"Any fool can carry sail on a ship . . ."

And so on and so on, the ship meanwhile rushing on her way with a heavier list, a noisier splutter, a more threatening hiss of the white, almost blinding, sheet of foam to leeward. For the best of it was that Captain S. seemed constitutionally incapable of giving his officers a definite order to shorten sail; and so that extraordinary vague row would go on till at last it dawned upon them both, in some particularly alarming gust, that it was time to do something.[1]

Captain Stuart's bad temper was due partly to the impossibility which he soon discovered of getting the speed out of his new ship which had earned him his reputation when he was in command of the *Tweed*. "There was something pathetic in it, as in the endeavour of an artist in his old age to equal the masterpieces of his youth. . . . It was pathetic, and perhaps just the least bit dangerous."

The weight of responsibility upon the young third mate was

[1] *Mirror of the Sea,* p. 40.

increased by the sickness of the second mate, which did not
make his relations with Captain Stuart any more easy; especially as the orders of the latter were generally laconic, and
confined to saying: "Don't take any sail off her!" Certainly a
pretty severe but profitable apprenticeship.[1]

The *Loch Etive* arrived at Sydney some time in November,
and sailed again early in December for London by the Cape
Horn route.[2] She reached London in April, and Conrad left
her on the 25th, having been away for more than eight months.
The letters of Uncle Thaddeus are still the only sources which
throw light upon Conrad's life during the year 1881. Fortunately, there are a good many of them covering the period
from May to September. In them his uncle shows himself
extremely satisfied: "You have proved this time," he writes,
"that you are more mature than your years," and he expresses
his pleasure in sending him money to enable him to pass his next
examination. Conrad had obviously shown in his own letters a
lively enthusiasm for his profession. His voyage in the *Loch
Etive*, however trying it might have been, had inspired him
with a sense, still obscure but already strong, of the dignity
of his life work. His uncle actually pleads for a little less enthusiasm. He would prefer not to see his young officer re-
embark for Australia or Cape Horn, but return to London
in September, in order that they may meet each other later
on at Wiesbaden, where Uncle Thaddeus intends to take a
cure; though, if an opportunity of going to sea again presents
itself, he does not wish his nephew to remain in idleness on
the chance of that possible meeting.[3]

After the end of May, Conrad gave up the hope of meeting his uncle at Wiesbaden or elsewhere, and he set his
thoughts on making certain of getting such experience as a
navigator as would qualify him for his two next examina-

[1] Conrad alludes to Captain Stuart in a letter to Alfred Knopf, September
13, 1913. "He is the Captain S. in the chapter 'Cobwebs and Gossamer' in my
Mirror of the Sea. His children, a son and daughter, recognized him there and
wrote to me very nicely a few months ago."

[2] See "Christmas Day at Sea," *Last Essays*, where Conrad alludes to spending Christmas on board shortly after leaving Sydney.

[3] Th. B., May 13 and 30, June 28, August 15, 22, and 30, September 23,
1881.

tions. He had but one aim now, to become a captain as soon as possible. The fire of youth was hot in him; never before had Conrad's physical and moral being reached such complete equilibrium. His uncle wrote:

Last post brought me your letter of June 10th.

It is all the more welcome as it breathes ardour and enterprise, in spite of the failure of our plans for meeting. Perhaps the disappointment affects me more than it does you. I do not mean to reproach you in saying that. When one is young one believes more in the future, one is certain of striking a favourable bargain with Fate. As for me, I have closed those accounts. You believe we shall see each other again, and I—I doubt it: I want it to be so, I hope it will be so, but at the same time I see how uncertain of fulfillment my plans are. Meanwhile, I assure you that this melancholy is not due to my health growing worse, it is merely a reasonable judgment upon life.[1]

In the same letter he expresses a wish particularly interesting to us, not only because it is the first literary compliment Conrad received, but because it indicates that, in his native language, Conrad had already shown a gift and that sense of style with which he was born. His uncle's encouragement was not dictated by family partiality: it came from a man who, in his memoirs, displayed a genuine literary talent. This is what he wrote to his nephew, June 20, 1881:

Personally, I hope you will visit new lands and seas, for I know that it is boring to have the same sights always before one's eyes. Since you do not forget your Polish tongue (may God bless you, you have my blessing!), and even write very well, I will revert to a subject I have already mentioned. It would be an excellent thing if you wrote for the *Wedrowiec* [the *Traveller*] at Warsaw. We have very few travellers or even correspondents of that kind. I am sure what you wrote would interest everybody greatly, and after a time they would pay you. It would form a tie with your own country, and it would be an act of piety to your father, who wished to serve, and did serve, his country with his pen. Think about this. Put together some recollections of your voyage to Australia and send them in as sketches. The address of the *Wedrowiec* is well known in Warsaw. Six letters a year from different countries will not take up much of your time. It would entertain you and others.

[1] Th. B., June 28, 1881.

In spite of this encouragement, Conrad did nothing. The desire for action was as yet uppermost in him, and his temperament had not yet begun to incline him toward reflecting upon and recording impressions. He found satisfaction in giving orders, meeting emergencies, in merely being just young and healthy, in getting to know the world—at least its oceans —and in having the prospect of possible adventure and probable danger in front of him. His state of mind, his youthful exaltation, would, perhaps, have found an outlet in writing had he been leading a confined and sheltered life instead of a free, wandering one.

Toward the middle of the year 1881, Conrad seems to have embarked in a ship, the *Anna Frost,* but of this there is no trace in official records. A letter from Thaddeus Bobrowski indicates that he had an accident while on board her.

> I received yesterday your agitated letter.
> Thanks be to God you escaped, that you are alive; that you have got off with only a few days' illness and that your stay in the hospital has done you good—which rarely happens. I send you the £10 you asked for and I shall not deduct it from your allowance. I send it to you as "a distressed seaman." [1]

Conrad, in his letter, had probably mentioned some commercial enterprise which he was contemplating, for his uncle adds:

> As you are a "Nalecz," beware of risky speculations which rest on nothing but hope, for your grandfather wasted his property in speculations, and your uncle got into debt and many awkward fixes through the same cause.

After his accident Conrad set about finding work. He did not find it easily. We catch, however, the reflected glow of his youthful ardour in his uncle's answers to his letters, the heat and flame of which Conrad recreates for us in *Youth.* In that story, his feelings and his adventures during the next eighteen months all find an exact transcription.

On September 21, 1881, Conrad sailed as second mate on board the *Palestine,* a London barque of 425 tons. She

[1] Th. B., August 15, 1881.

was an old ship, and her captain was an old, bent man, though it was his first command. He accepted the commission, failing anything better. Just before Conrad sailed, he received a letter from his uncle.

It seems to me you are not very pleased with your new post. In the first place, she is only a "barque," which is beneath your dignity, and then the pay is only £4 a month, which is not good for your pocket. The captain, too, seems a poor creature, whose intelligence leaves much to be desired. But perhaps that will give you an opportunity of showing yourself an expert in your profession. Anyhow, it is all settled now. Well, leave in good health, return in triumph. *Deus te ducat, perducat et reducat,* as our ancestors used to say to those who went to the wars, and as I say now to you, bidding you farewell and embracing you from the bottom of my heart.[1]

The same letter contains a passage which shows both Thaddeus Bobrowski's prophetic insight, and how keen Conrad's preoccupations and anxieties regarding things Polish must have been at this time.

What you write about our hopes for the future delighted me greatly, for I see that whatever touches our country affects you, though you are so far away. It is right that it should be so, and I count on you never to alter; but there are many who do not trouble about such matters at all, though they remain at home. For this reason what you tell me rejoices me, and I give you my double blessing. As to what you say about those of our hopes which rest upon the Panslavonic movement, though those hopes are comforting and plausible, they are likely to encounter great difficulties in practice. You do not lend sufficient weight to the prestige which force and mere numbers have in the eyes of the world. A more important nation which rests upon Panslavism and assures the world of its disinterestedness (though it is not disinterested) counts secretly upon its population to secure for it a hegemony. You make the same mistake in attributing qualities to us which are not, accurately speaking, ours. Russia only understands by Panslavism the Russification of all other Slav nations and their conversion to the Orthodox Church. She maintains that she is a country with eighty million of inhabitants (which is false), and that our culture, which is more advanced, and our national history, which is more ancient than hers, are only the culture and history of a single class pretending to be those of a whole people (up to

[1] Th. B., September 23, 1881.

a certain point this is true) ; and she maintains that it is *she,* Russia, who can develop the true, popular culture of Poland. She asserts that the Czechs are too small a nation to count; and that we and they represent a bastard culture, a cross between Slavonic and Western influences; while she herself represents the true Oriental Slav culture (which does not exist!). She tells to the other Slav nations that, in the first place, they are too weak to stand alone, and in the second, that being themselves of Eastern origin they ought consequently to submit to Russian sway; she is powerful: without her they will perish, etc. . . . I believe firmly there will be an end of all this some day; but when it comes I shall be in my grave. Meanwhile, though we are pariahs, robbed of political existence and the right to develop as a nation, we ought above all to preserve and defend our individuality to-day till what time the idea of a revenge long due shall at last become *a fact,* and give us a real national existence.

The barque *Palestine,* in which Conrad was about to sail, was none other than the barque he afterward immortalized in *Youth* under the transparent pseudonym, *Judea.* Readers will remember her story: how she left London, loaded a cargo of coal at Newcastle for Bangkok, was caught in a storm in the Channel, sprung a leak, put into Falmouth because the crew refused to work so old and unsound a ship, was drydocked, and took to sea again for Bangkok a year after her departure from London; how finally she caught fire in the Indian Ocean and had to be abandoned not far off the coast of Java. This story is precisely in every detail the story of the barque *Palestine.* The ship, her officers, the crew, and everything that happened to them, are recorded in *Youth;* and that sentiment of triumphant youth, which colours Marlow's story, was Conrad's own possession at the time. His mood is mirrored in the letter his uncle wrote to him at Falmouth, while the *Palestine* was being repaired:

Your misfortunes of the past year filled me with despair. I speak of it as a year already over, as I hope and trust fervently that your bad luck will be over with it. Fate is no doubt in part responsible, but your judgment is also to blame. This time, at least, after your accident, your cool judgment seems to have deserted you in accepting such a wretched ship as the *Palestine.* I quite understand that you made up your mind to do so to avoid being a burden to me in London, and to qualify by serving as a second officer for your final examination. But, my dear boy, you did not take into account the mishaps and accidents which in such a case were bound to follow. However, though you fall sick or injure yourself, I shall not abandon you. But if you succeed in drowning yourself it won't profit you to arrive at the Valley of Jehoshaphat in the rank of a third or second officer! I never think I have the right to control you now you are twenty-four, but all the same I advise you not to sail in such a lamentable ship as yours. Danger is certainly part of a sailor's life, but that does not preclude you having a sensible attachment to life, nor prevent you taking reasonable steps to preserve it. Both your Captain Beard [1] and you strike me as desperate men, who go out of their way to seek knocks and wounds, while your ship-owner is a rascal who risks the lives of ten brave men for the sake of a blackguardly profit.

Think well over, my dear fellow, what you ought to do. I shall not come down on you if you go back to London, and I shall try to help you. For, as can be imagined, I do not want, for the sake of saving three to five hundred roubles, to see you at the bottom of the sea, or ill or injured, or crippled with rheumatism for the rest of your life. So weigh the *pros* and *cons* and the chances of carrying through your project, curb your enthusiastic ambition, and do what reason dictates.

But Conrad could not listen to the voice of Reason. The voice of Youth was whispering in his ears of adventures, new lands, and the joy of taking risks. The ship was exceedingly old; she leaked—no matter! It was his first voyage to the East, which allured him by its legendary past and mysterious horizons, and it was his first voyage as a second mate. Conrad was bewitched.

It was one of the happiest days of my life [he wrote in *Youth*]. Fancy! second mate for the first time—a really responsible officer. I wouldn't have thrown up my new billet for a fortune.

The *Palestine* took more than a week to reach the roadstead of Yarmouth, weathered a tempest later on, and did not arrive at Newcastle till three weeks after her departure from London. When she reached Newcastle, she was not fit to put to sea for another six weeks. On November 29, 1881, she started for Bangkok with a crew of eight hands and two boys, and a load of 500 tons of West Hartley coal. The weather was at first magnificently fine, but, having met with heavy weather in the English Channel, she became leaky, and

[1] Conrad, in *Youth,* gives the captain his real name.

as the crew refused to proceed, she put in at Falmouth, where all her cargo, except ninety tons, was discharged and stored under cover. The vessel was repaired, and the cargo having been restored, she left Falmouth on September 17, 1882, and proceeded on her voyage to Bangkok.[1] Conrad, therefore, was held up at Falmouth by his ship's repairs for something like six months. He spent part of his time in reading Shakespeare, in a five-shilling one-volume edition, at odd moments of the day, to the noisy accompaniment of caulkers' mallets driving oakum into the deck seams of his ship in drydock.[2]

At first it was thought that it would only be necessary to unload part of the cargo and caulk the leak. After having been reloaded, the *Palestine* left Falmouth, but she was back again in a week leaking worse than ever. It was then that the crew struck, and she was drydocked. Repairs dragged on, and Conrad obtained three months' pay and five days' leave. He went straight to London:

It took me a day to get there, and pretty well another to come back; but three months' pay went, all the same. I don't know what I did with it. I went to a music hall, I believe, lunched, dined, and supped in a swell place in Regent Street and was back to time with nothing but a complete set of Byron's works and a new railway rug to show for three months' work.[3]

The old barque *Palestine* remained many long weeks yet at Falmouth. She had become a standing joke to the dockers and harbour men, who thought she would never put out again. But these delays and difficulties, though they weighed upon Conrad at the time, seemed also to have stiffened his resolve not to look for work elsewhere, and to have inspired in him a sort of affection for this ancient marine dowager of a ship. We can infer what his state of mind was from his uncle's replies to his letters.

Your last letter sent up my spirits, because it was filled with a genuine energy. It conveyed to me a sense of your longing to travel and your

[1] *A Personal Record,* Chap. IV.
[2] Extract from Board of Trade official caution re combustion of cargoes, September, 1897.
[3] *Youth,* p. 16.

splendid health. . . . You are infatuated, my dear fellow. Does the honour of your calling and the custom of the country really require one to go off in an old *rufian* and break one's neck? I know nothing of either one or the other. I don't understand the matter, and I can only send you my wishes for a happy departure and a happy return. I shall be much relieved to have you back again in time to see you this summer. I should indeed be well pleased if you could come to Cracow or Krynicka to breathe a little of your native air. If you return early enough we could meet at Cracow and go on and spend four weeks at Krynicka. If you come back in the autumn we could meet at Lwów and stay four weeks there. In any case, I consider our reunion next year as settled.

Toward August the departure of the *Palestine* was definitely decided upon, and his uncle had by that time already sent Conrad his farewell blessing on starting upon "a distant and year-long voyage"; but the vacillations of Wilson, the shipowner, again delayed matters.[1] Conrad, having thrown away a whole year in the hope of serving the necessary qualifying months, could not now throw up his job, though he was wasting his time and his salary was a poor one. Then, at last, the *Palestine* sailed from Falmouth on September 17, 1882. She had a good wind and calm sea as far as the Tropics, and she made about three miles an hour. For an interminable number of days, the weary old barque proceeded at this pace, entering the Indian Ocean and turning to the north toward Java Head. Weeks passed while she dragged herself along toward her destination, when suddenly the cargo was discovered to be on fire.

On March 11th, 1883, when in Latitude 2° 36 S. and Longitude 105° 45′ E., a strong smell was perceived, and on the next day smoke issued from the portside of the mainhole. Water was thrown on the coal until the smoke abated, and on the 13th four tons of coal was jettisoned, and more water poured into the hold. On the 14th the deck blew up, and the vessel was afterwards abandoned. The boats remained by her until 8.30 A. M. on the 15th, when her inside is stated to have been a mass of fire.[2]

[1] In *Youth* Conrad says: "She belonged to a man Wilmer, Wilcox—some name like that." The actual name was Wilson.

[2] Extract from Board of Trade official caution re combustion of cargoes, September, 1897.

In the account of these events in *Youth,* given with such amazing power of evocation, Conrad has lengthened a little the time which the ship took to burn. The above official version of the disaster shows that hardly four days passed between the discovery of the fire and the abandonment of the ship. It is unfortunately impossible to reproduce here Conrad's own account in *Youth* of this early adventure, though it is not only a masterpiece of vivid description, but far nearer to actuality than the official account. On March 14th, when the bridge blew up, Conrad was pitched sprawling on to the cargo of coal and half buried in splintered wood. He picked himself up as quickly as he could, and found his hair, beard, and eyebrows had been burnt. The captain still tried to save his ship and keep her head toward her destination, but the fire spread rapidly, and the ship became a furnace. The crew were distributed between three boats; Conrad was in the smallest with two other men. They had a sack of biscuits, some tins of preserved meat, and a barrel of water. His orders were to keep close to the large boat, so that in case of bad weather they might be taken on board her, but he could not bear to lose such an opportunity of showing self-confidence.

I thought I would part company as soon as I could. I wanted to have my first command all to myself. I wasn't going to sail in a squadron if there were a chance for independent cruising. I would make land by myself. I would beat the other boats. Youth! all Youth! the silly, charming, beautiful Youth! . . .

We made our way north. A breeze sprang up, and about noon all the boats came together for the last time. I had no mast or sail in mine, but I made a mast out of a spare oar and hoisted a boat awning for a sail, with a hoat-hook for a yard. She was certainly overmasted; but I had the satisfaction of knowing that with the wind aft I could beat the other two. . . . Next day I sat steering my cockleshell—my first command— with nothing but water and sky around me. I did sight in the afternoon the upper sails of a ship far away, but said nothing, and my men did not notice her. You see, I was afraid she might be homeward bound, and I had no mind to turn back from the portals of the East.[1]

Exactly how long they were in an open boat is uncertain. In *Youth* Conrad only says:

[1] *Youth,* pp. 34, 35, and 36.

I was steering for Java . . . I steered many days. . . . I remember nights and days of calm when we pulled, we pulled, and the boat seemed to stand still.

It is known, however, that he was at Singapore rather more than fifteen days later.[1] His first sight of the East had been an island near the coast of Java, and the impression which that first contact, so ardently longed for during an interminable voyage, made upon him never faded from his memory. It has inspired the last pages of *Youth* with a splendid and durable beauty.

Conrad remained at Singapore during the whole of April, waiting for the first chance to return to England, for in spite of the attraction the East had for him, his aim was first and foremost to get back and pass his examination without loss of time. At the beginning of May, he embarked for Europe as a passenger in a steamer. The adventure of the *Palestine* was over.

Eleven years later, in 1894, at a time when "Captain Korzeniowski" himself, though he did not then know it, had actually severed, for good and all, his connection with the sea, he met again the old captain who had shared that adventure with him.

He was a little grayer, a little more twisted and gnarled. He was very grimy and had a chocolate-coloured muffler round his throat. He told me he had piloted a foreigner down the North Sea. His eyes were perfectly angelic. This is not a sentimental exaggeration, but an honest attempt to convey the effect. He was so bent that he was always looking upwards, so to speak. In the poky bar of a little pub, he told me, "Since my wife died I can't rest." He had not been able to snatch her in his arms that time. He said he was glad I "got on" and did not allude to our voyage towards Bangkok. I should think he *can* rest where he is now.[2]

It is not likely that Captain Beard had really forgotten the peculiarly cruel circumstances in which he had lost at sea his first command, but rather that when he met his bygone mate again he was not inclined to recall painful memories. Those

[1] The certificate of discharge of the *Palestine* is dated Singapore, April 3, 1883.
[2] Letter to H. G. Wells, September 6, 1898.

events had affected his subordinate officer differently. In him the whole adventure, in spite of its dangers and, indeed, because of them, had left a sense of exaltation which remained for him the most glorious moment of his youth. It had been so vital and ardent an experience that, when Lieutenant Korzeniowski became the author, Joseph Conrad, the whole of that splendid story got itself written, almost straight off, in a few days, so freshly did he recall the enchanting and already regretted romance of his adventurous youth.

CHAPTER IV

LANDFALLS AND DEPARTURES

(1883–1886)

"Haven't we, together and upon the immortal seas, wrung out a meaning from our sinful lives?"

("THE NIGGER OF THE 'NARCISSUS.'")

ON the 13th May, 1883, the steamer in which Conrad had taken his passage from Singapore to Liverpool touched at Port Said, and by the beginning of June he was back again in London. He had two clear intentions before him: to pass his second examination, and to go to see his uncle, who was impatiently summoning him. They had not met for more than five years. Thaddeus Bobrowski again urged him to become a British subject.

I would rather see you [he writes] a little later, a free citizen of a free country, than that you should arrive earlier still a citizen of the world. But decide the question for yourself, arrange as you think best; for after all it is your skin that is at stake.[1]

Conrad, however, appears to have considered the question of his naturalization with extreme nonchalance. His uncle had first thought of meeting him at Cracow, but his doctor having recommended him to take the waters at Marienbad, it was there that the long-desired meeting between them was finally arranged to take place.

Meanwhile, Conrad passed, on the 4th of July, his mate's examination. Of the three Mercantile Marine examinations, this one remained in his memory as far the most trying. The examiner had the reputation for being "simply execrable," and on this occasion he showed himself worthy of it. Conrad

---

[1] Th. B., June 5, 1883.

74

Certificate delivered to Joseph Conrad Korzeniowski by E. Beard,
master of the barque *Palestine*. "As to the captain . . . he
could just write a kind of sketchy hand, and didn't care for
writing at all." (*Youth*, p. 5.)

has described the scene in the sixth chapter of *A Personal Record;* also the enigmatic, expressionless face of the examiner who did his best to trap the candidate into making blunders, and evidently relished putting an imaginary ship through a crescendo of imaginary catastrophes to see how the future officer would extricate himself from them. There was a touch of nightmare about the proceedings. However, after forty minutes of this torture, in spite of the drawbacks of his foreign birth, Conrad had the satisfaction of walking down Tower Hill knowing that he had passed. His thoughts at once turned to preparations for his journey to Marienbad.

He arrived there on July 24th and passed a full month with his uncle, first at Marienbad and then at Toplitz, near the frontier of Saxony.[1]

They must have had much to say to each other. They had not, as has been said, seen each other for five years, and Conrad all his life was wont as a talker to break long intervals of taciturnity with equally long discourses.

Among his other gifts, he was an extraordinary story-teller. He must have gone over all his memories of his five years' service in the Mercantile Marine, to which his last voyage had certainly contributed not the least arresting incidents.

He returned to London by way of Dresden, and from there he wrote a letter to which his uncle replied:

Your letter gave me real pleasure. Everything you say I shall remember in my heart. . . . You are right in supposing that when I returned to Toplitz I was sad and depressed when in the evening I sat down at table opposite your empty chair. . . . As for going to sea again, the sooner you do so the better, and I hope you will naturalize yourself at the very earliest moment, and that the "filthy lucre" which has been put aside for it will not be used for any other purpose.

During their talks at Marienbad, they had discussed together their present situation and their plans. Thaddeus Bobrowski had given Conrad a detailed account of the latter's finances. Thanks to different legacies and gifts from various

[1] They were at Toplitz on the 14th of August, as a letter from Stefan Buszczynski to Conrad shows. It was at Marienbad that the portrait of Conrad (1883) was taken, which, thanks to the kindness of Mlle Angela Zagórska, is reproduced in this book.

members of his family,[1] Conrad now possessed about 3,600 roubles.[2] Conrad had—we do not know under what circumstances—made the acquaintance in London of a man named Adolf P. Krieger, with whom he had soon come to terms of genuine friendship.[3] Krieger was employed by, and probably interested in, a transport firm, Barr, Moering & Co.[4]

Conrad now proposed that his uncle should put this little capital into the firm, and a good many of the letters of the following year deal at length with commercial considerations.

After his return from Marienbad and Dresden, he did not stay long in London. On the 10th of September, 1883, he embarked as second mate on board the sailing ship *Riversdale,* bound for Madras. She was a ship of 1,500 tons, of the port of London. We have no information about this voyage, but it seems to have suggested some scenes in the *Ferndale* episodes of *Chance.* It appears, however, that Conrad had a dispute with his captain, L. B. McDonald,[5] in consequence of which he threw up his berth and left the ship at Madras. From Madras he went to Bombay to look for a new commission. He was first offered one on board a mail boat of the British-India line, navigating in the Persian Gulf, but he was reluctant to serve on board a steamer if he could possibly avoid it. One evening he was sitting with other officers of the Mercantile Marine on the veranda of the Sailors' Home in Bombay, which overlooks the port, when he saw a lovely ship, with all the graces of a yacht, come sailing into the harbour. She was the *Narcissus,* of 1,300 tons, built by a sugar refiner of Greenock nine years before. Her owner had originally intended her for some undertaking in connection with the Brazilian sugar trade. This had not come off, and subsequently he had decided to employ her in the Indian Ocean

[1] Among others a relation of his father, Mlle Katherine Korzeniowski.

[2] About £300 in the currency of the day. His uncle reckoned it at £350 (letter of August 31, 1883).

[3] To whom afterward he dedicated *Tales of Unrest.*

[4] The British and Foreign Transit Agency, 36 Camomiie Street, London.

[5] On the back of Conrad's certificate of discharge from the *Riversdale* is written opposite "character for ability," in the captain's hand, "Very good," while "character for conduct" is annotated in the same hand with the single word, "Decline." This is the only example of an unfavourable comment in the thirteen certificates which were found among Conrad's papers.

and the Far East.[1] Some days later, Joseph Conrad Korzeniowski became her second mate.

She left Bombay on April 28th, and was dismantled at Dunkirk on the 17th of October following. Her name, the *Narcissus,* is, of course, familiar to all who know the work of Joseph Conrad. It has been immortalized in *The Nigger of the "Narcissus,"* one of his indisputable masterpieces describing ships and the sea. The spirit of that book is not only the creation of the writer's genius, it also owes much to his memory. *The Nigger of the "Narcissus"* is really a realistic and lyrical record of six months of Conrad's life during the year 1884.

I obtained from Conrad himself some details as to the extent to which the novel follows fact, and I write them down here just as he gave them to me in conversation a little before his death:

The voyage of the *Narcissus* was performed from Bombay to London in the manner I have described. As a matter of fact, the name of the Nigger of the *Narcissus* was not James Wait, which was the name of another nigger we had on board the *Duke of Sutherland,* and I was inspired with the first scene in the book by an episode in the embarkation of the crew at Gravesend on board the same *Duke of Sutherland,* one of the first ships the crew of which I joined. I have forgotten the name of the real Nigger of the *Narcissus.* As you know, I do not write history, but fiction, and I am therefore entitled to choose as I please what is most suitable in regard to characters and particulars to help me in the general impression I wish to produce. Most of the personages I have portrayed actually belonged to the crew of the real *Narcissus,* including the admirable Singleton (whose real name was Sullivan), Archie, Belfast, and Donkin. I got the two Scandinavians from associations with another ship. All this is now old, but it was quite present before my mind when I wrote this book. I remember, as if it had occurred but yesterday, the last occasion I saw the Nigger. That morning I was quarter officer, and about five o'clock I entered the double-bedded cabin where he was lying full length. On the lower bunk, ropes, fids and pieces of cloth had been deposited, so as not to have to take them down into the sail-room if they should be wanted at once. I asked him how he felt, but he hardly made me any answer. A little later a man brought him some coffee in a cup provided with a hook to suspend it on the edge of the bunk. At

[1] Information given me by Conrad himself.

about six o'clock the officer-in-charge came to tell me that he was dead. We had just experienced an awful gale in the vicinity of the Needles, south of the cape, of which I have tried to give an impression in my book. . . .

As to the conclusion of the book, it is taken from other voyages which I made under similar circumstances. It was, in fact, at Dunkirk, where I had to unload part of her cargo, that I left the *Narcissus*.[1]

From this beautiful book and *The Mirror of the Sea* we know what Conrad's life was like, not only during the voyage of the *Narcissus*, but during the twenty years he spent on board sailing ships. The atmosphere, the dangers, the fatigues of that life, become real to us; also its arduous beauty, which appealed intimately to Conrad, brought up from childhood, as he was, to be familiar with the sentiment of the sublime and with struggle against odds.

He passed the winter of that year in London. On April 24, 1885, he left Hull as second mate on board the *Tilkhurst,* a London sailing ship of 1,500 tons. He disembarked at Cardiff on the 31st of May, but signed on again five days later, his destination being this time Singapore.

At Cardiff he undertook a commission for a sailor whom he had met a short time before, and who was also of Polish origin. His name was Komorowski,[2] and he had come to Cardiff some time before on board a German ship as a stowaway, in order to avoid conscription in Russia. He had asked Conrad, if he should ever be in Cardiff, to pay back a small sum of money he had borrowed from another compatriot in that town, called Kliszczewski. This man had emigrated to England when he was quite young, after the Polish Insurrection of 1831, and had established himself in Cardiff as a watchmaker. On hearing again the Polish language in his shop, the watchmaker received Conrad with enthusiastic warmth, and a sympathy at once sprang up between them, which, on Conrad's side, included the whole of the watchmaker's

---

[1] These notes were taken in June, 1924, at Oswald's, Bishopsbourne, Kent, after a conversation with Joseph Conrad about *The Nigger of the "Narcissus,"* apropos of a new edition of Robert d'Humières' translation of that book into French.

[2] It is probably to this Pole that Conrad refers in Chapter VI of his *Personal Record*, p. 119.

family, and led to a friendship with the son Spiridion—a young man of about his own age—which lasted till Conrad's death.

The *Tilkhurst* loaded at Penarth [1] and left on the 5th of June. The voyage to Singapore was without incident, as is shown from the letters which Conrad wrote to Spiridion Kliszczewski, the son and partner of the Cardiff watchmaker. These letters are particularly valuable, as they are almost the only letters of Conrad extant written during his sea life, and are the earliest which have been found. They reveal his state of mind, his political ideas, his curiosity about things in general, and his intention—a sufficiently singular one which he entertained while navigating in tropical waters—to explore the polar seas and to try whaling. It may well be that the idea of joining the whale fisheries had been suggested by conversations the year before with the captain of the *Narcissus,* for in *The Nigger of the "Narcissus"* Conrad says of Captain Allistoun (who may well be a portrait) :

He was born on the shores of the Pentland Firth. In his youth he attained the rank of harpooner in Peterhead whalers. When he spoke of that time his restless gray eyes became still and cold, like the loom of ice. Afterwards he went into the East Indian trade for the sake of change.[2]

I have it from Mr. Spiridion Kliszczewski himself that it was he who dissuaded Conrad from this project.[3]

To Spiridion Kliszczewski

27th September, 1885,

Ship *Tilkhurst,*

Singapore.

DEAR SIR:

According to your kindly expressed wish and my promise, I hasten to acquaint you with my safe arrival.

[1] Docks near Cardiff.

[2] *The Nigger of the "Narcissus,"* Chap. II, p. 30.

[3] On my return from a voyage in Norway in 1921, in the course of which I met the captain of a Norwegian whaler returning from Brazil whose conversation had immensely interested me. As Joseph Conrad asked for my impressions, I mentioned the whaler and he showed an extremely wide and precise knowledge of conditions, past and present, of whaling. Used as I was to finding that Conrad knew everything, I was not particularly surprised at that, but he made no allusion to the intentions he entertained in 1885, to which his letters bear witness.—G. J.-A.

This globe accomplished almost half a revolution since I parted from you in the station at Cardiff: and old Father Time, always diligent in his business, has put his eraser over many men, things and memories: yet I defy him to obliterate ever from my mind and heart the recollection of the kindness you and yours have shown to a stranger, on the strength of a distant national connection. I fear I have not expressed adequately to your wife and yourself all my gratitude: I do not pretend to do so now, for in my case when the heart is full the words are scarce, and the more so the more intense is the feeling I wish to express.

I am in hopes of receiving a letter from you some time next month. Besides a natural desire to be assured of your and your family's welfare I await with anxiety the news of your father's health. We had a very fine passage, and my health is comparatively good.

Not wishing to take up more of your valuable time I shall bring this letter to a close, reserving any further intelligence that may be worth communicating for my next. In answer to yours, I hope.

My compliments to Mme Kliszczewska and a hearty handshake all round for the boys.

Believe me, my dear Sir,
Yours gratefully and faithfully,
CONRAD N. KORZENIOWSKI.

To Spiridion Kliszczewski
13th October, 1885,
Singapore.

MY DEAR SIR:
I need not tell you with what great pleasure I received your kind and friendly letter. I am exceedingly glad to know that your father, yourself and your family are all well, and your holidays were a success.

I also gratefully acknowledge the receipt of the *Daily Telegraph*. The Liberal Government was defeated on the budget vote a day or so before our departure from Penarth. As soon as we arrived here I looked anxiously through the papers expecting great things. Although somewhat disappointed, I saw with pleasure the evidence of improved relations with Germany, the only power with whom an Anti-Russian alliance would be useful, and even possible, for Great Britain. No wonder that in this unsettled state of affairs politics, at least foreign politics, are slightly dull. Events are casting shadows, more or less distorted, shadows deep enough to suggest the lurid light of battlefields somewhere in the near future, but all those portents of great and decisive doings leave me in a state of despairing indifference: for, whatever may be the changes in the fortunes of living nations, for the dead there is no hope and no salvation. We have passed through the gates where *"lasciate ogni speranza"* is written in letters of blood and fire, and nothing remains for us but the darkness of oblivion.

In the presence of such national misfortune, personal happiness is impossible in its absolute form of general contentment and peace of heart. Yet, I agree with you that in a free and hospitable land even the most persecuted of our race may find relative peace and a certain amount of happiness, materially at least; consequently I understood and readily accepted your reference to "Home." When speaking, writing or thinking in English, the word "home" always means for me the hospitable shores of Great Britain.

We are almost discharged, but our loading port is, as yet, uncertain. At any rate, I hope to be in England some time in July, when you may depend I shall gladly avail myself of your kindness and go down to Cardiff to see you all. As soon as my examination is over I shall be at liberty. I had a letter from my uncle, but he does not say if we could arrange an interview in Germany next year as we contemplated.

Accept a hearty handshake with many thanks for your kindness, and believe me, my dear Sir,

Yours very faithfully,
Conrad N. Korzeniowski.

To your father my dutiful respects. I am so glad to hear of his better health. My compliments for Mme Kliszczewska, and greetings for the boys.

We are ordered to Calcutta—Agents: Finlay, Muir & Co. We leave in ten days, and shall arrive there about the end of November.

To Spiridion Kliszczewski

25th November, 1885,
Calcutta.

MY DEAR SIR:

The second number of the *Standard* came to hand yesterday via Singapore. I suppose you are now in receipt of my second letter from Singapore advising you of our departure for this place, where we arrived only four days ago.

Everything is well with me, and I am also greatly cheered by the fact that we chartered for Dundee, and, according to all probabilities, we will leave here about New Year's Day to be home by the end of May or in the first week of June.

I am afraid this will be a long letter, and, moreover, entirely taken up with my personal concerns upon which I want your friendly advice. You have been so kind to me that I do not find great diffidence in addressing you; still I wish to apologize before beginning.

As you are aware, I shall pass (I take it for granted) [1] my last examination on my return, and, I consider, make a fresh start in the world. In what direction to shape my course? That is the question.

That question I have partly answered myself: I wish to start due North!

In other words and speaking (as everybody ought) plainly, my soul is bent upon a whaling venture.

And now here I must pray you take also for granted that I am brimful with the most exhaustive information upon the subject. I have read, studied, pumped professional men and imbibed knowledge upon whale fishing and sealing for the last four years. I am acquainted with the practical part of the undertaking in a thorough manner. Moreover, I have the assurance of active help from a man brought up in the trade, and although doing well where he is now, ready to return to his former pursuit (of whales). Finally I have a vessel in view, on very advantageous terms. And now for ways and means!

Upon that question I want your advice, or rather your opinion upon my plan to raise the necessary capital. From my uncle I cannot possibly ask the sum I require—£1,500, for reasons you no doubt understand. I do not know a man willing and able to advance me that amount of hard cash for the sake of my distinguished appearance, or any other sentimental consideration; having no tangible securities to offer, I have hit upon the idea of creating the same by insuring my life.

For, you see, although I cannot ask my uncle for the capital, I receive from him and from the London business (which I am advised is daily improving) yearly a sum sufficient for the payment of premium on life policy for £2,000, and the interest on the loan. *I suppose* I could raise on the security of the said policy (supposing the interest to be at the rate of 10 per cent) even should the venture for which the loan is destined turn out a dead failure: and I have special reasons to believe that such would not be the case. But let pass! Now, I want your advice on these points:

(1) Is such a transaction for a man in my position at all possible?

(2) If it is, what is the proper way to go about it? (for I am a very infant in business matters).

(3) Supposing the plan feasible, do you think, as a cool business man

---

[1] See *A Personal Record,* p. 113, "I was not frightened of being plucked; that eventuality did not even present itself to my mind."

Certificate delivered to Joseph Conrad Korzeniowski by Arch. Duncan, master of the ship *Narcissus* (1884).

not interested in the matter, that it would be sound to embark upon the undertaking (highly paying, *if successful,* as you know whaling is) on a capital borrowed at 12 per cent—for it will come to that with the premium and interest. (N. B. My idea is to pay the premium for the first year in advance, and then pay it every six months—always in advance.)

This is all the advice and "counsel's opinion" I require: I boldly ask for actual mental help in carrying the matter through, should it turn out to be more than the ravings of an unbusinesslike lunatic.

I have thought over it in all its aspects. Believe me, it is not the desire of getting much money that prompts me. It is simply the wish to work for myself. I am sick and tired of sailing about for little money and less consideration. But I love the sea: and if I could just clear my bare living in the way I suggested I should be comparatively happy. Can it be done? And if so: should it be done? I intended to ask you all those questions "viva voce" on my return, but I received here letters from Peterhead advising me of a sealing schooner—just the thing! This, together with the fact of us going actually to Dundee (next door to Peterhead), decided me to write to you on the matter. According to your answer, I shall, or shall not, run down to Peterhead before going to London; I shall, or shall not, give up plans carefully nursed for the last four years, and go on plodding in the old way, any way!

And now, dear Sir, will you kindly transmit to your father the expressions of my greatest respect and affection, my sincerest wishes for his good health and general welfare?

My dutiful compliments for Mme Kliszczewska, and friendly greetings for the boys, and always believe me, my dear Sir,

Yours gratefully and truly faithful,

CONRAD KORZENIOWSKI.

My address: Mr. Conrad, 2nd mate *Tilkhurst,* Sailors' Home, Dundee, to be delivered on arrival.

Write about the end of May, say the 20th.

To Spiridion Kliszczewski
19th December, 1885,
Calcutta.

MY DEAR SIR:

I received your kind and welcome letter yesterday, and to-day being Sunday, I feel that I could not make better use of my leisure hours than in answering your missive,

By this time, you, I and the rest of the "right thinking" have been grievously disappointed by the result of the General Election. The newly enfranchised idiots have satisfied the yearnings of Mr. Chamberlain's herd by cooking the national goose according to his recipe. The next culinary operation will be a pretty kettle of fish of an international character. Joy reigns in St. Petersburg, no doubt, and profound disgust in Berlin: the International Socialist Association are triumphant, and every disreputable ragamuffin in Europe feels that the day of universal brotherhood, despoliation and disorder is coming apace, and nurses daydreams of well-plenished pockets amongst the ruin of all that is respectable, venerable and holy. The great British Empire went over the edge, and yet on to the inclined plane of social progress and radical reform. The downward movement is hardly perceptible yet, and the clever men who started it may flatter themselves with the progress; but they will soon find that the fate of the nation is out of their hands now! The Alpine avalanche rolls quicker and quicker as it nears the abyss—its ultimate destination! Where's the man to stop the crashing avalanche?

Where's the man to stop the rush of social-democratic ideas? The opportunity and the day have come and are gone! Believe me: gone for ever! For the sun is set and the last barrier removed. England was the only barrier to the pressure of infernal doctrines born in continental back-slums. Now, there is nothing! The destiny of this nation and of all nations is to be accomplished in darkness amidst much weeping and gnashing of teeth, to pass through robbery, equality, anarchy and misery under the iron rule of a militarism despotism! Such is the lesson of common sense logic.

Socialism must inevitably end in Cæsarism.

Forgive me this long disquisition, but your letter—so earnest on the subject—is my excuse. I understand you perfectly. You wish to apply remedies to quell the dangerous symptoms: you evidently hope yet.

I do so no longer. Truthfully, I have ceased to hope a long time ago. We must drift!

The whole herd of idiotic humanity are moving in that direction at the bidding of unscrupulous rascals and a few sincere, but dangerous, lunatics. These things must be. It is fatality.

I live mostly in the past and the future. The present has, you easily understand, but few charms for me. I look with the serenity of despair and the indifference of contempt upon the passing events. Disestablishment, Land Reform, Universal Brotherhood are but like milestones on the road to ruin. The end will be awful, no doubt! Neither you nor I shall live to see the final crash: although we both may turn in our graves when it comes, for we both feel deeply and sincerely. Still, there is no earthly remedy for those earthly misfortunes, and from above, I fear, we may obtain consolation, but no remedy. "All is vanity."

Descending to common matters of life I transmit to your wife and yourself my best wishes for the coming year. May you have the winds fair and the seas smooth in the voyage of life. May the sail be long and pleasant, and if I wish your fine boys to walk straight in the path traced by their parents, I can wish them no better, for in the path of rectitude lies the true happiness!

With a hearty shake of the hand, believe me, my dear Sir and kind friend,

Yours very sincerely and faithfully,
K. N. KORZENIOWSKI.

To Spiridion Kliszczewski

6th January, 1886,
Calcutta.

MY DEAR SIR:

At last we are going to make a start for home! I am glad of it, being rather tired of the voyage and the ship—although very comfortable in all respects.

I hope all my letters reached you: they do get mislaid sometimes, as I know by experience. I venture to express the hope that you will kindly write to Dundee and pronounce your verdict upon my scheme. Even should all the arrangements (as I expect) strike you as foolish, yet I pray you to opine upon the insurance part as distinct from the whaling enterprise. What I should like to know is: can I reasonably expect to be able to raise a loan upon that security, should opportunity occur (to get command for instance) on moderate terms?

Should you opine that such a proceeding would be inadvisable or impossible I shall not trouble to insure, for not having a family, I do not see any necessity for doing so, unless for my own advantage.

I shall not, I think, start for Cardiff till I have passed my examination, when I shall be able, with my mind free of all immediate cares, to enjoy your society.

We are leaving to-morrow and a five months' passage is before us, then another month and I shall have the happiness to shake your friendly hand; till then believe me, my dear Sir,

Yours very faithfully,
KONRAD.

My compliments to Mme Kliszczewska and friendly greetings for the boys. My dutiful respects to Mr. Spiridion, Sen. with the hope of seeing him in good health on my return.

C. K.

Address

Mr. J. Conrad, 2nd Mate, Ship *Tilkhurst,* Sailors' Home, Dundee, to be delivered on arrival.

After remaining about a month at Singapore (September 25th to October 25th), the *Tilkhurst* weighed anchor for Calcutta, where she arrived on the 21st of November and remained six weeks.[1] Conrad's health seems to have been a little shaky, and during the years that followed he was more than once anxious about it. Like many men of nervous temperament, he was able to make efforts which were beyond his strength, when stimulated by his own will power and vivid sense of obligation. In spite of his antecedents and his often sickly childhood, an open-air life and an extreme sobriety had turned him into a healthy man, but the fatigues, often crushing, he had to endure as a sailor, though they did not really break his strength, undermined his constitution.

Writing on the 14th of August, 1885, his uncle says:

In exchange for the detailed news I am sending you, I am counting upon receiving the same from you. How is your general health, and your liver in particular? In spite of the assurances that you give me that the Indian climate is good from September to December, I am not so convinced about it as you seem to be, and I would much rather that you had sailed for other latitudes; for, if your first voyage to India has already affected your liver, the second may produce still graver trouble. Even if you become an admiral, at such a price your lot will not be an enviable one.

The voyage home was as normal and easy as the voyage out for the *Tilkhurst* and her crew; it contributes no dramatic adventures in Conrad's work.

She reached Dundee by the middle of June, and Conrad was discharged on the 17th. He accompanied Captain Blacke and his wife to London and his object was to pass as soon as possible his last examination. Conrad has described Captain

---

[1] A letter from Th. B., of April 24, 1886, shows that Conrad had dated his letter from the river Hooghly, January 8th.

Blacke in *The Mirror of the Sea,* under the appellation of
"poor Captain B—" as "the least sailor-like in outward aspect, but certainly one of the best seamen whom it has been
my good luck to serve under." On parting, Captain Blacke
said to him, "If you happen to be in want of employment remember that as long as I have a ship, you have a ship, too."
Alas! Captain Blacke was never able to put to sea again.
Some of the most touching pages Conrad ever wrote describe
his last visit in London to this old captain.[1]

Two things now occupied him: his naturalization and the
final examination which would give him his captain's certificate.
He was most anxious to visit Poland as soon as that examination should be over. His uncle was writing melancholy letters
from the Ukraine. Thaddeus Bobrowski's brother Casimir
was dangerously ill, and his wife and six children were dependent upon Uncle Thaddeus's bounty. He was now a lonely
man of sixty, who had lost his wife and daughter and was
about to lose his brother. Conrad's adventure-loving temperament filled him with misgivings. He had always urged him to
combine commerce with "the sea," partly, no doubt, in the
hope that such connections would keep him more in London.
He suggests that there might be a profitable connection between Poland and the firm of Barr, Moering & Co. Strange
as it may seem, Conrad, as the examination of documents
proves, did at this time think of giving up the sea and devoting himself to business. It is probable that the advice of his
uncle was reinforced by the prospect of profits held out to
him by his friend, Adolf P. Krieger. He may also have been
induced to entertain the idea as an alternative in the event
of failing to pass his captain's examination. Moreover, as the
answers from his uncle show, Conrad must have been just then
uneasy about his health. A meeting between them was impossible; Thaddeus Bobrowski, with new claims upon his
purse, could not afford to leave Poland, while Conrad could
not go there until he had been naturalized. At last the matter
of naturalization, about which his uncle had never ceased
to worry him for twelve years, was concluded. On August 19,
1886, Joseph Conrad Korzeniowski, "subject of the Russian

---

[1] *Mirror of the Sea,* Chaps. I–III, pp. 10 *et seq.*

Empire, of the age of twenty-nine years, mariner, unmarried," obtained a British certificate of naturalization.[1] His uncle wrote, "I clasp my Englishman to my breast as well as my nephew."

On November 11th he passed his examination and obtained his "Certificate of Competency as Master." The amiability of his chief examiner this time contrasted with the forbidding austerity of the last.[2] He was surprised to find that the candidate was a Pole. "Not many of your nationality in our service, I should think. I never remember meeting one either before or after I left the sea. Don't remember ever hearing of one. An inland people, aren't you?" For the rest, he gave Conrad a piece of advice he would not follow: he advised him "to go into steam." Eight years had sufficed for him to climb to the top of the ladder in the Merchant Service of a foreign country whose very language had been strange to him. Looking back, he might well feel some gratification on having falsified the predictions of his family.

It was a fact, I said to myself, that I was now a British master mariner beyond a doubt. It was not that I had an exaggerated sense of that very modest achievement, with which, however, luck, opportunity, or any extraneous influence could have had nothing to do. That fact, satisfactory and obscure in itself, had for me a certain ideal significance. It was an answer to a certain outspoken scepticism, and even to some not very kind aspersions. I had vindicated myself from what had been cried upon as a stupid obstinacy, or a fantastic caprice.[3]

His uncle, too, might well look back on the last twelve years with satisfaction. During the whole time, he had furnished the means necessary to his nephew's success and had never ceased to help him with advice and affection.

[1] The Oath of Allegiance is dated August 31, 1886, and in the certificate Conrad's address is given as 6 Dynevor Road, Stoke Newington, Middlesex. Conrad had lived in that place, when in London, at least for five years. In a letter from his uncle, dated June 13, 1881, one reads: "I'll write to you at 6 Dynevor Road, Stoke Newington."

[2] His examiners were Captain Steele, Captain Rankin, and Captain Sterry who passed him for master. (Information given by Conrad himself.) He has described all three in A Personal Record.

[3] A Personal Record, p. 120.

Long live "the Master British Merchant Service [sic]" [he wrote].
May he live as long as possible and may God grant him health and luck
on sea and land. Hearing of the *cachet rouge sur ton brevet* has made me
really happy. . . . Having been the humble provider of means to this
achievement, I can only congratulate my pennies on not having been
thrown away, but on having helped you to the top of the profession you
chose; on which account M. Antoine (inheritor of all the Greek and
Roman virtues), drew such a disastrous horoscope for the young man
who aspired to the service of Neptune. Monsieur my brother, you are
twenty-nine and the ball is at your feet. Do whatever seems good to
you.[1]

But his naturalization and his certificate are not the only
events which make 1885 a memorable year in his life: in 1885
he tried his hand for the first time at writing a story in English. The need for expression was in him; it had found vent
in his letters to Poland in his native language; he had been
an insatiable reader of English books. *Tit-Bits* had started a
prize competition for a story, and Conrad competed, un-
successfully, with one called "The Black Mate." A story with
the same title, and with the same subject, is to be found in
his collected works, but the existing version is no indication
of Conrad's command of English in 1886, for it was written
after that date.[2] It is true that in the final version there are
traces of the Conradian temperament, but the subject is more
in the vein of W. W. Jacobs; it shows the influence of the object for which it was written, and there is little or nothing of
the true quality of Conrad's work.

If the existing version is hardly Conradian, the original
one was probably even less so. It is only interesting as his first
step toward literary fame: a goal he had never dreamt of,
but one to which his profession was leading him.

The year 1886 marks a turning point in Conrad's life:

[1] Th. B., November 26, 1886. "M. Antoine" is presumably M. Antoine
Syroszczynski.

[2] In a letter to J. B. Pinker, January 19, 1922, Conrad wrote about "The
Black Mate": "I am surprised at the length of the thing. My feeling about it
is that there will be nothing actually disgraceful in its inclusion in my collected
edition. I don't remember whether I told you that I wrote that thing in '86 for
a prize competition started, I think, by *Tit-Bits.*" In Mr. Richard Curle's copy
Conrad has written: "My memories about this tale are confused. I have a notion
that it was written in the late 'eighties and retouched later."

chance events and some secret affinity within him had made him a British subject, a master in the Mercantile Marine and a budding author in a foreign language which was actually the second he had mastered; 1886 marks what amounts to a triple adoption by the country of his choice.

CHAPTER V

MEETING ALMAYER

(1887)

*"If I had not got to know Almayer pretty well it is almost
certain there would never have been a line of mine in print."*

("A PERSONAL RECORD")

A MASTER'S CERTIFICATE was no doubt a pleasant possession, but he could not live on it. The necessity to earn money
was urgent. His little capital in Barr, Moering & Co. brought
in, of course, only a tiny interest and Uncle Thaddeus had
now to support the widow and children of his brother Casimir. Conrad could not afford to wait for a command, so on
February 16, 1887, he took the post of first mate in the *Highland Forest* at Amsterdam, a Glasgow sailing vessel of a
thousand tons, bound for Samarang, in Java.

She could not put to sea at once; the cargo was delayed
and the severity of the winter postponed departure from
week to week. Conrad has described his surroundings in *The
Mirror of the Sea.*

I call to mind a winter landscape in Amsterdam—a flat foreground
of waste land, with here and there stacks of timber like the huts of a
camp of some very miserable tribe; the long stretch of the Handelskade;
cold, stone-faced quays, with the snow-sprinkled ground and the hard,
frozen water of the canal, in which were set ships one behind another
with their frosty mooring ropes hanging slack and their decks idle and
deserted because, as the master stevedore (a gentle, pale person with a
few golden hairs on his chin and a reddened nose) informed me, their
cargoes were frozen in up-country on barges and schuyts. In the distance,
beyond the waste ground, and running parallel with the line of ships, a
line of brown warm-toned houses seemed bowed under snow-laden roofs.
From afar at the end of Tsar Peter Straat, issued in the frosty air the
tinkle of bells of the horse tramcars, appearing and disappearing in the

opening between the buildings, like little toy carriages, harnessed with toy horses and played with by people that appeared no bigger than children." . . . [1]

As the days passed Conrad found it more and more irksome waiting for the cargo, which seemed to have been frost-bound somewhere in the interior of the country. There was nothing to do on board and it was bitterly cold. Every evening he used to go to a café in the centre of the town.

It was an immense place, lofty and gilt, upholstered in red plush, full of electric lights and so thoroughly warmed that even the marble tables felt tepid to the touch. The waiter who brought me my cup of coffee bore, by comparison with my utter isolation, the dear aspect of an intimate friend. There, alone in a noisy crowd, I would write slowly a letter addressed to Glasgow, of which the gist would be: there is no cargo and no prospect of any coming till late spring, apparently. And all the time I sat there the necessity of getting back to the ship bore heavily on my already half congealed spirits.[2]

The only thing that kept his heart warm was his sense of the importance of his job, though as yet it gave him nothing to do. During the day he used to visit a Mr. Hudig.[3]

Mr. Hudig always began by shoving me into a chair before I had time to open my mouth, gave me cordially a large cigar and in excellent English would start to talk everlastingly about the phenomenal severity of the weather. It was impossible to threaten a man who, though he possessed the language perfectly, seemed incapable of understanding any phrase pronounced in a tone of remonstrance or discontent. As to quarrelling with him it would have been stupid. The weather was too bitter for that. His office was so warm, his fire so bright, his sides shook so heartily with laughter that I experienced always a great difficulty in making up my mind to reach for my hat.[3]

After many visits to Mr. Hudig and having written many letters to the owners at Glasgow, at last the cargo did arrive, and the evening before the day fixed for sailing, the captain of the *Highland Forest* himself put in an appearance. He was no less a person than Captain John McWhirr, whose name,

[1] *The Mirror of the Sea*, pp. 48–49, "The Weight of the Burden."
[2] *Ibid.*, p. 49.
[3] This was the name Conrad gave later to the Dutch trader from Macassar in *Almayer's Folly* and in *An Outcast of the Islands*.
[4] *The Mirror of the Sea*, p. 51.

features, and temperament Joseph Conrad was to give later on to the hero of *Typhoon*. He is also mentioned in *The Mirror of the Sea*—at least his habit of remaining invisible in his cabin for the first few days of the voyage; a habit which left the entire responsibility to Conrad.

The voyage to Samarang "with a general cargo of which, alas! only one third in weight was stowed above the beams, was lively but not joyful." The manner in which she was loaded made the ship roll heavily, and the passage was unpleasantly rough.

There were days when nothing would keep even on the swing tables, when there was no position where you could fix yourself so as not to feel a constant strain upon all the muscles of your body. . . . It was a wonder that the men sent aloft were not flung off the yards, the yards not flung off the masts, the masts not flung overboard. . . . [1]

This unfortunate stowage of the cargo incidentally proved a misfortune to Conrad himself. He was struck in the back by "a piece of minor spar" which knocked him down, and after the accident he suffered from rather strange symptoms; "inexplicable periods of powerlessness, sudden accesses of mysterious pain," which mystified the doctor who treated him at Samarang. He had reached that port in June. The doctor was anxious about him and wanted him to leave the ship [2] and keep quiet for three months. He went to Singapore, where he was in the hospital some weeks. The hospital commanded the town and the bay, and he enjoyed recalling the dreadful cold and snow of Amsterdam while looking at the fronds of the palm trees, tossing and rustling at the height of the window.[3]

He recovered, however, more quickly than the doctor expected, and two months later he embarked as second mate in the S.S. *Vidar* (800 tons), though it was probably his shaky health alone which made him prefer a steamer, which he had done only once, ten years before, in the case of the *Europa*. The work on board was considerably lighter, and short voyages, involving no sudden change of climate, also proved bene-

[1] *The Mirror of the Sea*, p. 54, "The Weight of the Burden."
[2] Conrad did so on July 1st. (certificate of discharge).
[3] *The Mirror of the Sea*, p. 55.

ficial to his rheumatism and general health. They were not marked by startling incidents, but they were destined to play a considerable part in making a writer of him.

In 1924, I had the good luck to meet Captain C——, who commanded the *Vidar* when Conrad was her second mate. When I met him, he was carrying his seventy years and fifty years of seamanship lightly, and to him I am indebted for the following particulars:

The first time I met Conrad was at the Shipping Office of Singapore about the middle of August, 1887. He pleased me at once by his manners, which were distinguished and reserved. One of the first things he told me was that he was a foreigner by birth, which I had already guessed from his accent. I replied that that did not matter in the least as he had his certificate. (It was quite difficult at that time to find officers in the East who were not over fond of the bottle.) The *Vidar* belonged to an Arab called Syed Mosin Bin S. Ali Jaffree. He had been a rich man, but he had been nearly ruined by his two sons-in-law. I had navigated these waters for the past ten or twelve years, and I had got to know that Arab well. I respected him. Some of his creditors were on the point of making him bankrupt; the Chartered Bank had seized the ship, but they could not sell because I was a creditor with a prior claim—for wages, docking-costs, etc. During one voyage among the islands I collected several thousand guilders from his debtors, and on his instructions I placed them with a bank, which, after a creditors' meeting, made an arrangement; there was a sale, and the steamship *Vidar* became in part my property.

Such was the situation when Conrad joined her and we find reminiscence of her in Conrad's description of the ship he had just left, in *The Shadow Line* [1] :

She was an Eastern ship, inasmuch as then she belonged to that port. She traded among dark islands on a blue reef-scarred sea, with the Red Ensign over the taffrail and at her masthead a house-flag, also red, but with a green border and with a white crescent in it. For an Arab owned her, and a Syed at that. Hence the green border on the flag. He was the head of a great house of Straits Arabs, but as loyal a subject of the complex British Empire as you could find east of the Suez Canal. World politics did not trouble him at all, but he had a great occult power amongst his own people.

It was all one to us who owned the ship. He had to employ white men in the shipping part of his business, and many of those he so em-

[1] Pages 4-5.

ployed had never set eyes on him from the first to the last day. I myself saw him but once, quite accidentally on a wharf—an old, dark little man blind in one eye, in a snowy robe and yellow slippers. He was having his hand severely kissed by a crowd of Malay pilgrims to whom he had done some favour, in the way of food and money. . . . Excellent (and picturesque) Arab owner, about whom one needed not to trouble one's head. . . ."

She was not sailing under the British, but under the Dutch, flag, and she was registered at Banjarmassim, one of the chief ports of Dutch Borneo. Her course was to sail from Singapore through the Carimata Strait, from South Borneo to Banjarmassim, then between the Isle of Pulo Laut and the coast of Borneo. She coaled at Pulo Laut, touched at Dongala on the western coast of the Celebes, returned to Coti Broeuw, and finally reached Bulungan on the east coast of Borneo, whence she returned by the same route to Singapore. Most of these ports are in the estuaries of tortuous rivers, the banks of which are covered with a thick vegetation. Each little port was one long street, or rather row of houses and shops about six feet high, facing the river; among which the landing stage was the most prominent object. There was a profitable trade in natural products; in rubber, cane, gutta percha, gum, resin. The *Vidar* took as a rule three weeks over this voyage. Besides the captain and Conrad, the crew consisted of two European and one Chinese engineer, a second mate Mahamat, eleven Malayans, and eighty-two Chinamen; the latter were used for loading and unloading at the various ports. Conrad made, between August 22, 1887, and January 5, 1888, five or six of these voyages from Singapore to Bulungan in Borneo, which is the place to which he gave the name of "Sambir" in *Almayer's Folly* and *An Outcast of the Islands*. Its river he called the "Pantai."

It was during these voyages that he made the acquaintance of Almayer, also of Willems, Abdulla, Babalatchi, Lakamba, and Tom and Jim Lingard, characters who figure either in *Almayer's Folly,* or in *An Outcast of the Islands,* or in *The Rescue,* or in *Lord Jim;* and it was during these voyages that he absorbed that Malayan local colour which is so marked a feature in such work as "Karain," and "The Lagoon."

He made friends with his captain, and from him he learnt

many facts about the Malay Archipelago and the lives of its inhabitants. Captain C—— had navigated the dangerous rivers of the islands for ten years and had come into contact with European, half-caste, Arab, and Malayan traders. Few men could have been better qualified than he to enlighten the curiosity of his mate. Conrad's curiosity was keen, his memory was retentive, and his habit of brooding over what he had seen and heard was unsuspected by his companions. Years afterward Captain C—— told me he had been astonished to find, on reading the books, how completely Conrad had penetrated the spirit of these places and how thoroughly he had understood the characters of the men he had met. He had been there a very short time, yet he had reproduced places and men with amazing accuracy and vividness.

Almayer, the half-caste Dutchman, lived at Bulungan. According to Captain C——, Conrad has drawn an exact moral and physical portrait of him. In Chapter IV of *A Personal Record* he has described how he first encountered this strange person on one chilly early morning. Almayer's appearance, what he had heard of him before, and above all the contrast between his dilapidated condition and the enormous ambitions which he still nourished, made a deep impression on Conrad. He saw before him a vivid example of that discord between the imagination in man and his power to perform, which was to be one dominant theme, at once magnificent and pathetic, of his work as an artist. How charged with consequence this meeting was, Conrad's own words show: "If I had not got to know Almayer pretty well," he wrote in *A Personal Record,* "it is almost certain there would never have been a line of mine in print." [1]

Almayer was an Eurasian. He had married, as he is represented as having done in the book, a Malayan woman; only Conrad, for reasons connected with the story, made his child a girl and not, as was actually the case, a son. The real Almayer died of a wound he got on a python-hunt.

On one of these voyages, the *Vidar,* while clearing the Macassar Strait, encountered a long way from the coast a small canoe half-filled with water, in which a runaway Ma-

[1] *A Personal Record,* Chap. IV, p. 87.

layan slave was awaiting death. They picked him up and took him to Pulo Laut, where he worked some time on a pepper plantation before returning to his own island. This incident, according to Captain C——, must have given Conrad a hint for *An Outcast of the Islands*. As for Willems, the lamentable hero of that book, he was a Dutch sailor, once a fine, robust man, who had taken to drink and had become entirely dependent upon Almayer and the other residents in Bulungan. Conrad met him first when he went to dine with Almayer.

He was sitting with us in the manner of the skeleton at the feast. . . . Almayer, conversing with my captain, did not stop talking while he glared angrily at the retreating back. . . . It was clear that in those days Willems lived on Almayer's charity.[1]

It was during these Singapore and Borneo voyages that Conrad also came across that Tom Lingard whom he afterward made the hero of two of his books; creating him out of traits taken from the real man and others borrowed from Dominic Cervoni, who, from Conrad's first seafaring days to the end of his literary life, was a sort of familiar demon of his imagination.

The real Tom Lingard was the captain of a schooner which traded between Singapore, Benjarmassim, Cottu, Bulungan, and other Dutch places to the north. His nephew, Jim, had first served on board his uncle's ship and then established himself in Tom's interest as a trader at Bulungan. It was on board the *Vidar* that he was first dubbed Lord Jim, "thanks to the swaggering manner he assumed, when meeting our ship." [2]

Jim Lingard was married to a Malayan woman, by whom he had a numerous family. He made two or three voyages from Bulungan to Singapore on board the *Vidar* when Conrad was mate.

Of course, the real Jim Lingard and the Lord Jim of Conrad's novel have nothing in common except their name and physique. Babalatchi and Lakamba, whom we also meet

[1] See Author's Note in *An Outcast of the Islands*.
[2] Information from Captain C——.

in Conrad's Malayan books, were two natives of the Celebes established as merchants at Broeuw. They were much respected by the inhabitants, and their remarkable appearance attracted Conrad's attention. As to Abdulla, the appellation of Syed joined to his name signified that he was a descendant of Mahomet, which conferred on him high rank amongst Mussulmans. He was the elder son of Syed Mosin, the Arab to whom the *Vidar* still partly belonged. "Mr. Conrad," said Captain C——, "often called my attention to Abdulla and to the natives doing obeisance to him and kneeling to kiss his hand —their servility seemed repugnant to him." From Captain C——, James Allen, and John C. Niven [1] (first and second engineers) he got all the information he could about these people: their antecedents, morals, intimacies, and intrigues. Thus he mastered completely this corner of the world, where the clash of two races and many religions, the passions, follies, principles, and failures of men wove those intricate plots, of which he was to become the astonishing dramatist. [2]

It is not likely that he took more notes of what he heard and saw during this period than he did at any other. Conrad was never in the habit of taking notes, but Captain C—— asserts that, when he went down to the cabin to talk to his first mate, he usually found him writing. [3]

He could not resist those secret stirrings toward authorship, though he was still to wait seven years before publishing his first book. It may be said that, on board the *Vidar*, Captain Joseph Conrad Korzeniowski served in his spare moments his apprenticeship as a writer. No part of his life is richer in literary fruit than the second half of 1887, with the possible exception of the second half of 1890, which he passed in the Congo. There is a touch of irony in the fact that Conrad, the lover of sailing ships, was on board a steamer on both these occasions.

[1] This man appears as "John Nieven" in *The Shadow Line*, p. 6: "John Nieven was a fierce misogynist."

[2] "That part of the Eastern Seas from which I have carried away into my writing life the greatest number of suggestions." (*The Shadow Line*, Author's Note, p. ix.)

[3] We have traced only one letter written by Conrad from the *Vidar*, Singapore, November 3d.

CHAPTER VI

FIRST COMMAND

(1888)

"Youth is a fine thing, a mighty power—as long as one does not think of it. I felt I was becoming self-conscious."

("THE SHADOW LINE")

IN THE course of these five or six voyages of three weeks each, Conrad's health had recovered—so, at least, we gather from a letter Uncle Thaddeus wrote to him on his thirtieth birthday; and he found his fellow officers, the captain and the two engineers, the best of good fellows. More than thirty years later he wrote to Mr. Niven, the engineer:

> You could not really have believed that I had forgotten any time in the *Vidar*. It is part of my sea life to which my memory returns most often, since there is nothing to remember but what is good and pleasant in my temporary association with three men for whom, I assure you, I have preserved to this day a warm regard and sincere esteem.[1]

But, at the time, in spite of their friendship, the novelty of the country and the singularity of the characters he met, a certain weariness began to creep over the second officer of the *Vidar*. It was not a physical lassitude, but a kind of moral uneasiness, a melancholy without reason, an obscure nostalgia for—he knew not what. The want of variety in these regular voyages, the routine work on board began to weigh upon him. The calls upon him were too trivial to employ so active and ardent a temperament. From another of his uncle's letters we infer that Conrad was thinking of returning to Europe, and his impatience at a life so devoid of dash and go is reflected in the beginning of "The End of the Tether":

---

[1] Letter dated December 5, 1923.

He could not hope to see anything new upon this lane of the sea. . . . The old ship ought to have known the road better than her men, who had not been kept so long at it without a change. . . . She made her landfalls to a degree of the bearing and almost to a minute of her allowed time. At any moment as he sat on the bridge without looking up, or lay sleepless in his bed, simply by reckoning the days and the hours he could tell where he was—the precise spot of the beat. He knew it well, too, this monotonous huckster's round, up and down the Straits; he knew its order and its sights and its people. Malacca, to begin with, in at daylight and out at dusk, to cross over with a rigid phosphorescent wake this highway of the Far East . . . At noon the three palms of the next place of call, up a sluggish river. . . . Sixty miles farther on there was another place of call, a deep bay with only a couple of houses on the beach. And so on, in and out, picking up coastwise cargo here and there, and finishing with a hundred miles' steady steaming through the maze of an archipelago of small islands up to a large native town at the end of the beat. There was a three days' rest for the old ship before he started her again in inverse order, seeing the same shores from another bearing, hearing the same voices in the same places, back again to the *Sofala's* port of registry, on the great highway to the East, where he would take up a berth nearly opposite the big stone pile of the harbour office till it was time to start again on the old round of 1,600 miles and thirty days . . . not a very enterprising life for a man who had served famous firms, who had sailed famous ships. . . .[1]

In that pathetic story, "The End of the Tether," a captain goes blind without his crew realizing what is happening. Captain C—— informed me that at this time Conrad himself was very uneasy about his eyesight. It seems, therefore, as though he had only had to magnify his own past sensations to draw "Captain Whalley."

Physically and morally, he was passing through one of those transformations which are common enough in the lives of men, but differ in each case according to temperament and imagination and in being either restrained or explosive. Conrad has given a characteristic name to this inner crisis: he calls it "the shadow line."

One goes on. And the time, too, goes on, till one perceives ahead a shadow line warning one that the region of early youth, too, must be left behind.

[1] See *Youth and Two Other Stories,* pp. 166 and 167.

This is the period of life in which such moments of which I have spoken are likely to come. What moments? Why, the moments of boredom, of weariness, of dissatisfaction. Rash moments. I mean moments when the still young are inclined to commit rash actions, such as getting married suddenly or else throwing up a job for no reason. . . . A most excellent Scottish ship—for she was that from the keel up—excellent sea-boat, easy to keep clean, most handy in every way, and if it had not been for her internal propulsion, worthy of any man's love. I cherish to this day a profound respect for her memory. As to the kind of trade she was engaged in and the character of my ship-mates, I could not have been happier if I had had the life and the men made to my order by a benevolent Enchanter.

And suddenly I left all this. I left it in that, to us, inconsequential manner in which a bird flies away from a comfortable branch. It was as though all unknowing I had heard a whisper or seen something. Well—perhaps! One day I was perfectly right and the next everything was gone—glamour, flavour, interest, contentment—everything. . . . The green sickness of late youth descended on me and carried me off. Carried me off that ship, I mean.

We were only four white men on board, with a large crew of Kalashes and two Malay petty officers. The captain stared hard as if wondering what ailed me. But he was a sailor, and he, too, had been young at one time. Presently a smile came to lurk under his thick iron-gray moustache, and he observed that, of course, if I felt I must go he couldn't keep me by main force. And it was arranged that I should be paid off the next morning. As I was going out of the chart-room he added suddenly, in a peculiar, wistful tone, that he hoped I would find what I was so anxious to go and look for. A soft cryptic utterance which seemed to reach deeper than any diamond-hard tool could have done. I do believe he understood my case.[1]

On January 5, 1888, while at Singapore, he suddenly decided to throw up his berth on the *Vidar*, though he had no clear idea of what he would do next. What reason he gave Captain C—— for his decision we do not know. Captain

---

[1] See *The Shadow Line*, pp. 3, 4, 5, 6. Amongst J. C.'s sea papers was a personal certificate as follows: "Singapore, Jan. 5th, 1888. This is to certify that Mr. C. Korzeniouski [sic] has sailed with me as Chief Officer on the S.S. *Vidar* for a period of seven months, and during that time I found him a steady, sober and attentive officer at all times. I can recommend him to any Owner or Master to look after their interests, and a good seaman, James C——, Master." The period August 22d to January 5th was four and a half months and not seven as stated in that certificate.

C—— told me that he had been reluctant to separate from Conrad, with whom he had been quite satisfied, but that he did not want to prevent one of his subordinates from making a career for himself.[1]

At the moment when Conrad was preparing to return to Europe in search of a ship, circumstances unexpectedly put him in the way of getting just what he wanted: the command of a sailing vessel. These circumstances are related with careful literalness in *The Shadow Line*. We have the author's own authority for saying this. Moreover, the story was originally to have borne the title, *First Command*.[2] He was expecting no such good fortune, having hoped in vain for a whole year; now a command dropped out of the blue. In the story it is a Captain Giles who is the means of his getting it; the real man was called Patterson. Captain C—— of the *Vidar* appears as "Kent" and the novelist has left the marine superintendent at Singapore his proper name, Ellis. We must not conclude, however, that the singular character in *The Shadow Line* who, always by way of seeking a command, never finds one good enough, and prefers to live from hand to mouth at the Sailors' Home, was in fact called "Hamilton." But the conclusion of Chapter I, in which the hero is offered by the marine superintendent an English ship, then in the port of Bangkok, the captain of which had just died, is a literal transcription of fact:

I said I would be ready that very day if necessary. He caught me at my word with great readiness. The steamer *Melita* was leaving for

[1] After separating at Singapore in January, 1888, the two men corresponded for some time; then Conrad returned to Europe and proceeded to Africa. Captain C—— remained for over thirty years more in the East. He did not return finally until just before the novelist's death. But in 1896, on a visit of a few weeks to London, his eye happened to light on a book bearing the title *Almayer's Folly*, which was the nickname he himself had given to the house of his Almayer at Bulungan. He bought it and saw at once that it was the work of his first officer, recognizing in it, too, many of the talks they had had together. He did not know Conrad's address, so he neglected to write to him. When he returned for good and all in 1923, he got news of him from John Niven and he was thinking of paying Conrad a visit, when the latter died.

[2] "That piece of work is not a story really but an exact autobiography." (Letter to J. B. Pinker, 1917.) "The very speeches are (I won't say authentic, they are that absolutely) I believe verbally accurate. And all this happened in March–April, 1887." (Letter to Sir Sidney Colvin, February 27, 1917.)

Bangkok that evening about seven. He would request her captain officially to give me a passage and wait for me till ten o'clock.

It is possible to date this conversation exactly as having taken place on January 19, 1888, from the Memorandum signed by Henry Ellis [1] and addressed to Captain C. Korzeniowski:

This is to inform you that you are required to proceed to-day in the S.S. *Melita* to Bangkok and you will report your arrival to the British Consul which will show that I have engaged you to be Master of the *Otago* in accordance with the Consul's telegram on a voyage from Bangkok to Melbourne, wages at fourteen pounds per month and to count from date of your arrival at Bangkok, your passage from Singapore to Bangkok to be borne by the ship. Further to receive a passage from Melbourne to Singapore if you are not kept in the ship.

Conrad has vividly described the elation produced in him by this sudden appointment; that elation, however, was soon destined to give place to a very different emotion. He left Singapore the same evening after saying good-bye to Captain Patterson (alias Giles), whose parting words were, "I expect you'll have your hands pretty full of tangled up business." [2] The young captain, however, had no such apprehensions; he knew well that part of the Indian Ocean and the Malay Archipelago. True, he did not know the Gulf of Siam, or Captain Patterson's remark about it, "The Gulf . . . Ay! A funny piece of water—that," might well have inspired him with a faint uneasiness. But pride in his first command and joy at being master of a fine ship kept his spirits high during the four days' voyage to Bangkok—itself, that place of his dreams, which the burning of the *Palestine* had prevented him from seeing five years before. He was not even depressed by the captain of the *Melita,* "the first really unsympathetic man I had ever come in contact with," [3] though his eagerness to see his ship made the voyage seem long.

[1] The Captain H. Ellis appears also under the name of Captain Eliott in "The End of the Tether" (Chap. IV).
[2] *The Shadow Line,* p. 43.
[3] *Ibid.,* Chap. II, p. 47.

Suddenly I heard myself called by that imbecile. He was beckoning me to come up on his bridge. I didn't care very much for that, but as it seemed that he had something particular to say, I went up the ladder. He laid his hand on my shoulder and gave me a slight turn, pointing with his other arm at the same time.

"There! That's your ship, Captain," he said. I felt a thump in my breast—only one, as if my heart had ceased to beat. There were ten or more ships moored along the bank, and the one he meant was partly hidden from my sight by her next astern. . . . Directly my eyes had rested on my ship, all my fear vanished . . . Yes, there she was. Her hull, her rigging filled my eye with a great content. That feeling of life-emptiness which had made me so restless for the last few months lost its bitter plausibility, its evil influence, dissolved into a flow of joyous emotion. At the first glance I saw that she was a high-class vessel, a harmonious creature in the lines of her fine body, in the proportioned tallness of her spars. Whatever her age and her history, she had preserved the stamp of her origin. She was one of those craft that in virtue of their design and complete finish will never look old. Amongst her companions moored to the bank, and all bigger than herself, she looked like a creature of high breed—an Arab-steed in a string of cart-horses. . . . I knew that, like some rare women, she was one of those creatures whose mere existence is enough to awaken an unselfish delight. One feels that it is good to be in the world in which she has her being.[1]

She was the barque *Otago* which Conrad would have first to take to Melbourne.[2] The circumstances connected with his taking her over and his stay at Bangkok have also left traces in a story which he published before *The Shadow Line*, namely *Falk*.[3] From comparison between these two stories and documents in our possession we can reconstruct the events which followed accurately.

Conrad had been unexpectedly appointed to command the *Otago* upon the death of her captain. There was nothing very unusual in that. But her late captain had been a man of somewhat singular character. From the second officer he learnt that he had been sixty-five years old, and that he had spent the last weeks of his life playing the fiddle day and night in his cabin, without paying the smallest heed to the ship's

---

[1] *The Shadow Line,* pp. 48 and 49.
[2] She belonged to Messrs. Henry Simpson & Sons, of Port Adelaide, owners of the Black Diamond Line.
[3] Written in May, 1901.

course,—except to prevent her touching at a port; that he had seemed not so much indifferent to the welfare of his officers and crew, as desirous of seeing them all perish some day of hunger and boredom. One day, feeling himself to be ill, he had thrown his fiddle overboard and allowed himself to die; to the last completely indifferent to his crew.

Such a character when met in a book would naturally strike us as a strange creature of the imagination; but when we remember how much Conrad always took from actual experience, and observe how the details tally in the two stories, *Falk* and *The Shadow Line,* though fourteen years elapsed between the writing of them, there is good reason to suppose that this extraordinary captain was a real character. He left his successor "some suspiciously unreceipted bills, a few drydock estimates hinting at bribery, and a quantity of vouchers for three years' extravagant expenditure," all of which were discovered in disorder inside a dusty violin case. An account book was also found, not filled with figures, but with poems of a joyful and indecent character, together with a photograph of the captain himself taken at Saigon beside a woman dressed in an odd costume.[1]

The new captain must have been profoundly shocked by the evidences of his predecessor's complete disregard of the principles and traditions of the position he himself was about to fill for the first time. He found himself unable to clear up the accounts of the last two years, and the situation became still more intricate when he discovered that his predecessor had not taken the trouble to keep the owners informed of his movements. This detail is confirmed by a letter from Messrs. Henry Simpson & Sons, Port Adelaide, April 5, 1888, which was found among Conrad's papers. It is addressed to Captain Korzeniowski at Sydney "to await arrival" and runs as follows:

DEAR SIR:
Your favours dated Bangkok 2nd and 6th February, latter with P S.

---

[1] *Falk* (*Typhoon and Other Stories*), pp. 153 and 154. See the same details more developed in *The Shadow Line,* p. 59. Note that the subtitle of *Falk* is: "A Reminiscence" and that the circumstances correspond exactly with Conrad's when he took over the command of the *Otago.*

dated 7th on the eve of sailing, duly reached me, and have been interesting as detailing the melancholy circumstances under which you took charge of the barque *Otago*.

The accounts which you enclosed are no doubt at all in order but I have no means of comparing them with other documents as the late Captain never favoured me with a scratch of the pen [1] from the time of leaving Newcastle in August last and the acting Master Mr. Burns only wrote me a brief note acquainting me with his Captain's death. There-fore, I am at a loss to know what business was done by the ship after she arrived at Haiphong, whether she earned or whether she lost money. In fact, other than your documents, I have no record whatever of receipts and expenditure. Will you, therefore, please inform me whether any freight was obtained between Haiphong and Bangkok and if so, how much and generally what business was done by the ship for the ten months previous to your assuming command?

I presume the vessel will be entered inwards by the consignee of cargo, and you will no doubt telegraph your arrival to me. As to what will be done later on, nothing has yet been determined, but probably the late Captain's executors will wish the vessel sold in the interest of the widow and mortgages, and his two shares were fully pledged. It's quite likely, however, that before such sale I shall take a run over to Sydney, in which case I shall have the pleasure of making your acquaintance.

JAS. H. SIMPSON.

Captain Korzeniowski could not depend upon zealous sup-port from his two officers. The second officer, Mr. Burns, was a disappointed man. He had served on board the *Otago* for two years, but he was not qualified to be a master; yet he had navigated her to Bangkok after the death of the captain, in full expectation of getting his position confirmed.[2] As for the third officer, he was far from being a right-hand man to his captain, if we are to believe the description of him in *Falk*.

His name was Tottersen or something like that. His practice was to wear on his head, in that tropical climate, a mangy fur cap. He was, without exception, the stupidest man I had ever seen on board ship. And he looked it too. He looked so confoundedly stupid that it was a matter of surprise for me when he answered to his name.[3]

---

[1] See *Falk*, p. 154. "A letter from the owners complained mildly enough that they had not been favoured by a scratch of the pen for the last eighteen months."
[2] *Falk*, p. 154. See also *The Shadow Line*, p. 63.
[3] *Falk*, p. 154. See also *The Shadow Line*, p. 73.

The prospect of a voyage of sixty days from Bangkok to
Sydney in the company of these officers was not at all ex-
hilarating, nor was the situation satisfactory in other respects.
The young captain had to raise money to buy ship's necessities;
there was not a yard of sailcloth or rope on board. The
health of the crew was disquieting. Already stricken with
fever, it was urgent that the ship should leave the pestilential
river for the open sea as soon as possible; but the cargo
could not be procured at once, and meanwhile the health of
the crew deteriorated. The steward was the first to succumb;
he was taken to the hospital suffering from cholera and died
in a week;[1] the Chinaman who replaced him disappeared
after three days with thirty-two pounds, the whole of Conrad's painfully accumulated economies set aside against serious
emergencies. Mr. Burns next retired to his cabin with fever
and had ultimately to be taken to hospital. Mr. Burns, in his
first disappointment, had threatened to leave the ship, but he
had a wife and child in Sydney, and he now begged not to
be left behind. The cargo accumulated very slowly; delay was
inevitable, and delay meant that still more of the crew would
soon be down with fever. Thus difficulties and ominous responsibilities beset the young captain on every side. He might
well conclude, as he says in *Falk*, that,

Everything in this world, even the command of a nice little barque,
may be a delusion and a snare for the unwary spirit of pride in men.

This enforced delay lasted from January 24th to February
8th. If we are to believe what we read in *Falk*, the atmosphere
on board his own ship was so detestable at nightfall that he
spent most of his evenings on board a German ship anchored
near him in the river, which was more like a floating bourgeois
villa than an ordinary ship. Conrad had made the acquaintance of the *Diana's* captain on the occasion when he started
in pursuit of the runaway Chinaman. Captain Hermann had
joined with great good will in this fruitless search, and his
friendly cordiality afforded Conrad a little relief in the midst
of his worries. In the evenings he would go and smoke a

[1] *The Shadow Line*, p. 67.

pipe on board the *Diana* with Captain Hermann, who was surrounded by his wife and children; among the young people was that robust niece who became the silent heroine of *Falk*. It is likely enough that "Falk" himself is a real person, a Scandinavian captain, who actually refused Conrad the loan of his tug (the only one on the river), because he imagined that Conrad was running him down and spoiling his chances of marrying Captain Hermann's niece.

It was also at Bangkok that Conrad met that hotelkeeper to whom he gave the name of Schomberg,[1] who appears both in *Falk* and in *Victory*. It was to this unpleasant character that he was indebted for the introduction of the evasive Chinaman on board his own ship.

This fortnight at Bangkok, filled mostly with disagreeable incidents, left a permanent impression on Conrad's memory. Certain details belonging to it also appear in another of his stories, "The Secret Sharer." [2] The Gulf of Siam, the island of Koh-ring, the scenery at the mouth of the river, are clearly delineated in that story, though it does not embody any personal experience, but an incident which took place years before on board the *Cutty Sark,* of famous memory. Conrad has framed the story in the setting of memory to lend it an air of reality; and, in order to introduce an element of drama, the young captain in it is represented as having just stepped on board a strange ship, knowing nothing whatever about her or her crew—in fact, in precisely his own situation on board the *Otago,* when he sailed out of Bangkok harbour.

That the condition of the crew of the *Otago* was what it is represented to have been in *Falk* and *The Shadow Line* is proved by the following letter which was found among Conrad's papers:

---

[1] "A certain Schomberg, a big, manly, bearded creature of the Teutonic persuasion . . . he was by profession an hotelkeeper, first in Bangkok, then somewhere else and ultimately in Sourabaya." *Victory,* Chap. II. See also, Chap. III, p. 26: "He put a stress on the word Swede as if it meant scoundrel. He detested Scandinavians generally. Why? Goodness only knows." It has to be noted that Heyst, in *Victory,* is a Scandinavian like Falk and the feeling of Schomberg is the same in each story.

[2] See *'Twixt Land and Sea.*

Bangkok, Siam,
February, 1888.

DEAR SIR:

I think it is not out of place on my part that I should state, though not asked by you to do so, to prevent any misapprehension hereafter, that the crew of the sailing ship *Otago* has suffered severely whilst in Bangkok from tropical diseases, including fever, dysentery and cholera; and I can speak of my own knowledge that you have done all in your power in the trying and responsible position of Master of the ship to hasten the departure of your vessel from this unhealthy place and at the same time to save the lives of the men under your command.

Yours faithfully,
William Willis, M.D., F.R.C.S.E. [1]
Physician to H. M. Legation in Siam.

C. Korzeniowski, Esq.,
Master of the sailing-ship *Otago*.

At last the *Otago* left the river, with a sick crew, a second officer so ill that he had to be carried on board on a litter, and a third officer who was of very little use indeed. The most capable member of the crew was the cook, a first-rate sailor, who had been engaged for that job because he suffered from a weak heart; he and the captain were the only two men whose health had not suffered from the climate. It was Ransome who, morally and practically, helped Conrad most to run the ship. Her progress at first was extremely slow, and the young captain was soon to discover that the Gulf of Siam was indeed "a funny piece of water." Not a breath of wind filled her sails—and it was vital that they should leave behind them as soon as possible the malarious estuary! To crown everything, as Conrad has related in *The Shadow Line,* both his officers were unsympathetic to him. More than thirty years later, writing to Sir Sidney Colvin about *The Shadow Line,* he said:

The locality does not matter and if it is the Gulf of Siam it's simply because the whole thing is exact autobiography. . . . I am sorry you

[1] "A doctor is humane by definition, but that man was so in reality . . . he was the doctor of our Legation and, of course, of the Consulate too. . . . He was the only human being in the world who seemed to take the slightest interest in me." (*The Shadow Line,* p. 66.)

received an impression of horror. I tried to keep the mere horror out. It would have been easy to pile it on. You may believe me *j'ai vécu tout cela.*

The situation, too, was not without irony. When on board the *Palestine* in 1883, he had bitterly regretted not being able to reach Bangkok; now he was longing in vain to get away from it as soon and as far as possible. While he watched the sails above him in hope of at least a faint breeze, man after man of his crew fell sick. The supply of quinine on board had, he discovered, been squandered by his predecessor. Some malignant, invisible power seemed at work. It was a struggle against no palpable foe, but an implacable and sinister spiritual and physical stagnation. It was enough to drive many a captain mad. But Conrad clung to his sanity and his sense of responsibility, while the excellent Ransome of the weak heart kept an eye upon everything.

The *Otago* took three weeks to reach Singapore, a passage of about eight hundred miles. The crew were in such a lamentable condition that they disembarked, but the second officer, Mr. Burns, who had signed on for the voyage to Sydney, though he had not recovered, had to go there. But from thence onward Conrad tasted of the satisfaction of commanding a really good sailing ship. The *Otago* left Singapore for Sydney some time in March, for we gather from one of Thaddeus Bobrowski's letters that, on May 5th, Conrad had just reached Sydney. This letter brought him bad news of his uncle's health. He had been recommended a cure abroad, but his straitened means made that impossible. He expresses a great wish to see his nephew again and he inquires anxiously whether the authorities in St. Petersburg had sanctioned his naturalization.

In any case, do not neglect this matter. When you arrive in London go straight to the Russian Embassy and Consulate and renew your demand, for on this will depend our chance of seeing each other again.

The letter is written from Odessa, where he had gone in search of health, and he adds:

I hope in 1890 to have a railway station eight versts from here and I want to live to take advantage of it, for there I shall be nearer for M. le Capitaine.

We find only one mention in all Conrad's work and letters of his sojourn in Sydney. It was there he met again the old chief mate of the *Duke of Sutherland,* the Mr. B—— who, when he set foot on land, generally came back to the ship drunk.

He recognized me at once, remembered my name, and in what ship I had served under his orders. He looked me over from head to foot.

"What are you doing here?" he asked.

"I am commanding a little barque," I said, "loading here for Mauritius." Then, thoughtlessly, I added: "And what are you doing, Mr. B——?"

"I," he said, looking at me unflinchingly with his old sardonic grin, "I am looking for something to do."

I felt I would rather have bitten out my tongue. His jet-black, curly hair had turned iron-gray; he was scrupulously neat as ever, but frightfully threadbare. His shiny boots were worn down at heel. But he forgave me, and we drove off together in a hansom to dine on board my ship. He went over her conscientiously, praised her heartily, congratuated me on my command with absolute sincerity. At dinner, as I offered him wine and beer, he shook his head, and as I sat looking at him interrogatively, muttered in an undertone:

"I've given up all that."

After dinner we came again on deck. It seemed as though he could not tear himself away from the ship. We were fitting some new lower rigging, and he hung about, approving, suggesting, giving me advice in his old manner. Twice he addressed me as "My boy," and corrected himself quickly to "Captain." My mate was about to leave me (to get married), but I concealed the fact from Mr. B——. I was afraid he would ask me to give him the berth in some ghastly jocular hint that I could not refuse to take. I was afraid. It would have been impossible. I could not have given orders to Mr. B——, and I am sure he would not have taken them from me very long. He could not have managed *that,* though he had managed to break himself from drink—too late. He said good-bye at last. As I watched his burly, bull-necked figure walk away up the street, I wondered with a sinking heart whether he had much more than the price of a night's lodging in his pocket. And I understood that if that very minute I were to call out after him, he would not even turn his head.[1]

By the end of June, the *Otago* was at Melbourne, and, apparently, early in August she left Port Adelaide for Mauritius. Prompted by his craving for "that special intensity of existence which is the quintessence of youthful aspiration," a craving which never slept in him for long, Conrad suggested to his owners at Port Adelaide that the *Otago* should make for Mauritius by way of the Torres Strait between North Australia and New Guinea. Rather to his surprise, Messrs. Henry Simpson & Sons made no objection, although an additional insurance premium had to be paid for that route. This showed that the owners had already full confidence in their new captain.

The season was already advanced and there was no time to be lost; he set sail from Sydney in a severe southwest gale —to the dismay of the pilot and the tug master. Conrad has described his passage through the Torres Strait in one of the last essays he ever wrote.

It was not without a certain emotion that, commanding very likely the first and certainly the last merchantship that carried a cargo that way—from Sydney to Mauritius—I put her head at daybreak for Bligh's Entrance, and packed on her every bit of canvas she could carry. Wind-swept, sunlit empty waters were all around me half-veiled by a brilliant haze. The first thing that caught my eyes upon the play of green white-capped waves was a black speck marking conveniently the end of a low sand-bank. It looked like the wreck of some small vessel.

I altered the course slightly in order to pass close, with the hope of being able to read the letters on her stern. They were already faded. Her name was *Honolulu*. The name of the port I could not make out. The story of her life is known by now to God alone, and the winds must have drifted long ago around her remains a quiet grave of the very sand on which she had died. Thirty-six hours afterwards, of which about nine were spent at anchor, approaching the other end of the strait, I sighted a gaunt, gray wreck of a big American ship lying high and dry on the southernmost of the Warrior Reefs. She had been there for years. I had heard of her. She was legendary. She loomed up a sinister and enormous *memento mori* raised by the refraction of this serene afternoon above the far-away line of the horizon drawn under the sinking sun.

[1] *The Mirror of the Sea,* "In Captivity," p. 127.

And thus I passed out of Torres Strait before the dusk settled on its waters. Just as a clear sun sank ahead of my ship I took a bearing of a little island for a fresh departure, an insignificant crumb of dark earth, lonely, like an advanced sentinel of that mass of broken land and water, to watch the approaches from the side of the Arafura Sea.[1]

The *Otago* reached Mauritius without mishap, and her stay at that island is reflected on the pages of *'Twixt Land and Sea*. Mauritius is the scene of the adventure which Conrad entitled "A Smile of Fortune," the island which "the more enthusiastic of its inhabitants delight in describing as the Pearl of the Ocean."

The connection between the voyage of the *Otago* and that story is equally clearly shown by the presence in it of the somewhat surly chief mate, Mr. Burns, who also appears in *The Shadow Line*. I feel certain that the adventure narrated in "A Smile of Fortune," connected with the cargo of potatoes, actually happened as described, on account of an odd question which Conrad asked me one day when I was talking to him about this story. "Do you think," he said to me, "that Jacobus had seen something?" (He was alluding to the beginning of Chapter VI where Jacobus either surprises the young captain in the company of his daughter, Alice, or at least might have caught them at a compromising moment.) When I confessed that for my part I could not decide, and, in my turn, asked him the same question, he answered, "I never knew"—an answer which suggests that the incident is as autobiographic as that of the cargo of potatoes.

Conrad sailed on the 18th of November for Port Adelaide, and, on arriving there, he found two letters from his uncle, one of which showed that the latter was much disturbed about his health.

You do not tell me how long you think you are going to remain in Australia. You know that I do not wish to influence you, but for an old man who has not long to live, time is a matter of some interest, and also to know that he may possibly see again those who are dear to him. Cannot you ask Mr. Krieger to inquire at the Russian Embassy if the formality in excusing allegiance to the Czar is an accomplished fact? I

[1] *Last Essays*, "Geography and Some Explorers," pp. 20 and 21. A chart of Torres Strait kept by Conrad shows that the *Otago* sailed south of Timor from August 31 to September 4.

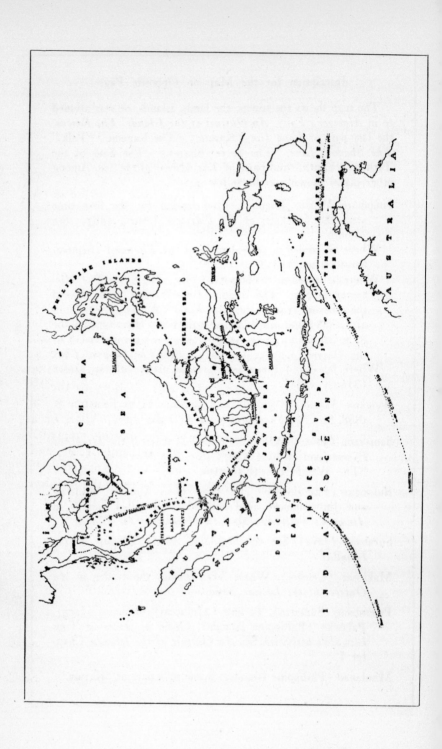

Inscription for the Map on Opposite Page

The map shows the towns, the lands, islands, or seas alluded to in *Almayer's Folly, An Outcast of the Islands, The Rescue,* the last part of *Lord Jim,* "Karain," "The Lagoon," "Falk," *The Shadow Line,* "The Secret Sharer," "The End of the Tether," "Youth," and parts of *The Mirror of the Sea.* Among other places shown are the following:

Singapore. Where Joseph Conrad landed for the first time after the wreckage of the *Palestine* (April, 1883). See "Youth."

Where he landed as second mate of the *Tilkhurst* (September–October, 1885).

Where he stayed at the hospital (July, 1887). See *The Mirror of the Sea:* "The Weight of the Burden," and between the different trips of the S. S. *Vidar* (August, 1887–January, 1888) and where he embarked as a passenger on the S. S. *Melita* to go to Bangkok and take the command of the *Otago* (January 19, 1888). See *The Shadow Line.*

Where he stayed for a few days as master of the *Otago* (March, 1888).

Bangkok. Where he stayed from January 24 to February 8, 1888. See *The Shadow Line* and "Falk."

Samarang (Java). Where he landed as mate of the *Highland Forest* (end of June, 1887). See *The Mirror of the Sea:* "The Weight of the Burden."

Bulungan (East Borneo). The place where Almayer, Willems, and Jim Lingard lived and which is called Sambir in *Almayer's Folly.* See also *An Outcast of the Islands.*

Surabaya (Java). See the beginning of *An Outcast of the Islands.*

Makassar (Celebes). Where Mr. Hudig, the trader in *An Outcast of the Islands,* lived.

Palembang (Sumatra), Ternate (Moluccas), Ombawa (Java), Palawan (Philippine Islands). Given as places of Tom Lingard's activities. See *An Outcast of the Islands,* Chapter I.

Mindanao (Philippine Islands). Scene of a part of "Karain."

read in the Polish newspapers that his grace had been afforded to twenty-seven persons. Perhaps you are one of them? No names were given. Perhaps it is all settled. In that case, we can hope to see each other in the country.[1]

In a second letter he informs his nephew about his disposition of his property.[2] He had placed with Mme Cécile Zaleska, or in the event of her death with her son, Stanislas, fifteen thousand roubles free of succession duty, which, a year after his death, would be handed over to Conrad. This news made Conrad decidedly uneasy, for neither distance nor an adventurous career had diminished his lively affection for his uncle. He thought of returning to Europe. A letter from his owners dated from Port Adelaide, January 19, 1889, and addressed to Melbourne, indicates that Conrad found himself at this port at the end of the year. During February and March he navigated the *Otago* between Melbourne, Sydney, and Port Adelaide, and at the end of March, that is to say, very probably on receiving the letter from his uncle which alarmed him, he resigned his command, as the following letter shows:

Port Adelaide,
April 2nd, 1889.

CAPTAIN J. CONRAD KORZENIOWSKI,
    Port Adelaide.

DEAR SIR:
    Referring to your resignation of the command (which we have in another letter formally accepted) of our bark *Otago,* we now have much pleasure in stating that this early severance from our employ is entirely at your own desire, with a view to visiting Europe, and that we entertain a high opinion of your ability in the capacity you now vacate, of your attainments generally, and should be glad to learn of your future success.
    Wishing you a pleasant passage home,
                We are, dear Sir,
                    Yours faithfully,
                        HENRY SIMPSON & SONS
                            Owners of the Black Diamond Line.

Twice again, three years later, Conrad visited the Australian ports, but his resignation of his command of the *Otago* ended for good and all his connection with the East.

---

[1] Th. B., September 24, 1888.   [2] Lipowiece, January 3, 1889.

CHAPTER VII

IN THE HEART OF DARKNESS

(1889–1890)

Land in a swamp, march through the woods, and in some in-
land post feel the savagery, the utter savagery, had closed
round him,—all that mysterious life of the wilderness that
stirs in the forest, in the jungles, in the hearts of wild men.

("HEART OF DARKNESS.")

THERE is no document which gives us the exact date of
Conrad's return to Europe, but everything leads us to believe
that he must have arrived in London at the end of May or
the beginning of June, 1889. If he did not immediately go
to Ukraine to see his uncle as he wished, it was because the
formalities of the Russian Administration were not yet completed; the release from his allegiance had indeed been noti-
fied in the Russian Official Gazette No. 49 of the 20th of
May, 1889, but besides this Conrad was obliged to apply for
the consent of the Governor of the province where he was
born, before he could enter Russian territory without difficulty. The three years that had passed since he had been
naturalized an English subject had not been enough to enable
him to regularize his situation in the land of the Czars.

Whilst waiting for the official document which would permit
his going to Poland, since Thaddeus Bobrowski's poor health
and limited means prevented his visiting his nephew, Conrad
had at his disposal some months of leisure—an experience
which had not been his for some time past. He was not long,
however, without thoughts of returning to sea; but a command is not always easy to find. Months passed before his
efforts were successful, and his situation was exactly that which
he gave to Marlow later on in his tale "Heart of Darkness": [1]

---

[1] "Heart of Darkness," as we shall see later, is a faithful transcript of most
of the episodes of Conrad's own life during the latter half of 1889.

I had then, as you remember, just returned to London after a lot of Indian Ocean, Pacific, China Seas—a regular dose of the East—six years or so, and I was loafing about, hindering you fellows in your work and invading your homes, just as though I had got a heavenly mission to civilize you. It was very fine for a time, but after a bit I did get tired of resting. Then I began to look for a ship—I should think the hardest work on earth. But the ships wouldn't even look at me. And I got tired of that game, too.[1]

Days and months passed without bringing any hope of a command; Captain Korzeniowski "loafed" about the town; he often journeyed to the City from Bessborough Gardens, where he was lodging, and visited his friend Adolf Krieger in the offices of Barr, Moering & Co., in Camomile Street, or else went to see whether kind Captain Froud,[2] the obliging secretary to the Masters' Association in Fenchurch Street, could not unearth him a job.

Days and months passed, summer was drawing to a close, and still Captain Conrad Korzeniowski was navigating only the streets of London, without maps or compass. After having traversed so many seas, this novel kind of wandering was by no means disagreeable to his humour of the moment. Until then he seemed to have lived only from day to day; but now —was it weariness, maturity, the impression of so many striking scenes, or all these things together, perhaps?—this thirty-three-year-old Polish captain, this recently naturalized Englishman, for the first time set about *remembering*. The carelessness, the adventurous curiosity of youth, were now succeeded by a state of reminiscence in which there took shape, at first confusedly, a whole series of human figures, of whom he had caught fleeting glimpses, and whom now, in his moments of London leisure, he was able to recall, with their actions, their desires, their illusions, and their disappointments.

One morning in the month of September, "an autumn day with an opaline atmosphere, a veiled, semi-opaque, lustrous day, . . . one of those London days that have the charm of mysterious amenity, of fascinating softness," in his lodgings of Bessborough Gardens, Captain Conrad Korzeniowski,

[1] "Heart of Darkness," Chap. I, pp. 51–52.
[2] For Captain Froud, see *A Personal Record*, Chap. I, pp. 6 *et seq.*

urged by a sudden and incomprehensible impulse, began to write the story of *Almayer's Folly,* in which he evoked the images of people he had met two years before on the east coast of Borneo. This novel, the first and the shortest of all those he was destined to write, took five years to complete; during all this time the work, which had been undertaken almost involuntarily, was pursued with a mingled obstinacy and indifference.

Joseph Conrad has given us an admirable account of this first day of his life as a writer in Chapter IV of *A Personal Record.* Never did the life of a writer begin so casually. On that September morning, if the sea captain, Korzeniowski, was beginning to make room for the novelist, Joseph Conrad, he was far from suspecting it—far from desiring it. He said afterward in *A Personal Record:*

I never made a note of a fact, of an impression or of an anecdote in my life. The conception of a planned book was entirely outside my mental range when I sat down to write; the ambition of being an author had never turned up amongst these gracious imaginary existences one creates fondly for oneself at times in the stillness and immobility of a daydream.[1]

However haunted he may have been by the misfortunes of Almayer, his chief preoccupation still remained his career as a sailor. He had no idea of giving up the sea; for fifteen years the sea had procured him his livelihood—meagre as it was, and seasoned, as we have seen, with dangers and risks; the profits which his year's command of the *Otago* had left him were not substantial enough to allow of his contemplating a long stay on shore. And besides, what could he have done during a long stay? He had very few friends in London, no relations, no home; there was nothing for him but to sail again.

Through his friend Adolf Krieger, the Antwerp shippers, Messrs. Walford & Co., had taken him as supercargo, and gave some hopes of the command of a ship to the West Indies and to New Orleans; but this command, too, was long in coming. The truest picture of Conrad's situation at this time

[1] *A Personal Record,* Chap. IV, p. 68.

can again be found in Marlow's account of himself at the beginning of "Heart of Darkness": [1]

. . . I have a lot of relations living on the Continent. . . .

I am sorry to own I began to worry them. This was already a fresh departure for me. I was not used to get things that way, you know. I always went my own road and on my own legs where I had a mind to go. I wouldn't have believed it of myself; but, then—you see—I felt somehow I must get there by hook or by crook. So I worried them. The men said, "My dear fellow," and did nothing. Then—would you believe it?—I tried the women. I, Charlie Marlow, set the women to work—to get a job. Heavens! Well, you see, the notion drove me. I had an aunt, a dear enthusiastic soul. She wrote: "It will be delightful; I am ready to do anything, anything for you. . . . I know the wife of a very high personage in the Administration, and also a man who has lots of influence with," etc., etc. . . .

As a matter of fact, Joseph Conrad himself possessed an aunt by marriage in Brussels—Mme Marguerite Poradowska, a Frenchwoman, married to a Pole. She was the daughter of a man of considerable note in the scientific world, Émile Gachet, and was herself beginning to acquire some reputation as a novelist.[2] It was by means of this aunt, whose sympathy was most useful to him at this early stage of his literary life, that Conrad now found himself attracted, not toward the Antilles, the scene of his youthful adventures, but to the very heart of Africa.

In this somewhat unexpected way, a wish formed in early childhood was accomplished. Many years ago, when he was a tiny boy in Poland, he had declared that he would go to this very spot; then he had forgotten all about his dream.

It was in 1868, when nine years old or thereabouts, that while looking at a map of Africa of the time and putting my finger on the blank space then representing the unsolved mystery of that continent, I said to

[1] P. 53.

[2] Mme Marguerite Poradowska was not in reality Conrad's aunt, but his maternal grandmother's first cousin.

She had published two years previously in the *Revue des Deux Mondes* her first novel, a sketch of Ruthenian manners and customs; she afterward published several others, besides translations from the Polish.

myself with absolute assurance and an amazing audacity which are no
longer in my character now:

"When I grow up I shall go *there*."

And of course I thought no more about it till after a quarter of a
century or so an opportunity offered to go there—as if the sin of childish audacity was to be visited on my mature head.[1]

Perhaps, as Marlow says, a map of the Congo seen in a
shop window in Fleet Street re-awoke these childish wishes,
but it is more probable that the thought of Mme Poradowska's
connections in the colonial world of Brussels was the most
important factor in his decision. It must not be forgotten
either that in 1889 the Congo was the topic of the day. Since
1875, the date when King Leopold II had founded the International Association for the Civilization of Central Africa,
the centre of Africa had been very much in men's minds.
Stanley's expedition from Zanzibar to the Lower Congo during the years 1876 and 1877 had aroused at once the deepest
interest and the most violent greed. On February 17, 1889,
Stanley had renewed the exploits of those years when he had
gone in search of Livingstone, by discovering and joining
Emin Pasha in Kavali's camp. All scientific, journalistic,
political, and commercial Europe had followed these excur-
sions with breathless interest. Brussels had become a focus of
adventure; daredevils from every part of the world congre-
gated there, as well as missionaries; honest folk and rogues
hurried there to enter upon engagements that would enable
them to exercise their various talents—their rapacity, their
faith, their violence, or simply their foolishness, in the heart
of what Stanley had called the Dark Continent.[2] People were
preparing at that very moment in England and Belgium to
give Stanley a triumphant welcome.[3]

[1] *A Personal Record*, p. 13. See also two other allusions to the same childish
recollection: *Heart of Darkness*, Chap. I, p. 52, and *Last Essays*, "Geography
and Some Explorers," p. 16.

[2] *Through the Dark Continent*, a work in four volumes published in 1878,
in which Stanley relates his expeditions of 1874–1878, to the sources of the
Nile, round the lakes Alexandra and Victoria Nyanza, and his descent of the
Congo from the Tanganyika to the sea.

[3] Between the 19th and 26th of April, 1890, Stanley was enthusiastically
received at Brussels and Antwerp by the King and Belgian people,

This atmosphere of adventure and discovery revived Conrad's childish enthusiasms and kindled the imagination of the young Pole, in whom the spirit of a novelist was just beginning to awake. He suddenly took it into his head that he must command a steamboat on the Congo. For a man accustomed for the greater part of his sailor's life to sailing boats of a respectable tonnage, it was undoubtedly a singular idea to take up the command of a miserable little steamboat of ten or fifteen tons. But Conrad's impulses were, as we have often seen, not to be gainsaid. Efforts were made in London, Brussels, and Ghent, to obtain for the young man the command that he wished. Through his friend Adolf Krieger, Messrs. Barr, Moering & Co. of London persuaded Mr. de Baerdemaecker of Ghent to write on Conrad's behalf to Captain Albert Thys, Acting-Manager of the Société Anonyme Belge pour le Commerce du Haut-Congo.[1]

The command of one of the Company's little steamboats necessitated a captain who spoke French. Captain Korzeniowski fulfilled this condition perfectly. After an exchange of letters, Joseph Conrad presented himself to Captain Albert Thys at Brussels at the beginning of November, and the impression he made was, no doubt, entirely favourable, for he was then and there promised by Captain Thys that he would be employed on the Congo as soon as a post fell vacant in the Company's flotilla.

The Société Anonyme Belge pour le Commerce du Haut-Congo [2] had only been formed in its final shape on the preceding 10th of December; but with energetic men at its head, this commercial enterprise was on the eve of considerable development. New stations were to be founded, new steamers built, plans were being studied for a new railroad from Matadi to Stanley Pool, which should insure rapid communication between the two navigable portions of the Congo. In

[1] Mr. de Baerdemaecker's letter recommending Conrad is dated September 24, 1889, and says, among many other things: "His general education is better than most sailors' and he is a perfect gentleman." Albert Thys was at that time aide-de-camp to King Leopold. He died a general in 1915 at the age of sixty-six.

[2] This company still exists in Brussels and forms part of the Banque d'-Outremer.

every direction new perspectives were opening out to adventurous activity.

Conrad's first step was to free himself from his engagements, such as they were, with the firm of Walford & Co.; but still the hopes of a command of a Congo steamboat failed to take shape. At this juncture he received an invitation from his uncle Thaddeus to pay him a visit. Conrad informed Captain Albert Thys by letter that he would be very glad to accept this invitation, but that it would involve a certain length of time, as a short visit would not be worth the trouble and expense of the journey, and he hoped the acting manager of the Upper Congo Company would let him know the date his services would be likely to be required, so that he might return to London in good time and hold himself in readiness.[1]

The answer, which came by return, must have given him to understand that there would still be some considerable further delay, for he decided to start for Poland a few weeks later. He stopped at Brussels on February 4th, in order to see his aunt, Mme Poradowska, whom he commissioned to look after his affairs in his absence, and in order to interview the secretary of the Société du Haut-Congo; after which he resumed his journey and arrived at his uncle's at Kazimierowka in Polish Ukraine, on February 16, 1890.[2]

His stay there lasted nearly two months; it was the first time he had revisited Poland since 1874, and it was not without emotion that he found himself again, after an absence of nearly sixteen years, in his native land and among old friends, who hurried to see this singular traveller in strange places, this Pole turned sailor. Nevertheless, he did not lose sight of his intention of going to the Congo, and on April 11th he wrote from his uncle's house at Kazimierowka to the acting manager of the Société du Haut-Congo to inform him he would be in Brussels on the last day of the month at latest and that he would lose no time in presenting himself at the company's offices in order to learn what had been decided on concerning him.

[1] Letter in French of the 27th of December.
[2] This date is furnished by a document in Thaddeus Bobrowski's hand, entitled, "For the guidance of my dear nephew Conrad Korzeniowski."

We know by another letter, written to his Zagorski cousins, that he came back by way of Lublin, where he spent a few days and which he left on April 22nd; on the 27th he was at Brussels. Then the pace of events, which had hitherto been so slow, began to quicken. At last the steps he had taken in September led to a result; it had needed no less than seven months to obtain the command of a small Congo steamboat, which he had so long coveted.

At the beginning of May he wrote to his cousin Marie Tyszka, née Bobrowska: [1]

MY DEAR MARIETTE:

I have not been able to write sooner. I have been exceedingly busy and have still a great deal to do. I am starting for the Congo in three days and I have to prepare for a stay of three years in the middle of Africa, so you will understand that every moment is precious.

The first chapter of "Heart of Darkness" gives us, under cover of Marlow, an authentic account of the circumstances which immediately preceded Conrad's departure for Africa, and reveals the reasons of the Company's sudden haste to engage him as captain:

I got my appointment—of course; and I got it very quick. It appears the Company had received news that one of their captains had been killed in a scuffle with the natives. This was my chance, and it made me the more anxious to go. It was only months and months afterwards, when I made the attempt to recover what was left of the body, that I heard the original quarrel arose from a misunderstanding about some hens. Yes, two black hens. Fresleven—that was the fellow's name, a Dane. . . .

Through this glorious affair I got my appointment, before I had fairly begun to hope for it.

I flew around like mad to get ready, and before forty-eight hours I was crossing the Channel to show myself to my employers, and sign the contract. In a very few hours I arrived in a city that always makes me think of a whited sepulchre. Prejudice, no doubt. I had no difficulty in finding the Company's offices. It was the biggest thing in the town, and everybody I met was full of it. They were going to run an over-sea empire, and make no end of coin by trade.

[1] Beginning of a letter in Polish, dated London, May 2d.

A narrow and deserted street in deep shadow, high houses, innumerable
windows with venetian blinds, a dead silence, grass sprouting between
the stones, imposing carriage archways right and left, immense double
doors standing ponderously ajar.[1]

Then follows the account of his visit to the Company's
offices. No one who has read this admirable tale can forget
the two women knitting black wool, as impassive as Fates, the
large many-coloured map of Africa, the forty-five seconds'
interview with the acting manager, the compassionate secretary, the visit to the doctor, the farewell to the aunt—a succession of scenes and details vividly painted and bearing in
their biting irony the very stamp of truth.

There is every reason to believe that these scenes took place
exactly as Conrad related them eight years later. He went to
the Company's offices in Brussels, which were then at 9 rue
Brederode; he exchanged a few words and a handshake with
Captain Albert Thys, the acting manager, "pale plumpness
in a frock coat," saw the secretary, the doctor Lebrun, the
aunt, and had to start hurriedly. It is equally true—as Marlow
says—that Captain Korzeniowski obtained his command because one of the Company's captains had just been killed on
the Congo by the natives. The captain was a Dane named,
not Fresleven, as Marlow called him, but *Freiesleben*.[2]

Joseph Conrad had no time to lose in farewells; we hear
of him in London on May 2nd; on the 7th he signed his contract in Brussels, and on the 12th he embarked at Bordeaux
in the French steamship the *Ville de Maceio,* bound for Boma.
The boat put in at Teneriffe, Dakar, Conakry, Sierra Leone,
Grand Bassam, Kotonou, Libreville, Loango, Banane (at the
mouth of the great river), and finally at Boma, the seat,
since 1886, of the Government of the Free State. Captain
Korzeniowski's work was only to begin some four hundred
kilometres farther away, at Stanley Pool. During the journey
from Bordeaux to Matadi, he had had as fellow traveller an
agent of the Free State, called Victor Harou, who was re-

---

[1] "Heart of Darkness," pp. 53, 54, 55.
[2] For Freiesleben, see *Mouvement Géographique,* September 8, 1889. See also
the *Rapport au Roi Souverain (Bulletin Officiel de l'Etat Indépendant du
Congo*), July, 1891.

joining his post; it is probable that he learnt in the course of conversations with him that the prospects of life in the Congo —in spite of official statistics—were far from rosy. This Belgian officer, who had already made several stays in the country, knew its risks. His revelations cast some gloom on the journey, but our traveller tried to put a good face on things, as we can judge from a letter written on board the *Ville de Maceio* and addressed to his cousin Charles Zagórski. We give here a translation from the Polish:

Freetown, Sierra Leone,
22nd May, 1890.

MY VERY DEAR CHARLES:

It is just a month to-day since you were scandalized by my hurried departure from Lublin. From the date and address of this letter you will see that I have had to be pretty quick, and I am only just beginning to breathe a little more calmly. If you only knew the devilish haste I had to make! From London to Brussels, and back again to London! And again to Brussels! If you had only seen all the tin boxes and revolvers, the high boots and the touching farewells; just another handshake and just another pair of trousers!—and if you knew all the bottles of medicine and all the affectionate wishes I took away with me, you would understand in what a typhoon, cyclone, hurricane, earthquake—no!—in what a universal cataclysm, in what a fantastic atmosphere of mixed shopping, business and affecting scenes, I passed two whole weeks. Two weeks spent at sea have allowed me to rest and I am impatiently waiting for the end of this trip. I shall reach Boma no doubt on the 7th of next month [1] and then leave Boma with my caravan to go to Leopoldville. [2] As far as I can make out from my "service letter" I am destined to the command of a steamboat, belonging to M. Delcommune's exploring party, which is being got ready; but I know nothing for certain as everything is supposed to be kept secret. What makes me rather uneasy is the information that 60 per cent. of our Company's employés return to Europe before they have completed even six months' service. Fever and dysentery! There are others who are sent home in a hurry at the end of a year, so that they shouldn't die in the Congo. God forbid! It would spoil the statistics which are excellent, you see! In a word, it seems there are only 7 per cent. who can do their three years' service. . . . Yes! But a

[1] He arrived at Boma on the evening of June 12th.
[2] On Stanley Pool where he had to take command of his steamboat.

Polish nobleman, cased in British tar! *Nous verrons!* In any case I shall console myself by remembering—faithful to our national traditions—that it is of my own free will that I have thrust myself into this business.

When you see—with the help of a microscope, no doubt—the hieroglyphics of my handwriting, you will, I expect, wonder why I am writing to you. First, because it is a pleasure to talk to you; next, because, considering the distinguished personage who is penning this autograph, it ought to be a pleasure to you too. You can bequeath it to your children. Future generations will read it, I hope with admiration (and with profit). In the meantime, *trêve de bêtises!*

I kiss my dear uncle and aunt's hands, and your wife's too. I think of you all, but can't write the whole list because this abominable lamp is going out.

Your affectionate
K. N. KORZENIOWSKI.[1]

We can see by this that Conrad was no longer unaware of the risks of his adventure—risks that had certainly not been laid openly before him at Brussels before his departure; but the Polish nobleman, underneath his British tar, kept his heart up. His uncle Thaddeus wrote to his nephew from Kazimierowka with the same appreciation of the dangers, but with less confidence and philosophy.

Ships of more than a certain tonnage were unable as yet to go up the river as far as Matadi, and the *Ville de Maceio* landed the traveller at Boma; from there he took a small boat which brought him to Matadi, the terminal point of navigation on the Lower Congo; above this point, indeed, the river presents, over a distance of about two hundred miles, a series of thirty-two impassable rapids. It is very probable that the journey of about thirty miles which separates Boma from Matadi was accomplished in the way that Marlow relates in "Heart of Darkness"; and it is possible that the Swedish captain, whose acquaintance he then made and whom he mentions in his tale, may have sat in a measure for Heyst, the Swedish hero of *Victory*.

Matadi, where he arrived on June 12th, could not fail

---

[1] Letter in Polish, communicated by the addressee's daughter, Mlle Angèle Zagórska.

to impress him unfavourably. In 1890 this station was a relatively important one, with 170 European inhabitants; it had four factories—English, Portuguese, Dutch, and French —without counting the Sanford Exploring Expedition's buildings, which had just been taken over by the Société Anonyme Belge pour le Commerce du Haut-Congo. Work on the railroad, which was to run from Matadi to Kinchassa, had been recently begun, giving the place an added animation. This railroad, which would considerably increase the importance of the station, was intended to unite the two navigable portions of the Congo and allow a more rapid transit of merchandise from the Upper Congo to the ports of embarkation on the sea—the only means of communication at that time consisting of caravan tracks and the backs of native porters. Matadi could have no attractions for Conrad. The Congo at this place has the appearance of a lake, surrounded on all sides by high mountains; its current, which elsewhere is rapid, here flows slowly and gently, spreading its waters till they attain a width of about twelve hundred yards; but, truth to tell, nature has not graced the spot with many charms, if we are to believe the description of that very Captain Albert Thys, who had interviewed Conrad so briefly in Brussels and who was well acquainted with the region. "On arriving at Matadi," he writes, "one seems to have reached an accursed land, set there as a barrier by Nature herself, to impede all progress." [1]

Conrad cared very little about so-called progress; he already felt doubts on the subject, which were to give rise later to "An Outpost of Progress" [2] as well as to "Heart of Darkness." His stay at Matadi seemed to him interminable; and it is he who speaks in Marlow's words, when he says: "I had to wait in the station [Matadi] for ten days—an eternity!" As a matter of fact, it was fifteen days and not ten that Conrad

[1] *Au Congo et au Kassai,* by Captain Thys (Bruxelles, Weissenbruch, pub. 1888).

[2] There is every reason to believe that it was Harou who told Conrad the story of the death of the two agents of the Company in circumstances exactly similar to those he describes in "An Outpost of Progress." I have Conrad's own testimony as to the authenticity of the facts. The real names of the characters have not been discovered; Conrad called them Kayerts and Carlier, the actual names of two men, an agent and a captain, whom he met in the Congo.

waited at Matadi, before he was able to start on the march of almost two hundred miles which was to take him to the spot where his boat awaited him.

Besides the literary transposition of the facts which we find in "Heart of Darkness," Conrad has left us a direct record of this part of his journey, in the form of a diary, which he kept from June 13th to August 1st, that is, from the day of his arrival at Matadi to the day preceding his arrival at Kinchassa. This diary, which has been recently published under the title "Congo Diary" in the volume *Last Essays,* is valuable not merely on account of the information it gives us about things and people, but also because of the notes of impressions, which evidently furnished the matter for certain passages in "Heart of Darkness."

Conrad stayed at Matadi from the 13th to the 27th of June. According to "Heart of Darkness" some of the characters he met there were indeed singular. According to the "Diary" he made the acquaintance of the head of the station, Mr. Gosse, a retired Belgian officer, who died six months later, and also of a person destined to attain extraordinary notoriety later on: Mr.—afterwards Sir—Roger Casement. At this period Casement was twenty-six years old and was on his third visit to the Congo; he was temporarily in the service of the Company and was one of the rare men he met in Africa who made a favourable impression upon Conrad. "Thinks, speaks well, most intelligent and very sympathetic," he notes shortly after his arrival at Matadi, and on June 28th, at the moment of leaving, he notes again: "parted with Casement in a very friendly manner." [1] But for the most part the impressions of these ten days at Matadi were far from favourable. On the first page of his diary we find this suggestive remark:

Feel considerably in doubt about the future. Think just now that my life amongst the people (white) around here cannot be very comfortable. Intend avoid acquaintances as much as possible.

[1] Another interesting allusion to Roger Casement will be found later on in a letter written to Mr. Cunninghame Graham thirteen years afterward, on December 26, 1903.

While waiting to start on the march of two hundred miles to Kinchassa, he employed himself as best he could, though often in occupations that had very little to do with his proper functions. "Have been busy packing ivory in casks. Idiotic employment." And the same day he notes again: "prominent characteristic of the social life here; people speaking ill of each other." The atmosphere of this colonial society was decidedly not in his line. At last, on June 28th, accompanied by Victor Harou, he left Matadi with a caravan of thirty-one men, after having taken leave of Casement and the head of the station, who accompanied the party as far as the beginning of the track they were to follow. At the first halt, before crossing the river at M'poso, two Danish officers joined the caravan, and together they traversed the mountainous region of Pataballa. In order to give some idea of the fatigue and unpleasantness of this part of the journey, we cannot do better than again quote Captain Thys:

If, on leaving Matadi, one takes the land route and goes towards the M'poso and the mountain range of Pataballa, the same impression continues; and when one reaches Pataballa, sweating, panting, and aching in every limb, there rises to the lips an exclamation which seldom varies: "What a dog's country!"

At the end of this long climb, Conrad's travelling companion, Harou, began to suffer from attacks of sickness which came on so constantly that he had to be carried almost the whole time during the greater part of the way. For eleven days, from Matadi to Manyanga, they marched at the rate of from fifteen to twenty miles a day, through forest and through plain—a weary and monotonous journey, of which Conrad has made a rapid and striking picture:

Paths, paths, everywhere; a stamped-in network of paths spreading over the empty land, through long grass, through burnt grass, through thickets, down and up chilly ravines, up and down stony hills ablaze with heat; and a solitude, a solitude, nobody, not a hut.[1]

[1] "Heart of Darkness," p. 70. See also *Vingt Ans de Vie Africaine*, p. 196, by Alex. Delcommune.

They started very early every morning on a wearisome march, which lasted till eleven o'clock. The track was broken now and then by a native market or a river that they forded or crossed on a bridge of creepers. They once met an officer of the Free State on a tour of inspection, and a few moments later they saw the body of a Negro killed by a bullet. On they marched through a yellowish gray landscape, "with reddish patches (soil) and clumps of dark green vegetation, scattered sparsely about," through steep gorges, or on the crest of a chain of mountains. The nights were damp and cool, the mornings misty, the middle of the day burning, the camping grounds were dirty, the water often brackish and the mosquitoes kept up their activity day and night. There were often arguments with the porters just before setting out. At the end of a week of this régime, Conrad notes in his diary, "getting jolly well sick of this fun."

At last, on the morning of the 8th of July, they arrived at Manyanga, where they were very kindly received by the manager of the Company, Reginald Heyn, who was an Englishman, and his assistant, Jaeger. Up till then Conrad's health had been satisfactory. During his stay at Manyanga he fell ill, probably of an attack of fever, and Harou's health did not improve. After sixteen days of rest, they set out again in rather a bad state. Once more they marched on day after day. The heat of noontide was rivalled by the chill of night. They spent the day of Sunday the 27th at the Sutili mission house, where they were received by the missionary's young wife, Mrs. Annie Comber.[1] During the two following days, they were accompanied on their way by another of the Company's agents. The monotony of the road which stretched out once more before them was only varied by an occasional skeleton tied to a post or a heap of stones in the shape of a cross to mark the grave of a white man. Then Harou fell seriously ill. He had one attack of fever after another, and

---

[1] Conrad little thought that, on that very day, July 27th, Dominic Cervoni, his master in the art of the sea, and the companion of his Mediterranean years, was dying in his native village of Luri (Corsica) at the age of fifty-six, after thirty-seven years of service at sea.

had to be carried. He was heavy, and the porters began to grumble and to desert at night with their loads. Conrad had to repress the beginnings of a mutiny. At last, after nine days of this expedition, they arrived at Kinchassa, which was the base harbour of the Upper Congo flotilla.

Here the Company had established ship-building premises, where shells of ships, sent out from Europe in parts and carried on men's backs from Matadi to the Pool, were assembled; and it was here also that damaged ships were repaired. When Joseph Conrad arrived, they were just repairing the vessel which had been intended for him and which had been sunk a few days before.[1] Unlike Captain Marlow in "Heart of Darkness," Captain Korzeniowski did not wait two months for his ship the *Florida* to be repaired: he embarked the same day on a little steamboat, the *Roi des Belges,* in the capacity of mate. Captain Koch, a Dane, undertook to initiate him in the difficulties and dangers of this freshwater navigation. Conrad had arrived at Kinchassa on August 2nd, and he left it the very next day, as we learn from the manuscript heading of the second of the notebooks which make up the complete Congo Diary. "Up River Book, commenced 3rd August, 1890, S. S. *Roi des Belges.*"

As soon as he arrived at Kinchassa he was received by the person whom Conrad calls "the manager."

My first interview with the manager was curious. He did not ask me to sit down after my twenty-mile walk that morning. He was commonplace in complexion, in feature, in manners, and in voice. He was of middle size and of ordinary build. His eyes, of the usual blue, were perhaps remarkably cold, and he certainly could make his glance fall on one as trenchant and heavy as an axe. . . . He was a common trader, from his youth up employed in these parts—nothing more. He was obeyed, yet he inspired neither love nor fear, nor even respect. He inspired uneasiness. That was it! Uneasiness. Not a definite mistrust—just uneasiness—nothing more. . . . He had no genius for organizing, for initiative, or for order even. That was evident in such things as the

---

[1] Conrad alludes to this circumstance in his diary under the date of July 29th. (See *Last Essays,* p. 168, and "Heart of Darkness," p. 72. A precise account may be found in the *Mouvement Géographique,* September 21, 1890. The accident had occurred on July 18th, and it was only five days later that it had been possible to bring the *Florida* back to Kinchassa.

deplorable state of the station. He had no learning and no intelligence. His position had come to him—why? Perhaps because he was never ill. . . .[1]

This manager, who as a matter of fact was only a temporary sub-manager, was a Belgian, named Camille Delcommune, then about thirty-one, who had started on his African career seven years earlier. The physical portrait which Conrad traces of him corresponds perfectly with the photographs which are to be found in the Belgian magazines of the time.[2] It is not for us to say how far the moral portrait was an accurate description of the man who was Camille Delcommune. All I can say is that Conrad, who was the most generous-minded person I have ever known, despised this man heartily. He often talked to me about the Congo, and I deeply regret not having made any notes, but what remains most vividly in my mind is, first, the landscape with the river wide as a sea and full of tree trunks, rocks and sand banks, which the great writer could raise up before his listeners' eyes as skilfully when he spoke as when he wrote; and second, the hostile and disagreeable figure of Camille Delcommune, whom he named to me without any circumlocution. During the last period of his life, when he used to take pleasure in recalling with a sort of tenderness the memories of his wandering life, he never showed any feeling of tenderness for the "pilgrims" (as he called them ironically in "Heart of Darkness"), whom he came across in the Congo, least of all for this one.

On August 2nd, the steamer *Roi des Belges,* with the assistant-manager Camille Delcommune, the captain Koch and the mate Conrad, the agents Keyaerts,[3] Rollin, and Van der Heyden, and the engineer Gossens on board, left Kinchassa with two lighters and two native canoes in tow. On August 26th, the boat had arrived at the confluent of the Oubanghi, and on September 1st, she had got near to the Stanley Falls, only twenty-eight days after her departure from Stanley

[1] "Heart of Darkness," p. 73.

[2] Amongst others, the number for February 26, 1893, of the *Congo Illustré.* Camille Delcommune died shortly after at Kinchassa on December 26, 1892.

[3] Conrad subsequently gave this name, merely altering it to Kayerts, to one of the two principal characters in his short story "An Outpost of Progress."

Pool.[1] This journey, which in those days was considered remarkably quick, had evidently given Conrad the impression of an interminable voyage, for he says in "Heart of Darkness": "It was just two months from the date we left the creek when we came to the bank below Kurtz's station."

Nothing could give one the very sensation of this up-stream journey on board a small boat of fifteen tons better than that admirable series of descriptions which forms the greater part of "Heart of Darkness," and from which we will now quote a few passages:

Going up that river was like travelling back to the earliest beginnings of the world, when vegetation rioted on the earth and the big trees were kings. An empty stream, a great silence, an impenetrable forest. The air was warm, thick, heavy, sluggish. There was no joy in the brilliance of sunshine. The long stretches of the waterway ran on, deserted, into the gloom of overshadowed distances. On silvery banks hippos and alligators sunned themselves side by side. The broadening waters flowed through a mob of wooded islands; you lost your way on that river as you would in a desert, and butted all day long against shoals, trying to find the channel, till you thought yourself bewitched and cut off for ever from everything you had known once—somewhere—far away—in another existence perhaps. There were moments when one's past came back to one, as it will sometimes when you have not a moment to spare to yourself; but it came in the shape of an unrestful and noisy dream, remembered with wonder amongst the overwhelming realities of this strange world of plants, and water, and silence. And this stillness of life did not in the least resemble a peace. It was the stillness of an implacable force brooding over an inscrutable intention. It looked at you with a vengeful aspect. I got used to it afterwards; I did not see it any more; I had no time. I had to keep guessing at the channel; I had to discern, mostly by inspiration, the signs of hidden banks; I watched for sunken stones; I was learning to clap my teeth smartly before my heart flew out, when I shaved by a fluke some infernal sly old snag that would have ripped the life out of the tin-pot steamboat and drowned all the pilgrims; I had to keep a look-out for the signs of dead wood we could cut up in the night for next day's steaming. When you have to attend to things of that sort, to the mere incidents of the surface, the reality—the reality, I tell you—fades. The inner truth is hidden—luckily, luckily. But I felt

[1] We take this piece of information from the *Mouvement Géographique* of November 2, 1890.

it all the same; I felt often its mysterious stillness watching me at my monkey tricks.[1]

The boat did not stay long at Stanley Falls, and there are no descriptions in "Heart of Darkness" of the farthest point that navigation can reach, but in another passage the writer recalls an impression that he felt in this part of the world. This passage gives us an echo of that feeling of solitude which came over him at this time, which was due, not only to his being plunged into a mysterious silence, "into the heart of an immense darkness," but also to the fact that he did not feel between his white companions and himself the innate fellow feeling, the common conception of human dignity, the fidelity to a few very simple and, so to speak, tacitly assumed principles, which had been since his childhood, and during fifteen years of sea, the atmosphere of his daily life, his safeguard and his pride.

Everything was dark under the stars. Every other white man on board was asleep. I was glad to be alone on deck, smoking the pipe of peace after an anxious day. The subdued thundering mutter of the Stanley Falls hung in the heavy night air of the last navigable reach of the Upper Congo, while no more than ten miles away, in Reshid's camp just above the Falls, the yet unbroken power of the Congo Arabs slumbered uneasily. Their day was over. Away in the middle of the stream, on a little island nestling all black in the foam of the broken water, a solitary little light glimmered feebly, and I said to myself with awe, "This is the very spot of my boyish boast."

A great melancholy descended on me. Yes, this was the very spot. But there was no shadowy friend to stand by my side in the night of the enormous wilderness, no great haunting memory, but only the unholy recollection of a prosaic newspaper "stunt" and the distasteful knowledge of the vilest scramble for loot that ever disfigured the history of human conscience and geographical exploration. What an end to the idealized realities of a boy's daydreams! I wondered what I was doing there, for indeed it was only an unforeseen episode, hard to believe in now, in my seaman's life. Still the fact remains that I have smoked a pipe of peace at midnight in the very heart of the African continent, and felt very lonely there.[2]

[1] "Heart of Darkness," pp. 92 et seq.
[2] Last Essays, "Geography and Some Explorers," p. 17.

The aim of this voyage of the *Roi des Belges* from Kinchassa to the Stanley Falls seems to have been—as Marlow says—to relieve one of the agents of the Company, who was stationed at the Falls and whose health was giving the gravest anxiety. This explains the departure from Kinchassa being hurried on and the haste with which the steamer left the Falls station.

The *Mouvement Géographique* of July 20, 1890, placed before me the following information:

M. Cloetens has taken over the direction of the Kinchassa branch, M. Heyn at Manyanga, Mr. Gosse at Matadi, Mr. Engeringh at Louebo, Mr. Mitchells at the Equator, Mr. Klein at the Falls" and at the beginning of "Heart of Darkness," Marlow says to his interrogators (p. 51):

"You ought to know how I got out there, what I saw, how I went up that river to the place where I first met the poor chap. It was the farthest point of navigation." [Stanley Falls.]

This dying agent, whom Conrad was one day to fashion into the singular hero of "Heart of Darkness" as Kurtz, was the agent at the Falls, Klein.

Georges Antoine Klein was a commercial agent of French nationality, who arrived at the Congo at the end of 1888 and was entrusted with the direction of the Company's establishment at Stanley Falls at the beginning of 1890. He died on the 21st of September, 1890, on board the steamer *Roi des Belges* and was buried at Bolobo by the crew of the steamer.[1]

It is impossible to assert without definite proof that the resemblance between Kurtz and Klein is *complete,* but there can be little doubt in the mind of anybody who knows Conrad's psychological methods that these two beings, the one real and the other imaginary, had much more in common than a mere similarity of names.

Although Captain Korzeniowski was only ship's mate on board the *Roi des Belges* when he travelled up the river, a fact which contradicts Marlow's statement in "Heart of Darkness," yet it was indeed in the capacity of captain that he

[1] Note communicated by the Société Anonyme Belge pour le Commerce du Haut-Congo.

took the steamer back from Stanley Falls to the Pool, as is proved by a letter from Camille Delcommune, dated 6th September 1890, to Captain Korzeniowski, requesting him to take over the command of the *Roi des Belges* until the recovery of Captain Koch.

Thus it was entirely owing to the illness of Captain Koch that Conrad obtained the official command of the ship—and this fact is a sufficient explanation of what happened later. It may be that this date of the 6th was that of the boat's departure from the Falls. The return journey was always much quicker owing to the current. At any rate, the date of Klein's burial (September 21st) necessarily coincided with the arrival of the vessel at Bolobo. On September 24th the *Roi des Belges* reached her base harbour at Kinchassa, and the only fresh-water voyage that Conrad ever accomplished was at an end.

It is clear to the reader of "Heart of Darkness," who knows how closely the story corresponds to the real facts of Conrad's life during this period, that Captain Korzeniowski's relations with his employers were rapidly becoming frigid and strained. The captain was disappointed; he felt that he was to be kept in a subordinate position and that he would not obtain in the Congo what had been promised him in Brussels. Morcover, the manner of life and the general spirit of these traders affected him most unpleasantly. All this had already found some outlet even before the meeting with Kurtz-Klein, of which Marlow says that it seemed to shed a kind of light on all the things around him and on his own thoughts. Already, before leaving Kinchassa to travel up the river, he had confided his first disappointments to his uncle, as the following reply clearly shows:

I see that you are very angry with the Belgians, who are exploiting you so unscrupulously. You must admit that this time there was nothing to force you to put yourself into the hands of the Belgians. *"Tu l'as voulu, tu l'as voulu, Georges Dandin!"* . . . If you had paid any attention to my opinion upon this matter, you would have gathered from our conversation that I was not very enthusiastic over this plan of yours. As a Polish gentleman I have always preferred more safe and less brilliant to more brilliant and less safe. . . . If you break your contract, you will be liable to pay expenses and to be accused of being unreliable, which might do you harm in your future career.[1]

The advice of the uncle, which, moreover, cannot have reached the nephew until long after, was not needed to make him cling pertinaciously to the adventure in which he found himself unfortunately entangled. Although he had had several attacks of fever, and even, at the Falls, an attack of dysentery, he was resolved not to give in yet.

In a passage of "Heart of Darkness" Conrad alludes to the arrival at Kinchassa of an expedition, which he describes in most ironical terms and to which he gives the still more ironical name of the Eldorado Exploring Expedition. "The uncle of our manager," says Marlow, "was the leader of that lot." This expedition is not an invention; it corresponds exactly with reality; Conrad alludes to it in a letter written on board the *Ville de Maceio* to his cousin Charles Zagórski. It was the Katanga expedition and was under the command of Alexandre Delcommune (the elder brother and not the uncle of the manager). The expedition arrived at the Pool not, as Marlow says, before the boat had left but after she had returned, and Conrad had every opportunity of seeing, hearing, and studying its members. His portrait of Alexandre Delcommune is no more flattering than that of his brother.

In exterior he resembled a butcher in a poor neighbourhood, and his eyes had a look of sleepy cunning. He carried his fat paunch with ostentation on his short legs, and during the time his gang infested the station, spoke to no one but his nephew. You could see these two roaming about all day long with their heads close together in an everlasting confab.[2]

But "Heart of Darkness" does not mention that Conrad had hoped at one moment to obtain command of the expedi-

[1] Th. B., September 14, 1890.
[2] "Heart of Darkness," p. 87. Alexandre Delcommune, born at Namur, October 6, 1855, went to Africa in 1873, managed the factory, then the station of Boma (1883-1884); explored the Kassai, the Kwango, the Lukenya, the Sankunu; headed the expedition of the Katanga Company (1890-1892). (*Congo Illustré*, No. 16, July 17, 1892.) Alexandre Delcommune died August 7, 1922.

tion's ship—that very *Florida* which had been intended for him. She had gone to the bottom in July shortly before his arrival and had just been put to rights again. He wrote a letter on this subject to his cousin, Mme Tyszka, the same day he returned to Stanley Pool.

I am very busy preparing for a new expedition on the Kassai River. I think that in a few days I shall once more leave Kinchassa for some months, perhaps for more than ten months. So don't be surprised if you don't hear of me for a long time.[1]

The head of the expedition, Alexandre Delcommune, did not get to Kinchassa before the beginning of October. During the voyage to the Falls the disagreement between Camille Delcommune and Conrad had no doubt become more acute; all hope of coming to an understanding was lost, and Camille Delcommune must have convinced his brother, if any such advice was necessary, not to intrust Conrad with the command of the boat, which was to take the expedition back on October 31st. The captain's health was already seriously undermined; it was only by an effort of will that he just managed to set out again. This tenacity is very much of a piece with the character which Conrad always displayed, both in his literary and in his seafaring career.

We have no first-hand account of the rupture with Camille Delcommune, but we have an indirect piece of evidence of the highest value. This is a letter dated November 29, 1890, from Lublin in Poland, written by Mme Marguerite Poradowska to Albert Thys, in which she says that she has just received a letter from her nephew, who is greatly affected in health and very much cast down in spirits.[2]

In addition, it appears that the ship that he is to command will only be ready in June, *perhaps,* and the manager, M. Delcommune, has told him straight out that he can hope for neither promotion nor a rise in salary as long as he stays in the Congo. He added, indeed, that any promises made in Europe do not bind him as long as they are not in the contract, and the promises that you were so good as to make him, Sir, are not in the contract.

[1] Letter in Polish, communicated by Mme Tyszka herself.
[2] Letter of November 29, 1890, communicated by the Company.

After expressing the state of anxiety into which Captain Korzeniowski's family had been thrown by the news of his health, Mme Poradowska transmitted to the administrator of the Company the wish expressed by Conrad that his name should be put down with a view to his obtaining command of some sea ship owned by one of the commercial companies of the Congo, travelling between Banana and Antwerp. If he could be recalled for this purpose, Captain Korzeniowski was quite willing to pay the expenses of his return journey himself. Mme Poradowska added the following significant sentence: "It is sad to think that a man of Captain Korzeniowski's abilities, accustomed to commanding ships, should be reduced to this inferior post and exposed to such deadly diseases."

It is clear from this letter that the chief reason for Conrad's dissatisfaction was Delcommune's refusal to give him command of a ship and his determination to keep him in a subordinate position, in spite of the promises that had been made in Brussels. It is quite certain that Conrad would never have left Europe, where he hoped to obtain a command, in order to be merely a mate on board a wretched little two-penny-halfpenny steamer.

The decision that was taken on the arrival of Alexandre Delcommune not to intrust Conrad with the command of the *Florida* [1] was the last blow to his endurance.

On October 19th he had already decided to abandon everything and to return to Europe, as he had but faint hope of obtaining the command of a sea-going vessel sailing between Banana and Antwerp. A few weeks later, when he was on the point of reaching Europe, his uncle Thaddeus wrote to him:

Although you assure me that the first sea breeze will restore your health, I found such a change in your handwriting—which I put down to fever and dysentery—that my reflections were not at all pleasant ones. . . .

Tell me also about the state of your finances, so that I may be able to help you as far as my means will go.[2]

[1] This command was intrusted to a captain named Carlier, a name which Conrad has given to the miserable hero of "An Outpost of Progress."

[2] Letter of December 27, 1890.

We know nothing of the circumstances which attended the return journey of Joseph Conrad. He must have left Kinchassa at latest at the beginning of November, for he was at Matadi on December 4th, and he made the journey from Kinchassa to Leopoldville in a native barque, as we are told in the following passage from *A Personal Record:*

A good many of my other properties, infinitely more valuable and useful to me [than the MS. of *Almayer's Folly*], remained behind through unfortunate accidents of transportation. I call to mind, for instance, a specially awkward turn of the Congo, between Kinchassa and Leopoldville—more particularly when one had to take it at night in a big canoe with only half the proper number of paddlers. I failed in being the second white man on record drowned at that interesting spot through the upsetting of a canoe. The first was a young Belgian officer, but the accident happened some months before my time, and he, too, I believe, was going home; not perhaps quite so ill as myself—but still he was going home. I got round the turn more or less alive, though I was too sick to care whether I did or not, and, always with *Almayer's Folly* amongst my diminishing baggage, I arrived at that delectable capital Boma, where before the departure of the steamer which was to take me home I had the time to wish myself dead over and over again with perfect sincerity.[1]

He did not reach Europe before the middle of January. The immediate consequence of this journey to the Congo was —as Conrad has said himself—a long, long illness and a dreary convalescence.

Conrad's health was affected during all the rest of his life by this African expedition. He suffered from attacks of gout which made his life an intermittent martyrdom. But, on the other hand, it is a not unlikely supposition that this journey to the Congo and its unfortunate consequences gave us the great writer.

Mr. Edward Garnett once told me that one day several years later, Conrad himself had said to him, "Before the Congo I was just a mere animal." By this he no doubt meant that during the first fifteen years of his seafaring career he had lived as though hardly aware of his own existence, without

[1] *A Personal Record,* p. 14.

ever reflecting on the reasons of his own or other people's activity, yet carried along by the ardour of his temperament and attracted by an almost unconscious longing for adventure. The illness which he brought back from the Congo, by limiting his physical activity and confining him to his room for several months, obliged him to withdraw into himself, to call up those memories with which his life, though he was only thirty-three, was already extraordinarily full, and to try to estimate their value both from the human and the literary point of view.

As we have already stated, it was just before he left that Captain Korzeniowski's literary vocation began to take shape, and amongst the baggage he had taken with him as far as the Stanley Falls was a copybook of some hundred pages, which he very nearly lost on his way back and which contained nothing less than the first seven chapters of *Almayer's Folly*. It would not, therefore, be correct to say that it was the Congo which aroused the potential novelist that Joseph Conrad Korzeniowski had carried within him ever since the years of his solitary childhood. But it was the Congo and its results on his health which finally settled his destiny and put the painful weight of illness into the balance on the side of the novelist, who was still struggling with the sailor for supremacy.

Until 1898, that is to say after having written not only *Almayer's Folly* but also *An Outcast of the Islands, The Nigger of the "Narcissus,"* and *Tales of Unrest,* Conrad still thought of taking to the sea once more.

He took steps to obtain a command; he longed to return to those great expanses which had been his domain for twenty years, but his longing for the sea was composed of both desire and distrust. It was certainly not the attractions of a literary career that kept him back, for he did not at first expect either profit or glory; he hoped for nothing more than a meagre subsistence, but he knew that he was now threatened every moment with disease, and in spite of his indomitable energy, he did not feel enough confidence in himself to take up once more the incessant struggle against his old and pitiless enemy the sea.

It may be said that Africa killed Conrad the sailor and strengthened Conrad the novelist.

It is not, perhaps, quite correct to say that "that lingering Congo fever which dogged his health fastened a deep, fitful gloom over his spirit." [1] This gloom was at the bottom of his nature, he had taken it in with his first breath, and contact with different countries and the solitude of the sea had only deepened it. But though it did not actually fasten this deep gloom on his spirit, yet the Congo certainly caused it to rise up from the depths of his soul, and thus no doubt contributed to those deep currents of bitterness which seem to well out like a great river from the very heart of human darkness and carry to the confines of the land of dreams the strength of an unquiet spirit and of a generous mind.

[1] John Galsworthy, "Reminiscences of Conrad."

CHAPTER VIII

'TWIXT LAND AND SEA

(1891–1894)

The sea is the sailor's true element, and Marlow, lingering on shore, was to me an object of incredulous commiseration, like a bird, which, secretly, should have lost its faith in the high virtue of flying.

("CHANCE," CHAP. I)

THE Congo had had a disastrous effect upon Conrad's health. During the last months of 1890 the fever never left him; and on his return to Europe in January he suffered from his first attack of gout. He had gone to Glasgow in search of another command, but he was obliged to give in, and spend the greater part of February and the whole of March in the German hospital in London to which he had been introduced by his friend, Adolf Krieger, who had met him on his arrival. His legs were now so swollen that he could not stand,[1] and he remained six weeks on his back; and although he tried to make light of his sufferings in writing to his uncle, both his strength and his spirits were very low.

At this time he writes to his cousin Mme Marie Tyszka:

London, 15. IV. 1891

MY DEAREST MARIETTE,

Your letter of February 24 found me ill, and this illness lasted so long that it was impossible to answer you till now. Do not suspect me of being indifferent or even lazy. I have been two months in bed: I got up quite lately and during three weeks had my hands swollen. It is only with the greatest difficulty that I was able to write a few words to Uncle Thaddeus.

Thank God that you have already recovered, my dear sister! You write me that you are leaving Elzbiecin, but you do not tell me why. I

---

[1] Letters of Th. B., March 10 and 24 and April 12, 1891.

hope you will let me know, if you can do so. I thought you were intending to live there. As to sorrows! Who has not got them? But you
have with you the tender solicitude of the very kind and esteemed Mr.
Theodor,[1] and you can stand all more easily than those who are obliged
to fight alone against the difficulties.

My congratulation to Zuria and to Martha [2] for the birth of their
children. I share their joy with all my heart and I ask you to remember
me to them. A cordial handshake for Mr. Theodor and all my kind
regards to you.

Your loving brother,
K. N. KORZENIOWSKI.

I kiss my Aunt's hands: please remember me to her.[3]

His health was bad enough to make a visit to Poland out
of the question. Dr. Ludwig, who attended him, decided to
send him to Switzerland, to a hydropathic establishment at
Champel near Geneva. He arrived there on May 21, 1891, in
a most melancholy, depressed state of mind. Conrad was now
thirty-three years old. After severe struggles, he had attained
what he wanted, a command, but his health was broken, his
future compromised, and his energies were undermined.

During his stay at Champel, which lasted until June 14th,
he lived at the Hôtel-Pension de la Roseraie.[4] It was a
square white house of three stories standing in a shady garden close to the river Arve, where the road runs along beside
the river. Just at this point there is a kind of weir, and the
steady sound of plunging water is pleasant to the ear. Beyond
the river is Pinchat hill, and behind, against the horizon, rises
the massive bulk of the Salève. The plain is covered with scattered, low houses and sheds and the factories of Carouge.
The bath-house is only a few steps from the hotel, on a little
eminence, and half an hour's walk along the Roseraie would
take him into the centre of Geneva. The treatment and the air
of this sheltered spot had immediately a good effect upon his
health, and his spirits rapidly recovered. He took up again the

[1] Mme Tyszka's husband.
[2] Mme Tyszka's sisters.
[3] The original is in Polish.
[4] When I visited it in November, 1925, it had not changed from what it
was when Conrad knew it. Dr. Glatz, who treated him on this occasion and
when he was there a second time, died in 1906.

manuscript of *Almayer's Folly*, which he had carried about with him for nearly two years. And he wrote later on:

Geneva, or more precisely the hydropathic establishment of Champel, is rendered for ever famous by the termination of the eighth chapter in the history of Almayer's decline and fall.[1]

While he was at Champel he was offered the chance—probably thanks to his friend, Adolf Krieger—of serving in a ship navigating the Niger, but he was decidedly sick of Africa, although he knew that the climate of the Niger was better than that of the Congo. He at once refused and set about returning to London, where he arrived toward the end of June, without knowing what he intended to do in the immediate future.

His uncle's letters show that Conrad must have visited Brussels several times during the summer to see his aunt Marguerite Poradowska; and it is probable that it was on one of these occasions that the meeting, described in the last pages of "Heart of Darkness," with the *fiancée* of Kurtz-Klein took place, and that the account is close to actual facts.

Did Conrad intend to live on the continent, and did he confide to his uncle his intention of turning author? We do not know for certain. In any case, from his uncle's letter dated July 30, 1891, in which he reproaches Conrad once more for changing his plans, we can surmise that what was in his mind at the moment was neither the pursuit of his profession nor an intention to go into business with Messrs. Barr, Moering & Co.

Your weakness comes from the Nalecz Korzeniowski. Your grandfather and uncle were always entertaining projects which had no validity except in their imaginations. . . . Your father was an idealistic dreamer; he loved mankind and wished them well, but he had two standards for judging them. He was indulgent to the poor and very hard on the rich. All three of them were ambitious and suffered acutely when they failed. Alas, in making plans, you too allow yourself to be carried away by your imagination, and, when those plans fail, to be far too deeply discouraged.

[1] *A Personal Record*, p. 14.

Conrad's discouragement sprang from a sense of his physical disabilities; his depression became worse during this summer and early autumn. His uncle wrote:

The tone of your letter of September 26th gave me very little comfort. To say that it is better to die young, a man must be either very discouraged or really ill. Such a philosophy could not proceed from a young man of thirty-four who was in good health.[1]

Meanwhile, Conrad fought his depression down. There was ever a store of energy in him which met and got the better of that melancholy which had, as we have seen, its roots in an unhappy childhood. An active life was his salvation, the one escape possible to a man of his temperament. Thus it was essential that he should first readapt himself to it, and the need of earning a living also compelled him in that direction. As his health did not allow him to go to sea, he accepted employment as manager of a waterside warehouse on the Thames which his friends, Adolf Krieger and G. F. W. Hope, obtained for him. "That work," he wrote afterward, "undertaken to accustom myself again to the activities of a healthy existence, soon came to an end. The earth had nothing to hold me with for very long." [2] He sought, too, distraction from his own mortifications in describing those of Almayer; in the course of the autumn he wrote the greater part of the ninth chapter of *Almayer's Folly*.

This year of compulsory leisure, of long meditations upon himself and upon life, drew up, little by little, from the depths of his being that inborn melancholy and energetic despair which underlie his work and which twenty hard, adventurous years had kept beneath the surface. One of his uncle's letters throws an interesting light upon Conrad's state of mind at this time:

MY DEAR BOY:
I begin as I always do, but I ought to address you as "my dear pessimist"; for judging from your letters that description would fit you best. I cannot say that I am pleased by your state of mind, or that I am

[1] October 8, 1891.
[2] *A Personal Record*, p. 14.

without apprehension about your future. Of course I am thankful for your frankness in not hiding from me what you really feel. I know human nature too well and I love you too much not to read between the lines of your letters. . . . Thinking over the causes of your melancholy most carefully I cannot attribute it either to youth or to age. In the case of one who is thirty-four and has had as full a life as you have had, I am forced to attribute it to ill-health, to your wretched sufferings on the African adventure, to your illness which resulted from them, and to the fact that you have had lately plenty of time to give yourself up to that habit of reverie which I have observed to be part of your character. It is inherited; it has been always there, in spite of your active life.

I may be mistaken, but I think this tendency to pessimism was already in you as long ago as the days when you were at Marseilles, but it was then part of youth. I am sure that with your melancholy temperament you ought to avoid all meditations which lead to pessimistic conclusions. I advise you to lead a more active life than ever and to cultivate cheerful habits.

Our country, as Slowacki well says (although he himself was not free from the reproach), is the "pan" of the nations, which, in plain prose, means that we are a nation who consider ourselves great and misunderstood, the possessors of a greatness which others do not recognize and will never recognize. If individuals and nations would set duty before themselves as an aim, instead of grandiose ideals, the world would be a happier place.

. . . Perhaps you will reply that these are the sentiments of one who has always had "a place in the sun." Not at all. I have endured many ups and downs; I have suffered in my private life, in my family life, and as a Pole; and it is thanks to these mortifications that I have arrived at a calm and modest estimate of life and its duties, and that I have taken as my motto *"usque ad finem,"* as my guide, the love of the duty which circumstances define.[1]

In spite of their affection for each other, there were deep divergences between uncle and nephew; the Polish country gentleman could not understand the passionate depth of melancholy in Conrad, or how inevitable it was that his ardour and intellect should suffer profoundly in contact with the mediocrity of the world. Such advice was impracticable just at a moment when the demands of his nature, long held in check, were imperiously asserting themselves. Nevertheless, feeling his strength returning, hoping that his illness was at last over,

[1] November 9, 1891.

and homesick, perhaps, for the sea after nearly two years' absence from it, Conrad eagerly accepted service on board a sailing ship, the offer of which was not only agreeable but flattering to him. The *Torrens,* in which he was offered a second command, was a vessel of about thirteen hundred tons, and "one of the most successful ships ever built, one of the fastest and for many years the favourite passenger ship to Adelaide," [1] the ship which was called "The Wonderful *Torrens."*

Her captain, H. R. Angel, who was also part owner and a very popular man in the Mercantile Marine, had lately retired. He had commanded her during fifteen voyages of, on an average, seventy-four days from Plymouth to Port Adelaide. "With the change of captains," as Mr. Basil Lubbock says, "her luck deserted her.[2] On her winter voyage (1890) she had lost her foremast and topmast, and when she had had to put in at Pernambuco to be repaired, part of her cargo had been burnt. On that occasion she had taken 179 days to reach Adelaide. Conrad thus narrowly missed a repetition of his experiences on board the *Palestine.* The second voyage of Captain Cope, on which he did accompany him, was not so eventful, although the *Torrens* on that occasion did not come up to her reputation for speed.

He signed on on November 20, 1891, and the vessel left Plymouth on the 25th; on February 28, 1892, Conrad disembarked at Adelaide after a voyage of ninety-five days. The references to this first voyage are scanty. A short letter addressed by him to one of the crew shows that she left for London on April 7th.[3] She touched at Capetown and at St. Helena on the way back and arrived at London at the end of August; his certificate of discharge is dated September 3, 1892.

[1] "The *Torrens* was launched in 1875, only a few months after I had managed, after lots of trouble, to launch myself on the waters of the Mediterranean. Thus we began our careers about the same time. From the professional point of view hers was by far the greater success." ("The *Torrens*": A Personal Tribute," *Last Essays,* p. 26.)

[2] *The Colonial Clippers,* by Basil Lubbock.

[3] To Geo. Mansfield: "Port Adelaide, Thursday, 31 March, 1892. Capt. Cope desires me to inform you that he is willing to accept your services as O.S. at £1. per month. As the ship is going to leave on the 7th proximo, you had better come over at once if you wish to join. J. Conrad, mate. Ship *Torrens."*

The voyage did him good. As might have been expected, responsibility and work reacted favourably on his temperament, and we find his uncle congratulating him on the recovery of his spirits, and in a later letter (October 17th) he suggests again that Conrad should visit him in July or August of the next year. In the same letter he reports that Conrad's cousin, Stanislas Bobrowski, has been arrested, for giving Polish lessons, by the Russian authorities; he was sent to jail for one and a half years; news which must have painfully reminded Conrad of his own childhood.

On October 25th the *Torrens,* with Conrad as mate, again left London, and reached Adelaide, ninety-seven days later, on January 30, 1893. It was during this voyage that Conrad first communicated to anyone his literary projects. From 1889 onward he had always carried about with him the unfinished manuscript of *Almayer's Folly,* but he had allowed no one to read it. He had not even told his uncle about it; and even if, as seems likely, his aunt, Marguerite Poradowska, had encouraged him to write down his recollections, it is by no means certain that he would have told her that he had begun to follow her advice.

There was a young Cambridge man called W. H. Jacques, on board the *Torrens,* who was taking the voyage for his health. The passengers were few and the voyage to Australia was long; naturally, officers and passengers got to know each other well up to a certain point. Conrad, being a great reader, had many talks with this youth fresh from the university, and they lent each other books. One evening, while they were talking in the mate's cabin, Conrad obeyed a sudden impulse, pulled out a drawer, and gave him the first nine chapters of *Almayer's Folly.*

"Would it bore you very much reading a MS. in a handwriting like mine?" I asked him one evening on a sudden impulse at the end of a longish conversation whose subject was Gibbon's History. Jacques (that was his name) was sitting in my cabin one stormy dog-watch below, after bringing me a book to read from his own travelling store.

"Not at all," he answered with his courteous intonation and a faint smile. As I pulled a drawer open his suddenly aroused curiosity gave him a watchful expression. I wonder what he expected to see. . . . In his

Champel near Geneva

Above: the Pension de la Roseraie, where Conrad lived for several
months in 1891, 1895, and 1907, and where he wrote parts of
Almayer's Folly and *An Outcast of the Islands.*   Below: the entrance of the hydropathic establishment of Champel.   "The hydropathic establishment of Champel is rendered for ever famous
by the termination of the eighth chapter in the history of Almayer's decline and fall."   (*A Personal Record,* p. 14.).

attractive, reserved manner, and in a veiled, sympathetic voice, he asked: "What is this?"—"It is a sort of tale," I answered with an effort. "It is not even finished yet. Nevertheless, I would like to know what you think of it." He put the MS. in the breast pocket of his jacket: I remember perfectly his thin brown fingers folding it lengthwise. "I will read it to-morrow," he remarked, seizing the door-handle, and then, watching the roll of the ship for a propitious moment, he opened the door and was gone. In the moment of his exit I heard the sustained booming of the wind, the swish of the water on the decks of the *Torrens,* and the subdued, as if distant, roar of the rising sea. I noted the growing disquiet in the great restlessness of the ocean, and responded professionally to it with the thought that at eight o'clock, in another half hour or so, at the furthest, the top-gallant sails would have to come off the ship. Next day, but this time in the first dog-watch, Jacques entered my cabin. He had a thick, woollen muffler round his throat and the MS. was in his hand. He tendered it to me with a steady look, but without a word. I took it in silence. He sat down on the couch and still said nothing. I opened and shut a drawer under my desk, on which a filled up log-slate lay wide open in its wooden frame waiting to be copied neatly into the sort of book I was accustomed to write with care, the ship's log-book. I turned my back squarely on the desk. And even then Jacques never offered a word. "Well, what do you say?" I asked at last. "Is it worth finishing?" This question expressed exactly the whole of my thoughts.

"Distinctly," he answered in his sedate, veiled voice, and then coughed a little.

"Were you interested?" I inquired further, almost in a whisper.

"Very much!" . . .

"Now let me ask you one more thing: Is the story quite clear to you as it stands?"

He raised his dark, gentle eyes to my face and seemed surprised.

"Yes! Perfectly."

This was all I was to hear from his lips concerning the merits of *Almayer's Folly.* We never spoke together of the book again.[1]

The incident took place, Conrad also notes, just as they were about to double the Cape; afterward, bad weather confined his first reader to his cabin for practically the rest of the voyage. The young man was gravely ill; he died shortly after reaching Australia.

In spite of this laconic encouragement, and in spite, too, of the truth of that quotation from Novalis which Conrad

[1] *A Personal Record,* p. 15.

was fond of quoting: "It is certain my conviction gains infinitely the moment another soul will believe in it," [1] he did
not work at his manuscript either during the rest of the voyage
or upon the return journey to London. The *Torrens* reached
Adelaide on March 19th, and sailed again a little later. This
is confirmed by the recollections of a passenger who embarked
in her at Adelaide, one who was destined to become one of
Conrad's most faithful friends and a famous man of letters.

Some months earlier, two young men, one from Oxford, the
other from Cambridge, attracted by the idea of a long cruise
and of visiting Robert Louis Stevenson at Samoa, set out
together for the Pacific Islands. One of them was Edward
Lancelot Sanderson, now headmaster of Elstree, the other
John Galsworthy.

They did not reach Samoa; they were obliged to return to
Europe. But if they missed knowing one great writer who had
achieved fame and was near his end,[2] they met another whose
literary career was just beginning—disguised as the mate of
the *Torrens*. Shortly after Conrad's death, Mr. Galsworthy
wrote:

It was in March, 1893, that I first met Conrad on board the English
sailing ship *Torrens* in Adelaide harbour. He was superintending the
stowage of cargo. Very dark he looked in the burning sunlight, tanned,
with a peaked brown beard, almost black hair, and dark brown eyes,
over which the lids were deeply folded. He was thin, not tall, his arms
very long, his shoulders broad, his head set rather forward. He spoke to
me with a strong foreign accent. He seemed to me strange on an English
ship. For fifty-six days I sailed in his company.

The chief mate bears the main burden of a sailing ship. All the first
night he was fighting a fire in the hold. None of us seventeen passengers
knew of it till long after. It was he who had most truck with the tail
of that hurricane off the Leeuwin, and later with another storm: a good
seaman, watchful of the weather; quick in handling the ship; considerate
with the apprentices—we had a long, unhappy Belgian youth among
them, who took unhandily to the sea and dreaded going aloft. Conrad
compassionately spared him all he could. With the crew he was popular;

---

[1] *A Personal Record*, p. 15. He also chose this sentence as a motto for *Lord
Jim*.
[2] Robert Louis Stevenson died in December, 1894.

they were individuals to him, not a mere gang; and long after he would talk of this or that among them, especially of old Andy the sail-maker: "I liked that old fellow, you know."

With the young second mate, a cheerful capable young seaman, very English, he was friendly; and respectful, if faintly ironic, with his whiskered, stout old captain. Evening watches in fine weather we spent on the poop. Ever the great teller of a tale, he had already nearly twenty years of tales to tell. Tales of ships and storms, of Polish revolution, of his youthful Carlist gun-running adventure, of the Malay seas, and the Congo; and of men and men; all to a listener who had the insatiability of a twenty-five-year-old.

On that ship he told of life, not literature. On my last evening he asked me at the Cape to his cabin, and I remember feeling that he outweighed for me all the other experiences of that voyage. Fascination was Conrad's great characteristic—the fascination of vivid expressiveness and zest, of his deeply affectionate heart, and his far-ranging, subtle mind. He was extraordinarily perceptive and receptive.[1]

They had long talks with him during his off-hours. His personality must have impressed them; but it is not true that either of them saw the manuscript of *Almayer's Folly* on board the *Torrens*.

She touched at Capetown in the middle of May, where Mr. Galsworthy left her; she arrived at London (so late that there was some anxiety about her) on July 26, 1893. There Conrad found a letter from his uncle waiting for him, urging him to come to Poland and giving him directions. Conrad seems to have left London early in August and to have spent most of August and September at Kazimierowka, returning to London early in October, after visiting his cousins Zagorski at Lublin. We learn from *A Personal Record* that in Berlin on his way to Poland he nearly lost his manuscript.

From certain passages in his uncle's letter we gather that Captain Cope, probably discouraged by the failure of the *Torrens* to live up to her reputation for speed under his command, was taking steps to be transferred to a steamer, steps which inspired in Conrad a brief hope of succeeding him. Up till the middle of October he remained nominally a member of the *Torrens's* crew.

[1] John Galsworthy: "Reminiscences of Conrad."

I ceased [he wrote in *Last Essays*] to "belong to her" on the 15th of October, 1893, when, in London Dock, I took a long look from the quay at that last of ships I ever had under my care, and, stepping round the corner of a tall warehouse, parted from her for ever and at the same time stepped (in merciful ignorance) out of my sea life altogether.[1]

It was not, however, his absolutely last connection with the sea, though the subsequent one was nominal rather than real. One afternoon, Captain Froud, the secretary of the London Shipmasters' Society, whose small office in Fenchurch Street Conrad used sometimes to visit, told him that the captain of a steamer wanted a mate who could speak French fluently. Such a man was not easy to find. It was not at all the kind of job Conrad was on the lookout for. His state of mind at this time was not unlike that in which, four years earlier, he had, while he was waiting care-free to embark for the Congo, begun to write the first pages of Almayer.

I had given myself up to the idleness of a haunted man who looks for nothing but words wherein to capture his visions. But I admit that outwardly I resembled sufficiently a man who could make a second officer for a steamer chartered by a French company. I showed no sign of being haunted by the fate of Nina and by the murmurs of tropical forests; and even my intimate intercourse with Almayer (a person of weak character) had not put a visible mark upon my features. For many years he and the world of his story had been the companions of my imagination without, I hope, impairing my ability to deal with the realities of sea life.[2]

He accepted the offer reluctantly and solely to rescue the excellent, obliging Captain Froud from a position of some embarrassment. The steamer in question was chartered by the Compagnie Franco-Canadienne to carry emigrants from France to Canada, plying from Rouen as its base. After an interview with her captain, Frederick Paton, and obtaining the promise of certain privileges as compensation for accepting a position which was beneath his naval status, Conrad embarked in the *Adowa* for Rouen on November 29, 1893.

She reached Rouen on the 4th of December.[3] The winter

[1] *Last Essays*, "The *Torrens*: A Personal Tribute," p. 26.
[2] *A Personal Record*, pp. 8–9.
[3] *Journal de Rouen*, December 5, 1893.

was exceptionally severe; great lumps of ice were riding down the Seine; all ferry services were interrupted. He has described exactly the conditions and surroundings in which he wrote the opening words of Chapter X of *Almayer's Folly:*

The round opening framed in its brass rim a fragment of the quays, with a row of casks ranged on the frozen ground and the tail-end of a great cart. A red-nosed carter in a blouse and a woollen night-cap leaned against the wheel. An idle, strolling custom-house guard, belted over his blue *capote,* had the air of being depressed by exposure to the weather and the monotony of official existence. The background of grimy houses found a place in the picture framed by my port-hole, across a wide stretch of paved quay brown with frozen mud. The colouring was sombre, and the most conspicuous feature was a little café with curtained windows and a shabby front of white woodwork, corresponding with the squalor of these poorer quarters bordering the river. We had been shifted down there from another berth in the neighbourhood of the Opera House, where that same port-hole gave me a view of quite another sort of café—the best in the town, I believe, and the very one where the worthy Bovary and his wife, the romantic daughter of old Père Renault, had some refreshment after the memorable performance of an opera which was the tragic story of Lucia di Lammermoor in a setting of light music.[1]

Not an emigrant appeared, only a company director or two from Paris who inspected the vessel. Idle citizens of Rouen, with their women and children, would occasionally also visit her, and Conrad in his smartest uniform did the honours. As he said himself, he had turned from being an officer of the Mercantile Marine into a Cook's interpreter. The projects of the Franco-Canadian Company ended in smoke; thirty days after his arrival the *Adowa* was ordered to return to London.

She arrived at London on the 12th, and on January 14, 1894, an important date in his life, Conrad left the marine service for good and all.

His career as a sailor ended, as it had begun, without will or purpose playing any part in the matter, and, as Conrad once pointed out to me in conversation, his twenty years' service as an English sailor began at one French port and closed at another.

[1] *A Personal Record,* p. 5.

At the time he had no intention of leaving the sea; the transition from a seafaring life to that of a man of letters was accomplished insensibly, without his wishing it or being conscious of it. Circumstances and the still secret impulse of his nature were the determining factors, and what he was later to call "the unknown powers that shape our destinies." [1]

[1] At this point in his biography it is not out of place to remind the reader how those who had worked with him remember him. During the long years to come he used to receive letters from them. We will quote two examples: "I would like to convey to you my appreciation of your great kindness to me during the voyage I served under you which was an epoch in my life," wrote a junior apprentice on the *Torrens*. Another wrote to the novelist in 1923: "From the reading of the chapter 'Poland Revisited' I gather that you have a son: if this is so, may I say something in this letter to him. I dislike flattery in any form, but I would like him to realize what a marvellous personality you have. I have loved you more than any man I ever knew except my own father and I revere the memory that was made upon the most irresponsible of human beings, the schoolboy, because I had only just left school when I had the honour of being your boy. I remember so distinctly the trouble you took in the silent watches of a tropical night to teach me the different ropes. This was thirty years or more ago."

CHAPTER IX

TALES OF UNREST

(1894–1904)

A free man, a proud swimmer striking out for a new destiny.

("THE SECRET SHARER.")

JOSEPH CONRAD had hardly got back to London and settled himself in his lodgings at 17 Gillingham Street, not far from Victoria Station, when, on the evening of January 29th, he received a telegram informing him that on the same day, at seven in the morning, his uncle Thaddeus Bobrowski had died on his estate of Kazimierowka. The distance was too great to allow Conrad to reach the Ukraine in time to attend his uncle's funeral. The executors informed him by letter of the terms of the will, which proved once more the peculiar affection and esteem which Thaddeus Bobrowski had for his nephew.[1]

The death of his uncle had not, indeed, severed Conrad's last link with Poland, but he had lost a being who was very dear to him, who had been the only person to know all his family intimately, who had taken care of him in childhood, watched over him during his youth, and never failed throughout his seafaring life to make him feel the support of constant kindness and affection.[2] In the course of his voyages, during the twenty years of his adventurous and wandering life, the Kazimierowka house had been the only fixed point round

[1] Amongst other bequests, Thaddeus Bobrowski left money to found a scholarship for a Polish student at the University of Kiev. The executors also sent Conrad twelve hundred roubles, representing the interest of the sum which Thaddeus Bobrowski had intrusted to Mme Zaleska in his nephew's name.

[2] "He had been for a quarter of a century the wisest, the firmest, the most indulgent of guardians, extending over me a paternal care and affection, a moral support which I seemed to feel always near me in the most distant parts of the earth." (*A Personal Record*, p. 31.)

157

which Conrad's thoughts could cluster. During twenty years uncle and nephew had met only four times, but these meetings seemed all the more precious for being long hoped for, often put off, and always desired. Rare as they were, however, they were sufficient, not only to keep alive his tenderness for his uncle, but also to enable him to hear many memories of past things, which Conrad had never known or had only dimly suspected during his boyhood. All these recollections of his uncle's had sharpened the contours of his own childish impressions and brought food to his meditations, thus contributing toward the formation of the spirit which he carried within him.

The death of his uncle deprived Conrad of the illusion of a home. He had not, during the long while he had been at sea, felt the urgent necessity of this home, but he felt its absence more acutely now that he could no longer think of returning to Kazimierowka, and that his undermined health, combined with the urgings of his unrevealed literary vocation, made him feel, though as yet confusedly, that he was no longer the sailor, whose only domain is the sea, whose only home is a ship.

About this time Conrad's impulse toward literature became stronger than it had ever been up till then, as we learn from the fact that from January to May, 1894,[1] he wrote the last three chapters of *Almayer's Folly,* that is to say, the last quarter of a book whose first three quarters had cost him nearly four and a half years to achieve.

When he had once finished the story of the illusions and the misfortunes of this Almayer, who had been the strange companion of his thoughts for several years past,[2] Joseph Conrad had no more intention than before of taking up a literary career. Indeed, it was actually from the offices of the Ship-

---

[1] The exact date of the completion of *Almayer's Folly* is somewhat vague. The MS. bears on its last page the date April, 1894, whereas the wrapper of the same MS. says "Finished on the 22nd May, 1894." The book was probably finished toward the end of April and the following month was taken up in correcting.

[2] "It took me three years to finish the *Folly,* there was not a day I did not think of it—Not a day." (Letter to Edward Noble, October 28, 1895.)

masters' Society, where he used to go in the hopes of finding
some employment, that, one day in the beginning of June, he
decided to send his MS. to a publisher just on the chance.
He had hesitated for a moment between two of them, but
that morning he made up his mind, and he called a messenger
boy to take his MS. to T. Fisher Unwin.[1] The following passage from one of Conrad's letters gives us the reason for his
choice:

At that period of his existence T. F. Unwin had published some paper-
bound books by various authors and I bought one or two of them, *Mademoiselle Ixe* and *The Pope's Daughters,* I believe. My ignorance was so
great and my judgment so poor that I imagined *Almayer's Folly* would
be just suitable for that series. As a matter of fact it was much too long,
but this was my motive in the choice of a publisher. I sent the MS. by
messenger boy, instructing him to get a receipt which the boy brought me
all right, but I did not preserve that document of the literary history
of our time. The acceptance came some three months later, in the first
typewritten letter I ever received in my life.[2]

The MS. had fallen into the hands of a very young man,
who had recently become reader to Fisher Unwin; his name
was Edward Garnett, and he was the son of the learned Dr.
Garnett who was then one of the keepers of the British Museum. Among the quantity of very poor stuff that he was
obliged in the course of his work to read, Edward Garnett
was immediately struck by the singular qualities of vision and
style which this book exhibited. As may be readily imagined,
he found it difficult to determine the social status of the author
from his MS. The exotic subject and some foreignisms in the
style seemed to indicate that the writer was not entirely of
British blood. But though he expected that the author would
turn out to be a rather strange character, Edward Garnett was
not a little surprised on finding himself shortly after confronted by a sea captain of Polish origin, who, in spite of his
undeniable qualities of vision and style and his astonishing

[1] The MS. of *Almayer's Folly* has written on it, "Submitted to F. Unwin
on 2nd June, 1894. Accepted in August same year."
[2] Letter to Mr. Chesson, May 6, 1918.

knowledge of the English language, yet could speak it only with a very strong foreign accent.[1]

As a rule, Mr. Fisher Unwin's reader was not brought into personal contact with authors, but this time Edward Garnett had taken such an interest in the acceptance of this MS. that Mr. Fisher Unwin arranged a meeting between the young reader and the strange writer. The almost immediate result of this meeting was a mutual sympathy between the two men, which soon turned into a friendship that death alone cut short. The part which Edward Garnett played in Conrad's literary career, not only by showing so great an interest in his first book but by encouraging him to write a second, was of the utmost importance and was due, not to chance alone, but to a perspicacity and a critical generosity for which the admirers of Conrad can never be too grateful.

Almayer's Folly, which was accepted in August, 1894, came out on April 29th of the following year.[2] Between whiles Conrad, who, thanks to his uncle's small legacy, could now enjoy a little leisure, still remained in contact with the sea, under the milder form of an amusement. Together with his friend G. F. W. Hope, he indulged in the pleasures of yachting in a little eighteen ton cutter.[3]

[1] The fact that Conrad was always incapable of accenting English correctly when he spoke is singular enough in a writer who had such a strong grasp of the peculiar cadence of the English language. This singularity seems the more striking when one knows that Conrad spoke French, not only with absolute grammatical correctness, but also with an accent so perfect that it never betrayed his Polish descent. None of the intonations and inflections which are noticeable even in those Poles who speak French best were discernible in his speech. At most a slight meridional accent could be observed in his pronunciation of certain words, no doubt as a result of the years he spent in Marseilles. Indeed, when he spoke English it was without any noticeable "Polonisms," but rather with a very strong French accent. We may also add that, although for fifty years Conrad had little occasion to speak his native tongue, yet he had kept the most correct and purest accent in Polish.

[2] *Almayer's Folly* was to have been dedicated to Thaddeus Bobrowski; it came out with the following dedication: "To the Memory of T. B."

[3] See letter to Arnold Bennett, November 25, 1912. "Some proofs of *Almayer's Folly* were corrected on board the *Ildegonda,* cutter." See also the beginning of "Heart of Darkness." Conrad places the meeting of the narrator and his listeners in the yacht *Nellie* on the lower Thames. The *Nellie* was a yacht belonging to his friend G. F. W. Hope, and it may be that Conrad actually told the story of his African experiences on this yacht more or less as he makes Marlow tell his.

But he did not remain long in complete idleness, for on November 18, 1894, he began to write his second novel, *An Outcast of the Islands*. Conrad himself has told us the state of mind and the circumstances which led to the creation of this second book:

> . . . no hesitation, half formed plan, vague idea, or the vaguest reverie of something else between *An Outcast of the Islands* and *Almayer's Folly*. The only doubt I suffered from, after the publication of *Almayer's Folly,* was whether I should write another line for print. Those days, now grown so dim, had their poignant moments. Neither in my mind nor in my heart had I then given up the sea. In truth I was clinging to it desperately, all the more desperately because, against my will, I could not help feeling that there was something changed in my relation to it. *Almayer's Folly* had been finished and done with. The mood itself was gone. But it had left the memory of an experience that, both in thought and emotion, was unconnected with the sea, and I suppose that part of my moral being which is rooted in consistency was badly shaken. I was the victim of contrary stresses which produced a state of immobility. I gave myself up to indolence. Since it was impossible for me to face both ways I had elected to face nothing. The discovery of new values in life is a very chaotic experience; there is a tremendous amount of jostling and confusion and a momentary feeling of darkness. . . .
>
> A phrase of Edward Garnett's is, as a matter of fact, responsible for this book. . . . One evening when we had dined together and he had listened to the account of my perplexities (I fear he must have been growing a little tired of them) he pointed out that there was no need to determine my future absolutely. Then he added: "You have the style, you have the temperament; why not write another?" . . . Had he said: "Why not go on writing?" it is very probable he would have scared me away from pen and ink for ever; but there was nothing either to frighten one or arouse one's antagonism in the mere suggestion to "write another." . . . At about eleven o'clock of a nice London night, Edward and I walked along interminable streets talking of many things, and I remember that on getting home I sat down and wrote about half a page of *An Outcast of the Islands* before I slept.[1]

The winter of 1894 and most of 1895 were devoted to the completion of *An Outcast of the Islands*. In March Conrad spent a short time in Brussels. In April he found so much

[1] *An Outcast of the Islands,* Author's Note.

difficulty in continuing work on this second novel that he decided to try a change of atmosphere:

I am going to look for Willems in Switzerland. . . . I find I can't work. Simply can't. I am going to try what mountain air combined with active fire-house (twice a day) will do for divine inspiration. I shall try it for about three weeks and may be the lenient gods will allow me to finish that infernal manuscript.[1]

The atmosphere of the Roseraie at Champel, which had been favourable four years earlier to *Almayer's Folly*, was equally favourable to *An Outcast of the Islands*. From Champel he wrote to Edward Garnett:

I am working every day: tolerably bad work. Like poor Risler the Elder's cashier: "I haf' no gonfitence." [2]

He returned from Champel on June 4th, after having written nearly a third of his book.[3] He spent the end of July and the beginning of August yachting between Chatham and Harwich with his friend, G. F. W. Hope, and two weeks of August going to and fro between Paris and London on some financial business for a friend. A month later, on September 4th, *An Outcast of the Islands* was finished. He had sold the rights to Fisher Unwin on August 23rd. Conrad's literary career was now settled upon. From this year, 1895, to that of his death, that is to say for nearly thirty years, the main adventures of Conrad's life are those connected with his books. The daily struggle against the intangible resistance of his imagination and the furtive evasion of words was made even harder to bear by material difficulties, which for twenty years were almost unceasing, and by repeated attacks of the gout, which tortured him intermittently during many of these thirty years. But in spite of the cries of anger, of bitterness or of pain, which disease sometimes tore from him, it never succeeded, even up to his last hour, in sapping that kind of desperate energy of which so many of his creations bear the mark

[1] Letter to Edward Garnett, May 1, 1895.
[2] Letter to Edward Garnett, May 12, 1895. Risler the Elder is an allusion to Alphonse Daudet's novel, *Fromont Jeune et Risler Aîné*.
[3] "There is nothing to prevent me writing in Champel (one third of my *Outcast* was written there.)"   (Letter to J. B. Pinker, March 13, 1907.)

—creations which are only the visible projections of his nature and of the inward warfare that he never ceased to wage.

Henceforward it must be the biographer's task to efface himself behind the numerous documents which Conrad has left.[1] These are the letters which he addressed in the course of thirty years to his earliest literary friends, to those which his books brought him, to his admirers, English or foreign, old or young, to whom he wrote with an inexhaustible and generous warmth. These letters show the man and the author to have been in complete accord. They not only shed better light than anything else on the figure of this great artist, but they also reveal, without indiscretion, his constant kindness. While keeping to himself all his own weariness, doubts, and bitterness, he lavished the most generous encouragement upon his friends.

It will be enough if we add as briefly as possible a few circumstances and dates which may help the reader to understand the letters that follow.

The publication of the *Outcast* was delayed owing to a fire which destroyed the printer's stereo-plates, and the book only came out on March 4, 1896. At that moment Conrad's thoughts were taken up with an event of quite a different nature, for three weeks later he married Miss Jessie George, a young girl whose acquaintance he had made eighteen months earlier at his friends', the Hopes. On the evening of March 24th they embarked at Southampton for St. Malo. They went on as far as Lannion, where a worthy Breton called Prijean, who was taking them for a drive round the country, pointed out to them a house to let in the Île-Grande. It was in this little house, a description of which will be found farther on, that the young couple spent the first few months of their marriage, from April 7th to the end of August. Their stay in the island was broken by an occasional sail in a little boat called *La Pervenche*. The passion with which Conrad flung himself into

[1] More than two thousand of Conrad's letters, in English, French, and Polish, have come into my hands. The French letters will shortly come out in a separate volume. With the exception of about ten Polish letters, which have been translated into English, all those that are printed here were chosen from the eighteen hundred English letters. (See Bibliography.)

his work was so great that he did not even wait to be settled in the Île-Grande before beginning again, and, though he had been for three days very anxious about his young wife's health, he had, during their short stay at the Hôtel de France at Lannion, already written the first eleven pages of *The Rescue,* which he thought was to be his third book. As in his two preceding novels, the background of this book was the Malay islands, and it was to have completed what may be called the Malay trilogy or the cycle of Lingard in Conrad's work.[1] But this novel among all his books was to have a very special fate; despite the constant efforts that he made during five or six years, taking it up, leaving it, taking it up once more, it was destined not to be completed until twenty years later.

In spite of an extremely violent attack of gout, which kept him motionless for some weeks in July, and in spite of the discouraging news that almost all his uncle's little legacy had been engulfed in an unlucky mining speculation, yet Conrad's stay in Brittany was particularly fruitful. Besides all the first part of *The Rescue,* Conrad wrote several tales: "The Idiots," suggested by impressions he had received on the spot in Brittany;[2] "An Outpost of Progress," which was a memory of his Congo experiences; and finally, the first ten pages of *The Nigger of the "Narcissus."* The couple returned to England in September, and after spending some weeks in Conrad's Gillingham Street lodgings, they settled into a little cottage, Ivy Walls, at Stanford-le-Hope, Essex, the village where their friends Mr. and Mrs. G. F. W. Hope were living.

During the autumn of 1896 Conrad set aside *The Rescue* and devoted himself entirely to writing *The Nigger of the "Narcissus,"* which he at first intended to be only a short story.

---

[1] "If the virtues of Lingard please most of the critics, they shall have more of them. The theme of it shall be the rescue of a yacht from some Malay vagabonds and there will be a gentleman and a lady cut out according to the regulation pattern," he wrote to his publisher on April 9th. It may be pointed out that Conrad composed the cycle of Lingard in the reverse of chronological order, going from Lingard's old age in *Almayer's Folly* to his youth in *The Rescue.*

[2] This is the only work that Conrad ever wrote immediately after an actual experience on the spot.

I crawl on with it. It will be about 30,000 words. I must enshrine my old chums in a decent edifice. Seriously, do you think it would be too long? There are so many touches necessary for such a picture.[1]

But, as often happened in the course of Conrad's literary life, the work grew in the making and *The Nigger of the "Narcissus"* was not finished till February 19th of the following year. The only interruption he allowed himself during this work was a few days' visit at Christmas-time to his old friend, Spiridion Kliszczewski, at Cardiff.

In the meantime, the young novelist's reputation was beginning to spread, not only in England, but also in his own country, as is shown by the following passage from a letter to his friend Garnett:

They have heard of me in Poland, through Chicago (of all God-forsaken places!) and think of trying for translations of *A. F.* and *Outcast*. So I am unofficially informed by a Warsaw friend.[2]

H. G. Wells, in an important article which appeared in the *Saturday Review* of May 16, 1896, drew the attention of the cultivated public to the new writer. Though making some reservations as to his style, Mr. Wells nevertheless said:

An Outcast of the Islands is perhaps the finest piece of fiction that has been published this year, as *Almayer's Folly* was one of the finest that was published in 1895. . . . Surely this is real romance, the romance that is real! . . . He imagines his scenes and their sequence like a master, he knows his individualities to their hearts; he has a new and wonderful field in this East Indian novel of his.[3]

Although Conrad was already complaining of the difficulties of his task, he had hardly finished *The Nigger* in February, 1897, when he set to work on "Karain," made another attempt at *The Rescue*, and, in the course of the summer, composed *The Return*. In the meantime *The Nigger* was appear-

[1] Letter to Edward Garnett, October 16, 1896. This tale was originally to have been called *The Forecastle: A Tale of Ship and Men.*

[2] *Ibid.*, November 16, 1896. *A. F.* = *Almayer's Folly.*

[3] *Saturday Review*, May 16, 1896, p. 509. Conrad wrote to H. G. Wells in reply to this article, but his letter has unfortunately not been found. H. G. Wells's answer is to be seen in *Twenty Letters to Joseph Conrad.* (First Edition Club. London, 1926.)

ing in the *New Review,* edited by W. E. Henley. The close of
the year 1896 brought him the first of his literary friendships
(after Edward Garnett's)—a friendship which, as we shall
see by his letters, remained one of his dearest until the end
of his life. It was that of Robert Bontine Cunninghame
Graham, who, on reading "An Outpost of Progress" in
Cosmopolis, was so filled with enthusiasm as to write immediately to the author and express a desire to become acquainted
with him.

In December, 1897, *The Nigger of the "Narcissus"* appeared in book form—a masterpiece which met with only a
limited success; it brought him, however, the encouragement
of two new friends (in addition to Garnett and Galsworthy),
who were none other than the distinguished Americans
Henry James and Stephen Crane, the latter of whom asked
to be introduced to the author of *The Nigger* immediately on
his first arrival in London from New York. In March, 1898,
appeared *Tales of Unrest.* In the preceding January his son
Borys was born.

His work was now progressing much too slowly to please
Conrad. To the end of his life he was familiar with what
Baudelaire so justly calls "the sterilities of nervous writers."

At times, I am myself amazed at my impudent desire to be able to live.
And, at times, I feel sick—sick at heart with doubts, with a gnawing un-
belief in myself. It's awful.[1]

Once more he set himself to work upon *The Rescue,* but
once more the same difficulties confronted him and he put the
book aside for the third time. In May and June he wrote
"Youth" in a few days and began *Lord Jim,* which he intended
at first to be also a short story. In the meantime, in the nervous
depression caused by his failure to finish *The Rescue,* and in
view of the small financial profits of his new career, his
thoughts turned once more to the sea. Cunninghame Graham
promised to use his influence in Scotland, and in September
Conrad went to Glasgow in search of a job; but as he wrote
to his friend Garnett:

[1] Letter to Edward Garnett, September 27, 1897.

Joseph Conrad in 1896.

Nothing decisive happened in Glasgow: my impression is that a command will come out of it sooner or later—most likely later when the pressing need is past and I have found my way on shore.[1]

No command was offered him, and as he had promised *The Rescue* to the *Illustrated London News* and to the American publisher McClure of New York, he was obliged to give up all other thoughts and confine himself entirely to his literary work; he complained of not being able to work at Ivy Walls and toward the end of September he settled at Pent Farm, Kent, near Hythe. He made no other attempt to return to his first vocation, and the labours of the second were just then particularly fruitful. "Youth" was soon followed by "Heart of Darkness"—two of his finest and most technically perfect tales. At the beginning of 1899 he obtained a prize of fifty guineas from *The Academy*.[2] The year 1900 was spent in working at *Lord Jim,* which, before it was completed, began to appear in *Blackwood's Magazine* in October. In spite of a kind of breakdown in February, 1900, he continued his work with renewed courage, and in a letter to Garnett, dated March

[1] Letter to Edward Garnett, September 29, 1898.
[2] Mrs. Craigie, who wrote novels under the pseudonym John Oliver Hobbes, was the proprietor of *The Academy* and founded this prize. It was divided between Conrad for *Tales of Unrest,* Mr. Maurice Hewlett for *The Forest Lovers,* and Mr. Sydney Lee for *A Life of William Shakespeare.* An anonymous and singularly understanding article accompanied the announcement of the prizewinners' names in the number of January 14th, in *The Academy.* Amongst other things the author says: "Mr. Conrad, in the five years or so that he has spent on land, setting down for our beguilement some of the stories that had come to him during his life at sea, has produced only four books: but they have been, in the fullest sense of the word, written. It might be said that the work of no novelist now working gives so much evidence of patient elaboration of style, without, however, leaving any sense of elaborateness. Mr. Conrad's art conceals art. . . . He blends human beings and nature. The puppet never fills the universe, as with certain other novelists. Everything is related and harmonized. This comprehensiveness of vision, this amplitude of outlook, makes Mr. Conrad more than just a story-teller. He seems to have some of the attributes of the Greek tragic dramatists. He has their irony. He sees so much at once, and is so conscious of the infinitesimal place a man can fill. Hence his work belongs never to cheerful literature: it is sombre, melancholy, searching. Yet, Mr. Conrad is a poet too. At the same time that he is aware of man's shortcomings, he is profoundly in love with his capacity for grandeur, with his potential nobility. He recognizes that an emotion may be as beautiful as a night of stars, a passion as tremendous as a typhoon."

26th, he writes with an enthusiasm which is unusual in his correspondence:

I am still at *Jim*. I've been beastly in February. I am old and sick and in debt,—but lately I have found I can still write. *It* comes, *it* comes and I am young and healthy and rich.[1]

Hardly was *Lord Jim* finished (July 16, 1900)[2] than he went to Bruges, accompanied by his wife and child, in order to meet Ford Madox Hueffer, with whom he had already begun to collaborate; but his stay at Bruges and Knocke was disturbed by considerable anxiety about his child's health. In the course of the winter of 1900 and during the year 1901, Conrad wrote, one after the other, "Typhoon," "Falk," "Amy Foster," [3] and set to work on a book entitled *Romance,* which he wrote in collaboration with Hueffer. The year 1902 was spent partly in finishing *Romance,* partly in working at "The End of the Tether." This strenuous labour had no interruption but a few visits to F. M. Hueffer at Winchelsea, to Henry James at Rye, to H. G. Wells at Sandgate, and from time to time a short stay in London where he met a few friends such as Edward Garnett, W. H. Hudson, E. V. Lucas, Stephen Reynolds, Edward Thomas, Percival Gibbon, etc., generally lunching with them at the Mont Blanc Restaurant in Gerrard Street, or seeing others of his friends, (Sir) Hugh Clifford, (Sir) Edmund Gosse, Sir Frank Swettenham, etc., at the Wellington Club. Few writers of his generation have drawn to themselves a more devoted little band of friends than Conrad, by his genius and by the magic of his personality.

---

[1] Letter to Edward Garnett, March 26, 1900.

[2] The very day the final number of *Lord Jim* appeared, Henry James wrote Conrad an enthusiastic letter, which has, unfortunately, not been found.

[3] "Typhoon" was completed on January 11, 1901: "Falk" in the following May; "Amy Foster" in June; *Romance* in March, 1902; "The End of the Tether" in October, 1902. Apropos of *Romance:* "The tale as it stands here is based on Ford Madox Hueffer's MS. of 'Seraphina,' a much shorter work and quite different in tone. On this we went to work together, developing the action and adding some new characters. We collaborated right through, but it may be said that the middle part of the book is mainly mine with bits of F. M. H.— while the first part is wholly out of 'Seraphina': the second part is almost wholly so. The last part is certainly three quarters MS. F. M. H. with here and there a par. by me." (Joseph Conrad's handwritten note on T. J. Wise's copy of *Romance,* 1923.)

Their loyalty to him was as unswerving as his affection for them.

Then, from the beginning of 1903 until September 3, 1904, Conrad shut himself up at Pent Farm and plunged into the formidable task of writing his longest, most complicated, most powerful work, *Nostromo*. He has himself given us a description of the terrible strain in a well-known passage of *A Personal Record*, which, however often it has been quoted, may well be quoted here once more:

All I know is that, for twenty months, neglecting the common joys of life that fall to the lot of the humblest on this earth, I had, like the prophet of old, "wrestled with the Lord" for my creation, for the headlands of the coast, for the darkness of the Placid Gulf, the light on the snows, the clouds on the sky, and for the breath of life that had to be blown into the shapes of men and women, of Latin and Saxon, of Jew and Gentile. These are, perhaps, strong words, but it is difficult to characterize otherwise the intimacy and the strain of a creative effort in which mind and will and conscience are engaged to the full, hour after hour, day after day, away from the world, and to the exclusion of all that makes life really lovable and gentle—something for which a material parallel can only be found in the everlasting sombre stress of the westward winter passage round Cape Horn. For that too is the wrestling of men with the might of their Creator, in a great isolation from the world, without the amenities and consolations of life, a lonely struggle under a sense of overmatched littleness, for no reward that could be adequate, but for the mere winning of a longitude. . . .

. . . a long, long, desperate fray. Long! I suppose I went to bed sometimes, and got up the same number of times. Yes, I suppose I slept, and ate the food put before me, and talked connectedly to my household on suitable occasions. But I had never been aware of the even flow of daily life, made easy and noiseless for me by a silent, watchful, tireless affection. Indeed, it seemed to me that I had been sitting at that table surrounded by the litter of a desperate fray for days and nights on end.[1]

And during all this time there were unceasing material difficulties to contend with—the failure of a bank which had advanced him money and his own incessant ill-health, which sometimes prevented him from writing and almost from thinking for a week on end. And yet at the same time that he was

[1] *A Personal Record*, pp. 98–101.

writing *Nostromo,* and almost by way of distraction, he was able to compose several chapters of *The Mirror of the Sea,* which contain some of his finest and most beautiful pages.

In the letters which follow, we find proof of this surprising energy, which seemed constantly tottering and yet never gave way, and which in the course of ten years, amidst daily money difficulties,[1] continual illness and terrible nervous exhaustion, was yet able to produce six novels, twelve short stories (in *Tales of Unrest, Youth, Typhoon and Other Stories*), and half of *The Mirror of the Sea.* These letters show, moreover, the warmth of his friendship, his enthusiastic and unselfish interest in the efforts of others, the conscientiousness of a great artist, and an unfailing generosity of heart and mind.

[1] *"Quelle sacrée misère* having to think of these things (money difficulties) which interfere with one's mind in a sort of sterilizing way, driving all images and expressions clean out of it." (Letter to William Rothenstein, June 9, 1904.)

LETTERS OF JOSEPH CONRAD

LETTERS OF JOSEPH CONRAD

TALES OF UNREST (1895–1904)

To Edward Garnett

Friday
17, Gillingham St., S. W.
March 8, 1895.

DEAR GARNETT,

I send you 4 chapters of the *Outcast* who—as you will perceive—is very much so. More than ever.—Your talk yesterday put so much life into me that I am reluctantly compelled to suspect you of good nature. Do not be offended for I do not mean any harm in charging you with such a *bourgeois* (or Philistine) failing. Even our friends are not perfect! This world is a dreary place and a prey to minor virtues. A dreary place —unless a fellow is a Willems [1] of some kind and is stuffed full of emotions—without any moral—when he may discover some joviality or other at the bottom of his load of anguish. But that's a lottery; an illegal thing; the invention of the Devil.

In Chap. XII beginning with the words: [2] "And now they are . . ." are the two pars. in the new style. Please say on the margin what you think. One word will do. I am very much in doubt myself about it; but where is the thing, institution or principle which I do not doubt?!

I shall advise you by autograph of my return from the Continent: because the fashionable intelligence of the *Pall Mall* neglects me in a most unaccountable way. Till then

Vale.

To Edward Garnett

Friday morning.
17, Gillingham St., S. W.
March 15, 1895.

DEAR GARNETT,

I arrived from Brussels about an hour ago and found your letter. I've read it with my hat on, rug over the arm, and umbrella hanging by its

[1] The principal character in J. C.'s novel *An Outcast of the Islands.*
[2] The division of the book was altered later on. There is no longer a chapter XII nor a chapter beginning with those words in *An Outcast of the Islands.*

tassel-string to my finger. Then I undressed, unpacked and before break-
ing bread read once more. I could not have had a more charming welcome. To be read—as you do me the honour to read me—is an ideal experience—and the experience of an ideal; and as I travel from sentence
[to sentence] of your message I feel my unworthiness more and more.
Your appreciation has for me all the subtle and penetrating delight of
unexpected good fortune—of some fabulously lucky accident like the
finding of a gold nugget in a deserted claim, like the gleam of a big
diamond in a handful of blue earth.

Theory is a cold and lying tombstone of departed truth (for truth is
no more immortal than any other delusion). Yet a man is nothing if not
perverse.—That's why Willems lies buried under my pet theory even
while I stand by, lamenting and grinning with the spade in my hand. I
cannot weep, by all the devils! I cannot even sneer at my dead. All you
say is true. All, absolutely—and the only thing that I can think of is to
administer to myself a moral bastinado—say five hundred on the soles
of my unsteady and erring feet.

Having propitiated you by the barbarous cruelty of my punishment I
proffer my request. Will you meet me next Thursday? any time after
six. Or name a day and the time that would suit you best. We shall *not*
talk of Willems. Just simply dine—feast of body—not of soul. Soul be
hanged!

This is only to let you know that letter and MS. received—also that
your words have not fallen into barren ground. The crop will ripen in
good time. You shall see.

To Edward Garnett

Friday, 7th June '95.
17, Gillingham St., S. W.

MY DEAR GARNETT,

You must think me as faithless as Willems and think of me as hiding
the blackness of my soul in epistolary silence.

I came back last Tuesday [1] and called upon the Enlightened Patron
of Letters.[2] Meant to call again in Pater er Bdgs. yesterday to see you.
I received in the morning an invitation *by wire!!!!* to dine with the
E.P.L. and had to waste all my day to find a man, just to tell him I
could not see him. Do you understand the pathos of the situation? I had
accepted the electric invitation, having forgotten a very good fellow that
was coming to smoke with me in the evening. It was easier, then, to put
him off than the Patron.

---

[1] From Champel near Geneva.
[2] Conrad's pet name for his first publisher, Mr. T. Fisher Unwin.

So I have added the festive and hospitable board of "my publisher" to my other experiences—and life seems tolerably complete. What else may I expect? What else that is new? Don't you think, dear Garnett, I had better die? True—there is love. That is always new—or rather startling, being generally unexpected and violent—and fleeting. Still one must have some object to hang his affections upon—and I haven't. Oh! the world—since this morning—is one big gray shadow and I am one immense yawn. Do come to the rescue early next week and put some heart into me with your dear, precious brazen flattery. Will you? If so—please say so. Say when, and I shall try to go to sleep till then.

The Patron has sent me McCarthy's [1] letter. I was as pleased as a dog with two tails till the notion came that it may be the white-bearded one's small joke. Perhaps the venerable man of politics felt frivolous. The letter seems to me at times as weird and unreal as Irving's knighthood. Isn't it funny? The whole thing is so characteristic of the Art, or profession or priesthood—or by whatever name you call play-acting. I have smiled several times. Mr. Brodribb in the part of Sir Henry Irving! Hang it. Now if that astonishing Lord Rosebery gives a peerage to Sir John Falstaff and makes Bardolph Secretary of State, it will put the finishing touch to the fairy tale of the most misty and elusive administration of this practical country.

I have 6 more chapters for you and the end is not yet. [2]

To Edward Noble

July 17th 1895 [London]
Monday evening.

MY DEAR NOBLE,

Just got your letter,—as I dress to go out to dinner,—but I must answer, if only a few words, at once.

I am inexpressibly touched by the appreciation, more touched by the manner of its expression. I am also immensely flattered by your good opinion which you state with such evident sincerity,—with no ring of reservation in it.

I thank you with all my heart. Letters like yours are rewards of all trouble,—of a sweet trouble if you will,—but still a trouble. It is made up of doubt, or hesitation, of moments silent and anxious when one listens to the thoughts,—one's own thoughts,—speaking indistinctly, deep down somewhere, at the bottom of the heart.

Why do you misjudge so blindly your own personality? And why do

[1] Mr. Justin McCarthy, M.P.
[2] Of *An Outcast of the Islands.*

you belittle your own temperament? You have your own distinct individuality that may—and in time will—appeal to hundreds, thousands, or millions,—as blind fate shall will it. And it is an individuality that will stand wear and tear, that has resistance and power,—while I shall be used up in a short and miserable splutter of dim flame. It is so. Hope is the best and the worst of life. Half of it comes from God and half from the devil, but it behoves men to take gifts and curses with a steady hand and an equable mind,—because of such is made up Fate,—the blind, the invincible.

I should like to see the beginning of your novel very, very much. Shall drop you a line. Thanks for all your kindness. My duty to Mrs. Noble and my love to Miss Noble.

To E. L. Sanderson

24 Aug. 1895.
17, Gillingham Street, S. W.

MY DEAREST TED,

Yesterday I came home rather late from a dinner with that Enlightened Patron of Letters,—Fisher Unwin,—and found your welcome letter looking up at me reproachfully from the table. I only then clearly realized what ages we have not spoken to each other. Till that moment (my life has been so strangely full lately) I have,—often thinking of you,—said to myself: "I shall write to-morrow: it's but one short day more." And so, wondering vaguely what your address might be, I have let the time slip by:—all regardless of the stealthy approach of Eternity which waits not for a day,—and knows everybody's address.

Then coming home (as related above) with a fixed intention to write before I slept,—there was your letter. Into the hot, noisy and dissipated night of my neighbourhood I shouted "Hooray,"—read your letter with a pang, . . . and went to bed.

Flesh is weak: and spirit is but of little account.

So you had a tussle with the old enemy! You speak of it slightingly with the affectation of those who come off victorious,—and I rejoice to know that you can speak of it so. Still, my dear Ted, the wise man does not get wet (unless under the stress of extreme necessity), because wet brings dysentery:—the infamous thing! The wise man is also careful of his food. You tell me who grooms and drives the horse (happy horse!— I present my humble duty to the distinguished groom), but I yearn to know who does your cooking for you? That's the thing! my dear boy. What and how you eat! Believe my wisdom (I don't mind telling you in confidence that I have lately torn out by the roots a good many white hairs). Remember likewise that dysentery (like salmon) lurks in water: in the babbling brook and the smooth-flowing river,—and is caught without a fly. A tumbler will do. Avoid this form of your beloved sport.— Your idea of elevating yourself above the low-ranging microbe by means of a pair of stilts is very praiseworthy, and I commend it heartily. For, that is your motive,—is it not?—since I cannot comprehend a man of your gravity and idealistic tendencies taking to such ungainly exercises except for weighty,—nay, imperative,—reasons.

I am inexpressibly happy to hear such a good account of your Mother and Father. I shall not write to dear Mrs. Sanderson for another week. I want to enjoy to the full my privilege and for that I must shake off the various trammels of mind, which worry me now,—and shall worry for a few days more.

We extended our cruise [1] to the Dutch coast, having strong winds and moderately heavy seas all the time. We lived mostly in our oilskins and all our various guests that came from time to time were very seasick. The last two days were ideally beautiful. We spent them at the mouth of the Thames from Rochester to Burnham and then to Harwich where we left the yacht for good.

That was on the 7th and ever since I have been extremely busy and half the time in Paris. I have crossed the Channel six times (three trips) in a fortnight. I got back from my last flight on the 21st, having accomplished my purpose. As you may imagine Willems [2] has been considerably neglected during that time and is not dead yet. I had, really, no time to attend to that murder.

Yesterday I sold him. I've sold him for about 12½ per cent. royalty, and fifty pounds cash payable on the 1st of December. I have half serial and American rights. F[isher] U[nwin] wants to get the book accepted for a serial by some magazine or newspaper. I hate the idea but have given in to his arguments. My opinion is he shall not be able to place it. As a book it will be a 6/.- edition uniform with *Almayer!*

Strangely enough I also had a great disturbance of internal machinery, —very much like dysentery,—with a slight fever. It left me depressed. I could take no rest, for I could not let go what I had in hand out of regard for other people. I travelled in a Pullman and generally pampered myself—and so went through,—but it left me rather flabby and cynical.

All this came about unexpectedly (I do not mean the illness but the occupation) and in a rather curious chain of circumstances. First of all I was induced to look up and make use of my old French acquaintances for the sake of a very good fellow called Rorke (of Rorke's Drift) whom I

[1] A yachting cruise in a cutter with his friend G. W. F. Hope.
[2] In *The Outcast of the Islands.*

knew some years ago and who is Hope's brother-in-law.[1] That man owned some 150 claims on the Roodeport gold reef for the last 6 or 7 years. Of course he tried many times to sell, but during the period of depression (since 1889) nobody would look at them. Now the boom came a few months ago and a French Syndicate approached Rorke (out there in Johannesburg) and actually concluded the sale, paid £500 deposit and induced Rorke to part with documents. Then various hitches occurred. Rorke waited, paying meantime the Statutory licences,—to keep his title to the claims. For that purpose he parted with every penny he could scrape,—sold his freehold, farms, etc., etc.: and at the end of last June found himself without a penny, with his documents somewhere on the Continent of Europe,—so that he could not sell to anybody else. He wrote a despairing letter to Hope praying to be saved. There was no time to lose. The unsophisticated Rorke was at his last gasp. As the Syndicate was in Paris, I went over there on the 8th and looked up people I know or used to know. They were good enough to remember me with apparent pleasure. I enlisted many influential and sympathetic people for my cause. Pascalis of the *Figaro*,—Guesde (a deputy) and the bankers Jullien and Epstein. All acquaintances of my young days.[2] We found out (to my intense satisfaction) that the French Syndicate were all Germans. We sat upon them with an order from the President from the X court and ascertained that they have been trying to sell already to some shady people in London. The documents, reports and plans were also in London. Epstein got very interested and proposed to come back with me. Agreed. He snored ignobly all the way. At 8.30 in Victoria. At 10 in Hope's office. At 3 P. M., same day, the London people (called Thompson) parted with all the papers for the sum of £100! They had no more chance, of course, to float a company than any crossing sweeper. As a matter of fact they are penniless Jews. They tried to bluff and bully,—but collapsed before a firm attitude. Next day Epstein, Hope and I met some people of good standing here and before evening a Memorandum of Association of an Anglo-French Syndicate was signed by which they agreed to buy Rorke's claims for £8,000 cash and 25,000 shares. We cabled Rorke the terms and he cabled consent. Meantime power of attorney for Hope arrived from Africa. We concluded the sale. On the 11th Aug., I was on my way back to Paris with Epstein. He snored all the way. For two days there was much cabling and rushing about. In my two trips I managed to get rid of £117. On the 14th (evening) I left Paris with a check of the French Syndicate of £4,000 in my pocket. On the 15th the English half was paid up and £8,000 less expenses (some 370

---

[1] His friend G. W. F. Hope.

[2] People he was acquainted with probably in Marseilles in the seventies.

pounds) were cabled through African Banking Corporation to the unsophisticated Rorke,—and we all sat down and wiped our perspiring brows.—Epstein (previously unknown to me) is a very straightforward Jew and the French part is in very good hands. The English undertaking is practically floated and shall be put on the market within the next fortnight as Rorke-Roodeport Goldmine. There are two Rhodesia directors on the board and the thing is sound. Of course I do not make anything. My expenses are paid and I shall take 200 shares as acknowledgment of my services. They wanted to give me 1,000, which I declined. Yet I must say I was very smart. Nobody was more surprised than myself!

On the 16th while I sat patting myself on the back I received a cable from a man called Maharg—also an old acquaintnce of mine, who is now in Johannesburg. Dazzled by my success with Rorke that fellow offered me the selling of 50 claims on the black reef next to the Minerva Mine (whose shares stand now at 20 per cent. premium). He was so certain of the value of that property that he did not want any cash for it. Was content to get paid in shares only,—but there were conditions about working capital and such like,—all calculated to guarantee the safety of future investors,—and therefore difficult to obtain from the common, garden kind of promoter. After a due amount of reflection I took the thing up. You know that I wanted funds for the base purpose of carrying on a wretched and useless existence. The thing was as honest as such things can be. In fact exceptionally so. It is a first-class property and offered cheap. I could with all due care for my honour (which is my only hereditary property) take it up. And I did so. I went over to Paris again but ultimately I have sold it here in London to people of high repute. It was exciting and interesting work and I had a glimpse into curious depths! Very curious!

To Edward Garnett

17 Sept. 1895.
17, Gillingham Street, S. W.

DEAR GARNETT,

It is my painful duty to inform you of the sad death of Mr. Peter Willems, late of Rotterdam and Macassar,[1] who has been murdered on the 16th inst. at 4 P. M. while the sun shone joyously and the barrel organ sang on the pavement the abominable *Intermezzo* of the ghastly Cavalleria. As soon as I recovered from the shock I busied myself in arranging the affairs of the two inconsolable widows of our late lamented

---

[1] The leading character in *An Outcast of the Islands*.

friend and I am glad to say that—with the help of Captain Lingard who took upon himself all the funeral arrangements—everything was decently settled before midnight. You know what strong affection I had for the poor departed, so you won't be surprised to hear that to me since yesterday life seems a blank—a dumb solitude from which everything, even the shadows, have completely vanished.

Almayer was the last to go, but, before I succeeded in getting rid of him, he made me perfectly wretched with his grumblings about the trouble and expense connected with the sad event and by his unfeeling remarks about the deceased's little failings. He reviled also Mrs. Willems, who was paralyzed with grief and behaved more like a cumbersome dummy than a living woman. I am sorry to say he wasn't as sober as he ought to have been in these sad conjectures and as usual he seemed not aware of anybody's grief and sufferings but his own—which struck me as being mostly imaginary. I was glad to see him go, but—such is the inconsequence of the human heart—no sooner he went than I began to regret bitterly his absence. I had for a moment the idea to rush out and call him back, but before I could shake off the languor of my sorrow he was gone beyond recall.

There's nothing more to tell you except that the detailed relation of the heartrending occurrences of the last two days will be deposited to-morrow in Paternoster Bdgs. for your perusal.

I can write no more! Assured of your precious sympathy I shake tearfully your trusty hand.

To Edward Garnett

[September 24, 1895]
Tuesday.

DEAR GARNETT,

I got your letter and the MS. about an hour ago and I write at once under the impression of your criticism—of your kind and truly friendly remarks. I want to tell you how much I appreciate your care, the sacrifice of your time, your evident desire to help me. I want to tell you all that, but do not know how to express myself so as to convey to you clearly the sense of the great obligation, of my indebtedness towards you. You gild the pill richly—but the fact remains that the last chapter is simply abominable.[1] Never did I see anything so clearly as the naked hideousness of that thing. I can also see that you do faithfully try to make the best of it with a delicacy of feeling which does honour to your heart however much it may be wrong from an ethical standpoint.

[1] This refers to *An Outcast of the Islands.*

I am glad you like the xxiii chapter. To tell you the honest truth I like it myself. As to the xxiv I feel convinced that the right course would be to destroy it, to scatter its ashes to the four winds of heaven.[1] The only question is: can I?

I am afraid I can't! I lack the courage to set before myself the task of rewriting the thing. It is not—as you say—a matter of correction here and there—a matter of changed words or lines—or pages. The whole conception seems to me wrong. I seem to have seen the wrong side of the situation. I was always afraid of it.—For months I have been afraid of that chapter—and now it is written—and the foreboding is realized in a dismal failure.

Nothing now can unmake my mistake. I shall try—but I shall try without faith, because all my work is produced unconsciously (so to speak) and I cannot meddle to any purpose with what is within myself. —I am sure you understand what I mean.—It isn't in me to improve what has got itself written.

Still with your help I may try. All the paragraphs marked by you to that effect shall be cut out. For Willems to want to escape from *both* women *is* the very idea. Only—don't you see—I did not feel it so. Shame! The *filiation* [2] of feelings in Willems on the evening when Aïssa speaks to him arises from my view of that man—of the effect produced upon him by the loss of things precious to him coming (the loss) after his passion is appeased. Consequently—his deliberate effort to recall the passion as a last resort, as the last refuge from his regrets, from the obsession of his longing to return whence he came. It's an impulse of thought, not of the senses. The senses are done with. Nothing lasts! So with Aïssa. Her passion is burnt out too. There is in her that desire to be something for him—to be in his mind, in his heart—to shelter him in her affection— her woman's affection which is simply the ambition to be an important factor in another's life. They both long to have a significance in the order of nature or of society. To me they are typical of mankind, where every individual wishes to assert his power, woman by sentiment, man by achievement of some sort—mostly base. I myself—as you see from this— have been ambitious to make it clear and have failed in that, as Willems fails in his effort to throw off the trammels of earth and of heaven.

So much in defence of my view of the case. For the execution I have no word to say. It is very feeble and all the strokes fall beside the mark. Why?—If I knew that—if I knew the causes of my weakness I would

[1] The division and numbering of the chapters were altered before the completion of the book and it is impossible now to know to what passages of the book Conrad was alluding.

[2] A rare example of Conrad's using a French word for lack of an English equivalent.

destroy them and then produce nothing but colossal masterpieces—which "no fellow could understand." As it is I am too lazy to change my thoughts, my words, my images, and my dreams. Laziness is a sacred thing. It's the sign of our limitations beyond which there is nothing worth having. Nobody is lazy to accomplish things without any effort—and things that can only be attained by effort are not worth having.

In the treatment of the last scenes I wanted to convey the kind of placidity that is caused by extreme surprise. You must not forget that they are all immensely amazed. That's why they are so quiet—(At least I wanted them to be quiet and only managed to make them colourless). That's why I put in the quiet morning—the immobility of surrounding matter emphasized only by the flutter of small birds. Then the sense of their position penetrates the hearts—stirs them. They wake up to the reality. Then comes violence: Joanna's slap in Aïssa's face, Aïssa's shot—and the end just as he sees the joy of sunshine and of life.

Forgive me this long rigmarole. I wanted you to see what I meant—and this letter itself is a confession of complete failure on my part. I simply could not express myself artistically. It is a small loss to me and I notice that the world rolls on this morning without a hitch.

Once more, thanks. I shall set to at once and grub amongst all these bones. Perhaps! Perhaps!

P. S. On Friday at 7 with joy.

To Edward Noble

17, Gillingham Street, S. W.
28 Oct. '95

MY DEAR NOBLE,

I received your discouraged letter this morning and can assure you I felt very sorry for your disappointment ending the long-drawn hope.

It is hard to say anything. You must remember that true worth is never recognized at once. If Macmillans refused, then some other should be tried. Why not send to F. Unwin,—it might do for the pseudonym series,—or autonym if you do not like the idea of a "nom de guerre."

You shall get certainly a careful consideration. Do make them purely river stories (about 30–40 thousand words).

Only, my dear Noble, do not throw yourself away in fables. Talk about the river,—the people,—the events, as seen through your temperament. You have a remarkable gift of expression, the outcome of an artistic feeling for the world around you, and you must not waste the gift in (if I may say so) illegitimate sensation. You remember perhaps what I said about the vampire story. A capital thing,—wonderfully well put, as far as the impressionism of the thing went,—only,—only to me all the charm, all the truth of it are thrown away by the construction,—by the mechanism (so to speak) of the story which makes it appear false.

Do not be angry with me. I have thought your letter over many times during the day and now I put down here my exact thoughts,—right or wrong.

You have any amount of stuff in you, but you (I think) have not found your way yet. Remember that death is not the most pathetic,—the most poignant thing,—and you must treat events only as illustrative of human sensation,—as the outward sign of inward feelings,—of live feelings,—which alone are truly pathetic and interesting. You have much imagination: much more than I ever will have if I live to be a hundred years old. That much is clear to me. Well, that imagination (I wish I had it) should be used to create human souls: to disclose human hearts,—and not to create events that are properly speaking *accidents* only. To accomplish it you must cultivate your poetic faculty,—you must give yourself up to emotions (no easy task). You must squeeze out of yourself every sensation, every thought, every image,—mercilessly, without reserve and without remorse: you must search the darkest corners of your heart, the most remote recesses of your brain,—you must search them for the image, for the glamour, for the right expression. And you must do it sincerely, at any cost: you must do it so that at the end of your day's work you should feel exhausted, emptied of every sensation and every thought, with a blank mind and an aching heart, with the notion that there is nothing,—nothing left in you. To me it seems that it is the only way to achieve true distinction—even to go some way towards it.

It took me 3 years to finish the *Folly*. There was not a day I did not think of it.[1] Not a day. And after all I consider it honestly a miserable failure. Every critic (but two or three) overrated the book. It took me a year to tear the *Outcast* out of myself and upon my word of honour,—I look on it (now it's finished) [2] with bitter disappointment. Judge from that whether my opinion is worth having. I may be on the wrong tack altogether. I say what I think and from a sincere desire to see you succeed,—but I may be hopelessly astray in my opinions.

Meantime you should try F. Unwin, 11, Paternoster Buildings, E. C. I shall see Garnett (the reader) and mention your manuscript and your name to him. He is young but very artistic. He is also a very severe critic. Of course your book will be judged strictly on its merits. I am sure you would not wish for anything else.

[1] It refers to Chapters VIII to XII written from February, 1891, to May 22, 1894.

[2] It had just been finished on the 14th of September.

Keep a good heart. You have many stories by you. Rewrite some of them from an inward point of view. In that point of view anything may be made interesting and the faculty to do it is in you, or I am much mistaken.

I have finished correcting my proofs,[1] a ghastly occupation. I come out in November 25th or 30th. I shall send you a copy of course.

To Edward Noble

2nd Nov. '95.
17, Gillingham Street.

DEAR NOBLE,

I have your letter in answer to mine. Your argument is perfectly just and your point of view perfectly legitimate. There's nothing to say on my part in the way of controversy. On one point I think you misunderstood me. When I speak about writing from an inward point of view,— I mean from the depth of your own inwardness. I do not want you to drag out for public inspection the very entrails of your characters. Lay bare your own heart, and people will listen to you for that,—and only that is interesting.

Everyone must walk in the light of his own heart's gospel. No man's light is good to any of his fellows. That's my creed from beginning to end. That's my view of life,—a view that rejects all formulas, dogmas and principles of other people's making. These are only a web of illusions. We are too varied. Another man's truth is only a dismal lie to me. I am telling you things that I would never dream of telling anybody, but I don't want to speak to you from the shelter of false pretences.

You can see now how little anything I may say is worth to anybody. Good luck to you!

To Charles Zagórski[2]

17 Gillingham Street, London, S. W.
10 March, 1896.

MY DEAR CHARLES,

I am again sending you a masterpiece, the second one this time.[3] Last year I sent three copies of my novel to my native place. Two of them arrived all right but the third addressed to you and your wife no doubt

---

[1] Of *An Outcast of the Islands.*
[2] The original of this letter is in Polish.
[3] *An Outcast of the Islands.*

failed to reach its destination. I now make another attempt and I hope
that this time my book and my letter will find you.

At the same time I am announcing to my dear Aunt Gabrielle—and to
you both, dear friends—and I do so solemnly (as the occasion requires)
that I am getting married. Perhaps nobody is more astonished than I am.
But I cannot say that I am terrified, being, as you know, accustomed to
lead a life full of adventure, and to wrestle with terrible dangers. Besides
I must add that my fiancée does not appear at all dangerous. Her Christian name is Jessie; her surname George. She is a little person who is
very dear to me. . . . She has eight brothers and sisters. . . . Our
marriage will take place on the 24th of this month and then we shall
leave London immediately to hide from the purview of the world our
happiness (or our absurdities) on the wild and picturesque shores of
Brittany, where I intend renting a little cottage in a fishing village—
probably at Plouarec or Pervengan (not far from St. Malo). It is there
that I shall set about writing my third book [1] since one must write to
live. A few days ago I was offered the command of a sailing ship. This
idea pleased Jessie (who is fond of the sea) very much, but the conditions
were so unsatisfactory that I refused. Only literature remains to me as a
means of existence. You understand, my dear friend, that if I have undertaken this thing, it is with the firm resolution to make a name—and I
have no doubt that I shall be successful in this connection. I know what
I can do. The question is only to earn the money *"qui est une chose tout-
à-fait à part du mérite littéraire,"* yet I am not sure of it—but my needs
are very moderate and I can wait. I therefore look towards the future
rather calmly.

I trust that on my wedding day, you—who are to me my only family—
will be with me, at least in spirit. I kiss the hands of my dear Aunt and
ask her to send me her blessing. I commend myself to your wife's kind
thoughts as well as to yours.

Your affectionate
CONRAD KORZENIOWSKI.

To Edward Garnett

Monday [London]
[March 23, 1896.]

DEAR GARNETT,

I am very glad you wrote to me the few lines I have just received. If
you spoke as a friend I listened in the same manner,—listened and was
only a little, a very little, dismayed. If one looks at life in its true aspect

---

[1] *The Rescuer.*

then everything loses much of its unpleasant importance and the atmosphere becomes cleared of what are only unimportant mists that drift past in imposing shapes. When once the truth is grasped that one's own personality is only a ridiculous and aimless masquerade of something hopelessly unknown, the attainment of serenity is not very far off. Then there remains nothing but the surrender to one's impulses, the fidelity to passing emotions which is perhaps a nearer approach to truth than any other philosophy of life. And why not? If we are "ever becoming—never being," then I would be a fool if I tried to become this thing rather than that; for I know I never will be anything. I would rather grasp the solid satisfaction of my wrong-headedness and shake my fist at the idiotic mystery of Heaven.

So much for trifles. As to that other kind of foolishness: my work,[1] there you have driven home the conviction and I *shall* write the sea-story —at once (12 months).[2] It will be on the lines indicated to you. I surrender to the infamous spirit which you have awakened within me and, as I want my abasement to be very complete, I am looking for a sensational title. You had better help, O Gentle and Murderous Spirit! You have killed my cherished aspiration and now must come along and help to bury the corpse decently. I suggest

THE RESCUER

A Tale of Narrow Waters

Meditate for a fortnight and by that time you will get my address and will be able to let me know what your natural aptitude for faithlessness and crime has suggested to you.

My dear Garnett, you are a perfect nuisance! Here I sit (with ever so many things to do) and chatter to you (instead of being up and doing) and what's worse I have no inclination to leave off. (Surrender to impulses—you see.) If I was not afraid of your enigmatical (but slightly venomous) smile I would be tempted to say with Lingard: "I am an old fool!" But I don't want to give you an opportunity for one of your beastly hearty approvals. So I won't say that, I will say: "I am a wise old man of the sea"—to you.

Tell Mrs. Garnett with my most respectful and friendly regards how grateful I am to her for the kind reception of myself and Jessie.[3] I

---

[1] "The Sisters," which was to remain an unprinted fragment.

[2] It refers to *The Rescuer*. The title of the book when it was published in 1920, was *The Rescue, A Romance of the Shallows*.

[3] Miss Jessie George, who was to become Mrs. Joseph Conrad.

commend myself to her kind remembrance and look forward to my next visit to your hermitage, with pleasure unalloyed by the fear of boring her to death. I have the utmost confidence in her indulgence—and the goodness of her heart will come to the rescue in the distress of her mind. As to you, I, of course, do not care what happens to you. If you expire on your own hearthstone out of sheer ennui and weariness of spirit, it will only serve you right.

Good-bye, my dear friend.

To Mrs. Sanderson [1]

6th April, 1896.
Lannion.
Côtes-du-Nord.

DEAR MRS. SANDERSON,

The joyful sight of your dear missive brought, besides the sense of satisfaction, a small pang of remorse. I am glad to say your first letter to me as a man married and done for has not miscarried. I had it one day after dispatching to you my dismal note with the news of Jessie's indisposition,—and how grateful I was for it and how much cheered by it,—words cannot express.

My very best thanks for your gracious kindness to my wife and myself. The dear girl is herself again,—nearly,—and so am I. For I must tell you, that,—unaccustomed as I am to matrimonial possibilities,—I was alarmed,—not to say horribly scared! However she had convincing proofs of my nursing qualifications: and no doubt in a year or two I will be disposed to take things with much more composure,—not to say coolness. But I must tell you under seal of confidence that I would not go through such three days again for a diamond mine! I am delighted to think Miss Monica liked the wretched *Outcast* book. Please tell her so. I have a great opinion of her mental powers and of her judgment. This last you had better not tell her, for of all people of the world I should like her the least to think me gushing. I had a few reviews.[2] Nothing remarkable. The *Illustrated London News* says I am a disciple of Victor Hugo, and is complimentary! Very! So are the Irish papers,—the *Whitehall Review* and the *World*. But there is plenty of criticism also. They find it too long, too much description,—and so on. Upon the whole I am satisfied.

---

[1] Mr. Edward Lancelot Sanderson's mother.
[2] About *An Outcast of the Islands.*

To-morrow we take possession of the home on Île-Grande.[1] I have written 11 pages of the *Rescuer*.

Believe me always your most obedient and affectionate servant.

Letter to dearest Ted soon. Beg him to excuse delay. My great love to him.

To E. L. Sanderson

14 April, 1896.
Île-Grande, par Lannion
Côtes-du-Nord

DEAR TED,

At last, from my new (and very first) home, I write you to say that I am quite oppressed by my sense of importance in having a house,—actually a whole house!!,—to live in. It's the first time,—since I came to years of discretion,—that such an event happened in my life.

Jess is immensely amused by the kitchen (the fireplace alone is big enough for her to live in) and spends most of her time trying to talk with the girl (who is a perfect treasure). The kitchen is the most splendid and the best furnished apartment of the palace,—and the only way in or out, anyhow. So we see it pretty often. Our sticks and caps have their domicile there altogether.

The coast is rocky, sandy, wild and full of mournful expressiveness. But the land, at the back of the wide stretches of the sea enclosed by the barren archipelago, is green and smiling and sunny,—often even when the sea and the islets are under the shadow of the passing clouds. From beyond the rounded slopes of the hill the sharp spires of many village-churches point persistently to the sky. And the people that inhabits these shores is a people of women,—black-clad and white-capped,—for the men fish in Iceland or on the banks of Newfoundland. Only here and there a rare old fellow with long hair, forgotten by the successive roll-calls of the sea, creeps along the rock between beaches and looks sad and useless and lone in the stony landscape.

The first chapter of *The Rescuer* is gone to London yesterday. I want Unwin to have a sample to show to the Mag.[azine] Editors.

Write to me about yourself as I write to you about myself. So we shall have the illusion of nearness.

[1] See the following letter about the new home.

To Edward Garnett

Sunday, May 22, 1896.
Île-Grande.

MY DEAR GARNETT,

I swear by all the gods that I haven't had such a sunshiny day since I came here—as to-day. I could not believe my eyes! If you knew how many bitter speculations, hesitating hopes, frightened longings, I have known since your wife's last letter. On Friday I could not stand it any more and wrote F. U.[1] asking for news about you. We—Jessie and I—used to spend our evenings in dismal suppositions as to what happened in the Cearne, and came to the ghastly conclusion that you were no better, Mrs. Garnett had broken down—and the end of the world seemed— to me—somehow within sight.[2] We are both rejoiced! We have danced with loud shouts round your letter. We are hoarse and very tired. I sit down to answer! I haven't anything to say for the moment! There is nothing to say except that I am glad. Glad like a man relieved from rack or thumbscrew—that kind of profound inexpressible satisfaction. Your letter is so cheerful that I feel you must be in the state of real con- valescence. I tell you what. I simply did not dare to write again to your wife. I kept quiet like a man who, afraid to start an avalanche, keeps deadly still on a narrow ledge—and waits.

It is good of you to think of me—to write to me—and such a long letter too! Don't you read the *Resc:* read nothing but Rabelais—if you must read. But I imagine you so weakened by disease that the bare effort of looking at the page must make you pant. However, I trust that Mrs. Garnett has some control over your actions—and will withhold this letter if she thinks it necessary.

Any amount of reviews![3] Heaps! It's distracting if one could take it all in. But one does not—fortunately. You are the best of invalids to send me the commented *Sat. Rev.* I had seen it! I was puzzled by it, but I felt confusedly what you say in your letter. Something brings the im- pression off—makes its effect. What? It can be nothing but the expres- sion—the arrangement of words, the style. Ergo: the style is not dis- honourable. I wrote to the reviewer. I did! And he wrote to me. He did!! And who do you think it is?—He lives in Woking. Guess. Can't

---

[1] Fisher Unwin.
[2] Edward Garnett has been severely ill for the previous four or five weeks.
[3] Of *An Outcast of the Islands.*

tell? I will tell you. It is H. G. Wells.[1] May I be cremated alive like a miserable moth if I suspected it! Anyway he descended from his "Time-Machine" to be as kind as he knew how. It explains the review. He dedicates his books to W. Henley—you know.

I have been rather ill. Lots of pain, fever, etc., etc. The left hand is useless still. This month I have done nothing to the *Rescuer*—but I have about 70 pages of the most rotten twaddle. In the intervals of squirming I wrote also a short story [2] of Brittany. Peasant life. I do not know whether it's worth anything. My wife typed it and it is in London now with a friend.[3] I shall direct him to send it to you soon. The worst of it is that the Patron knows of it. I don't know why I told him about it. . . . I want to know (when you are quite well) what you think of it. The title is: "The Idiots" (10,000 words).—This is all the news. I've been living in a kind of trance from which I am only waking up now to a sober existence. And it appears to me that I will never write anything worth reading. But you have heard all this before. To-night I shall go to bed with a light heart at last. Do not tire yourself writing. It's enough for me at present to know you are getting on. I shall write tho' whenever the spirit moves me or loneliness becomes insupportable.

Jess sends her love. My affectionate regards to Mrs. Garnett.

To Vernon Weston

Île-Grande, par Lannion.
26 May 1896.

DEAR MR. WESTON,

I have just got your card and hasten to thank you and all friends for your kind thought and good wishes. I am not likely to forget my early days in Well Street and the good will shown to a stranger by all there—and especially by your late Father, who so kindly assisted me in becoming (I hope not altogether an unworthy) British subject; and your own uniform friendliness.

Kindly give my best regards to Mr. Newton—my only Teacher—and Mr. Bachard my first Watch-Officer.

I trust everybody is well and happy.

[1] Mr. H. G. Wells's undated letter sent in May from Lynton, Maybury Road, Woking, has been reproduced in *Twenty Letters to Joseph Conrad* with an introduction and some notes by G. Jean-Aubry (First Edition Club, London, 1926).
[2] "The Idiots."
[c] Adolf Kriege

I expect to be in London in October when I shall make a point of calling on you.

I see some newspapers prophesy that my seagoing days are over. It is not my feeling. I do hanker after the sea—it's only the want of opportunity that keeps me on shore. I am now writing my third novel. It is an occupation of much trouble and little profit—and a man can't live on praise alone. I get enough of that.

To Mme Angèle Zagórska [1]

12. 6. 1896.
Île-Grande—par Lannion.

DEAR COUSIN,

Forgive my long silence: I have been ill. I had an attack of rheumatism in my hand and foot. This attack not only kept me in bed for two weeks, but it has so shaken me that I still feel giddy. My hand is also swollen, which does not make writing easy.

I cannot express to you, my dearest Angèle, what a great pleasure your letter has given me—seeing the news you sent me of you all and your so very artistic appreciation of my book.[2] The expressions in your letter inspire me with confidence and the desire to continue my work. I again read your letter to-day and it is with a fresh sense of gratitude that I send you my thanks.

Forgive me for not being able to write a longer letter to-day. I am not yet recovered either in body or in mind. Fortunately I was able to finish before I was taken ill the first part of my new novel and naturally my illness has made my wife very tired, but otherwise she is well. As for me, I feel better and better every day.

I wish to be remembered to you all, my dear ones. I hope that you will find a moment to write to me. We shall be here for three months longer.

Your affectionate brother and servant,
K. N. KORZENIOWSKI.

To Edward Garnett

19th June 1896
Île-Grande.

MY DEAR GARNETT,

I got your letter to-day. Need I tell you how delighted I am with your approval? The warm commendation is to me so unexpected that if I had

---

[1] The original of this letter is in Polish.
[2] *An Outcast of the Islands.*

not a perfect confidence in your sincerity I would suspect that the despondent tone of my accompanying letter induced you perhaps to force the note of satisfaction with my effort. However, if I don't believe in the book [1] (and I don't somehow) I believe in you—in you as a last refuge: somewhat as an unintelligent and hopeless sinner believes in the infinite mercy on high.

Since I sent you that part 1st (on the eleventh of the month) I have written one page. Just one page. I went about thinking and forgetting—sitting down before the blank page to find that I could not put one sentence together. To be able to think and unable to express is a fine torture. I am undergoing it—without patience. I don't see the end of it. It's very ridiculous and very awful. Now I've got all my people together I don't know what to do with them. The progressive episodes of the story *will* not emerge from the chaos of my sensations. I feel nothing clearly. And I am frightened when I remember that I have to drag it all out of myself. Other writers have some starting point. Something to catch hold of. They start from an anecdote—from a newspaper paragraph (a book may be suggested by a casual sentence in an old almanack), they lean on dialect—or on tradition—or on history—or on the prejudice or fad of the hour; they trade upon some tie or some conviction of their time—or upon the absence of these things—which they can abuse or praise. But at any rate they know something to begin with—while I don't. I have had some impressions, some sensations—in my time;—impressions and sensations of common things. And it's all faded—my very being seems faded and thin like the ghost of a blonde and sentimental woman, haunting romantic ruins pervaded by rats. I am exceedingly miserable. My task appears to me as sensible as lifting the world without that fulcrum which even that conceited ass, Archimedes, admitted to be necessary.

I know the Patron has "The Idiots." I trust he has sent them to you but I haven't heard from him at all. I did write to the *Cornhill* [2] a suitable answer and informed the Patron of their offer.

Thanks with all my heart for the time, the care, the thoughts you give to me so generously. I am getting so used to your interest in my work that it has become now like a necessity—like a condition of existence. Why don't you tell me how you are? How are the veins—for I trust that is now the only trouble and I long much to know that it is over.

My affectionate regards to Mrs. Garnett.

I am nearly right. Had a 3 days' cruise along the coast.

[1] *The Rescuer.*
[2] The *Cornhill Magazine,* which published "The Lagoon," in January, 1897.

To Edward Garnett

14th August, 1896.
Île-Grande.

DEAR GARNETT,

Thanks ever so much for your letter—or rather for your two letters. I suppose you are now in possession of my howl of distress. Perhaps the not unnatural exasperation of a man condemned to read such lamentations has subsided somewhat and you will be able to look at this missive with a—comparatively—kind eye.

You are right in your criticism of "Outpost."[1] The construction is bad. It is bad because it was a matter of conscious decision, and I have no discrimination—in the artistic sense. Things get themselves written —and you like them. Things get themselves into shape—and they are tolerable. But when *I* want to write—when *I* do consciously try to write or try to construct, then my ignorance has full play and the quality of my miserable and benighted intelligence is disclosed to the scandalized gaze of my literary father. This is as it should be. I always told you I was a kind of inspired humbug. Now you know it. Let me assure you that your remarks were a complete disclosure to me. I had not the slightest glimmer of my stupidity. I am now profoundly thankful to find I have enough sense to see the truth of what you say. It's very evident that the first 3 pages kill all the interest. And I wrote them of set purpose!! I thought I was achieving artistic simplicity!!!!!! Now, of course, the thing—the *res infecta*—is as plain as a pikestaff. It does not improve my opinion of myself and of my prospects. Am I totally lost? Or do the last few pages save the thing from being utterly contemptible? You seem to think so—if I read your most kind and friendly letter aright.

I must explain that that particular story was no more meant for you than "The Idiots"—that is all the short stories (*ab initio*) which were *meant alike* for a vol. to be inscribed to *you*.[2] Only then I had not heard from you so long that you were naturally constantly in my thoughts. In fact I worried about it, thinking of the treachery of disease and so on. And then I thought that the story would be a good title-story—better than "The Idiots." It would sound funny, a title like this: *Idiots and Other Stories*. While *Outposts of Progress and Other Stories* sounds nice and proper. That's why your name has been typed by my devoted wife on the title page of the infamous thing. The question is—is the inf: thing too infamous to go into the vol.?—I leave it to you.

[1] "An Outpost of Progress," the story, included afterward in *Tales of Unrest* and written between the 17th and 21st of July.

[2] That volume was dedicated to Adolf Krieger; and to Edward Garnett *The Nigger of the "Narcissus."*

Meantime the E. P. of L. has bombarded the *Cosmo.*[1] with it. It appears it will do. At any rate the secretary of the *Cosmo.* accepts and refers to his editor who is away. The price put upon that ghastly masterfolly by the E. P. of L. is £50, which seems to be also agreed to provisionally. I must say that the Patron has behaved generally in a friendly manner which is touching. He writes often and seems to want really to push me along. I will want a lot of pushing, I fear.

I've sent a short thing[2] to the *Cornhill.* A Malay tells a story to a white man who is spending the night at his hut. It's a tricky thing with the usual forests, river—stars—wind—sunrise, and so on—and lots of second-hand Conradese in it. I would bet a penny they will take it.[3] There is only 6,000 words in it so it can't bring in many shekels. . . . Don't you think I am a lost soul?—Upon my word I hate every line I write. I wish I could tackle the *Rescuer* again. I simply *can't!* And I live in fear that is worse than mortal. But I have told you all that.

To Edward Garnett

27th Oct. 1896
[Ivy Walls Farm]
Stanford-le-hope, Essex.

MY DEAR GARNETT,

I am very much touched by your promptitude in writing to cheer me up. You ease my mind greatly—and in this juncture no man could do it but you. I have nothing to do but to follow your advice, which is the more easy because it accords with my inclination. I am at your disposition on Friday or any other day, only, my dearest fellow, invite those men in my name for I cannot let you stand my business dinners; I can always break your bread (and argue with you impudently while I do so) in the commission of friendship, but this is another matter. You will render me an immense service if you will undertake to arrange everything and let me know of the place of feeding. It seems almost an impertinence to ask you to do that, but I know you want to help me. On second thoughts perhaps it is better that you should ask them—(I only know Lucas) [4]— but I want you to understand that I *won't* let you pay for it. That's all. Blessings on your head!

[1] The magazine *Cosmopolis,* which published "An Outpost of Progress" in June and July, 1897. "The E. P. of L.," the Enlightened Patron of Letters, Conrad's humorous designation of Mr. Fisher Unwin.
[2] "The Lagoon."
[3] They did, and published the story in January, 1897.
[4] E. V. Lucas.

Your proposal to introduce me to Longman and also to Heinemann smiles at me. Only I do not want you to give any cause for a grievance to the Patron. And I would never forgive myself if I was the cause of any inconvenience to you. Perhaps I am an old donkey to mention this, but somehow the idea struck me. Don't be angry!—As to Watt[1] I think I ought to know him. It would be a great relief to have someone to do one's "dirty work," as the sailors say of any occupation they dislike.

I must tell you that you have sent me an incomplete letter. There are two *full sheets* (8 pages each) and a half sheet which is evidently a P. S. —The last page of the *full sheet* ends "Don't however commit" and there is nothing more! Frightful! I have looked everywhere under tables and chairs and can't find the part which tells me what *I* mustn't commit. So, I am left in a state of trepidation. It is just possible there was something in the envelope which I have burnt. I did look in however before throwing it on the coals. I assure you I will commit nothing of any kind till I hear from you. The P.[atron] has not as yet replied to my farewell letter. I won't yield an inch, for my "dander is riz" (as Bret Harte's men say). Thanks a thousand times.

I have sent *Outcast* to H[enry] James with a pretty dedication.

To E. L. Sanderson

Stanford-le-Hope.
21st Nov. 1896.

DEAREST TED,

I swear by the lyre of Apollo and by the sandals of all the Muses that I haven't the slightest idea why you suspect me of not liking "An Episode of Southern Seas."

My dearest fellow, I received it one evening just at the moment when my wife was treating me to one of her fainting fits. Well! That business over I read it,—read it at once,—read it more than once. If my first letter was incoherent, it only reflected the exact state of my mind,— which, I hasten to add, was *not caused* by the reading of your stanzas. I waited till I had something like mental leisure to write to you at length and the very day I was going to write I received the glad tidings from the North. This for a time, I own, put the verses out of my head. And since I had no mental leisure. It is the sorry truth. Hang it all! I *love* the thing. My dearest Ted, don't suspect me of being conceited enough to think that my opinion can matter to you one way or another,—except

---

[1] A. P. Watt, the literary agent.

for the affection I have for you and you for me. Headlam and Richardson were the men to ask and I am proud to know that my instinct, impulse (call it as you like), was right. I thought the poem good at first reading, —I mean in point of expression. And I took it as complete. When you said, "I won't finish it" I was surprised and took it for an expression of indifference which I could not encourage. I also wondered what more you would say. I own I was curious, for I could see the idea was completely expressed. And even now I think that if there is something more to say,—something which I do not see,—which others do not see,—but what you see yourself you should say it,—now, or later on.

I am very glad you are going to send it somewhere. Jess tried very hard to copy correctly and I think that one of the copies is absolutely correct. The other I have corrected according to the manuscript, which I keep of course. I want your handwriting and your thought and your melody.

That I prefer the "Gray Hour" proves nothing. I simply mean that, if under irresistible compulsion I had to burn one of the two poems, I would keep the "Gray Hour." I think it written in a much more spiritual,—in a much more "rare" mood. But your inherent distinction is in both,—the same quality of it,—the same individual note: something very fine, a little elusive: something pervading, impalpable and distinct: like in the morning the glorious charm of a golden haze. In point of workmanship, of course, the two are perfectly on a level,—I think. And what must strike anyone possessed of a *human* kind (as differentiated from scholarly) of discrimination is the perfect genuineness of expression, the straight flow of inspiration, the unfaltering felicity of thought. I say nothing about felicity of phrase. You know there are lines I cherish.

If I do not talk to you much about my work it only means that I am working,—with difficulty, as ever. The more I go, the less confidence in myself I feel. There are days when I suspect myself of inability to put a sentence together: and other days when I am positively incapable to invent anything that could be put into a sentence. Gone are, alas! those fine days of *Alm: Folly* when I wrote with the serene audacity of an unsophisticated fool. I am getting more sophisticated from day to day. And more uncertain! I am more conscious of my unworthiness and also of my desire of perfection which,—from the conditions of the case,— is so unattainable. I would blaze like a bonfire and shall consume myself to give the feeble glimmer of a penny dip,—if even so much.

I won't come out in *Cornhill:* and *Cosmopolis:* till next year. There will be next year one vol. of short stories. Smith Elder offered me £50 down for the privilege of locking them up till after the publication of the *Rescuer.* They are rather keen to get hold of the *Rescuer,* but I have concluded nothing. Their promises were rather vague. But one of the short stories (a pretty long one too,—about half the length of *Almayer*) is now under Henley's consideration for serial publication in the *New Review*.[1] If accepted by Henley, then Heinemann will publish it afterwards in a small volume. I want £100 for serial and book rights and of course some percentage on the sales.

Still I will take any offer (not absurdly low) they may make, because I do wish to appear in the *New Review*.

As soon as I get my 2nd proof of story for the *Cosmopolis* I shall send it to you.[2] I want to know what you think of it. I also wished to ask where it could best be cut without spoiling the effect too much. It is too long for one number, they say. I told the unspeakable idiots that the thing halved would be as ineffective as a dead scorpion. There will be a part without sting,—and the part with the sting,—and being separated they will be both harmless and disgusting. But if they must cut, then you will help me to minimize the disaster. Next week I shall hear from Henley and let you know what the patron of Kipling and Stevenson thinks. I haven't said half of what I intended to say. (To be continued in our next.)

To Edward Garnett

29th Nov. 1896. Sunday.

DEAR GARNETT,

I send you seventeen pages more—*65-82*—of my beloved *Nigger*. Send them on to Mr. Pawling,[3] but first look at them yourself. I am ashamed to think how much of my work you have not seen. It is as if I had broken with my conscience, quarrelled with the inward voice. I do not feel very safe.

Of course nothing can alter the course of the *Nigger*. Let it be unpopular, it *must* be. But it seems to me that the thing—precious as it is to me—is trivial enough on the surface to have some charm for the man in the street. As to lack of incident, well—it's life. The incomplete joy, the incomplete sorrow, the incomplete rascality or heroism—the incomplete suffering. Events crowd and push, and nothing happens. You know what I mean. The opportunities do not last long enough. Unless in a boy's book of adventures. Mine were never finished. They fizzled out before I had a chance to do more than another man would. Tell me what you think of what you see. I am going on. Another 20 pages

---

[1] *The Nigger of the "Narcissus,"* which Conrad was writing at that moment but which turned out to be longer than he expected at first.

[2] This refers to "An Outpost of Progress."

[3] A partner of the firm of William Heinemann.

of type—or even less—will see the end, such as it is. And won't I breathe! Till it's over there's no watch below for me. A sorry business, this scribbling.

To Edward Garnett

Monday morning.
December 7. 1896.

DEAR GARNETT,

Of course—as old Pendennis used to say—I am *monstrously* pleased to see Pawling, monstrously pleased begad! You are raising for yourself a fine crop of ingratitude—for I don't see any other course of action opened for me.

Shall I meet you at Compton Street? I suppose it is the place where we had dinner together once or twice.[1] At the back of Palace music hall. If you don't write I shall take it as being so. It seems an awful thing to sleep in a Museum right along-side fellows who have slept for 2,000 years or so, but I am brave.[2] Now I have conquered Henley I ain't 'fraid of the divvle himself. I will drink to the success of the *Rescuer*. I will even get drunk to make it all safe—no morality! I feel like, in old days, when I got a ship and started off in a hurry to cram a lot of shore-going emotions into one short evening before going off into a year's slavery upon the sea. Ah! *Tempi passati*. There were then other prejudices to conquer. Same fate in another garb. I shall look for you downstairs first. But I will be in Monico's entrance hall at 5.30 for a vermouth. Won't you call in?

To Charles and Angèle Zagórska [3]

Stanford-le-Hope, Essex,
20. 12. 1896.

MY DEAREST CHARLES AND ANGÈLE,

This is the first Christmas I shall be able to spend with my wife. Now that I am no longer alone, on behalf of two of us—so to speak—I send you our sincerest wishes for your happiness, peace and successes great and small; for it is the latter which for most of us go to make up the joys of life. And we both send the same to our darling Aunt, whilst

---

[1] The "Restaurant d'Italie" in Old Compton Street.

[2] Conrad had been asked to stay with Dr. Garnett, librarian of the British Museum, Edward Garnett's father.

[3] The original of this letter is in Polish.

asking her—at this time, when families are united at least in thought—to remember us in her heart for she has known those whose memory is the guide of our lives.

I had the intention of coming home for the holiday—home, that is to say, to you. It was a vague and uncertain plan, although a fervent wish. I did not tell you about it. I hardly dared myself think of it. Nevertheless, it is a cruel disappointment. There will be no holidays for me this year—but I comfort myself with the thought that another year will follow and also other years—and that dreams come true sometimes (not often). Meanwhile one must work, for we cannot live on praise, neither my wife nor myself. I used to write and to write ceaselessly, but now the sight of an inkpot and a penholder fill me with rage and disgust—and yet I am still writing! Do not be angry with my long periods of silence. I will describe my state of mind to you; I do not wish to fill your ears with my lamentations. You can be sure that if I had something to be pleased with, I would hasten to manifest my joy to you. I boldly commend myself to your affection. I hope that this is not effrontery. I kiss the hands of Cousin Angèle, I embrace her and kiss my little cousins,[1] after the fashion of a seaman, on both cheeks.

With all my heart I remain your devoted brother,
K. KORZIENOWSKI.

To Miss Watson [2]

Stanford-le-Hope.
27th Jan. 1897.

DEAR MISS WATSON,

Thanks very much for the "Outpost,"—and more for your kind note. I am delighted to hear you both had such a happy time. I've heard already from Ted: he is in a state of perfect felicity, and has already begun to count days to Easter. I trust the beginning of your new life of content and peace shall not be too long delayed. It is a great trial to him—this waiting. Women have a more penetrating vision, and a greater endurance of life's perversities. But man longs for the actual,—because he is less able to look afar into days and years.

I understand the "Fortune" is to be *the* home. I am very glad. I would rather see you live in a tent on the lawn than sharing the big house with another household. This is said with all respect to every individual of both households. No doubt you understand me. It is almost incredibly

---

[1] Angela and Karola, the little daughters of Mr. and Mrs. Zagórska.
[2] Miss Watson was to be, soon after, Mrs. E. L. Sanderson.

good of you to think and talk of me when you have one another to contemplate and comment upon. But I am more than delighted,—I am much touched by the unselfishness of your thoughts. And yet it is what I expected! The greater the affection the more exacting it is: and I only hope that later on you will not find I exact or expect too much!

The story just finished is called *The Nigger: A Tale of Ships and Men*. Candidly, I think it has certain qualities of art that make it a thing apart. I tried to get through the veil of details at the essence of life. But it is a rough story,—dealing with rough men and an immense background. I do not ask myself how much I have succeeded. I only dare to hope that it is not a shameful failure, that perhaps, here and there, may be found a few men and women who will see what I have tried for. It would be triumph enough for me.

Once more thanks for your thought,—for your gracious words.

I am, dear Miss Watson, your very affectionate and obedient servant.

To E. L. Sanderson

27th Jan. '97.

DEAREST TED,

I've just finished a letter to Miss Watson,—acknowledging receipt of "Outpost" and thanking her for a charming note she sent with it. I am happy with your happiness and together with you suffer from this delay of your wishes. Not that I think the sweetness of expectation will change to bitterness, but I do not like to think you are gnawing at your heart,— and I know that in a more or less decorous way it is what you are engaged upon.

I suppose that at Easter, Mehemet-Ali (on whom I invoke the blessing of the Prophet) will undertake the rôle of Cupid again. O! lucky mortal whose love is served by princes! I never could understand before the advantages of Egyptian occupation: but since your engagement I see the hidden wisdom of the inscrutable Gladstonian policy of many years ago.

I wish you would come and talk things over. I have a certain compunction in asking a man to go to the end of the civilized world, just to talk. Still when I think of it I see that I would ask you to do more difficult things for my sake. When you find time, do come. Galsworthy did come last Sunday and returned safely, none the worse for his desperate adventure. And what's more he had the pluck to volunteer for it too! Now, what do you think of that! Are you fired with envy and emulation?

I did not explain (being naturally muddle headed) that I wanted your advice upon "Outpost." It is not cutting down; it's cutting *in two* that bothers me. They want to publish in two numbers (March–April) [1] and I do not see where it can be cut.

The sting of the thing is in its tail,—so that the first instalment, by itself, will appear utterly meaningless,—and, by the time the second number comes out, people would have forgotten all about it and would wonder at my sudden ferocity. Henley likes my story, but there is some hitch about the [*New*] *Review*. What I do not know, but expect to hear soon.

My wife is anxious to see you under our temporary roof and sends her regards.

To Edward Garnett

13th Febr. 1897.

DEAR GARNETT,

I had this morning a charming surprise in the shape of the *Spoils of Poynton* sent me by Henry James, with a very characteristic and friendly inscription on the flyleaf.[2] I need not tell you how pleased I am. I have already read the book. It is as good as anything of his—almost—a story of love and wrong-headedness revolving round a houseful of artistic furniture. It's Henry James and nothing but Henry James. The delicacy and tenuity of the thing are amazing. It is like a great sheet of plate glass—you don't know it's there till you run against it. Of course I do not mean to say it is anything as gross as plate glass. It's only as *pellucid* as clean plate glass. The only fault I find is its length. It's just a trifle too long. Personally I don't complain, as you may imagine, but I imagine with pain the man in the street trying to read it! And my common humanity revolts at the evoked image of his suffering. One could almost see the globular lobes of his brain painfully revolving and crushing, mangling the delicate thing. As to his exasperation, it is a thing impossible to imagine and too horrid to contemplate.

I send you some thirty pages of MS.[3] I am heartily ashamed of them and am afraid that this instinct of shame is right. I feel more of a humbug than ever—and yet I lay my shame bare to you because you wish it. My

---

[1] "The Outpost of Progress," owing to the publication in the April and May numbers of Rudyard Kipling's "Slaves of the Lamp," was delayed till the issues June and July, 1897, of *Cosmopolis*.

[2] The inscription was: "To Joseph Conrad in dreadfully delayed but very grateful acknowledgment of an offering singularly generous and beautiful. Henry James. Feb. 11, 1897."

[3] Very probably a part of his short story "Karain."

wife is this moment reading reverently James' book, and trying honestly to distinguish its head from its tail. Her reverence is not affected. It is a perfectly genuine sentiment inspired by me: but her interest is, I suspect, affected for the purpose of giving me pleasure. And she will read every line! 'Pon my word it's most touching and only women are capable of such delicately penetrating sacrifices. I do nothing but yawn and tear my hair.

To Miss Watson

14th March 1897.
Stanford-le-Hope.

DEAR MISS WATSON,

I trust you will pardon me the delay in answering your delightful letter,—and the most delightful of all was the evidence in your own writing that you are better,—but I was finishing another story, a promised and belated story! I am so sure of your generosity that I shall say no more in extenuation.

Languidness was to be expected; only you must permit me to point out that the kind of languidness following upon influenza must not be combated otherwise than in spirit: *think* cheerfully,—even uproariously! —but do not overtax your physical powers.

I am right glad to know you like the "Lagoon." To be quite confidential I must tell you it is, of my short stories, the one I like the best myself. I did write it to please myself,—and I am truly delighted to find that I have also pleased you.

I am sorry to think there is opposition to the "Fortune." The name is of good omen,—and I see no other acceptable alternative but a marble palace on one of the Fortunate Isles. Failing that,—it must be *the* Fortune in Elstree.

And I shall come,—of course,—anywhere,—even to a marble palace! Only you must not ruin yourself in wings. You must trust Ted's love,— friend's discrimination: and the sincerity of your own nature. Then indeed we shall not only see wings, but even hear music,—and a song of serenity and peace.

And here I must end. A mass of neglected correspondence awaits me, —and work (but that is always waiting),—and some sad thoughts.

Your letter has cheered me. Thanks for your inestimable friendship and for the proof of your memory.

I am, dear Miss Watson, always your most faithful and obedient servant and friend.

To E. L. Sanderson

Friday, 26th March, 1897.
Stanford-le-Hope.

DEAREST TED,

I had your letter on the last day of my first year of married life. It was good of you to remember me and even accident was kind by bringing your missive on an ominous day. A year of anything gone is a great loss, or a great gain,—and in any case a fitting opportunity to desire some kind of consolation. At the end of many conventional periods of time, one is apt to think overmuch about oneself. A barren occupation! But a friend's voice turns the current of thought into a more fruitful valley in the reamed land of the past.

I need not tell you how sorry I was to hear of the illness at Corsbie West. You did well to go. Well! It's the past already and it is an easier matter to remember than to bear.

Only the other day I've re-read Miss Helen's [1] letter, the letter to me. It is laid away with some of my very particular papers. It is so unaffectedly, so irresistibly charming, and profound too. One seems almost to touch the ideal conception of what's best in life. And—personally—those eight pages of her writing are to me like a high assurance of being accepted, admitted within the people and the land of my choice. And side by side with the letter I found the printed paper signed by the Secretary of State. The form of nationalization and its reality,—the voice of what is best in the heart of peoples.

I don't count the weeks since I've seen you. Not now! There are too many. A stream seems to flow between us. Surely it is not a stream of life: I feel like a man in a desert. It is not the deadly stream of ambition, interest, personal thoughts. Let those who live in the world splash in that muddy current. And it is not the black waters of forgetfulness. It is but a trickle,—a trickle of small worries, of insignificant and vital accidents. I wish I could wade through it and grasp your hand on the other side. Well! In time, in time! The thought is faithful: and that "amicitia *Torrente* inchoata" [2] shall live as long as you and I, dear Ted, have eyes to look upon the sea where it was born.

I feel horribly sentimental,—no joking matter this, at my age, when one should be grave, correct, slightly cynical,—and secretly bored. I am none of those things and, feeling my shortcomings, withdraw from the gaze of my fellow beings. Now, note the inconsequence of the human

[1] Miss Watson.
[2] An allusion to their first meeting in 1893 on board the *Torrens*.

animal: I want to rush into print whereby my sentimentalism, my incorrect attitude to life,—all I wish to hide in the wilds of Essex,—shall be disclosed to the public gaze! Do I do it for money? *Chi lo sa!* Oh no! —it would be too indecent. I am in a bad way. Now if I could only attain to become (is that English?) a minor Thackeray, decency would be preserved and shekels gathered at the same time. Alas! I have been born too far East, where not many cultivate the virtue of reticence.

From the above you will (justly) conclude that I am growling and snarling over my work,—and cherishing it at the same time. In short, behaving like a dog with a bone. Very true. I am an old dog and nevertheless am tired of the hard road. Preserve us from lying proverbs! A lying prophet must ultimately die but the folly of nations is practically immortal. There is also a French proverb which says that "a wise man does not tie up his dog with a string of sausages." This one seems rather true—and the publishers are wise men.

Galsworthy came here last week. He stayed with me just one hour and forty-five min: by the watch. He wrote since saying he had been in Elstree. I trust Miss Agnes is beyond convalescence now. I was on the point of writing to Mrs. Sanderson but refrained, for I know that she would answer and I do not know how her eyesight is now: so I denied myself that pleasure. Give her my affectionate and respectful regards. We live in the Farm house. Jess is busy with the garden. I think I saw her digging with a spade the size of a shoe horn. It reminded me of seaside and children. I've done nothing since finishing the *Nigger,* but am at something now.[1] Lots of writing but not much else in it. The "Outpost" begins in *Cosmopolis* for April. When you write to Corsbie West spare me the space for a few words of sympathy and of the greatest regard. You know how I feel. Write soon to me. Come, if you can! With love.

To E. L. Sanderson

Wednesday. May 1897.

MY DEAREST TED,

I send you on the *Nigger.* Galsworthy had seen a couple of sheets when he was here last, so I let him have the lot first. He returned it to-day and I dispatch it at once to you.

I address it rather to you than to your dear Mother because I want you to see it first. I know, my dear fellow, that *you* will never suspect me of ingrained coarseness of thought and language. But I want you to read and judge before you hand it over to Mrs. Sanderson. Not that I mis-

[1] The tale "Karain."

trust her comprehension and indulgence, but I want to spare to her (even at the cost of my self-love) any unpleasant experience. Not, perhaps, because I think that the thing is not worth it. I am conceited enough about it,—God knows,—but He also knows the spirit in which I approached the undertaking to present faithfully some of His benighted and suffering creatures; the humble, the obscure, the sinful, the erring upon whom rests His Gaze of Ineffable Pity. My conscience is at peace in that matter, and it is with confidence and love that I send the work to you,—to read and to judge.

Love to all. Write soon again. Now in haste for post.

To Miss Watson

27th June, 1897.

MY DEAR MISS WATSON,

It is a real sorrow for me to hear such news of poor Ted: but it was very friendly and very dear of you to write. I am very grateful to you for the friendship and the confidence. The pang of regret comes when one realizes one's helplessness to remedy the ills of the people one loves.

Dear old Ted takes life hard as higher natures always do,—for him relief must come from changed circumstances, for it will never come from within. He is not the man to abandon the ethical position in which his sensitive conscience has placed him for his fight with life. He has no idea of sparing himself. My comfort is in thinking that, for a time at least, you are by his side. But I can imagine how large a part of suffering falls to your share. One hates to preach a lower creed. I have ventured before to do so to him,—at a personal risk, you will own,—and I did earnestly, if without belief in my success. Abnegation and self-forgetfulness are not always right. They are not always right even in the noblest cause. I've said so without fear for him. In such a saying one runs the risk of being misunderstood. A man's duties are wide and complex: the balance should be held very even, lest some evil should be done when nothing but good is contemplated. These are truisms which choice characters,—like Ted,— do not condescend to see.

It seems too hard to have nothing to offer you but words. One would like to *do* something. And one is too far, and one is blind,—and sympathy is only the refuge of helplessness. If you can't help him, no one,— no one,—can. But I am sure you help him,—and much more than you think or would believe if the secret of hearts could be put into words.

I trust you will let me know soon how he progresses. Without the slightest exaggeration I may say that since this morning I am very miserable about both of you. Let me entreat you,—as Ted's friend,— to spare yourself any very trying fatigue. The knowledge that you are near *and well* will make him more happy than the knowledge you are over-exerting yourself for his sake. You must sacrifice the best of your impulses to do the most good.

It is very good of you,—at this anxious time,—to think and speak of my book.[1] The pleasure of your appreciation,—which I prize so highly,— is overshadowed by the news you send. I must however assure you that there was no intention of levity in my treatment of the cook. I did not try to,—and I trust I did not make—him ridiculous. Nothing was further from my thoughts than irreverence. It would have been untrue to my convictions. The worst that can be charged against me is artistic failure,—failure to express the mixed sentiments the men (whom I knew) awakened in me. I close to catch the post.

I am, dear Miss Watson, your most obedient and faithful friend and servant.

To E. L. Sanderson

19th July, 1897.

DEAREST TED,

I heard from Galsworthy that you have returned from Lowestoft and that you are better. I write to offer my congratulations on recovery and also to tell you that I did not write before because I was in such a frame of mind, that to write an epistle of mine would have been poison to a man depressed by influenza. Just now I also feel better,—at any rate well enough not to endanger your health by my writing.

I am glad to say that the *Blackwood Maga[zine]* accepted my last short story which is called "Karain." They demurred at first at my price, but I stuck to it heroically (while I felt very vile all the time),—tho'— really,—£2. 10. per thousand words of my painful prose is not extortionate. What do you think?

At last Wm. Blackwood wrote himself saying he would accept my terms on the understanding that I should give him the first refusal of any short story I may write! This, coming from Modern Athens, was so flattering that for a whole day I walked about with my nose in the air. Since this morning, however, it occurred to me that Blackwood won't help me to write the stories,—and with me, I see, the trouble is not in the publishing: it is in the writing.—Alas!—I've been ten weeks

---

[1] *The Nigger of the "Narcissus."*

trying to write a story of about 20 pages of print.[1] I haven't finished yet! and what I've written seems to me too contemptible for words. Not in conception perhaps,—but in execution. This state of affairs spells Ruin, —and I can't help it,—I can't.

Tell Miss Watson all about "Karain." A letter of hers had something to do with the shaping of that story. She informed me your taste has grown so hopelessly depraved that you can no longer conceal your craving for my prose. I understand even that you have refused all other literary food. I am sorry for you, my dear Ted. You'll starve. However, I'll do my best and you shall have the proofs as soon as practicable.

There is no other news,—unless the information that there is a prospect of some kind of descendant may be looked upon in the light of something new. I am not unduly elated. Johnson says it may mend Jess's health permanently,—if it does not end her. The last he does not say in so many words, but I can see an implication through a wall of words. This attitude does not contribute to my peace of mind,—and now, when I think of it, there is nothing very shocking in my not being able to finish a short story in three months. The old practitioner here tho' is very cheerful about it. Well! we shall see,—in December I believe.

Here's a letter all shop and family. As soon as you feel up to it do write, dear old chap. I want to know what you do, what you think,— how it is with you generally.

With love.

The most affectionate regards to Mrs. Sanderson. Remember me to all.

To R. B. Cunninghame Graham [2]

5th Aug. 1897.
Stanford-le-Hope, Essex.

DEAR SIR,

You've given me a few moments of real, solid excitement. I scuttled about for the signature,—then laid the letter down. I am a prudent man. Very soon it occurred to me that you would hardly go out of your way (in the month of August) to kick an utter stranger. So, I said to myself, "These,—no doubt,—are halfpence. Let us see." And,—behold! it was real gold, a ducat for a beggar,—a treasure for the very poor! You'll ruin yourself: but (I am a white man) what does it matter to me as long as the profit is mine?

[1] "The Return," which he finished on the 24th of September, and which was rejected by Chapman & Hall in October.

[2] Mr. R. B. Cunninghame Graham, prompted by his admiration, had just written to Joseph Conrad after having read "An Outpost of Progress" in *Cosmopolis*.

And I feel distinctly richer since this morning. I admire so much your vision and your expression that your commendation has for me a very high value,—the very highest! Believe that I appreciate fully the kind impulse that prompted you to write.

Mr. Kipling has the wisdom of the passing generations,—and holds it in perfect sincerity. Some of his work is of impeccable form and because of that *little* thing, he will sojourn in Hell only a very short while. He squints with the rest of his excellent sort. It is a beautiful squint: it is an useful squint. And—after all,—perhaps he sees round the corner? And suppose Truth is just round the corner, like the elusive and useless loafer it is? I can't tell. No one can tell. It is impossible to know. It is impossible to know anything, tho' it is possible to believe a thing or two.

Pray do not regret your letter: I mean to hold my beliefs,—not that I think it matters in the least. If I had your eyesight, your knowledge and your pen, it would matter. But I haven't. Nevertheless I shall persist in my beastly attitude. Straight vision is bad form,—as you know. The proper thing is to look round the corner, because, if Truth is not there, there is at any rate a something that distributes shekels. And what better can you want than the noble metal?

You did not expect such a *tuile sur la tête* as this in answer to your letter. Well! it's only five pages at the most, and life is long,—and art is so short that no one sees the miserable thing. Most of my life has been spent between sky and water and I live so alone that often I fancy myself clinging stupidly to a derelict planet abandoned by its precious crew. Your voice is not a voice in the wilderness,—it seems to come through the clean emptiness of space. If, under the circumstances, I hail back lustily I know you won't count it to me for a crime.

I am very sincerely delighted to learn that you can stand my prose. It is so hard to realize that I have any readers!—except the critics, who have been very kind and moral and austere, but excessively indulgent. To know that you could read me is good news indeed,—for one writes only half the book: the other half is with the reader.

To R. B. Cunninghame Graham

9th Aug. 1897,
Ivy Walls Farm,
Stanford-le-Hope, Essex.

DEAR SIR,

I was delighted to see your handwriting which, by the bye,—I had not the slightest difficulty in reading,—this time.

Of course I would be most happy to come whenever you say the word: and I'll be still happier if your recklessness carries you as far as Stanford. I presume Bohemianism has no terrors for you. It isn't pretty at my age, but it's one of those facts one must face,—with concealed disgust. My wife (she's a good girl *et pas du tout gênante*) shall cook something and —please God!—we may find for you some place to sleep,—not absolutely on the floor.

I am both touched and frightened by what you say about being the prophet of my inarticulate and wandering shadow. I cannot help thinking with alarm of the day when you shall find me out, or rather find out that there is nothing there. How soon will you begin to regret your magnificent imprudence?—and will you ever forgive me the triumph of your friends when they assail you with reproaches and a great clamour of "I told you so!"

You understood perfectly what I tried to say about Mr. Kipling,— but I did not succeed in saying exactly what I wanted to say. I wanted to say, in effect, that in the chaos of printed matter Kipling's *ébauches* appear by contrast finished and impeccable. I judge the man in his time,— and space. It is a small space and as to his time I leave it to your tender mercy. I wouldn't in his defence spoil the small amount of steel that goes to the making of a needle. As to posterity, it won't smile. Not it! Posterity will be busy thieving, lying, selling its little soul for sixpence (from the noblest motives), and will remember no one, except perhaps one or two quite too atrocious mountebanks: and the half-dozen men lost in that *bagarre* are more likely to weep than to smile over those master-pieces of our time.

I am very unhappy just now, not being able to squeeze three consecutive sentences out of myself. The world, however, seems to be rolling on without a check,—which is of course very offensive to me. I want to ask you a favour. There is a thing of mine coming out in the *New Review*.[1] Being, as you inform me, my *prophète en titre,* I am afraid you must consider it your sacred duty to read everything over my signature. Now in this special case *please don't.* In November I shall send you the book,—if you allow me,—and then you shall see the whole. I am conceited about that thing and very much in love with it, and I want it to appear before you at its best. The instalment plan ruins it. I wouldn't make that fuss if I didn't value your opinion.

I shall be here from now till the end of time, I fancy. So whenever you are in town and have absolutely nothing better to do, drop me a line. I am always ready to drop my work.

[1] *The Nigger of the "Narcissus."*

To Edward Garnett

1897. 28th Augst.
Stanford-le-Hope, Essex.

DEAREST GARNETT,

Thanks many many times for your sympathetic and wise letter. I put sympathy first—the gift—the unchanging thing—the most precious to me. But as to your wisdom I am ready to admit without discussion that it surpasses the sagacity of the most venomous serpents.

As you may imagine I do not care a fraction of a dam' for the passage you have struck out [1]—that is, the personal part. But I think that the eight lines at the end (of the paragraph struck out) conveying the opinion that in "art alone there is a meaning in endeavour as apart from success" should be worked in somehow. And whether your wisdom lets me keep them in or not I tell you plainly—fangs or no fangs—that there is the saving truth—the truth that saves most of us from eternal damnation. There!

I shall promptly patch the hole you have made and show you the thing with the infamous taint out of it.—If, then, there is the slightest chance of it doing some good to the *Nigger* it shall *not* go to the *Saturday* or any other Review. Hang the filthy lucre. I would do any mortal thing for Jimmy—you know.

I have a bit of news which I am bursting with. The other day I wrote to Blackwood's asking them to send me proofs early and so on—just to give them my address. Yesterday I had a charming, friendly letter from Wm. Blackwood, saying he would have the story set up on purpose and at once—asking me whether I would mind the story [2] coming out in November instead of October, but leaving it to me—and so on in that unheard of tone. At the end he asks me whether I have a long story "on the stocks" and wishes to know whether there is enough of it for him to see with a view to running it as a serial in the magazine. Imagine my satisfaction! I answered in a befitting manner and by and by shall let him have the *Rescuer*. All the good moments—the real good ones in my life, I owe to you—and I say it without a pang; which is also something of which you may boast, O wiser than the serpents! You sent me to Pawling—you sent me to Blackwood—when are you going to send me to heaven? I am anxious to depart soon so as not to be too late for the next batch of immortals—but I don't care to go without an introduction from you. May your days be steeped in serenity and your visions be only of sevenfold Perfection.

[1] In the Preface to *The Nigger of the "Narcissus."*
[2] "Karian."

To Edward Garnett

5th Dec. 1897.

MY DEAR GARNETT,

The *Nigger* came out to-day I believe but is not advertised in the *Sat. Review*. As soon as I get my copies I shall forward a specimen to the Cearne.

I had Crane here last Sunday.[1] We talked and smoked half the night. He is strangely hopeless about himself. I like him. The two stories are excellent. Of course, "A Man and Some Others" is the best of the two but the boat thing [2] interested me more. His eye is very individual and his expression satisfies me artistically. He certainly is *the* impressionist and his temperament is curiously unique. His thought is concise, connected, never very deep—yet often startling. He is *the only* impressionist and *only* an impressionist. Why is he not immensely popular? With his strength, with his rapidity of action, with that amazing faculty of vision —why is he not? He has outline, he has colour, he has movement, with that he ought to go very far. But—will he? I sometimes think he won't. It is not an opinion—it is a feeling. I could not explain why he disappoints me—why my enthusiasm withers as soon as I close the book. While one reads, of course he is not to be questioned. He is the master of his reader to the very last line—then—apparently for no reason at all—he seems to let go his hold. It is as if he had gripped you with greased fingers. His grip is strong but while you feel the pressure on your flesh you slip out from his hand—much to your own surprise. This is my stupid impression and I give it to you in confidence. It just occurs to me that it is perhaps my own self that is slippery. I don't know. *You* would know. No matter.

My soul is like a stone within me. I am going through the awful experience of losing a friend. Hope [3] comes every evening to console me but he has a hopeless task. Death is nothing—and I am used to its rapacity. But when life robs one of a man to whom one has pinned one's faith for twenty years the wrong seems too monstrous to be lived down. Yet it must. And I don't know why, how, wherefore. Besides there are circumstances which make the event a manifold torment. Some day I will tell you the tale. I can't write it now. But there is a psychological point in it. However this also does not matter.

[1] Joseph Conrad and Stephen Crane met, in London, for the first time, two months before. (See *Stephen Crane,* by Thomas Beer, with an Introduction by Joseph Conrad, p. 2.)

[2] "The Open Boat."

[3] His friend G. F. W. Hope.

The *Nigger* is ended and the *New Review* stops. I suppose you've heard already. Henley printed the Preface at the end as an Author's Note. It does not shine very much, but I am glad to see it in type. This is all the news. No criticisms have appeared as yet. I am trying to write the *Rescuer* and all my ambition is to make it good enough for a magazine—readable, in a word. I doubt whether I can. I struggle without pleasure like a man certain of defeat. Drop me a line.

To R. B. Cunninghame Graham

> 6th Dec. 1897.
> Stanford-le-Hope,
> Essex.

MY DEAR SIR,

I am horribly ashamed of myself. I ought to have written last week to thank you for the Stevenson. My inadequate excuse is I've been strangely seedy—nothing very tangible, but for nearly a week I have thought not at all and eaten very little,—and didn't see the use of doing anything. This may seem to you an impertinent excuse but I assure you it is a very sad and fiendish,—well, indisposition, and too real for words. I throw myself on your mercy. I shook myself at the sight of your letter and now what between shame and pleasure I am able to sit here like a galvanized corpse to write this flat and miserable apology.

The *Xmas at Sea* is all that you said. I was glad of the book and still more of your thought. I was glad to know I haven't been seen,—and forgotten. Only,—*parce que c'est vous!* There are people from whom I would beg on my knees the favour of an eternal oblivion. Would I get it? *Croyez-vous qu'on se retrouve, là-bas?* To me *"là-bas"* appears sometimes as a big hole,—a kind of malefactors' cavern—very crowded (think how long mankind has been in the habit of dying!) with perspiring shades,—a moral perspiration of squeezed spirits exhaling the unspeakable meanness, the bareness, the lies, the rapacity, the cowardice of souls that on earth have been objects of barter and valued themselves at about two-and-six. But this is morbid,—and I sat down intending to produce a good impression! I take it all back and declare my belief in lilies, gold harps,—and brimstone, like my Podmore in the *"Narcissus."* [1]

And apropos of Podmore,—I am afraid the *Nigger* will bore you. *C'est vécu,—et c'est bête.* There are twenty years of life, six months of scribbling in that book,—and not a shadow of a story. As the critic in to-day's *D'ly Mail* puts it tersely: "The tale is no tale at all." The man

---

[1] The cook of the *Narcissus* in *The Nigger of the "Narcissus."*

complains of lack of heroism! and is, I fancy, shocked at the bad language. I confess reluctantly there is a swear here and there. I grovel in the waste-paper basket, I beat my breast. May I hope you, at least! won't withdraw your esteem from a repentant sinner?

No man can escape his fate! You shall come here and suffer hardships, boredom and despair. It is written! It is written! You,—as a matter of fact,—have written it yourself (at my instigation,—very rash of you) and I shall be inexorable like destiny and shall look upon your sufferings with the idiotic serenity of a benevolent Creator (I don't know that the ben: Crea: is serene:—but if he is (as they say) then he *must* be idiotic) looking at the precious mess he has made of his only job. This letter reminds me of something I used to know years ago: Algebra,—I think. Brackets within brackets and imbecility raised to the nth power.

I heard of the H. & S. play [1] through G. B. S. in the *S. R.* [2] More Algebra. Do you understand? I allude in this luminous way to *Admiral Guinea*. I haven't seen a play for years, but I have read this one. And that's all I can say about it. I have no notion of a play. No play grips me on the stage or off. Each of them seems to me an amazing freak of folly. They are all unbelievable and as disillusioning as a bang on the head. I greatly desire to write a play myself. It is my dark and secret ambition. And yet I can't conceive how a sane man can sit down deliberately to write a play and not go mad before he has done. The actors appear to me like a lot of *wrong-headed* lunatics pretending to be sane. Their malice is stitched with white threads. They are disguised and ugly. To look at them breeds in my melancholy soul thoughts of murder and suicide,—such is my anger and my loathing of their transparent pretences. There is a taint of subtle corruption in their blank voices, in their blinking eyes, in the grimacing faces, in the false light, in the false passion, in the words that have been learned by heart. But I love a marionette-show. Marionettes are beautiful,—especially those of the old kind with wires, thick as my little finger, coming out of the top of the head. Their impassibility in love, in crime, in mirth, in sorrow,—is heroic, superhuman, fascinating. Their rigid violence when they fall upon one another to embrace or to fight is simply a joy to behold. I never listen to the text mouthed somewhere out of sight by invisible men who are here to-day and rotten to-morrow. I love the marionettes that are without life, that come so near to being immortal!

Here's the end of paper. It is to-morrow already and high time for me to go to bed,—to dream, perchance to sleep. You must forgive the writer, the letter, the mistakes of spelling, the obscurity of the grammar,—the

[1] Henley's & R. L. Stevenson's play.
[2] George Bernard Shaw in *Saturday Review.*

imbecility of the nth power. Forgive! Forgiveness has been invented to prevent massacres.

P. S. I haven't yet had *St. Thérèse*.[1] Expect it next week. I have looked lately again at the scenery article,—and am confirmed in my opinion that your wife has said what is really fundamental, essentially true in the matter, and said it charmingly. Sorry to hear of Hudson's [2] illness. A lovable man, a most lovable man.

To R. B. Cunninghame Graham

14 Dec. 1897.
Stanford-le-Hope,
Essex.

MY DEAR SIR,

Your good letter cheered me immensely, but with my usual brutal ingratitude I've let the days pass without saying so. It was a friendly thought to send me the *Glasgow Herald's* cutting. It came in the nick of time and sent me to bed in peace with my fellow men.

I've been thinking over the letter you have written me about the *Nigger*. I am glad you like the book. Sincerely glad. It's clear gain to me. I don't know what the respectable (hats off) part of the population will think of it. Probably nothing. They never think. It isn't respectable. But I can quite see that, without thinking, they may feel an instinctive disgust. So be it. In my mind I picture the book as a stone falling in the water. It's gone and not a trace shall remain. But the words of commendation you and a few other men have said will be treasured by me as a proof that the book has not been written in vain—as the clearest of my reward.

So you may rest assured that the time you have given to reading the tale and to writing to me has not been thrown away,—since, I presume, you do not believe that doing good to a human being is throwing away effort and one's own life. And you have done me good. Whatever may be the worth of my gratitude, you have it all: and such is the power of men to show feeling that *hélas! vous ne vous en apercevrez même pas!*

But as I said I have been meditating over your letter. You say: "Singleton, with an education." [3] Well, yes! Everything is possible, and most things come to pass (when you don't want them). However I think Singleton with an education is impossible. But first of all,—what education? If it is the knowledge of how to live, my man essentially pos-

---

[1] *Santa Teresa: Her Life and Times,* by Gabriela Cunninghame Graham. 2 vols., London, Black, 1897.

[2] W. H. Hudson.

[3] Singleton, one of the characters in *The Nigger of the "Narcissus."*

sessed it. He was in perfect accord with his life. If by education you mean scientific knowledge then the question arises,—what knowledge? How much of it,—in what direction? Is it to stop at plane trigonometry or at conic sections? Or is he to study Platonism or Pyrrhonism, or the philosophy of the gentle Emerson? Or do you mean the kind of knowledge which would enable him to scheme, and lie, and intrigue his way to the forefront of a crowd no better than himself? Would you seriously, of malice prepense, cultivate in that unconscious man the power to think? Then he would become conscious,—and much smaller,—and very unhappy. Now he is simple and great like an elemental force. Nothing can touch him but the curse of decay,—the eternal decree that will extinguish the sun, the stars, one by one, and in another instant shall spread a frozen darkness over the whole universe. Nothing else can touch him,—he does not think.

Would you seriously wish to tell such a man "Know thyself! Understand that you are nothing, less than a shadow, more insignificant than a drop of water in the ocean, more fleeting than the illusion of a dream?" Would you?

But I hear the postman. Au revoir till next week. I won't now delay. Many thanks for your good and friendly letter.

To R. B. Cunninghame Graham

20th Dec. 1897.
Stanford-le-Hope.

MY DEAR SIR,

Your letter reached me just when I was preparing to write to you. What I said in my incoherent missive of last week, was not for the purpose of arguing really. I did not seek controversy with you,—for this reason: I think that we do agree. If I've read you aright (and I have been reading you for some years now) you are a most hopeless idealist,— your aspirations are irrealizable. You want from men faith, honour, fidelity to truth in themselves and others. You want them to have all this, to show it every day, to make out of these words their rules of life. The respectable classes which suspect you of such pernicious longings lock you up and would just as soon have you shot,—because your personality counts and you cannot deny that you are a dangerous man. What makes you dangerous is your unwarrantable belief that your desire may be realized. This is the only point of difference between us. I do not believe. And if I desire the very same things no one cares. Consequently I am not likely to be locked up or shot. There is another difference,—this time to your manifest advantage.

There is a,—let us say,—a machine. It evolved itself (I am severely scientific) out of a chaos of scraps of iron and behold!—it knits. I am horrified at the horrible work and stand appalled. I feel it ought to embroider,—but it goes on knitting. You come and say: "This is all right: it's only a question of the right kind of oil. Let us use this,—for instance, —celestial oil and the machine will embroider a most beautiful design in purple and gold." Will it? Alas, no! You cannot by any special lubrication make embroidery with a knitting machine. And the most withering thought is that the infamous thing has made itself: made itself without thought, without conscience, without foresight, without eyes, without heart. It is tragic accident,—and it has happened. You can't interfere with it. The last drop of bitterness is in the suspicion that you can't even smash it. In virtue of that truth one and immortal which lurks in the force that made it spring into existence it is what it is,—and it is indestructible!

It knits us in and it knits us out. It has knitted time, space, pain, death, corruption, despair and all the illusions,—and nothing matters. I'll admit however that to look at the remorseless process is sometimes amusing.

I've got *Sta. Teresa*[1] at last. I've just finished reading that wonderful introduction. Of course what I find in it is mostly new to me,—new as impression. It seems as though I were reading of Spain for the first time. I am delighted and intensely interested. I feel in sympathy with the book. I shall breathe its atmosphere and track its style for some time now,—a charming prospect. As to the style I can't just yet "locate" its charm. For one thing I find it unexpectedly masculine,—in the best sense. Don't you think so too?—And the Saga?[2] Where haven't you been? I want more of the Saga. Why the devil did they divide it? I want the whole Saga and nothing but the Saga!

To Mme Angèle Zagórska[3]

20.12.1897.
Stanford-le-Hope.

MY DEAR ANGÈLE,

I know that you do not forget my existence and I know also that this is not due to my merit, but to your goodness. Silence may be a sin, but

[1] Mrs. Cunninghame Graham's book.

[2] "Snaekroll's Saga," a tale which was included later on in the volume: *The Ipané*.

[3] The original of this letter is in Polish. The sentences or words here in French are in French in the original.

it is not always a mortal one; there are circumstances when one may obtain pardon. Naturally, I think that my sins deserve forgiveness. *Du reste tout le monde pense de même, au point de vue personnel bien entendu.* In all sincerity I may add in earnest that there is in me so much of the Englishman, the sailor and the adventurer, that I do not care to write—even to my nearest and dearest relatives—when things do not go well. This is the reason for my long silence. I do not want to count the months. I prefer to ask you to forget them. We have lived another year. *Autant de gagné!* Therefore we must wish one another happiness—*ce bonheur dont personne ne connaît le premier mot*—and wish it sincerely with all our hearts; try to forget that man's wishes are seldom fulfilled.

I write here words of affection, words that vanish when once spoken—but the feeling remains. May the next year bring you health, peace and the realization of your dreams—without disenchantment. And if you think that this is not possible—I shall tell you that my wishes do reflect, if not the possibility, at least my feelings for you all.

My wife joins me in my wishes. She knows you all—*comme les enfants connaissent les personnages de Contes de Fées,* and like children eager for stories, she is always ready to listen, and I, (a real story-teller), am always ready to relate. In this way you live two lives. Over there, at Lublin, where life is hard, no doubt—and here in Stanford, Essex, on the banks of the Thames—under the spell of my words: for the one you have never seen, *vous avez la douceur des Ombres et la splendeur de l'Inconnu!*

I have worked during the whole year. I have finished two volumes.[1] One came out a fortnight ago and the other is ready for the press. *Voilà.* And while waiting I live in a state of uncertainty. I enjoy a good reputation but no popularity. And as to money I have none, either. *Triste.* But things are going better at present. That I shall some day attain material success there is no reason to doubt. But that requires time and meanwhile???

The worst is that my health is not good. *Les nerfs, les nerfs!* Uncertainty torments me. It is very foolish, no doubt—*mais que voulez-vous? l'homme est bête.*

And this is how I battle with time. At my age *ce n'est pas drôle.* I fear that "before the sun rises, the dew will have destroyed the eyesight:" [2]

Enough wailings. A few days ago I had news from good-natured Margot [Marguerite Porodowska]. Her life is not very easy either. I do

[1] *Tales of Unrest* and *The Nigger of the "Narcissus."*
[2] Polish proverb.

not know if she has written to you that we expect a baby here. Jessie is very happy with this expected event, which will take place in about a week—*si le diable ne s'en mêle pas. Moi je suis plus calme.* As a matter of fact, not very calm, as, possessing a certain amount of imagination—*je m'imagine toutes sortes de désastres.* As I have already had the honour to inform you, man is silly. I must close, it is already late. I only hear the bells of the ships on the river, which remind me how far I am from you. Do not forget me *malgré tout!* I kiss the hands of Aunt Gabrielle and yours, dear Angèle. I embrace Charles, whose photo stands on the mantel-piece in the room where I work at my chefs-d'œuvre.

Yours affectionately
K. KORZENIOWSKI.

To E. L. Sanderson

26th Dec. '97.
Stanford-le-Hope.

DEAREST TED,

We got your card this morning but I was not so covered with confusion as you may imagine,—since I had already asked Miss Watson (in a letter sent on Thursday to Corsbie West) to give you all the wishes suitable to the season and which friendship may dictate. By that clever move I disarm any resentment you may feel for my apparent neglect to write,—and go on to explain that it isn't neglect at all. I simply desired to write you with plenty of time for a long palaver,—and it seemed as though I would never get the time! I declare solemnly to you that for all that I haven't done anything for ages. After all perhaps it was not so much time I wanted as freedom of mind. And that seems to-night as far off as ever,—but I write anyhow.

Life passes and it would pass like a dream were it not that the nerves are stretched like fiddle strings. Something always turns up to give a turn to the screw. Domestic life would be tolerable if,—but that soon will be over. The larger life (including many large hopes) rolls on like a cart without springs,—that is jolting me fearfully. It's true also I never knew how to drive. Driving bores me: and yet one must attend to it in a way, to avoid an upset,—a dismal death in a ditch. How do you like driving, dear Ted? What kind of road have you been travelling over lately? Methinks, O most fortunate of men, whom Egyptian princes serve (tho' not on bended knees) that you also have your share of ruts and jolts. Still you know where you're driving to. A great thing,—in fact everything! But I don't,—I don't.

The clearest gain so far from the *Nigger* was the other day a letter from Q.[1] The excellent man,—may his star ever be propitious,—writes enthusiastically a message short but packed full of sweetness. He is struck in his very vitals by the tale (which the *Standard* indignantly declares is "no tale") and apologizes for saying so "in a private letter of thanks." I wrote him back four pages to explain that this apology is the only thing I find it hard to forgive him, but that, otherwise, I am not angry. I hope that my letter got to Cornwall before the remorse for his indiscretion quite overpowered him.

In this way I am paid for the life and the writing that went up to the making of the book, the "like of which" (the *D. Chronicle* says) "we have never read before." Apart from that I am afraid that Mr. Conrad "who is in fact unique" (*Pall Mall Gaz.*) will not gain much from the book. Yet in a sense it is enough. When writing one thinks of half a dozen (at least I do) men or so,—and if these are satisfied and take the trouble to say it in so many words, then no writer deserves a more splendid recompense. On the other hand there is the problem of the daily bread which cannot be solved by praise, public or private.

I went up to town at the beginning of this month to dine with Cunninghame Graham on his return from the captivity amongst the Moors. We had exchanged 4 or 5 letters before. He is a most interesting man, not at all bigoted in his socialistic-republican ideas, which I treated to his face with a philosophic contempt. We got on very well. Of course, as is often the case, the groundwork of his ideas is, I may say, intensely aristocratic. We talked in two languages.[2] I like him,—and I verily believe he likes me.

This is all I can find to say in a hurry. The future is as mysterious as ever and every added happiness is another terror added to life. Sometimes I think I am following an *ignis fatuus* that shall inevitably lead me to destruction: sometimes I try not to think at all. And all the time I am trying to write. Here you have the essence of my existence unveiled.

Good luck to you, dear Ted, health and peace of mind. The peace of heart you have, and no one rejoices more at it than I do. Think of me often,—write to me sometimes,—but only when you feel the need. Our friendship can withstand silence,—because silence is not forgetfulness.

My affectionate regards and duty to Miss Watson. I've sent off a copy of the *Nigger* for her. You must wait for yours a little. With love.

[1] Sir Arthur Quiller-Couch.
[2] In English and in French.

To R. B. Cunninghame Graham

Stanford-le-Hope.
7th Jan. '98.

CHER AMI,

Business first. If a damned stack fetched away in a gale it would have to stay down, I fancy. But if it got only loose then chains, wire rope, any blamed thing you could lay hands on would serve to secure it. Never saw a stack quit its post, tho' I saw a cold green sea go right down into one.

Yes. A fore-staysail and a main-staysail (if carried) could be set to steady the roll of a steamship, providing the gale was not too heavy. Fore-staysail alone, hardly: tho' it's quite conceivable. In a serious affair they would be useless and in any case would speedily vanish: the necessity of steaming head to sea causing a tremendous strain on the canvas.

And in exchange will you tell me whether that lifeboat that capsized (of which you wrote) was a steam lifeboat? And what does your brother think of steam lifeboats? I hate machinery but candidly must own that it seems to me that in most cases steam's the thing for that work.

A year of happy life for every word spoken of the *Nigger*,—to you! Had you the pluck to read it again? Eh! Man! Ye are perfectly fearless. What mad thing will you do next?

Read the *Badge*.[1] It won't hurt you,—or only very little. Crane-ibn-Crane el Yankee is all right. The man sees the outside of many things and the inside of some.

I am making preparations to receive the "Impenitent Thief"[2] with the honours due to his distinguished position. I always thought a lot of that man. He was no philistine anyhow,—and no Jew, since he had no eye for the shent-per-shent business the other fellow spotted at once. I hope your essay is sympathetic.

So send everything you write,—it does a fellow good. Or at any rate let us know where the things are, so that I may scuffle around to get them.

As to the Saga it confirms me in my conviction that you have a fiendish gift of showing the futility, the ghastly, jocular futility of life. *Et c'est très fin,—très fin. C'est finement vu et c'est exprimé avec finesse, presque à mots couverts, avec de l'esprit dans chaque phrase.*

Excuse the polyglot epistle to the faithful ever yours.

P. S. Ah! *Amigo!* I've thought of Rajah Laut in London and if not

[1] *The Red Badge of Courage* by Stephen Crane.
[2] A tale, included later in the volume *Success* (Duckworth, London, 1902).

in the W. H.[1] then next thing to it. But I haven't the heart! I haven't! Not yet! I am now busy about his youth,—a gorgeous romance,—gorgeous as to feeling, I mean. Battles and loves and so on.[2]

To R. B. Cunninghame Graham

10 P. M. 14 Jan. '98.
Stanford-le-Hope,
Essex.

CHER AMI:

A really friendly letter and my conscience smote me at every word read when I thought of your work upon which I intrude with my miserable affairs.

Semm! Pronounce the Name,—and write to Frank Harris.[3] This *is* a service and a most important one. I would rather owe it to you than to anyone else,—in fact don't *see* myself owing it to anyone else. Frankly (you may have guessed) I was pretty nearly in my last ditch before I thought of attacking Harris. I talked to you in my letter as if I was ready to face fire and water and an Editor, but my heart was in my boots. Yours is a helping hand. And if you don't think you are thus sacrificing an old friend to a new one,—well then say the Name,—and write.

And since you offer to do me this good turn I had better tell you that it would be rather important to have the publication begin as soon as possible: say in two,—three months. By that time there would be a good lot of copy to go on with while I twisted the remainder out of my bowels. (It's wonderful how this fool business of writing is serious to one.)

The book is by no means near its termination.[2] About 30,000 out of 90,000 words are ready. Won't it be too cheeky approaching H. with such a small beginning?

I would be very glad, very, to see him,—in any case. But you know I am shy of my bad English. At any rate prepare him for a "b . . . y furriner" who will talk gibberish to him at the rate of 10 knots an hour. If not forewarned the phenomenon might discourage him to the point of kicking me downstairs. This is submitted to your wisdom, which embraces the world and the men in it from Patagonia to Iceland. Our ears are open.

[1] Western Hemisphere. Rajah Laut, i. e., Tom Lingard, the character in *An Outcast of the Islands.*
[2] *The Rescuer.*
[3] Frank Harris was then the editor of the *Fortnightly Review.*
[4] *The Rescuer.*

Was the fire serious? And has your wife got over the emotion? You know when I sprung that affair of mine on you I had no idea of the accumulation of troubles in Gartmore. But all the same it was dam' unkind of you to lead me on gently to make an ass of myself about smoke-stacks and staysails and then fire off at me a lot of sailor talk about going down the leech of a topsail. What don't you know! From the outside of a sail to the inside of a prison! When I think of you I feel as tho' I had lived all my life in a dark hole without ever seeing or knowing anything.

Nothing would be more delightful to me than to read a review of the *Nigger* by you. I never dreamed you would care to do this thing! I do not know who, when and how it is to be reviewed. But is the *N.* worthy of your pen and especially of your thought? Is it too late? Do you really mean it? There will be a vol. of short stories appearing in March. One of them "The Outpost." Now if you are really anxious to give me a good slating . . .

"Put the tongue out," why not? One ought to really. And the machine will run on all the same. The question is whether the fatigue of the muscular exertion is worth the transient pleasure of indulged scorn. On the other hand one may ask whether scorn, love, or hate are justified in the face of such shadowy illusions.

The machine is thinner than air and as evanescent as a flash of lightning. The attitude of cold unconcern is the only reasonable one. Of course reason is hateful,—but why? Because it demonstrates (to those who have the courage) that we, living, are out of life,—utterly out of it. The mysteries of a universe made of drops of fire and clods of mud do not concern us in the least. The fate of a humanity condemned ultimately to perish from cold is not worth troubling about. If you take it to heart it becomes an unendurable tragedy. If you believe in improvement you must weep, for the attained perfection must end in cold, darkness and silence. In a dispassionate view the ardour for reform, improvement, for virtue, for knowledge and even for beauty is only a vain sticking up for appearances, as though one were anxious about the cut of one's clothes in a community of blind men.

Life knows us not and we do not know life,—we don't know even our own thoughts. Half the words we use have no meaning whatever and of the other half each man understands each word after the fashion of his own folly and conceit. Faith is a myth and beliefs shift like mists on the shore: thoughts vanish: words, once pronounced, die: and the memory of yesterday is as shadowy as the hope of to-morrow,—only the string of my platitude seems to have no end. As our peasants say: [1] "Pray,

[1] The Polish peasants.

brother, forgive me for the love of God." And we don't know what forgiveness is, nor what is love, nor where God is. *Assez!*

Yesterday I've finished the *Life*.[1] *Ca m'a laissé une profonde impression de tristesse comme si j'avais vécu toutes les pages du livre.* I can say
no more just now.

P. S. This letter misses this morning's post because an infant of male
persuasion arrived [2] and made such a row that I could not hear the postman's whistle. It's a fine commentary upon this letter. But salvation lies
in being illogical. Still I feel remorse.

To John Galsworthy

Sunday, Jan. 16, 1898.
Stanford-le-Hope.

DEAR GALSWORTHY,

Writing to F. Unwin I would say: "as to terms of publication, I would
suggest the following arrangement. . . ." I wouldn't take up an un-
yielding position.

The good lady in the North judges from a remote standpoint. It
never probably occurred to her to ask herself what you intended doing,
how near you've come to that intention. Now I contend that (if I
understood your attitude of mind) you have absolutely done what you
set out to do. I contend that the people you take being what they are,
the book is *their* psychology. This is my opinion. And the merit of the
book, (apart from distinguished literary expression) is just in this: You
have given the exact measure of your characters in a language of great
felicity, with measure, with poetical appropriateness to characters, tragic
indeed but within the bounds of their nature. That's what makes the
book valuable, apart from its many qualities as a piece of literary work.

I am anxious to see the added chapter. If you have a duplicate copy
please send the three chapters without delay. Interpolating like this is a
dangerous experiment.

An infant of male persuasion arrived yesterday. All is going well here.
I feel relieved greatly and hope to do some work now.

I should like to know what agreement you make with Unwin. I've
told Garnett to look out for your MS. He is simply overwhelmed with
work.

I am glad to hear your club reads the *N. H.*[3] *The Nigger length
50,000 words.* You are well within the limits of a 6/- book.

---

[1] *Santa Teresa.*

[2] Joseph Conrad's first child, Borys.

[3] *The Nigger of the "Narcissus,"* published in book form a fortnight before.

P. S. In fact the force of the book is in the fidelity to the surface of life, to the surface of events,—to the surface of things and ideas. Now this is not being shallow. If the episode of life you describe strikes your critic as without profundity, it is not because the treatment is not deep. To me you have absolutely touched the bottom, and the achievement is as praiseworthy as though you had plumbed the very ocean. It is not your business to invent depths,—to invent depths is no art either. Most things and most natures have nothing but a surface. A fairly prosperous man in the state of modern society is without depth,—but he is complicated,— just in the way you show him. I don't suppose you admire such beings any more than I do. Your book is a dispassionate analysis of high-minded and contemptible types, and you awaken sympathy, interest, feeling in an impartial, artistic way. It is an achievement. I am rather angry with your critic for so wholly missing the value and the *fundamental* art of the book. As to the executive beauty of the work she could not very well have said less. The book is desperately convincing. She quarrels with you for not making it inspiring! Just like a clever woman. You and I know that there is very little inspiration in such a phase of life, but women won't have it so. Prepare yourself to be misunderstood right and left. The work is good. And *as work,* it *is* inspiring. Even so!

To Mme Angèle Zagórska [1]

21.1.98.
Stanford-le-Hope.

DEAR COUSIN,

I received the consecrated bread and your bitter reproach which I do not quite deserve. *Les apparences mentent quelquefois.* But that does not altogether explain my silence.

The child was born on the 17th of this month and I purposely waited these three days so as to be able to tell you *que tout va bien.* The doctor says it is a magnificent boy. He has dark hair, huge eyes and he resembles a monkey. What pains me is that my wife pretends that he also resembles me. *Enfin!* Do not draw too hasty conclusions from this astonishing concurrence of circumstances. My wife is certainly mistaken.

He will be christened at the Chapel in the cloisters of the Carmelites at Southwark, London. The principle which determined my choice of his Christian names is the following: the rights of the two races

[1] The original of this letter is in Polish.

should be respected. My wife representing the Anglo-Saxon has chosen the Saxon name of Alfred. As for me I was in a dilemma. I wanted to choose a name that was purely Slavonic and yet easy for foreigners to pronounce and write. I therefore decided on the name of Borys, remembering that my friend Stanislas Zaleski gave that name to his eldest son—from which I conclude that a Pole may bear that name. Therefore, my dear Angèle, until you advise something prettier (there is still time) condescend to remember that there is a certain Alfred Borys Conrad Korzeniowski whom I commend to your kind thoughts in the name of God and in the name of those who, after a life full of suffering and anguish, rest in your memory and in mine.

I kiss your hands. I embrace Charles with affection. *My wife sends her dear love to all of you.*

Your devoted
C. KORZENIOWSKI.

She says that it is now only that she feels she belongs to the family. She is extremely pleased with herself and with the whole world. *C'est naif mais touchant.*
Both our love to the dear girls.

To R. B. Cunninghame Graham

31. Jan. '98.

CHER ET EXCELLENT AMI,

In the wrist there was gout or some other devil which rendered it quite powerless, besides it being horribly painful. It's all over now.

It is good of you to push my fortunes. You are the only man,—in this or any other country,—who took any effective interest in them. Still I think that F. Harris should not be pressed. You have given him two broadsides and if the man will not surrender, well, then let him run.

Now the first sensation of oppression has worn off, a little that remains with one after reading the *Life of St. Teresa* is the impression of a wonderful richness: a world peopled thickly, with the breath of mysticism over all,—the landscapes, the walls, the men, the women. Of course I am quite incompetent to criticize such a work: but I can appreciate it. It is vast and suggestive: it is a distinct acquisition to the reader,—or at least to me: it makes one *see* and reflect. It is absorbing like a dream and as difficult to keep hold of. And it is,—to me,—profoundly saddening. It is indeed old life. And old life is like new life after all,—an uninterrupted agony of effort. Yes. Egoism is good, and altruism is good, and fidelity to nature would be the best of all, and systems could be built and rules could be made,—if we could only get rid of consciousness. What makes mankind tragic is not that they are the victims of nature, it is that they are conscious of it. To be part of the animal kingdom under the conditions of this earth is very well,— but as soon as you know of your slavery, the pain, the anger, the strife, —the tragedy begins. We can't return to nature, since we can't change our place in it. Our refuge is in stupidity, in drunkenness of all kinds, in lies, in beliefs, in murder, thieving, reforming, in negation, in contempt,—each man according to the promptings of his particular devil. There is no morality, no knowledge and no hope: there is only the consciousness of ourselves which drives us about a world that, whether seen in a convex or a concave mirror, is always but a vain and floating appearance. *Ote-toi de là que je n'y mette* is no more of a sound rule than would be the reverse doctrine. It is however much easier to practise.

What made you suspect that I wanted *vous faire une querelle d'Allemand* about the technique of the "Impenitent Thief?" I leave that to Wells, who is in the secret of the universe,—or at least of the Planet Mars. It struck me when reading your essay that the style was not the Cunninghame Graham I've known hitherto. As to the matter, however, there was not the slightest doubt,—and as I have said, every word has found a home. As to form; *c'est plus d'un seul jet,* if I may say so. It grips in a different way. The pictures and the figures are drawn without lifting pencil from paper. I like it very well. It's just the thing for that essay, whether you did it of set purpose, or by caprice, or, perhaps, unconsciously?

I am glad your brother liked the *Nigger.* Symons [1] reviewing *Trionfo della Morte* (trans[lation]) in the last *Sat. Rev.* went out of his way to damn Kipling and me with the same generous praise. He says that *Captains Courageous* and the *Nigger* have no idea behind them. I don't know. Do you think the remark is just? Now straight!

I haven't written to your brother. I am not going to inflict myself upon the whole family. I shall devote all my spare time and what's left of my energy to worrying you alone of the whole of your House. And why not? Haven't you rushed upon your fate? I am like the old man of the sea. You can't get rid of me by the apparently innocent suggestion of writing to your brother.

Seriously speaking I was afraid of trespassing,—and then each is so busy with his own futility that the handwriting of a stranger cannot be

[1] Arthur Symons.

very welcome to him. Is he a naval officer? I *am* glad he liked the *Nigger*. Please tell him so,—if you ever do write to him.

The Rescuer, A Romance of Shallow Waters, spreads itself more and more shallow over the innumerable pages. Symons (who lives on ideas) shall have no indigestion if he reads it. It would be for him like swallowing a stone: for there, *I know,* there are no ideas. Only a few types and some obscure incidents upon a dismal coast where Symons' humanity ends and raw mankind begins.

And so the end! The lamp is dim and the night is dark. Last night a heavy gale was blowing and I lay awake thinking that I would give ever so much (the most flattering criticism) for being at sea, the soul of some patient faithful ship standing up to it, under lower topsails and no land anywhere within a thousand miles. Wouldn't I jump at a command, if some literary shipowner suddenly offered it to me! .

Thanks for your inquiries. My wife and the boy are very well. I was sorry to hear of your wife's indisposition. Nothing serious, I hope. If your horse has not eaten you up entirely I trust you will write before the end of the week.

To E. L. Sanderson

3rd. Feb. '98.

MY DEAR TED,

I haven't yet thanked you for your congratulations and the classical greetings to the boy. I liked it immensely. May your wishes expressed in the words of old Ajax come true. But the child is born to a dismal heritage. I like sometimes to forget the past.

There isn't much to say. All goes well here,—and for that I am inexpressibly thankful. I work. I reproach myself with my incapacity to work more. Yet the work itself is only like throwing words into a bottomless hole. It seems easy, but it is very fatiguing.

And so I've taken to writing for the press. More words,—another hole. Still the degradation of daily journalism has been spared to me so far. There is a new weekly coming. Its name: *The Outlook:* its price: threepence sterling: its attitude: literary: its policy,—Imperialism, tempered by expediency: its mission,—to make money for a Jew: its editor Percy Hurd (never heard of him): one of its contributors, Joseph Conrad,—under the heading of "Views and Reviews."

The first number comes out on Saturday next. There will be in it something of mine about a Frenchman who is dead and therefore harmless.[1] I've just sent off a second contribution. It is a chatter about Kipling provoked by a silly criticism. It's called,—"Concerning a certain criticism": I'll send you the number in which it appears, probably No. 2.

Stephen Crane is worrying me to write a play with him. He won't believe me when I swear by all the gods and all the muses that I have no dramatic gift. Probably something will be attempted but I would bet nothing shall be done.

This is all my news. And now your turn—when you really can spare the time. Do not think hardly of me because I don't write often. I think of you more perhaps than I would if I saw you every day: and when the good time comes we shall foregather,—and find no change.

To Mme. Angèle Zagórska [2]

6.2.98.—Stanford-le-Hope.

MY DEAREST ANGÈLE,

It is still more painful and hard to think of you than to realize my loss;[3] if it was not so, I would pass in silence and darkness these first moments of suffering. Neither you, nor he, know—can know—what place you occupy in my life—how my feelings, my thoughts and my remembrances have been centred round you both and your children. And perhaps I myself did not know until now how much I depended on his memory, his sympathy and his personality—who, even when seen only once, could arouse such feelings of devotion and confidence. He had the gift of drawing all hearts to him and from the moment when I saw him for the first time, fourteen years ago, I was overcome with affection for him, as the man most akin to me in thought and by blood —after my Uncle, who took the place of my parents. Not a single day passed but I found myself thinking of you both—and during the most painful moments *l'idée qu'il y aurait un jour où je pourrais lui confesser ma vie toute entière et être compris de lui: cette pensée était ma plus grande consolation. Et voilà que cet espoir—le plus précieux de tous— s'est éteint pour toujours.*

The sound of human words does not bring consolation—there is no consolation on this earth. Time can soften but not efface sorrow. I have never felt so near to you and your little girls until this moment when

---

[1] An article on Alphonse Daudet, which was published in *The Outlook*, April 9, 1898.

[2] The original of this letter is in Polish.

[3] Charles Zagórski died on the 4th of February.

we feel together the injustice of Fate which has loaded you with the burden of life without any support. In the presence of your grief I dare not speak of mine. I only ask you to believe in my attachment to you and to the memory of the mourned husband and father who, with you, was my whole family.

My wife said to me with tears in her eyes: "I felt as if I knew him" —and seeing her tears, it seemed to me that never had I cared for him so much as now. Unfortunately she never knew him—altho' she had often heard me speak of him—for I was not capable of appreciating the worth of such a man. I did not know him thoroughly; but I believe that I understood him. I had a profound affection for him, I always went to him in my thoughts. And now I feel quite alone—even as you.

I kiss your hands, my poor dear Angèle, I also kiss your little daughters, for whose sake you must be courageous. My affection and my sympathy are always yours.

C. KORZENIOWSKI.

To R. B. Cunninghame Graham

Sunday Feb. 1898.

CHER AMI,

I've got a bad wrist: that's why I did not write sooner. I gave it complete rest. Much better now.

The "Impenitent Thief" has been read more than once. I've read it several times alone and I've read it aloud to my wife. Every word has found a home. You and your ideals of sincerity and courage and truth are strangely out of place in this epoch of material preoccupations. What does it bring? What's the profit? What do we get by it? These questions are the root of every moral, intellectual or political movement. Into the noblest cause, men manage to put something of their baseness: and sometimes when I think of you here, quietly, you seem to me tragic with your courage, with your beliefs and your hopes. Every cause is tainted: and you reject this one, espouse that other one as if one were evil and the other good, while the same evil you hate is in both, but disguised in different words. I am more in sympathy with you than words can express, yet if I had a grain of belief left in me I would believe you misguided. You are misguided by the desire of the Impossible,—and I envy you. Alas! what you want to reform are not institutions,—it is human nature. Your faith will never move that mountain. Not that I think mankind intrinsically bad. It is only silly and cowardly. Now you know that in cowardice is every evil,—especially, that cruelty so characteristic of our civilization. But, without it, mankind would vanish. No great matter truly. But will you persuade humanity to throw away sword and shield? Can you persuade even me,—who write these words in the fulness of an irresistible conviction? No, I belong to the wretched gang. We all belong to it. We are born initiated, and succeeding generations clutch the inheritance of fear and brutality without a thought, without a doubt, without compunction, in the name of God.

These are the thoughts suggested by the man who wrote an essay on the "Impenitent Thief." Forgive their disconnected impertinence. You'll have to forgive me many things, if you continue to know me on the basis of sincerity and friendship.

I wanted to say a word or so about the technique of the essay but I can't. *A la prochaine, donc!*

To R. B. Cunninghame Graham

5th March '98.
Stanford-le-Hope.

CHER AMI,

I see you don't bear malice for my delays in correspondence so I don't apologize.

The Guide book is simply *magnificent*. Everlastingly good! I've read it last night, having only then returned home. During my visit to the Cranes we talked of you and your work every day. Stephen is a great admirer of yours. The man after all knows something. Harold Frederic [1] also enthused with perfect sincerity. My opinion of them has gone up a hundred points.

Your engineer is immense! Wish I had seen him. It is good of you to think of me when such a subject comes in your way. I never seem to meet any one of that kind,—now. I am on the shelf,—I am dusty.

Yes, we Poles are poor specimens. The strain of national worry has weakened the moral fibre,—and no wonder when you think of it. It is not a fault: it is a misfortune. Forgive my jeremiads. I don't repine at the nature of my inheritance but now and then it is too heavy not *to let out* a groan!

I've sold my American *serial* rights of the *Rescuer* for £250 to McClure (of New York): I'll get another £50 on accept. of book rights in the States (15% royalty). I think,—upon the whole,—this is not bad. Pawling arranged it all for me,—free of charge. The worst is the book

---

[1] One of the most able American authors and journalists of the day; author of *Illuminations:* a friend of Stephen Crane. He died suddenly, very soon after.

is not finished yet and must be delivered end July at the latest. Pawling told me they (Heinemann) are going to publish your book,—the Morocco book I understand. I wait for it anxiously.[1]

My short tales,—*Tales of Unrest,*—shall appear (from Unwin's shop) on the 25th of this month.

Well! Till next time!

P. S. It was Harold Frederic who wrote the criticism of the *Nigger* in the *Sat. Rev.:* He affirmed to me that Runciman had cut out the best passages. I tried to persuade him I did not care a hang,—which is true.

To Edward Garnett

29th March [1898].

MY DEAR GARNETT,

I am ashamed of myself. I ought to have written to you before, but the fact is I have not written anything at all. When I received your letter together with part IInd. of *R.*[2] I was in bed—this beastly nervous trouble. Since then I've been better but have been unable to write. I sit down religiously every morning, I sit down for eight hours every day— and the sitting down is all. In the course of that working day of 8 hours, I write 3 sentences which I erase before leaving the table in despair. There's not a single word to send you. Not one! And time passes —and McClure waits—not to speak of Eternity, for which I don't care a damn. Of McClure however I am afraid.

I ask myself sometimes whether I am bewitched, whether I am the victim of an evil eye? But there is no "jettatura" in England—is there? I assure you—speaking soberly and on my word of honour—that sometimes it takes all my resolution and power of self-control to refrain from butting my head against the wall. I want to howl and foam at the mouth, but I daren't do it for fear of waking that baby and alarming my wife. It's no joking matter. After such crises of despair I doze for hours still half conscious that there is that story I am unable to write. Then I wake up, try again—and at last go to bed completely done-up. So the days pass and nothing is done. At night I sleep. In the morning I get up with the horror of that powerlessness I must face through a day of vain efforts.

In these circumstances you imagine I feel not much inclination to write letters. As a matter of fact I have a great difficulty in writing the most

---

[1] *Mogreb-el-Acksa. A Journey in Morocco,* by R. B. Cunninghame Graham, was about to be published by William Heinemann.

[2] *The Rescuer.*

commonplace note. I seem to have lost all *sense* of style and yet I am haunted, mercilessly haunted, by the *necessity* of style. And that story I can't write weaves itself into all I see, into all I speak, into all I think, into the lines of every book I try to read. I haven't read for days. You know how bad it is when one *feels* one's liver, or lungs. Well, I feel my brain. I am distinctly conscious of the contents of my head. My story is there in a fluid—in an evading shape. I can't get hold of it. It is all there—to bursting, yet I can't get hold of it, any more than you can grasp a handful of water.

There! I've told you all and feel better. While I write this I am amazed to see that I can write. It looks as though the spell were broken, but I must hasten, hasten lest it should in five minutes or in half an hour be laid again.

I tried to correct Part II. according to your remarks. I did what I could—that is I knocked out a good many paragraphs. It's so much gained. As to alteration, rewriting and so on I haven't attempted it— except here and there a trifle—for the reason I could not think out any- thing different to what is written. Perhaps when I come to my senses I shall be able to do something before the book comes out. As to the serial it must go anyhow. I would be thankful to be able to write any- thing, anything, any trash, any rotten thing—something to earn dis- honestly and by false pretences the payment promised by a fool.

That's how things stand to-day; and to-morrow would be more mys- terious if it were not so black! I write you a nice cheery letter for a good-bye:[1] don't I, dear old fellow? That's how we use our friends. If I hadn't written I would have burst.

Good luck to you and *buon' viaggio, signore.* Think of me sometimes. Are you going to Milan? It's twenty-four years since I saw the Cathedral in moonlight.[2] *Tempi passati*—I had young eyes then. Don't give all your time to the worship of Botticelli. Somebody should explode that superstition. But there, *you* know better. It is good of you to think of the boy. He is bigger every day. I would like to make a bargeman of him: strong, knowing his business and thinking of nothing. That is *the* life, my dear fellow. Thinking of nothing! O bliss! I had a lunch with Blackwood, a good old smoothbore. Also Cunninghame Graham came down to see me the day before dining with your father. Has been in bed since but writes every second day. Recommend my short stories to your friend. Have you seen the *Nigger* notice in *Literature* of last week?— Amazing. Jess sends her best love.

Vale frater.

[1] E. G. was about to take a holiday in Italy.
[2] In the summer of the year 1873 (see Chap. I).

To Miss Helen Watson

2nd April 1898
Stanford-le-Hope
Essex.

DEAR MISS WATSON,

Permit me to answer informally and through you the invitation we have had to your wedding since it is to your friendly feeling and your memory that we owe it.

That we cannot give way to our very strong desire to be present at the ceremony is, believe me, the fault of unbending circumstances. The despotism of the baby, my wretched health and the necessities of my work prevent me from leaving home. And, indeed, were there no inexorable obstacles, I would perhaps, perhaps, hesitate out of my sincere affection for you both to show my sour face and (let me charitably say) my constitutional melancholy on the day of all days when all the omens should speak of unalterable serenity, and peace, and joy.

But if the face is sour and the mind (more or less) diseased, the heart, I trust, has not been touched by a subtle evil: and though you who found your worldly welfare upon the uncorruptible promises of Eternity have no need of men's wishes to be the forerunners of your happiness, yet you will allow me to send mine the most true,—the most sincere,— straight from a heart, let us hope, untouched by evil.

Jess joins me in this imperfect expression of feeling. She is happy with your happiness and begs you to believe that her thoughts, like mine, will be with you both on the momentous day. Believe me, dear Miss Watson, with true affection and profound respect.

Your most faithful and obedient servant,
J. CONRAD KORZENIOWSKI.

To R. B. Cunninghame Graham

Thursday. April, 1898.

CHER ET EXCELLENT AMI,

Yesterday I hobbled out and away to London. Not hearing from you, I imagined all kinds of serious things. So I called at Chester Square. The bird was flown! I thought, very good! but had a suspicion you went away too early. Your letter confirms my surmise. I thought it wasn't a common cold you had. If I were you (or rather if you were me) I would take it easy for a couple of weeks. It would pay better in the long run.

The cutting is valuable. Do you possess Lavery's portrait of yourself?

Of Lavery I know only *The Girl in White*, but I know he has done some oriental things.

Don't you take it into your head you are getting old. You are simply run down, and strong men feel it so much more than weaklings like me,—who have felt overtasked ever since the age of 28. True! And yet I had another ten years of sea,—and did my work too. It isn't your body,—it's your brain that is tired. The battery wants re-charging. Time, with common caution, will do that.

My wife was very much concerned about you. Women have a curious insight sometimes. She said to me after you left, "I am sorry Mr. Cunninghame Graham came. He ought to have been at home. I am sure he will be ill."—I said, "Oh bosh! You don't know anything: that kind of man is never ill." I consider you played a mean trick on me with your affectation of influenza. My position as an infallible man is badly shaken at home. I never had it elsewhere.

I am glad you like "Karain." [1] I was afraid you would despise it. There's something magazine'ish about it. Eh? It was written for *Blackwood's*.

There is twilight and soft clouds and daffodils,—and a great wearying. Spring! *Excellentissime,*—Spring! We are annually lured by false hopes. Spring! Another illusion for the undoing of mankind.

Enough!

Do spare yourself, if not for your own sake then for the sake of the horse.

To Mme. Angèle Zagórska [2]

12. 4. 98. Stanford-le-Hope.

MY DEAR ANGÈLE,

Forgive my long silence. The bad state of my health is the reason why the news of our terrible bereavement has put me in such a state of nervous excitement that I am quite unable to follow my thoughts or to write a couple of lines.

I am filled with admiration for your courage and the strength of mind with which you bear this awful blow inflicted by Fate. I have not written, but all the same I can tell you that every day I have been with you in spirit.

The exigencies of life do not bring relief—they only drive back the

---

[1] "Karain" had been published in *Blackwood's Magazine* in November of the previous year and was republished in *Tales of Unrest*.

[2] The original of this letter is in Polish.

outward show of grief. The day before yesterday I returned to my work; it could not be otherwise. And it is thus, with poignant grief in my heart, that I write novels to amuse the English.

I thank you for your letter which I read with much sadness and which brings me nearer to your grief; in sharing your feelings and your sorrow, I do not feel so much alone! I feel as if in sorrow, at least, I were near you. Alas! it is impossible to remove the consciousness of the distance which separates us. There is a wish to take the hand and to hear the sound of the voice, but it cannot be. My wife and child are well, thanks be to God. As for me, I am not ill, but I am not well either. And then the uncertainty of our destiny oppresses me. We live with difficulty, from day to day—*et c'est tout!* My reputation grows, but popularity remains behind. The work is not easy and every day seems more difficult to me. *Que la vie est cruelle et bête!* But enough for to-day.

To ——[1]

23rd April, 1898

MY DEAR SIR,

It is a sore temptation, but I don't think I ought to review Crane's last book. The excellent fellow in the goodness of his heart has been praising me beyond my merits on his own side of the water and his generous utterances have been quoted here. I've not enough standing and reputation to put me above the suspicion of swinging back the censer. Consequently my review would do no good to Crane's work, which deserves a warm appreciation. I've seen many of these stories in MS. and others in proofs and have discussed them all ends up with him; yet what can be said and explained during an all-night talk may wear a different complexion in the cold austerity of print. Upon the whole then I think I had better not. Pardon all this long letter, for the simple purpose of saying no. But I wished you to understand why I can't avail myself of your flattering offer.

To R. B. Cunninghame Graham

1st May, 1898.

CHER ET EXCELLENT AMI,

I take it for granted you are not angry with me for my silence. Wrist bad again, baby ill, wife frightened, damned worry about my work and

---

[1] It has been impossible to trace to whom the above letter was addressed. A copy of it has been sent by Mr. Arthur Stiles of New York, who bought the original a number of years ago.

about other things, a fit of such stupidity that I could not think out a single sentence,—excuses enough in all conscience, since I am not the master but the slave of the *péripéties* and accidents (generally beastly) of existence.

And yet I wanted badly to write, principally to say: *"Je ne comprends pas du tout!"* I had two letters from you. The first announced an enclosure which was not there. The next (a week ago, by the gods!) alluded no doubt to the absent enclosure and said you corrected proof (of a sea-phrase) by wire. It being Saturday I jumped at my No. of the *S. R.*,[1] making sure to see there the story of the Scotch tramp on a Christmas Eve. Nix! Exasperation followed by resignation on reflecting that, unless the world came to a sudden end, I would worm out of you the secret of these letters. I want to know! Istaghfir Allah! O! Sheikh Mohammed! I take refuge with the One, the Invincible.

By all means *Viva l'España!!!!* I would be the first to throw up my old hat at the news of the slightest success.[2] It is a miserable affair whichever way you look at it. Will the certain issue of that struggle awaken the Latin race to the sense of its dangerous position? Will it be any good if they did awaken? Napoleon the Third had that sense and it was the redeeming trait of his rule. But, perhaps, the race is doomed! It would be a pity. It would narrow the life, it would destroy one side of it which had its morality and was always picturesque and at times inspiring. I am sorry, horribly sorry. *Au diable! Après tout, cela doit m'être absolument égal.* But it isn't, for some obscure reason or other. Which shows my folly. Because men are *fourbes, lâches, menteurs, voleurs, cruels,* and why one should show a preference for one manner of displaying these qualities rather than for another, passes my comprehension in my meditative moments.

However, I need not worry about the Latin race. My own life is difficult enough. It arises from the fact that there is nothing handy to steal, and I never could invent an effective lie;—a lie that would sell, and last, and be admirable. This state of forced virtue spreads a tinge of fearsome melancholy over my wasted days. But I am ever yours.

To Edward Garnett

Tuesday (May 1898).

DEAREST G.,

Thanks for your letter. I am glad you like C. Graham, who certainly is unique.

---

[1] *Saturday Review.*
[2] It evidently refers to the Spanish-American War.

As to *Rescue* you are under a "misapyrehension" as Shaw would have said. I intend to write nothing else. I am not even going to finish *Jim* now. Not before Septer. The talk about short stories has been commenced by those men Blackwood and McClure, and, seeing them willing to discuss the future, I gave them an idea of what I would do. The fact however remains that this *Rescue* makes me miserable—frightens me—and I shall not abandon it—even temporarily. I must get on with it, and it will destroy my reputation. Sure!

B[1] has returned yesterday and Meldrum wrote me saying I shall hear from him very soon.

Thanks for your care, for your thought. Alas, no one can help me. In the matter of *Rescue* I have lost all sense of form and I can't see *images*. But what to write I *know*. I have the action, only the hand is paralyzed when it comes to giving expression to that action. If I am too miserable I shall groan to you, O best of men!

To (Sir) Hugh Clifford

Pent Farm.
17 May, 1898.

DEAR MR. CLIFFORD,

It is very good of you to have forgiven me my review of your *Studies*.[2] I suppose you have seen between the lines the feeling which dictated the words. For me to review your work would have been a mere impertinence and I would have left it to some journalist who lives by that kind of thing, had it not been that I meant it for a tribute not only to the charm of the book but to the toil of the man; to the years of patient and devoted work at the back of the pages. This is why, when approached by the *Academy*, I stipulated for my signature. Reviewing is not in my way; I had never done any before and none since. I had rather use my ignorance in other ways—for writing novels, for instance.

I appreciate the more the kind things you say in your letter because I suspect my assumption of Malay colouring for my fiction must be exasperating to those who *know*. It seems as though you had found in my prose some reason for forgiving me. Nothing could be more flattering to a scribbler's vanity or more soothing to the conscience of a man who, even in his fiction, tries to be tolerably true.

---

[1] William Blackwood.

[2] "An Observer in Malay," Joseph Conrad's review of *Studies in Brown Humanity* by Hugh Clifford. This review was published in the *Academy*, April 23, 1898, and was reprinted in *Notes on Life and Letters*.

To Mrs. E. L. Sanderson

3 June, 1898.

DEAR MRS. SANDERSON,

Your letter is all that's good and kind and charming to read and I thank you very much for it. I can't imagine any letter from you that could be anything else to me. So your remarks at the end,—since you know my feeling towards the House of Sanderson, in all its ramifications, —seem not so much the outcome of modesty as of mistrust of my own peevish disposition. You are humbly (but firmly) requested not to do it again. To hint that reading your letter could be for me a loss of time is at least unkind,—if not bitterly ironic. My dear Mrs. Sanderson, the friendships contracted at Elstree, Ted's solid affection, your friendly feeling,—are the clearest gains of my life: and such letters as yours assure me that I've not lost that without which I would be forlorn indeed, and ruined beyond retrieving.

When your letter arrived I was finishing a short story[1] and I put off my answer till the end was reached. Half an hour ago I've written the last word and without loss of time after a short stroll up the meadow, sat down to expostulate with you,—a little,—but mostly to thank you for all you say and for the kindness that shines between the lines of your letter.

I am anxious to see you and Ted in your new house. The servant trouble, the financial shortcomings, are of the kind one gets used to. Just as well one should,—since they are unavoidable. And in time the household machine will run smooth,—but you must not let it grind you small.

And you mustn't let other things grind you at all. In these matters the great thing is to be faithfully yourself. I am quite alive to the circumstances, to the difficulties that surround you. They must be faced *in propria persona,* so to speak. You and Ted,—Ted and You, the two, the one, must meet them by being faithful to yourselves,—and by that alone. This seems vague,—yet it is my clear thought for which I cannot find another form. Nothing more difficult than expression. And if,—at times,—you feel defeated, believe me, it will be a delusion, because no circumstances of man's contriving can be stronger than a personality upheld by faith and conscience. There! I wish I could say something really helpful,—something practical to you,—and here I am unable to present anything but a belief. I believe it is truth. For the rest, I so completely trust your tact and Ted's *instinct* of the world (his knowledge of

---

[1] "Youth."

it of course being greater) that I contemplate your future with interest, with sympathy, but without uneasiness.

There's hardly room left to thank you for the invitation. Of course I am eager to come,—and I shall very soon,—my visit being to St. Mary's.

> Believe me, dear Mrs. Sanderson,
> Your most faithful friend and servant.

Hand-shake to Ted. I am inexpressibly glad to hear good news of his health.

To R. B. Cunninghame Graham

11 June, 1898.

CHER ET EXCELLENT AMI,

Thanks ever so much for the book.

I have read it once so far.

The more I read you the more I admire. This is a strong word but not a bit too strong for the sensation it is supposed to describe. In your wife's sketches I came again with delight upon the hand that had called to life the incomparable saint [1] and the mankind of that place and time.

I and Garnett have used up most of the adjectives we know in talking you over yesterday. He has sent me the "Bloody Niggers" [2] and the "Labour Leader." *Très bien!!*

You are the perfection of scorn,—not vulgar scorn, mind, not scorn that would fit any utterance. No! Scorn that is clear in the thought and lurks in the phrase. The philosophy of unutterable scorn.

Ah! *Amigo de mi corazón* (is that right?) you may fling contempt and bitterness, and wit and hard wisdom, hard unpractical wisdom, at this world and the next,—*l'ignoble boule roulera toujours portant des êtres infimes et méchants dans un univers qui ne se comprend pas lui-même.*

I put first (of yours) *Horses* [3] then *Father Arch.* [4]—or bracket them. But I like every line of the others. Of your wife's *The Will* is a perfect little thing and *Yuste Batuecas* and *Plasencia* [5] are pictures of a rare charm. They breathe like things of life seen in a dream.

---

[1] *Santa Teresa.*

[2] Probably *Niggers,* now in the volume entitled *The Ipané.*

[3] *The Horses of the Pampas.*

[4] "Father Archangel of Scotland and Other Essays," by G. and R. B. Cunninghame Graham. London, Adam & Charles Black, pub. 1896.

[5] *La Vera de Plasencia.*

P. S.—You are the most *undemocratic* of men. By what perversion of sentiment, *vous êtes-vous fourré dans une galère qui n'arrivera nulle part? Du reste, ça importe peu.* The truth of your personality is visible, would be visible anywhere.

P. P. S.—No. *The Vanishing Race* [1] is decidedly first in my affection.

To E. L. Sanderson

15th June '98.

DEAREST OLD TED,

I do not deserve the display of your patience and endurance towards me. It was good and next to angelic to write to me when I had not answered your letter after the end of the honeymoon. I did not answer. I do nothing: I have no time: I shall take arrears of correspondence with me into my grave,—I fear. I am incorrigible.

And by the by: what a good title for a play,—a serious comedy in five acts: *The Incorrigible.* Almost any phase of life could be treated under that title.

Excuse me: I have play on the brain: nothing definite: but *play* in the abstract.

I am coming to see you in your own nest. Every day counts. When I'll get there is another matter. I am in a state of deadly, indecent funk. I've obtained a ton of cash from a Yank under, what strikes me, are false pretences. The Child of the Screaming Eagle is as innocent as a dove. He *thinks* the book he bought will be finished in July while I know that it is a physical and intellectual impossibility to even approach the end by that date. He sends on regular checks which is,—according to his lights,—right: but I pocket them serenely, which,—according to my lights,—looks uncommonly like a swindle on my part. And would you believe it? Sometimes I feel a kind of guilty exultation, a kind of corrupt joy in living thus, on the proceeds of dishonesty. As we get older we get worse. At least some of us do. Others again remain young for ever. Thus the supply of tolerably decent people is kept up.

But as I don't wish to see your door closed against me, I hasten to inform you that, partly from fear and partly from remorse, I have invited the Yank to lunch here to-morrow. In that way I return some part of my ill-gotten gains and may have an opportunity to break the fatal news gently to him. If I survive the interview you shall certainly see me very soon.

[1] *A Vanishing Race,* dealing with the Gauchos of the Pampa.

I am glad you liked my thing in the *Outlook*. Was it the "Views and Reviews" article about Marryat and Cooper? It seems to have pleased various people,—and the Editor (a decent little chap) most of all.[1]

However that kind of thing does not pay.

I have written a species of short story for Blackwood. That pays pretty well. It is a sort of sea narrative without head or tail.[2] When it will appear I don't know, and care not since the cash I've had, I have spent, alas, already.

I am so-so. My wife is pretty well and the boy thrives alarmingly well. To-day is his fifth (monthly) birthday and he has two teeth. Jess sends her kindest regards to you both and I am, speaking to both of you, ever yours.

To R. B. Cunninghame Graham

19 July, 1898.

CHER AMI,

Thanks for *Cyrano*.[3] I haven't yet read it but shall do so before the sun rises again.

I've seen Sir Francis Evans this morning. He was full of business, with twenty people waiting for an interview, but he received me at once and was kindness itself. The upshot of it is this. It is of course impossible to place me in the Union Line,—I said I did not even dream of such a thing but explained that I thought he might have some tramp or good collier. The Company, he said, owns no tramp or colliers, but he might hear of something of the kind and in such a case would let me know. He has my card, but my address is not on it. Perhaps you would drop him a line *pour l'entretenir dans la bonne voie* and mention where I live. He said he would be "extremely pleased to do anything for a friend of Mr. Cunninghame Graham." Thereupon I salaamed myself out and another man rushed in.

Something may come of it. In any case many thanks. Since you have begun that trouble yourself I feel less compunction in asking you to keep it up when an opportunity offers. Now some shadow of possibility to go to sea has been thus presented to me I am almost frantic with the longing to get away. Absurd!

[1] Published under the title of "Tales of the Sea," June 4, 1898. (Now in *Notes on Life and Letters*.)

[2] "Youth" was to be published in *Blackwood's Magazine*, September, 1898.

[3] Edmond Rostand's *Cyrano de Bergerac*, which had just been published.

I return Don Jaime's letter.[1] It is amusing. The glimpse into the *cuisine* of criticism is very entertaining. I would expect anything from a man like Traill.[2] *C'est une vieille ganache.* He wrote once a book about Flaubert for which he deserves to be disembowelled and flung to die on a garbage-heap. Who's Watt? And why is he inimical to the Ingenious Hidalgo, as presented by Don Jaime? *Moi je suis naïf et je ne comprends pas.* Enough of this twaddle.

Mes devoirs à Madame votre femme. Jessie, who sends her kind regards, is as anxious for the sea as I am. She is very touched by your references to Borys in your letters, and full of gratitude for your efforts in my behalf.

To R. B. Cunninghame Graham

Saturday, July 1898.

TRÈS ILLUSTRE SEIGNEUR,

I write at once because to-morrow is Sunday *et dans le village arriéré* where you sojourn now there is no postal delivery to-morrow.[3]

Pourquoi pas? It is a jolly good idea for the play. Of that particular bit of history (and of every other) I have but the slightest, the haziest, idea. In the way of writing I *do not* see your limitations. *Rêvez là-dessus* and something very good may come out of it. You are as romantic as the rest of us. *Nous sommes tous dans cette galère.* The thing is the expression. Now as to that I have no doubt. You'll find it, for the simple reason it is in you. *Il s'agit de fouiller au plus profond* and you will reach the vein. I am only afraid you would make it too good,—much too good for scenic success. The gods are stupid. You'll not be conventional enough for them to understand you.

These are brave oaths! *Ils me mettent du cœur au ventre.* I shall write to you re Sir F. E.[4] when I hear. It seems to me however that it may not happen for a long time,—may never happen! *Quien Sabe? La plus belle fille du monde ne peut donner que ce qu'elle a.* You know this proverb? Therefore if before you return to your native wild you come across the Donald creature,[5] just whisper softly into his ear. I've served in so many Scotch ships (from the *Duke of Sutherland* to the *Highland*

---

[1] A letter from Prof. Fitzmaurice Kelly, professor of Spanish literature at the University of Liverpool.

[2] The Irish poet and critic.

[3] R. B. Cunninghame Graham was then in Scotland.

[4] Sir Francis Evans.

[5] Allusion to Walter Scott's "The Dougald Creature."

Forest,—the list is too long) that I imagine myself to possess some sort of claim. A word from Sir Donald [1] would go a long way with any firm north of the Tweed. Let the big-wigs compete for the honour of employing the immortal author of . . . of . . . I forget now.

I conclude from your letter I shan't see you here this time. *Tant pis.* Let me know when you are passing through London on your way to Morocco. *Veuillez présenter mes très respectueux devoirs à Madame votre femme.*

Borys is better. I find it difficult yet to forgive him for preventing your visit here. *On ne rattrape pas l'occasion qui passe, qui est passée!*

To R. B. Cunninghame Graham

Saturday 30th July, '98.

TRÈS CHER AMI,

This morning I had the *Aurora* [2] from Smithers, No. 2 of the 500 copies.

C'est, tout simplement, magnifique, yet I do not exactly perceive what on earth they have been making a fuss about.

I am afraid Henley [3] is a horrible bourgeois. Who drew the frontispiece? I can't imagine anybody whose name I know. Is it an English drawing? It does not look like it. I notice variations in the text as I've read it in the typewritten copy. This seems the most finished piece of work you've ever done. *Il y a une note, une résonnance là-dedans, vibrant de ligne en ligne. C'est très fort.* No one will see it.

I've read the little book three times, this morning,—and behold! I am disgusted with what I write. No matter.

Blackwood's Magazine for this month has an appreciation of F. M. Kelly's edition of *Don Quixote.* Very fair. Nothing striking, but distinct recognition.

I do like the attitude of the Maga [4] on the Spanish business. [5]

Viva l'España! Anyhow.

Do you believe in a speedy peace? Write me all you know. I would like to see the thing over and done with, though, mind, I think that

---

[1] Sir Donald Currie—head of the Castle Line.

[2] *Aurora la Cujini, a Realistic Sketch in Seville,* by R. B. Cunninghame Graham, with a frontispiece [an ancient Spanish printing]. Leonard Smithers, pub. 1898.

[3] W. E. Henley.

[4] *Blackwood's Magazine.*

[5] The War.

Spain is perfectly invulnerable now and may keep the Yanks capering around for an indefinite time.

When do you start for Morocco?

I've been seedy,—in my head,—in my idiotic *cabeza*. I feel lazy (always did) and sleepy. When I've written a page, I feel it ought to be sold to the ten-cent paper man in New York. This is all it's good for.

C'est Zolaesque ce que je viens d'écrire, hein? But look at the circumlocution. If you want to know how I exactly feel towards my work put the above into plain Zola language and it will give you a faint idea then.

Assez. Toujours le vôtre.

Mes devoirs à Madame votre femme.

To R. B. Cunninghame Graham

3rd Aug. 1898.

EXCELLENT AMI,

Thanks for letter with commission from Sir Donald.

It is sound advice, but does not meet the case. If I wanted to do what he advises I would hunt up some of my old skippers. That however I can't do. It would be giving up everything to begin life for the third time, and I am not young enough for that.

Do not worry about that affair. If I thought that, in the midst of your troubles, my silly desire to get out to sea added to your occupation, my conscience wouldn't let me sleep.

Je suis triste à crever. I think of you preparing your capitulation [1] with fate *et j'ai le cœur gros*. Fourteen years! How much that means in the past,—and for the future too,—since this fight must have grown and taken root in your life.

Toujours à vous de cœur.

Jess sends her best regards. She understands enough to be very sorry. Write only when you have time. Could I do anything in the way of reading the proofs for you?

To R. B. Cunninghame Graham

26th Aug. '98.

CHER ET BON,

I return the pages "To Wayfaring Men." [2] I read them before I read your letter and I have been deeply touched. I think I can understand the

---

[1] R. B. Cunninghame Graham had to sell his Gartmore estate.
[2] Which were to be the preface to *"Mogreb-el-Acksa."*

mood from which the thing flowed. And if I can't understand your mood,—which is probable,—I can understand my own emotion at the reading of these pages,—a silly thing for which you should disclaim responsibility because your words are meant for better men.

Ah! the lone tree on the horizon and then bear a little (a very little) to the right.[1] Haven't we all ridden with such directions to find no house but many curs barking at our heels? Can't miss it? Well, perhaps we can't. And we don't ride with a stouter heart for that. Indeed, my friend, there is a joy in being lost, but a sorrow in being weary.

I don't know whether it is because I know too much,—but there seems to me to be a deeper note in this preface than in any of your writings I've seen. But what business have you, O Man! coming with your uncomprehended truth,—a thing less than mist but black,—to make me sniff at,—the stink of the lamp?

Ride to the tree and to the right,—for verily there is a devil at the end of every road. Let us pray to the poor bellied gods, to gods with more legs than a centipede and more arms than a dozen windmills: let us pray to them to guard us from the mischance of arriving somewhere. As long as we don't pray to the gods made in man's image we are sure of a most glorious perdition.

Don't know tho' I wouldn't give twopence for all its glory,—and I would pray to a god made like a man in the City, and do you know for what? For a little forgetfulness, say half an hour.

Oh bliss! I would give him my soul for it and he would be cheated. To be cheated is godlike. It is your devil who makes good bargains: legends notwithstanding.

Meantime let us look at Soheil[2] and reflect that it is a speck in the eternal night, even as we are. Only we don't shine. At least some of us don't. But we are as celestial as the other bodies,—only we are obscure. At least some of us are. But we all have our illusion of being wayfarers. No more than Soheil, *amigo!*

The appointed course must be run. Round to the left or round to the right, what matters if it is a circle? Ask Soheil. And if you get an answer I shall with my own hands give you a piece of the moon.

I've got your short note. Thanks for sending on my papers. Look here! Shorter[3] of the *Illustrated London News* who bought *Rescue* from McClure suddenly decided to put it into the last quarter of the *News*. Begins in October. I thought I had months before me and am caught. The worst is I had advances from McClure. So I must write or burst.

---

[1] Allusion to the last sentence of the Preface.

[2] The Arab name of a small star. "Show me Soheil and I will show you the Moon," an Arab proverb.

[3] Clement Shorter.

It is too awful. Half the book is not written and I have only to 1st Nov. to finish it. I could not take a command till December because I am in honour bound to furnish the story to time. Yet to go to sea would be salvation. I am really in a deplorable state, mentally. I feel utterly wretched. I haven't the courage to tackle my work.

To R. B. Cunninghame Graham

27 Aug. 1898.

CHER ET EXCELLENTISSIME,

I have been thinking of you every day and more than once a day.

Garnett just left. He showed me your preface to the Fisher Unwin volume of your sketches.[1] We howled with satisfaction over it. *Vous êtes tout-à-fait unique et inimitable.*

He read *Aurora* here. He thinks it is simply great. On the other hand, he abused you bitterly for spoiling the effects of *Victory*. As he said he had written to you about it I shan't repeat his criticism. Moreover I dissent.

Sometimes I feel deeply distressed. At times a little angry. But I think and think,—*et la terre tourne.* How long? O Lord! How long?

If this miserable planet had perception, a soul, a heart, it would burst with indignation or fly to pieces from sheer pity.

I am making desperate efforts to write something. Why the devil did I ever begin? *Que tonteria!*

I am writing *coglionerie,* while I don't know how the Teufel I am going to live next month. The very sea breeze has an execrable taste. *Assez.*

Mes devoirs très respectueux à Madame votre femme. Jess sends her kind regards.

Can't understand Rimbaud [2] at all. You overrate my intelligence. *Je ne suis bon qu'à lire Cyrano* and such like *coglionerie.* That's what I am fit for only since I am no longer fit to carry sacks of wheat in a hold. I wish you would come to shoot me.

To Mrs. E. L. Sanderson

31 August, 1898.

DEAR MRS. SANDERSON,

Thanks for your kind and friendly letter. I have been passing through

[1] *The Ipané.* T. Fisher Unwin, pub. London, 1899.
[2] Arthur Rimbaud, the French poet.

a period of ill health and worries and had no heart to write. It is good of
you to remember me.

I am glad of the good news. Of course I will come if you still want
me. Don't I want to come! If there is a place I wish to see, it is Elstree.

I am in the midst of various difficulties,—but the baby is well. He is
very large and noisy and (they say) intelligent. He has broken ever so
many things,—a proof of intelligence indubitably. He has not put anything together yet and it is that I am anxious to see. He is very preco-
cious and very objectionable. I want Ted to let me know what is the
very earliest age a boy may be sent to school,—say to Elstree?

The *Rescue* is to appear as a serial in the *Illustrated London News,*
to begin on October the first and end with the year. This is sprung on
me suddenly: I am not ready: the "artist" is in despair: various Jews are
in a rage: McClure weeps: threats of cancelling contracts are in the air,
—it is an inextricable mess. Dates are knocked over like ninepins: proofs
torn to rags: copyrights trampled under foot. The last shred of honour
is gone,—also the last penny. The baby, however, is well. He is singing
a song now. I don't feel like singing,—I assure you.

My head feels as if full of sawdust. Of course many people's heads are
full of sawdust,—the tragic part of the business is in my being aware of
it. The man who finds out that apparently innocent truth about himself
is henceforth of no use to mankind. Which proves the saving power of
illusions.

I am like a tight-rope dancer who, in the midst of his performance,
should suddenly discover that he knows nothing about tight-rope danc-
ing. He may appear ridiculous to the spectators, but a broken neck is
the result of such untimely wisdom. I am trying to be as serious as I
know how,—for indeed the matter is serious enough to me.

Still I have till November the 15th to find out whether I can dance
on a tight-rope. That honourable occupation shall engross all my energies,—up to that date. Afterwards,—the deluge, probably. Should I
break my neck, I hope you will sometimes remember the acrobat. If his
head was full of sawdust, his heart,—well, we will not talk of his heart,
since that also must die and turn to dust.

If you catch sight of the brown covers of *Blackwood's Magazine* (for
September) there is a thing of mine there called "Youth: a Narrative,"
and if you have time perhaps you will look at it. I would like you to see
it very much. A bit of life,—nothing more,—not well done,—"a small
thing,—but mine own."

After all,—*chi lo sa?*—perhaps I may yet save my neck. And then
won't I inflict myself on all my friends! It shall be a pilgrimage, beginning at Elstree. Received with kindness, I shall make myself insupport-

able out of pure lightness of heart, and shall depart in the midst of rejoicings. It is too good to come to pass, I fear!

Jessie sends her love. She is pretty well and under proper subjection to the baby.

Believe me, dear Mrs. Sanderson, your most affectionate and obedient friend and servant.

My immense love to dear old Ted. I shall write to him soon,—or at least as soon as I can. I am going to stay with my friend Garnett for a fortnight to do a monstrous heap of work: if a silly novel may be so called.

To H. G. Wells

6th Sept. 1898.
The Cearne.[1]

MY DEAR SIR,

I am profoundly touched by your letter—and [E. V.] Lucas whom I expect to see this evening shall have my warmest thanks for his share in procuring me this unexpected piece of real good fortune.

A few days ago I heard with great concern the news of your illness. It saddened me the more because for the last two years (since your review of the *Outcast* in *Saturday Review* compelled me to think seriously of many things till then unseen) I have lived on terms of close intimacy with you, referring to you many a page of my work, scrutinizing many sentences by the light of your criticism. You are responsible for many sheets torn up and also for those that remained untorn and presently meeting your eye have given me the reward of your generous appreciation.

It has been treasured, and if two letters I wrote to you in that time were never sent it is only a further proof of our intimacy. I had obtained so much from you that it was unnecessary to presume further. And, indeed, there was perhaps a deficiency of courage. I am no more valorous than the rest of us. We all like in our audacities to feel something solid at our backs. Such a *feeling* is unknown to me. This confession is induced by honesty, which you will take for what it is worth. To be dishonest is a dangerous luxury for most of us, I fancy, and I am sure it is so for me.

As to the flaws of "Youth"[2] their existence is indisputable. I felt what you say myself—in a way. The feeling however which induced me to write that story was genuine (for once) and so strong that it poked its way through the narrative (which it certainly defaces) in a good many

---

[1] Joseph Conrad was then at Edward Garnett's.
[2] "Youth" had just been published in *Blackwood's Magazine*.

places. I tell you this in the way of explanation simply. Otherwise the thing is unjustifiable.

Looking at your letter, so dim in the sunlight, I cannot help thinking what a lucky day it was for me when in 1880 [1] I shipped in the *Palestine*. And it was a gloomy, rainy day too. Well. Peace to its ashes. Only four years ago poor old Beard [2] ran after me outside the South West India Dock gates. He was a little greyer, a little more twisted and gnarled. He was very grimy and had a chocolate coloured muffler round his throat. He told me he had piloted a foreigner down the North Sea. His eyes were perfectly angelic. This is not a sentimental exaggeration but an honest attempt to convey the effect. He was so bent that he was always looking upwards, so to speak. In the poky bar of a little pub he told me "Since my wife died I can't rest." He had not been able to snatch her in his arms that time. He said he was glad I "got on" and did not allude to our voyage towards Bangkok. I should think he *can* rest where he is now.

Yes. The story should have been ended where you say or perhaps at the next paragraph describing the men sleeping in the boats. I am afraid I am wearying you not a little, but it has been such a pleasure to talk to you a bit that I gave rein to my ferocious selfishness for once. I would like to hear how your recovery progresses and when you are *going back to work*. May it be soon! I—for one—cannot have enough of your work. *You* have done me good. You have been doing me good every day for many months past. Some day you will perhaps deny me—cast me out—but it will be too late. I shall be always yours.

To H. G. Wells

11th Sept. '98.
Stanford-le-Hope.

MY DEAR MR. WELLS,

I am writing in a state of jubilation at the thought we are going to be nearer neighbours than I dared to hope a fortnight ago. We are coming to live in Pent Farm, which is only a mile or so from Sandling Junction. The other day I met [Edwin] Pugh [3] who told me you are much better and in good spirits. We render thanks to Echmûn the Liberator, the same who in the country of the Greeks is called Æsculapius, and we pour, after the Phœnician manner, a libation of clear water out of a

---

[1] Not in 1880, but in 1881, September 21st.
[2] The late captain of the *Palestine*.
[3] Edwin Pugh had already attracted attention by his publication of some "Sketches" in the *National Observer,* and of a novel, *Tony Drum.*

glass cup, for our means do not run to a cup of gold. As to sacrifices of goats, bulls, lambs and pigs, these are for kings or rich merchants to be offered on altars of temples with priests and ceremonies—but when we meet (soon—let us hope) we shall offer up a piece of ox-flesh on the altar of domestic gods and partake of the holy viands according to prescribed rites in gratitude for your return to health and work.

I am still wretched and ashamed of what I am doing, and only the hope that you all for whose opinion I care will forgive me for the sake of what went before gives me the courage to struggle on. We "take up our residence" at Pent on the 26th of this month and I shall wander out your way soon after that date.

To the Hon. Mrs. Bontine [1]

16th October 1898.
Stanford-le-Hope.
Essex.

DEAR MRS. BONTINE,

I need not tell you with what pleasure I've read your letter so full of that kind of appreciation for which the author's heart yearns and so seldom obtains: and thanks, being mostly ineffective, I will not enlarge on my sentiments of gratitude. The commendation of your son, Charles, is very precious to me. He can appreciate the intention and also the *detail* of my work. His praise has an especial significance to me, for, though no two lives could have been more dissimilar, there is between us that subtle and strong bond of the sea,[2]—the common experience of aspects of sky and water,—of the sensations, emotions, and thoughts that are in greater or lesser degree the companions of men who live upon the ocean. Perhaps you would let him know my feelings, lamely expressed above. I would have written direct had I not been held back by the thought he is a busy man,—and a sailor,—and, in this double capacity, no doubt averse to increasing his correspondence.

My last letter from Robert was from Tangiers, the day after he landed. I can well understand your anxiety. Want of water and wild tribes are dangers, but the absolute magnitude of such perils depends in a great measure upon the man who affronts them. Robert is courageous

---

[1] Anna Elizabeth Elphinstone married in 1851 Major William Cunninghame Graham Bontine of Gartmore and was R. B. Cunninghame Graham's mother. She was seventy years old at the time of the above letter and died a little after Conrad in 1925 at the age of ninety-seven.

[2] "Between the five of us there was the strong bond of the sea," at the beginning of "Youth," which had just been published in *Blackwood's Magazine*.

and foresighted. He has also experience. With his qualities and knowledge he is not likely to proceed rashly. Firmness and tact,—which he
possesses,—go a long way towards minimizing the danger from wild
tribes. The scarcity of water means privation and a call upon endurance,
perhaps, but not necessarily serious danger. I have the greatest confidence
in his management and in the success of his journey. We shall get news,
—and good news,—soon, I think.

"Higginson's Dream" [1] is super-excellent. It is much too good to remind me of any of my work, but I am immensely flattered to learn you
discern some points of similitude. Of course I am in complete sympathy
with the point of view. For the same accomplishment in expression I can
never hope,—and Robert is too strong an individuality to be influenced
by any one's writing. He desired me to correct the proofs, but the *Sat.
Rev.* people did not send me the proofs. I am very much annoyed, for
there is a misprint which makes nonsense of a French phrase. I wrote
them reproachfully when sending the MS. of "Pulperia," [2] which I did
four days ago, and now I clear my character before you as Robert's literary representative.

To your kind inquiries about my wife and boy I am lucky enough to
say they are both very well. In fact, Jessie is better than she has been
for some time. We are leaving Stanford-le-Hope on the 26th Oct. for
good. Our new residence is also a farmhouse, in Kent, near Hythe, and
thus near the sea, though not absolutely in sight of it. I have no ship
(but I still have *la nostalgie de la mer*), though Robert has really done
almost the impossible for me. I did take a run to Glasgow for a day and
saw Dr. McIntyre, who was kindness itself. I am afraid nothing will
come out of it. *Il y a trop de tirage* from novel writing to the command
of a ship, I fear. Moreover I am tied just now by my engagements to
American and English publishers,—engagements I failed lamentably to
keep through nervous ill-health—and I can't think of going away till
I've liberated myself from the incubus of that horrid novel I am trying
to write now. Early next year, when that torment is over (and I am
hardly able to realize that such a time will ever come), I will without
scruple use and abuse everybody's goodwill, influence, friendship to get
back on the water. I am by no means happy on shore.

The fact is that in the *Academy* photograph, it is not my clothes that
are *endimanchés* but my face. The artistic photographer's aim being
always to obliterate every trace of individuality in his subject,—so as
to make a respectable picture. *Voilà! La bêtise étant respectable,* he did
not obliterate that. *"Je trouve que j'ai l'air idiot là-dedans."* But the

---

[1] Published in the *Saturday Review,* October, 1898.

[2] "La Pulperia," published a few days later on in the *Saturday Review,*
October 22, 1898. "Higginson's Dream" and "La Pulperia" are now part of the
book called *Thirteen Stories.*

notice is sympathetic and not commonplace.[1] The man who wrote it is Edward Garnett, a great and discriminating admirer, not only of Robert's works but of his personality, which, he,—in a measure,—understands. This cannot be said of many men (especially literary men) in England.

I do not know whether I outrage *"les règles de la bienséance"* by writing such a long letter. If so, you must forgive me in consideration of my answer to your first letter having been telegraphic. I did not do it for the sake of conciseness however. I was far from home when your letter arrived and on my return, knowing you were about to start on a journey, I wished my answer to find you at home yet. If this excuse is not valid, then by invoking the name of the absent I am sure to be pardoned. Since I learned it was you who first put my work before Robert I consider I owe to you alone one of the most fortunate events of my life,—and they are not numerous. With such a thought and such an obligation a purely ceremonious attitude is impossible. Hence the *abandon* in the matter of the length of this letter. I promise however not to sin very often.

I have grievously sinned towards your nephew. He gave me in the kindest way an invitation to call on him, which I promised to do and did not do. It is not so much through my fault as it may look. I beg for your intercession in getting my *pardon* for what looks like inexcusable negligence. May I be permitted to keep the invitation for future use,— as soon as possible? I have been worried horribly and I have not been well at all. I am haunted by the idea I cannot write,—I dare say a very correct idea too. The harm is in its haunting me. For the last six months, I've not known a minute's real peace of mind. *Enfin! On se fait à tout.* I have got hardened now,—*mais j'ai eu de bien mauvais moments*. With many thanks for remembering me, I beg you to believe me, dear Mrs. Bontine,

Your most faithful and obedient servant.

To John Galsworthy

Pent Farm Postling
Stanford near Hythe.
28 Oct. '98.

MY DEAR JACK,

I turned to you confidently. Your words of cheer are more valuable than all the money in the world,—they help one to live,—while the

[1] The portrait and the notice were published in the *Academy* 15 October, 1898, p. 82.

money enables one only to exist. And yet one must exist before one can even begin to live.

I feel pretty hopeful,—not extravagantly so, which is rather a good sign than otherwise.

I concluded arrangement for collaboration with Hueffer. He was pleased. I think it's all right. Details when we meet.

The first letter in my new home was from you, and you must be the first visitor,—the first friend under the new roof.

To R. B. Cunninghame Graham

Pent Farm,
9th Nov. '98.

TRÈS CHER ET EXCELLENT AMI,

I only got your letter on Monday and the tray came this morning. And for both thanks. We shout cries of welcome. Travelling is victory. As to returning *bredouille,* well, that's better than a crack on the head, —if not for yourself, perhaps (note how the habit of cynicism clings to me) then for your friends. A virtuous man lives for his friends. "Remember this," as the edicts of the Emperor of China conclude.

I was just thinking of sending a note to the Devonshire Club to meet you, when your letter arrived "announcing presents." Days had slipped disregarded, full to the brim with the botheration of moving. Now I am here I like it. I can write a little, a very little. A little is better than nothing, but it is so little that out of the present worries I look with terror into the future still. Oh! the weariness of it, the weariness of it!

They did not send me the proofs of "Higginson's Dream." There is a misprint in French. When sending "Pulperia" I reproached them. They sent me proofs of that but without the MS., so if there is anything wrong, it is not so much of my fault as it may look.

I had a most enjoyable trip to Glasgow. I saw Neil Munro and heaps of shipowners, and that's all I can say. The fact is from novel writing to skippering *il y a trop de tirage.* This confounded literature has ruined me entirely. There is a time in the affairs of men when the tide of folly taken at the flood sweeps them to destruction. *La mer monte, cher ami; la mer monte* and the phenomenon is not worth a thought.

My letter is disjointed because I can't think to-night. I am touched to think that when wandering through the brass-workers' bazaar (in Fez,—was it?) you thought: "There's that Conrad." Well, yes, there he is,—for a little while yet. I have been looking at the thing all day. It has a fascination. I seem to see the face bending over it, the hands that touched it. A brown meagre hand, a hooked profile, a skullcap on a shaven head, lean shanks ending in splay slippers, thus I picture the man who hammered the brass according to the design known to his remote forefathers. Pressing both your hands. Ever yours,

I didn't know the review was by your wife. I liked it immensely. I noted it. I hope her health is good. *Mes hommages les plus respectueux.* I shall levy toll of one copy upon your book,—*comme de juste.*

To H. G. Wells

Pent Farm.
17. Nov. '98.

MY DEAR WELLS,

I was glad to find you well enough to be out for an airing, though of course horribly sorry to miss you. I couldn't wait. A man was coming to see me whom I had to meet at Sandling. I only made a dash to Sandgate to hear how you were getting on. My dear fellow, don't you talk of sunsets in connection with your health or your anything else. Nothing more beastly than a sunset—in the abstract. But practically it argues the possibility of sunrise. I ain't clear. I want to say—think of sunrises. This is obscure. Try to understand and believe I am not intoxicated. Too early. It is the first hour of the day and after breakfast I will be more articulate—but the post will be gone. So I write now— 1 A. M. One is still capable of heroism.

I've been bothering Pugh to come and see me. He may turn up next Saturday week in sheer desperation. If he comes in decent time we might invade you for a couple of hours. Or would you be well enough to come along and sit on us, boys? *Veni, vidi, vici.* You may *veni* by a train that gets to Sandling about 12.40. I would meet you on wheels if you write in time. There is a return train about five—another at six.

We would have called together before this, but Jess is tied to the house. Our girl's temperament was too artistic. She would wander off and disappear for hours at a time. What she found to dream about on country roads, in the mud and after dark, I can't imagine. We aren't straitlaced ourselves but—dash my buttons—she was too unconventional. So we parted suddenly. The noise of that wrench had a melancholy shrillness like the screams of sea gulls. I kept my head throughout, but wouldn't like to go through it again. She departed; another's coming soon, of a philistinish aspect; meantime we stop at home and look after the baby. It takes a minimum of two wideawake persons to ward off the dangers besetting his reckless infancy. So, as I said, we sit at home—and watch.

Let me know about your health. I am not very bright myself. I beg to be remembered to Mrs. Wells. The first fine day (baby permitting) I shall bring my wife to be introduced to her.

To the Hon. Mrs. Bontine

Pent Farm.
22nd Nov. 1898.

DEAR MRS. BONTINE,

Many thanks for your good letter and the enclosed Max Nordau's autograph. Would Robert let me keep it? I own myself surprised. There is not the slightest doubt Max Nordau has understood my intention. He has absolutely detected the whole idea. This to me is so startling that I do not know what to think of myself now. However I am pleased. Praise is sweet, no matter whence it comes. What strikes me as strange is that he writes as though Robert had asked him why he (Robert) liked the book! The expounding attitude is funny,—and characteristic too. He is a Doctor and a Teacher,—no doubt about it. But for all that he is wondrous kind.

When I heard of Robert's decision to return, my first impulse was to rush to a telegraph office and wire you my jubilation, exultation, congratulation. You will not deny he has justified my trust in his judgment and good sense. He has done so much in his life and knows so well what he can do that he would not attempt the impossible, as an untried man could be tempted to do. We exchanged two letters. I think that the trip anyhow has done him good.

My wretched novel begins in April in the *Illustrated London News* as a serial to run 3 months. It will appear in book form in October next.[1] I am afraid that you and Robert will be disappointed. You will *see*, but you will be disappointed. Everybody else won't see,—the idea has the bluish tenuity of dry wood smoke. It is lost in the words, as the smoke is lost in the air. Attempting to tell romantically a love story in which the word love is not to be pronounced seems to be courting disaster deliberately. Add to this that an inextricable confusion of sensations is of the very essence of the tale, and you may judge how much success, material or otherwise, I may expect. *Le lecteur demande une situation nette et des motifs définis.* He will not find it in the *Rescue.*

I can't imagine where we could find a reviewer worthy of Robert and

---

[1] *The Rescuer* was not published in the *Illustrated London News* and had to wait till 1919 for its completion.

of Robert's book. If I could review myself I would do it, and, under the mask of anonymity, give full play to the baseness of my nature. Robert being my friend, *the* friend, it would be sweet to abuse him, with safety and propriety. But seriously speaking, I do not see anybody. Wells (H. G.) does that kind of thing, has intelligence, partly understands Robert, (only partly) and perhaps would like to review. Yet he is scarcely the man. There is Garnett also. But the man is slow and sometimes inarticulate out of the fulness of his heart. There would be no doubt of *his* sympathy and intelligence. Shall I write to him? Perhaps I could work the *Academy*.[1] Ask Garnett first and then set Lucas (one of the *Academy* gang) to work the oracle within the temple, so as to get the book sent to Garnett? I live like a silly hermit and can be of no good to my friends. *Je ne suis pas dans le mouvement.*

On Henry James's last I share your opinion. The second of the *Two Magics* is unworthy of his talent. The first evades one, but leaves a kind of phosphorescent trail in one's mind. *Frederic* for me is unreadable. Mr. Fitzmaurice Kelly's book I have not seen yet but would like to and shall before long.

Thanks for your kind inquiries. My wife and boy are well. We like our new place. I have been horribly seedy with some kind of gout. It always leaves me demoralized and gloomy. I only got up yesterday. Tears besprinkle my manuscript, but my bad language can be heard across the fields even as far as the sea.

Believe me, dear Mrs. Bontine, always your most faithful and obedient servant.

To H. G. Wells

Friday [end of Nov.] '98.
Pent Farm.

MY DEAR WELLS,

I did not nourish robust hopes of seeing you on Sat., the weather was infamous. I have been laid up also, with a kind of gout entertainment which lasted 3 days and of course I can only hobble now it is over. As to struggling over darkling hills, I thought I made it plain enough there are wheels—not of chance,[2] but of certitude. Of course our carcasses, for the sake of their inhabitants, require careful handling, but at all events I am telling you that I shall be (on wheels) at Sandling Junction on Sat. at 12.30 to remove Pugh. Thereafter same wheels could take

---

[1] The magazine of that name.
[2] Allusion to H. G. Wells's *Wheels of Chance*.

you back at five or six. Bringing P. to lunch is another matter. As I tell you, one of my propellers is damaged and done up in flannel—an obscene sight—not to speak of the pain and impiety, for swear words issue from my lips at every step I take. I don't think I really could undertake a journey to Sandgate either to-morrow or on Sunday. I go to the station because P. is a stranger and may starve or otherwise perish in the fields like any other beast unless he is taken care of. But I shall not leave the fly, and I intend to hoot like a sick Martian outside the station.[1] He is sure to be interested by such a remarkable noise and thus he shall find me.

Re Henley.[2] There is a furnished house in Hythe standing isolated at the Sandgate end of Hythe High Street. A red brick thing, rather large. It would do at a pinch—perhaps.

If you have a copy of the *Invisible Man* send it to me. I lent mine to a god-fearing person who stole it. Thus wags the world. I ain't cadging for a gift—it's a loan I want and I will try my best not to steal.

Really, why shouldn't you both come? I take all the transport arrangements upon myself on this end. They *won't* fail. At your end you have omnibuses, if you are not too high-toned to use them. And you may be home at six—and that is virtuous enough. Well, well, I don't want to be a nuisance, I throw out a suggestion like the angler his hook—the rest is with fate—and the gullibility of the fish. Let me also mention that with Mrs. Wells to take care of you you can't come to any harm. On the other hand, Mrs. Wells with your support can affront for a few hours our shabby, wretched, rural bohemianism with a fair chance of surviving the adventure. And we will leave it at that.

To. R. B. Cunninghame Graham

Pent Farm.
1st Dec. 1898.

CHÉRISSIME ET EXCELLENTISSIME,

Your photograph came yesterday (It's good!) and the book arrived by this evening's post.[3] I dropped everything,—as you may imagine,—and rushed at it paperknife in hand. It is with great difficulty I interrupt my reading at the 100th page,—and I interrupt it only to write to you.

A man staying here has been reading over my shoulder, for we share our best with the stranger within our tent. No thirsty men drank water

---

[1] Allusion to H. G. Wells's *The War of the Worlds,* which had just been published in book form.

[2] W. E. Henley.

[3] *Mogreb-el-Acksa. A Journey in Morocco,* by R. B. Cunninghame Graham. William Heinemann, London, 1898.

as we have been drinking in, swallowing, tasting, blessing, enjoying, gurgling, choking over, absorbing, your thought, your phrases, your irony, the spirit of your vision and of your expression. The individuality of the book is amazing even to me who know you or pretend to. It is wealth tossed on the roadside, it is a creative achievement. It is alive with conviction and truth. Men, living men, are tossed to these dogs, the readers; pictures are flung out for the blind; wisdom,—brilliant wisdom,— showered upon fools. You are magnificently generous. You seem to be plunging your hand into an inexhaustible bag of treasure and fling precious things at every paragraph. We have been shouting, slapping our legs, leaping up, stamping about. There was such an enthusiasm in this solitude as will meet no other book. I do not know really how to express the kind of intellectual exultation your book has awakened in me: and I will not stay to try: I am in too great a hurry to get back to the book. My applause, slap on the back, salaams, benedictions, cheers. Take what you like best of these, what you think most expressive. Or take them all.

I can't be too demonstrative.

Ever yours with yells.

Why did you tug in J. C. into your pages. Oh why? Why take a sinner on your back when crossing a stream?

To the Hon. Mrs. Bontine

Pent Farm.
4th Dec. 1898.

DEAR MRS. BONTINE,

Just a word or two about Robert's book.[1] It is a glorious performance. Much as we expected of him, I, and two men who were staying with me when my copy arrived, have been astonished by the completeness of the achievement. One said: "This is *the* book of travel of the century." It is true. Nothing approaching it had appeared since Burton's *Mecca.* And, as the other man pointed out, judging the work strictly as a book, —as a production of an unique temperament,—Burton's *Mecca* is nowhere near it. And it is true. The *Journey in Morocco* is a work of art. A book of travel written like this is no longer a book of travel,—it is a creative work. It is a contribution not towards mere knowledge but towards *truth,*—to truth hidden in men,—in things,—in life,—in nature, —to the truth only exceptional men can see, and not every exceptional man can present to the ordinary dim eyes of the crowd.

[1] *Mogreb-el-Acksa. A Journey in Morocco,* by R. B. Cunninghame Graham.

He is unapproachable in acuteness of vision,—of sympathy: he is alone in his power of expression: and through vision, sympathy and expression runs an informing current of thought as noble, unselfish and human as is only the gift of the best.

The book pulled at my very heartstrings. *Et voilà!* I've been trying to tell you this,—and only this,—from the first page to this line. *Je ne parle pas de son esprit. Chaque page en est un exemple, chaque phrase en est une preuve. Le livre est rempli d'un charme étrange et pénétrant. C'est bien là la terre, les hommes, le ciel, la vie! Cette œuvre brilliante* [sic] *laisse dans l'âme du lecteur comme une traînée de lumière.*

I must close this macaronic letter. I could write on for ever and just to so little purpose. Believe me, dear Mrs. Bontine, your most faithful and most obedient servant.

Je viens de recevoir une lettre du Sérénissime Seigneur.[1] *Il se dit triste. Pourquoi!* He seems also uncertain about the book. Exactly. The poor man is quite incapable of judging impartially, or even sensibly, the work of Mr. C. Graham. A man who can write like this is a creator,— not a critic.

To H. G. Wells

Pent Farm.
4th Dec. 1898.

MY DEAR WELLS,

Thanks ever so much for the *Invisible Man*. I shall keep him a few days longer.

Frankly—it is uncommonly fine. One can always *see* a lot in your work—there is always a "beyond" to your books—but into this (with due regard to theme and length) you've managed to put an amazing quantity of effects. If it just misses being tremendous, it is because you didn't make it so—and if you didn't, there isn't a man in England who could. As to b—— furriners they ain't in it at all.

I suppose you'll have the common decency to believe me when I tell you I am always powerfully impressed by your work. Impressed is *the* word, O Realist of the Fantastic! whether you like it or not. And if you want to know what impresses me it is to see how you contrive to give over humanity into the clutches of the Impossible and yet manage to keep it down (or up) to its humanity, to its flesh, blood, sorrow, folly. *That* is the achievement! In this little book you do it with an appalling

---

[1] R. B. Cunninghame Graham.

completeness. I'll not insist on the felicity of incident. This must be obvious even to yourself. Three of us have been reading the book (I had two men staying here after Pugh left) and we have been tracking with delight the cunning method of your logic. It is masterly—it is ironic—it is very relentless—and it is very true. We all three (the two others are no fools) place the *I.M.* above the *War of the Worlds*. Whether we are right—and if so why—I am not sure, and cannot tell. I fancy the book is more strictly human, and thus your diabolical psychology plants its points right into a man's bowels. To me the *W. of the W.* has less of that sinister air of truth that arrests the reader in reflexion at the turn of the page so often in the *I.M.* In reading this last, one is touched by the anguish of it as by something that any day may happen to oneself. It is a great triumph for you.

My compliments to Mrs. Wells. How are you? I am not well—I am eating my heart out over the rottenest book that ever was—or will be.[1]

To R. B. Cunninghame Graham

Pent Farm.
9th Dec. 1898.

MY DEAREST AMIGO,

I wrote to your mother about your book. I found it easier to speak to a third person,—at first. I do not know what to tell you. If I tell you that you have surpassed my greatest expectations you may be offended, —and this piece of paper is not big enough to explain how great my expectations were. Anyway, thus left behind, I am ashamed of my moderation and now I am looking at the performance I ask myself what kind of friend was I not to foresee, not to understand, that the book would just be *that*,—for our joy, for our thought, for our triumph. I am speaking of those who understand and love you. The preface [2] is a gem,—I knew it, I remembered it, and yet it came with a fresh force. To be understood is not everything,—one must be understood as one would like to be. This probably you won't have.

Yes, the book is Art. Art without a trace of Art's theories in its incomparably effective execution. It isn't anybody's art,—it is C. Graham's art. The individuality of the work imposes itself on the reader, from the first. Then come other things, skill, pathos, humour, wit, indignation. Above all a continuous feeling of delight: the persuasion that there one

---

[1] It refers to *The Rescuer.*
[2] Preface in the way of a dedication "To Wayfaring Men."

has got hold of a good thing. This should work for material success. Yet who knows! No doubt it is too good.

You haven't been careful in correcting your proofs. Are you too *grand seigneur* for that *infect* labour? Surely I, twenty others, would be only too proud to do it for you. *Tenez-vous le pour dit*. I own I was exasperated by the errors. Twice the wretched printers perverted your meaning. It is twice too often. They should die!

I write because I can't come. Can't is the truth. I am sorry to hear of your depression,—but O friend, who isn't,—(I mean depressed). I am not able to say one cheering word. It seems to me I am disintegrating slowly. Cold shadows stand around. Never mind.

I thought it was next Tuesday you were coming to town. Stupid of me. Now this letter'll be probably too late to catch you. I am very sorry to hear of your wife's indisposition. Remember me to her, please. I trust she is better.

I daren't ask you to come down. I am too wretched, and it's worse than the plague.

Au revoir.

To Mme Angèle Zagórska [1]

Pent Farm, Stanford.
18. 12. 1898.

MY DEAR ANGÈLE,

If I did not believe in the constancy of your sentiments towards me I would not dare write to you after so long a silence. As a matter of fact, my dear, I have been in a wretched state of health—miserable rather than bad—and I preferred not to weary or tire you with the sadness of my letters. And also I was ashamed to display before you—who are so brave among the difficulties and trials of life—my foolish and not very praiseworthy pessimism.

This is how the days, weeks and months go by; I waited—always thinking of you, with my pen ready to write—I waited for a moment of lucidity, of calmness, of hope. It is long in coming. And now the end of the year festivities are upon us. I must implore your pardon, express what I feel—promise to amend for the hundredth or thousandth time, according to the sinner's ways.

As you will see, we have come to live here; this is also a farmhouse, somewhat small, but more convenient and, what is most important, it is situated on higher ground. I found that I could not work in our old place.

---

[1] Original of this letter in Polish.

It is better here although I have nothing to boast about. We are only five kilometres from the sea. The railway station is 3 kilometres and Canterbury 1½ kils. away. Before my window I can see the buildings of the farm, and on leaning out and looking to the right, I see the valley of the Stour, the source of which is almost behind the third hedge from the farmyard. Behind the house are the high Kentish Downs which slope in zigzag fashion down to the sea, like the battlements of a fortress. A path runs along the foot of the hills along the house—a very lonely and straight path, and along which (so it is whispered) old Lord Roxby —he died 80 years ago—rides sometimes at night in a four-in-hand which he drives himself. What is rather strange, however, is that he has no head. Why he should leave his head at home while he takes a ride, nobody can explain. But I must tell you that during the two months we have lived here, we have not yet heard the noise of any wheels and although I sometimes walk along this road near midnight, I have never met a four-in-hand. On the other side of the little garden stretch out quiet and waste meadows intersected by hedges and here and there stands an oak or a group of young ash trees. Three little villages are hidden among the hillocks and only the steeples of their churches can be seen. The colouring of the country presents pale brown and yellow tints—and in between, in the distance, one can see the meadows, as green as emeralds. And not a sound is to be heard but the laboured panting of the engines of the London-Dover express trains.

We live like a family of anchorites. From time to time a pious pilgrim *appartenant à la grande fraternité des lettres* comes to pay a visit to the celebrated Joseph Conrad—and to obtain his blessing. Sometimes he gets it and sometimes he does not, for the hermit is severe and dyspeptic *et n'entend pas la plaisanterie en matière d'art*. At all events, the pilgrim receives an acceptable dinner, a Spartan's bed—and he vanishes. I am just expecting one to-day. The author of *Jocelyn*,[1] which he dedicated to me! The novel is not remarkable, but the man is very pleasant and kind —and rich, *que diable fait-il dans cette galère*—where we are navigating whilst using pens by way of oars—on an ocean of ink—*pour n'arriver nulle part, hélas!*

Jessie is dreaming of a visit to Poland—which to her means a visit to you. And I am dreaming the same. *Pourquoi pas?* It costs nothing to journey in thought amongst those we love. It costs nothing—only a little heartache when we find how far the dream is from the reality. Now the holidays are drawing near.

[1] John Galsworthy.

To H. G. Wells

Pent Farm.
23rd Dec. 1898.

MY DEAR WELLS,

We called yesterday by an act of inspiration, so to speak, and with the neglect of common civilities did so at 2.45 P. M., for which we were very properly punished by not finding you at home. We would have waited, but we'd left the baby in the gutter (there was a fly under him tho') and the days are too short to allow of camping in a friend's drawing room. So we went despondently. And by the by, there was an Invisible Man (apparently of a jocose disposition) on your doorstep, because when I rang (modestly), an invisible finger kept the button down (or in, rather) and the bell jingling continuously to my extreme confusion (and the evident surprise of your girl). I wish you would keep your creations in some kind of order, confined in books or locked up in the cells of your brain, to be let out at stated times (frequently, frequently of course!) instead of letting them wander about the premises, startling visitors who mean you no harm—anyhow my nerves can't stand that kind of thing—and now I shan't come near you till next year. There!

Coming back we found your card. We haven't cards. We ain't civilized enough—not yet. But the wishes for the health, happiness and peace of you both I am writing down here in mine and my wife's name are formulated with primitive sincerity, and the only conventional thing about them is the time of their voicing prescribed by the superstitions of men. Thus are we the slaves of a gang of fools unable to read your work aright and unwilling to buy a single entire edition of any of mine. Verily they deserve to have the Heat-Ray turned upon them [1]—but I suppose it would be unseasonable just now. Conventions stand in the way of most meritorious undertakings.

Has Henley come down here after all? When you favour me with a missive let me know how he is, if you know.

To Mme. Angèle Zagórska [2]

Christmas 1898.

DEAR ANGÈLE,

I have just received your letter and I am replying to it at once. The news that you give me distresses me. For me also, my dearest, *la vie est dure—très dure.*

[1] Allusion to *The War of the Worlds.*
[2] Original of this letter in Polish.

I shall send you some cuttings (in envelopes, like letters) from the *Saturday Review* and other reviews which deal with literature—and I shall add occasionally some notes taken by myself.

With regard to Grant Allen's *Woman Who Did, c'est un livre mort.* The *Woman Who Did* had a kind of success, of curiosity mostly and that only amongst the philistines—the sort of people who read Marie Corelli and Hall Caine. All three are very popular with the public— and they are also puffed in the press. There are no lasting qualities in their work. The thought is commonplace and the style (?) without any distinction. They are popular because they express the common thought, and the common man is delighted to find himself in accord with people he supposes distinguished. This is the secret of many popularities. (You can develop this idea as an explanation of the enthusiasm of the public for books which are of no value.) As to Allen, he is considered a man of letters among scholars and a scholar among men of letters. He writes popular scientific manuals equally well. Marie Corelli is *not* noticed critically by the serious reviews. She is simply ignored. Her books sell largely. Hall Caine is a kind of male Marie Corelli.

Among the people in literature who deserve attention the first is Rudyard Kipling (his last book *The Day's Work,* novel), J. M. Barrie —a Scotsman. His last book *Sentimental Tommy* (last year). George Meredith did not bring out anything this year. The last volumes of the charming translation of Turgeniev came out a fortnight ago. The translation is by Mrs. Constance Garnett. George Moore has published the novel *Evelyn Innes—un succès d'estime.* He is supposed to belong to the naturalistic school and Zola is his prophet. *Tout ça, c'est très vieux jeu.* A certain Mr. T. Watts-Dunton published the novel *Aylwin,* a curiosity success, as this Watts-Dunton (who is a barrister) is supposed to be the friend of different celebrities in the world of Fine Arts (especially in the pre-Raphaelite School). He has crammed them all into his book. H. G. Wells published this year *The War of the Worlds* and *The Invisible Man.* He is a very original writer with a very individualistic judgment in all things and an astonishing imagination.

But, my dearest, really I read nothing and I never look at the papers, so I know nothing of politics or literature. I have barely time to write, for I find work very hard and it is only with difficulty that I can earn a little bread. This is the whole truth.

I shall see Mr. Wells in a few days and I will ask him on your behalf for permission to translate *The Invisible Man* into Polish. If I can arrange this I will send you the book. The language is easy—the story very interesting; it would make a very good serial for a paper. If you undertook this work and if you would send me the sheets as and when you finish them, I shall put notes in the margin which may help you. But you certainly know English as well as I do—and I do not speak of your Polish!

For the moment I am not writing anything. Since the month of January, I have been in such a state that I have been unable to write anything. It was not until November that I started to work. The novel which was ordered from me is 6 months behind. This is ruin! and even now I am not at all well.

I kiss your hands. I embrace my little cousins.

Yours with all my heart,
K. KORZENIOWSKI.

P. S. With what I have written you and two books to review, *on peut faire un article,—pas une chose profonde, mais du bon journalisme.* Try. I will send you, at the same time as the cuttings, a few notes about the authors—if I know anything about them. This is what the papers want. A chat, an appreciation, something light and interesting. *Du journalisme tout pur.* If you begin writing, try to do it. It always pays.

To the Hon. Mrs. Bontine

Pent Farm.
12th Jan. 1899.

DEAR MRS. BONTINE,

My humble apology for not thanking you before for the volume of verses.[1] I share your opinion of Maupassant. The man is a great artist, who sees the essential in everything. He is not a great poet,— perhaps no poet at all, yet I like his verses. I like them immensely.

To-day, from your kindness, I received the *Chronicle* with Robert's letter. *C'est bien ça,—c'est bien lui!*

Is he in London now? I have it on my conscience that I did, not reply yet to his last letter. I couldn't. A fit of silence. I had too much to say perhaps,—and perhaps nothing. *Je deviens bête et sauvage.*

Pardon this hurried scrawl. I am finishing in a frightful hurry a story for *B'wood* and it's an immense effort.[2]

With many thanks I am, dear Mrs. Bontine, always your most faithful and obedient servant.

[1] Guy de Maupassant's *Des Vers*.
[2] "Heart of Darkness."

To R. B. Cunninghame Graham

Pent Farm.
2nd Feb. 1899.

CHER ET EXCELLENT AMI,

I haven't two ideas in my head and I want to talk to you all the same. Horrid state to be in.

Pawling says your book is going off. The reviews are *good* tho' positively repulsive. *Que voulez-vous!* They are good selling reviews.

We sang songs of praise before your greatness this morning, with E. G.[1] preparing your Unwin vol.[2] for the press. May the best of luck attend it.

A thing of mine began in *B'wood's* 1000th No. to conclude in Feb.[3] I am shy of sending it to you,—but have no objection to you looking at it if it should come in your way.

Don't, don't ask about the *Rescue*. It will be finished about end March unless it makes an end of me before.

I was in London one day, amongst publishers and other horrors. My heart is heavy but my spirits are a little better.

McIntyre[4] is really "impayable,"—and so are you. D'ye think the shipowners of "Glesga" are gone mad? They will never, never give a ship to a "chiel" that can write prose,—or who is even suspected of such criminal practices.

I am writing an idiotic letter. If I could tell really what I feel for you, for your work and for the spirit that abides in the acts and the thoughts of your passages amongst this jumble of shadows and—well—filth which is called the earth, you would think it fulsome adulation. So I won't say anything and shall hug myself with both hands in the assurance of your friendship.

This is stupidly put and a cynic would say it was stupidly felt. *Are* you a cynic?

Quelle bête de vie! Nom de nom, quelle bête de vie! Sometimes I lose all sense of reality, as a kind of nightmare effect produced by existence. Then I try to think of you,—to wake myself. And it does wake me. I don't know how you feel about yourself but to me you appear extremely real,—even when I perceive you enveloped in the cloud of your irremediable illusions.

[1] Edward Garnett.
[2] *The Ipané.*
[3] It was published in *Blackwood's Magazine,* February, March, and April issues, under the title, "The Heart of Darkness."
[4] A doctor of Glasgow.

I had better stop before I say something that would end in bloodshed.
Now I haven't said anything and that's enough.

> Ever desperately yours,

To Mme Angèle Zagórska [1]

> Pent Farm, 7. 2. '99.

DEAR ANGÈLE,

Just a few lines in answer to your letter, for which I thank you.
I have seen Mr. Wells, who considers it an honour that his works
should be translated into Polish. You must know that the *Mercure de
France* has finished the publication of his novel, *Time-Machine*.

In two days I will send you the book. You can introduce the translation as being authorized by the author. If a newspaper publishes it,
you could suggest a short sketch to the Manager and an appreciation of
the author—introduced to the Polish public, as it were—by myself—
about 500–1000 words. But only in the event of this being of any use
to place the novel.

I am not sending you any cuttings, as there is nothing of any interest.
I will send you soon a notice on Miss Kingsley's book on Africa. *C'est
un voyageur et un écrivain très remarquable.* Her opinions on questions
dealing with colonies are thought a great deal of.

Here is the photo of Mr. Borys, *agé d'un an et deux jours.* His
mamma, who sends you "lots of love," is not good. She looks like a
very stout old woman—which she is not yet.

Your card written in English is almost without a mistake. Evidently
you have a practical knowledge of the language. *Cela se voit.*

Forgive this hasty letter, but I am awfully busy and surrounded
with these wretched editors.

> A thousand embraces
> Your KONRAD KORZENIOWSKI.

To (Sir) Algernon Methuen

> Pent Farm,
> 7th Feb. 1899.

DEAR SIR,

Forgive the delay in answering your friendly and flattering letter;
but I was away from home and on my return having a story to finish

---

[1] The original of this letter is in Polish.

for "Maga" [1] I left, according to my practice, all my letters unopened. Thus the delay is the fault of the system not of the man.

Frankly, I am such an unsatisfactory person that giving promises for books should be the last thing for me to do. I am so unsatisfactory that I am not at all sure of appearing in the *Ill: London News*. I've inconvenienced Mr. Shorter. I know it because he said so to me in writing a few days ago. I made a suitable reply—I mean suitable to my state of mind. And this is the last I know of the affair. However, the book is promised; has been so for this year past.

Candidly I dare not make any promises. I write with difficulty, I don't keep my word, I worry my publishers, I try their tempers. I am afraid it would take much better writing than mine to make up for these defects—of character.

To R. B. Cunninghame Graham

8th Feb. 1899.

CHÉRISSIME AMI,

I am simply in the seventh heaven to find you like the "H. of D." [2] so far. You bless me indeed. Mind you don't curse me by and bye for the very same thing. There are two more instalments in which the idea is so wrapped up in secondary notions that you,—even you!—may miss it. And also you must remember that I don't start with an abstract notion. I start with definite images and as their rendering is true some little effect is produced. So far the note struck chimes in with your convictions,—*mais après?* There is an *après*. But I think that if you look a little into the episodes, you will find in them the right intention, though I fear nothing that is practically effective.

Somme toute, c'est une bête d'histoire qui aurait pu être quelque chose de très bien si j'avais su l'écrire.

The thing on West. Gar. is excellent, excellent. I am most interested in your plans of work and travel. I don't know in which most. *Nous allons causer de tout cela.*

As to the peace meeting. If you want me to come I want still more to hear you. But,—I am not a peace man, not a democrat (I don't know what the word means really), and if I come, I shall go into the body of the hall. I want to hear you,—just as I want always to read you. I can't be an accomplice after or before the fact to any sort of fraternity that includes the westerness [?] whom I so dislike. The

---

[1] *Blackwood's Magazine.*
[2] "Heart of Darkness."

platform! *Y pensez-vous? Il y aura des Russes. Impossible!* I cannot admit the idea of fraternity, not so much because I believe it impracticable, but because its propaganda (the only thing really tangible about it) tends to weaken the national sentiment, the preservation of which is my concern. When I was in Poland 5 years ago [1] and managed to get in contact with the youth of the University in Warsaw I preached at them and abused them for their social democratic tendencies. *L'idée démocratique est un très beau phantome,* [sic] and to run after it may be fine sport, but I confess I do not see what evils it is destined to remedy. It confers distinction on Messieurs Jaurès, Liebknecht & Co. and your adhesion confers distinction upon it. International fraternity may be an object to strive for, and, in sober truth, since it has your support I will try to think it serious, but that illusion imposes by its size alone. *Franchement,* what would you think of an attempt to promote fraternity amongst people living in the same street, I don't even mention two neighbouring streets? Two ends of the same street.

There is already as much fraternity as there can be,—and that's very little and that very little is no good. What does fraternity mean? Abnegation,—self-sacrifice means something. Fraternity means nothing unless the Cain-Abel business. That's your true fraternity. *Assez.*

L'homme est un animal méchant. Sa méchanceté doit être organisée. Le crime est une condition nécessaire de l'existence organisée. La société est essentiellement criminelle,—ou elle n'existerait pas. C'est l'égoïsme qui sauve tout,—absolument tout,—tout ce que nous abhorrons, tout ce que nous aimons. Et tout se tient. Voilà pourquoi je respecte les extrêmes anarchistes.—"Je souhaite l'extermination générale." Très bien. C'est juste et ce qui est plus, c'est clair. On fait des compromis avec des paroles. Ça n'en finit plus. C'est comme une forêt où personne ne connaît la route. On est perdu pendant que l'on crie: "Je suis sauvé."

Non. Il faut un principe défini. Si l'idée nationale apporte la souffrance et son service donne la mort, ça vaut toujours mieux que de servir les ombres d'une éloquence qui est morte, justement parce qu'elle n'a pas de corps. Croyez-moi si je vous dis que ces questions-là sont pour moi très sérieuses,—beaucoup plus que pour Messieurs Jaurès, Liebknecht et Cie. Vous,—vous êtes essentiellement un frondeur. Cela vous est permis. Ce sont les nobles qui ont fait la Fronde, du reste. Moi, je regarde l'avenir du fond d'un passé très noir et je trouve que rien ne m'est permis hormis la fidélité à une cause absolument perdue, à une idée sans avenir.

Aussi, souvent, je n'y pense pas. Tout disparaît. Il ne reste que la vérité,—une ombre sinistre et fuyante dont il est impossible de fixer

---

[1] Conrad means in August, 1893.

l'image. Je ne regrette rien,—je n'espère rien, car je m'aperçois que ni le regret ni l'espérance ne signifient rien à ma personnalité. C'est un égoïsme rationnel et féroce que j'exerce envers moi-même. Je me repose là-dedans. Puis, la pensée revient. La vie recommence, les regrets, les souvenirs et un désespoir plus sombre que la nuit.

Je ne sais pas pourquoi je vous dis tout cela aujourd'hui. C'est que je ne veux pas que vous me croyiez indifférent. Je ne suis pas indifférent à ce qui vous intéresse. Seulement mon intérêt est ailleurs, ma pensée suit une autre route, mon cœur désire autre chose, mon âme souffre d'une autre espèce d'impuissance. Comprenez-vous? Vous qui dévouez votre enthousiasme et vos talents à la cause de l'humanité, vous comprendrez sans doute pourquoi je dois,—j'ai besoin,—de garder ma pensée intacte comme dernier hommage de fidélité à une cause qui est perdue. C'est tout ce que je puis faire. J'ai jeté ma vie à tous les vents du ciel, mais j'ai gardé ma pensée. C'est peu de chose,—c'est tout, ce n'est rien,—c'est la vie même.

Cette lettre est incohérente comme mon existence, mais la logique suprême y est pourtant,—la logique qui mène à la folie. Mais les soucis de tous les jours nous font oublier la cruelle vérité. C'est heureux.

Toujours à vous de cœur.

P. S. Jessie sends her kind regards and thanks for message about the story. It delights. I shall talk with Garnett about your work. He is a good fellow. Eye and ear? Eh? Not so bad. Only if I *could* write like you—if I *knew* all you know,—if I *believed* all you believe! If, if, if!

To John Galsworthy

Pent Farm.
Sunday evening [Feb. 11, 1899].

DEAREST JACK,

Yes, it is good criticism. Only I think that to say Henry James does not write from the heart is maybe hasty. He is cosmopolitan, civilized, very much *homme du monde* and the acquired (educated if you like) side of his temperament,—that is,—restraints, the instinctive, the nurtured, fostered, cherished side is always presented to the reader first. To me even the R. T.[1] seems to flow from the heart because and only because the work, approaching so near perfection, yet does not strike cold. Technical perfection, unless there is some real glow to illumine and warm it from within, must necessarily be cold. I argue that in H. J.

[1] *The Real Thing and Other Tales* published in 1893.

there is such a glow and not a dim one either, but to us used, absolutely accustomed, to unartistic expression of fine, headlong, honest (or dishonest) sentiments the art of H. J. does appear heartless. The outlines are so clear, the figures so finished, chiselled, carved and brought out that we exclaim,—we, used to the shades of the contemporary fiction, to the more or less malformed shades,—we exclaim,—stone! Not at all. I say flesh and blood,—very perfectly presented,—perhaps with too much perfection of *method*.

The volume of short stories entitled, I think, *The Lesson of the Master* contains a tale called "The Pupil," if I remember rightly, where the underlying feeling of the man,—his really wide sympathy,—is seen nearer the surface. Of course he does not deal in primitive emotions. I maintain he is the most civilized of modern writers. He is also an idealizer. His heart shows itself in the delicacy of his handling. Things like "The Middle Years" and "The Altar of the Dead" in the vol. entitled *Terminations* would illustrate my meaning. Moreover, your cousin admits the element of pathos. Mere technique won't give the elements of pathos. I admit he is not *forcible*,—or let us say, the only forcible thing in his work is his technique. Now a literary intelligence would be naturally struck by the wonderful technique, and that is so wonderful in its way that it dominates the bare expression. The more so that the expression is only of delicate shades. He is never in deep gloom or in violent sunshine. But he feels deeply and vividly every delicate shade. We cannot ask for more. Not everyone is a Turgeniev. Moreover Turgeniev is not civilized (therein much of his charm for us) in the sense H. J. is civilized. *Satis*. Please convey my defence of the *Master* with my compliments. My kindest and grateful regards to Mrs. Sauter [1] and love to the boy. The finishing of "H. of D" [2] took a lot out of me. I haven't been able to do much since.

To Mrs. E. L. Sanderson

Pent Farm.
26th Feb. 1899.

DEAR MRS. SANDERSON,

I ought to have thanked you for your letter before. We have read it with delight, and we take the full share of friendship in your happiness and joy.

How good of you to write at length of your dear daughter. The names

[1] John Galsworthy's sister.
[2] "Heart of Darkness" had just been completed.

are pretty, very pretty, and I have not the slightest doubt she lives and shall live up to her names.

I am glad to hear Ted makes a satisfactory nurse. I was a complete duffer at that business, being, as a matter of fact, horribly frightened of the baby. I've now got over my timidity, but then the boy is no longer a baby. He only disconcerts me by his unexpected knowledge of the world and of human nature, so that I feel I cannot be cautious enough in my dealings with him. As it is, he has me always at a disadvantage in every personal discussion. He is also very rowdy and can be naughty in more different ways than I could have imagined. One is amused, and at the same time one has a feeling of being confronted by a grave problem.

I don't mind owning I wished for a daughter. I can't help thinking she would have resembled me more and would have been perhaps easier to understand. This is a selfish feeling, I admit: but boy or girl, they are very interesting and infinitely touching. I can't confess to any reverential feeling for childhood. I've heard people, more or less sentimental, talk about it, but I question whether it is not a rather artificial attitude. It is their humanity that is so endearing, their nearness to the angels. Perhaps it is only my propensity to make the best, not of things in general, but to make the best of the worst which induces me to take their view. It may be bad for me, but I am sure it is good for Borys, because if my affection for him depended on his angel-like qualities, it would be very evanescent. At the age of thirteen months he is an accomplished and fascinating barbarian full of charming wiles and of pitiless selfishness. It is not his innocence but his unconsciousness that makes him pathetic,—besides making him just bearable.

I am writing you a twaddling letter. You must forgive,—if you can detect,—the tinge of cynicism upon my opinions. It is a false light after all. At the bottom of all these cheap reflections there is love for the young souls committed to our blind guardianship, which must fit them for the hazard of life.

I would immensely like to meet Mr. Lynch,—but in any case as soon as I am out of my difficulties I shall come to Elstree. My difficulties may appear to you interminable. It seems to me it is years and years since I first began to afflict and exasperate my friends with these dark allusions to a perfectly clear matter, my inability to work fast enough to get my living. It is ridiculous and sad and wearisome, and that it is true does not make it any less offensive.

Jess sends her love to you and the baby. She has declared to me she "imagines" the baby perfectly. I fancy I also do. We trust we may hear often from you three, but I've become such a wretched correspondent that I hardly dare to hope for forgiveness from my best friends.

Believe me, dear Mrs. Sanderson, your very affectionate friend and obedient servant.

To R. B. Cunninghame Graham

Pent Farm.
26th Feb. 1899.

TRÈS CHER ET EXCELLENT AMI,

The portrait came. It is gorgeous. I like its atmosphere. It is a likeness too besides being a picture.[1]

In a little while came the books. *Vous me gâtez.* I've read *Vathek* [2] at once. *C'est très bien.* What an infernal imagination! The style is cold and I do not see in the work that immense promise as set forth by the introduction. Chaucer I have dipped into, reading aloud as you advised. I am afraid I am not English enough to appreciate fully the father of English literature. Moreover I am in general insensible to verse.

Thereupon came "The Stealing of the Mare." [3] This I delight in. I've read it at once and right through. It is quite inspiring, most curious and altogether fascinating. I've written to your wife a few words in the language of the Franks about "Family Portraits," which is a delicious bit. The tenderness of the idea and the feeling for the past have delighted me. *C'est tout-à-fait dans sa note.* The quality that made the extraordinary charm of *Sta. Teresa* is in that short article, as visible as in the great work.

To Mr. Spiridion Kliszczewski

12th April [1899].

MY DEAR OLD FRIEND,

Here's the latest volume of my works I beg you to accept for yourself and dear Mrs. Spiridion.

I haven't written for a very long time, as it seems to me: but both you and I are busy men, each in our way. I daresay you will forgive me. After six hours pen in hand, one does not seem to have anything more to write,—even to one's best friend.

[1] A photograph after Sir John Lavery's portrait of R. B. Cunninghame Graham now in the Glasgow Municipal Gallery.

[2] William Beckford's *Vathek.*

[3] Translation of an Arab poem by Wilfrid Blunt and his wife, Lady Ann Blunt.

The book I've been writing [1] since last December and am writing still is sold already for serial appearance both in America and also here. The price is not so bad, considering I get £250 for *serial* rights in both countries. Then, for *book form* I shall probably get £100 in all. Well, one can live on that. But meantime I am living on these prospects, the book being not finished as yet. I am trying to complete it by end July and, if the heart holds out, I shall no doubt do it.

When you have a moment of spare time give me the news of your wife's and your own health and tell us all about your boys. We often talk of them and especially of Clement, for whom my wife has a soft spot. May your prosperity always increase and your shadow never grow less.

What do you think of foreign affairs? I am simply sick to see the blind and timid bungling of the man at the head of affairs. This is this country's very last chance to assert itself in the face of Russia and indeed of the whole of Europe. I am convinced that at this moment all the chances would be in favour of England and after a first success there would be no lack of friends and allies. But there! What's the use of talking; I am not foreign minister.

Jessie sends her love to all. She is pretty well. The baby flourishes exceedingly. He is very big and seems very strong. I am afraid he is tasking my wife's strength to the utmost.

Well! Good-bye for the present. My affectionate greetings to you all.

To Mme. Angèle Zagórska [2]

Pent Farm,
12th April, 1899.

DEAR ANGÈLE,

Excuse these few words. I am anxious about Karola.[3] Please let me know how she is—and how you all are. Since your last letter I have sent: 1.—the photo of the boy; 2.—3 packets of cuttings; 3.—a number of *Literature;* 4.—Wells's novel *The Invisible Man.* Let me know, my dearest, if you have received all this; especially the photo and the book. If the cuttings have gone astray, it will be necessary to send them in envelopes. If you have received *Literature* I will send it to you regularly. If the book has not reached you, I will send another copy at once.

---

[1] *Lord Jim.*
[2] The original of this letter is in Polish.
[3] Mme Zagórska's daughter.

I have been in bed a whole week with gout. I do not feel at all well. But that does not matter. My wife and the youngster are both well. God grant that all may go well with you. Send me a few lines to re-assure me. I embrace you affectionately and kiss your hand.

Your K. KORZENIOWSKI.

To R. B. Cunninghame Graham

Pent Farm.
17th April, 1899.

TRÈS CHER AMI,

Your letter this morning made me feel better. Is it possible that you like the thing[1] so much? Well, you say so and I believe you, but,— do you quite believe it yourself, *soit dit sans vous offenser?* The element of friendship comes in. But still I am willing, even eager, to believe in your scrupulous literary honesty. And in any case my blessing on your intention.

I hold *Ipané*[2] Hoch! Hurra! Viva! May you live! And now I know I am virtuous because I read and had no pang of jealousy. There are things in that volume that are like magic, and through space, through the distance of regretted years, convey to one the actual feeling, the sights, the sounds, the thoughts: one steps on the earth, breathes the air, and has the sensations of your past. I knew of course every sketch: what was almost a surprise was the extraordinary good, convincing effect of the whole. It is not always so with a collection. The style grows on one from page to page. It is as wonderful in a slightly differ-ent way as the Morocco book. How do you do it? How? I do not say which I like best. I like best the one I happen to be reading. I think the sequence of the sketches has been arranged very well.

I have read it already three times.

I am cursed and tongue-tied. Not only in my own work but when I want to talk of a friend's work too. And from a full heart nothing comes. A weariness has laid its hand on my lips.—I ask myself at times whether it is for ever. Then I ought to die. However, one is never sure and thus one hangs on to life. Can there be anything more awful than such an incertitude and more pathetic than such hanging on? Shall I see you before you leave for the Sahara, O fortunate man?

I'll come to town on purpose, you know!

Jess sends her kindest regards.

[1] *Lord Jim.*
[2] *The Ipané*, by R. B. Cunninghame Graham. London, Fisher Unwin, 1899.

To John Galsworthy

Pent Farm.
17 April, 1899.

DEAREST JACK,

We were awfully disappointed, but perhaps you are right. It would have been like the glimpse of a ship in a fog, tormenting, disturbing, conveying no sense of companionship. I have nothing to show you, so you haven't lost much: but I am anxious about these thousand words you've written. At this juncture *every* word is an object to be considered anxiously with heart searchings and in a spirit of severe resolution. Don't write them (words) hurriedly. I am glad you have written no more than one thousand. If it had been only one hundred I would have said: it is well. Don't smile and think that it is only my own cursed tongue-tied state that gives me that point of view. There may be something of that, of course,—but for the most part it is sheer conviction. And I think of your prose just as I think of mine own.

I am sincerely pleased with what you say of Elstree.[1] You know that I am loyal enough: that my memory is good and sane even if my mind is diseased and on the verge of craziness.—I am glad they think well of me: it is the only kind of treasure I want to lay up, the only sort of wealth I prize. And I am not ungrateful to those who contribute. I have been more moved by your letter than I intend telling you. I watch as patiently as I can for your return, trusting that you will come here with the MS. without loss of time.

Jess sends her kindest regards.

To (Sir) Hugh Clifford

Pent Farm.
24th May, 1899.

MY DEAR SIR,

If we haven't met last Saturday it is the P.O.'s fault.

Thanks very much for your kind letter. I am sure you won't take it ill if I confess my inability to take immediately advantage of your friendly invitation. The reasons that keep me at home just now are too many to be set down, but you may well believe that, if they are not good, they are uncommonly strong or else I would break through them, for

---

[1] He refers to their mutual friends, the Sandersons, who were living at Elstree.

my desire to meet you is not only prompted by a very natural gratitude for your appreciation (the most flattering and welcome recognition my work has brought me) but by a profound regard for your personality, for your life-work, for your large and generous sympathies—as far as it is given to my ignorance to understand these things.

The institution of domestic slavery having broken down in this country, and my wife being far from well just now, I simply dare not take you at your word, tho' my restraint costs me something, I assure you. You would probably get nothing to eat, and though you have known worse hardships, think how black my face would be after such a misfortune.

I take it I have your permission to let you know when I come to town next, and if then you can spare an hour, I will be most happy (this is no conventional phrase) to call on you; and live even in hopes that before next November you'll sacrifice a whole day to seek me out in my jungle.

To (Sir) Algernon Methuen

Pent Farm.
25th May, 1899.

MY DEAR SIR,

My letter to you was not a coy manœuvre with a view to a vast amount of shekels. The facts are these: I am engaged to Mr. Heinemann here, and to the McClure Co. over there, for the *Rescue*. I am almost a year behind my date with that extremely long story and I am beyond measure distressed by the delay. The thing simply *won't* come out as quick as I fondly hoped. I am also engaged to Mr. Blackwood for a vol. of three stories which is still 80,000 words short. It is clear to me that my power of production is as uncertain as the weather of these Isles. If H. and McC. get tired of my irregularity (to pick out a mild name) I shall come to you and I don't think you'll find me exceptionally rapacious. I have no reason, however, to think that such would be the case, and these two houses have treated me with such consideration, patience and friendliness, that I don't see myself going elsewhere of my own movement. Apart from very friendly relations, *Blackwood's* is the only periodical *always* open to me—and is the only one for which I really care to work. Such being the true state of the case, to talk about any future work of mine would be futile and not very sincere. Nevertheless I am very grateful to you for your generous suggestions. The disposal of my work cannot be governed purely by questions of payment.

That is at least how I feel about it, tho' nowise bound to these firms except by their good offices rendered to me at a time when they were needed rather badly.

Pardon the length of this. It is just because I appreciate the spirit of your offer that I am anxious to make my position clear to you.

To J. B. Pinker [1]

Pent Farm.
23rd August 1899.

DEAR SIR,

Thanks very much for your letter. The American publisher need not be ashamed, tho' the fact is that all my prose has been published in the States. Publishers are not supposed to be able to read. I can write a little, but God forbid that I should break upon the blessed ignorance of a stranger far from his native land.

My method of writing is so unbusinesslike that I don't think you could have any use for such an unsatisfactory person. I generally sell a work before it is begun, get paid when it is half done and don't do the other half till the spirit moves me. I must add that I have no control whatever over the spirit—neither has the man who has paid the money.

The above may appear fanciful to you, but it is the sober truth. I live in hopes of reformation, and whenever that takes place you and you alone shall have the working of the new Conrad. Meantime I must be content to pander to my absurd weaknesses and hobble along the line of the least resistance.

To John Galsworthy

Pent Farm.
2nd Sept. 99.

DEAREST JACK.

Horrors! I think I am too late in writing. The days slipped by so fast, so fast!

Dear of you to drop me a line, to think of me and my work. You have no idea how your interest in me *keeps me up*. I am unutterably weary of thinking, of writing, of seeing, of feeling, of living.

[1] Joseph Conrad's literary agent.

Jim [1] will be finished end of this month. I plod on without much faith.

I think of your work. Hueffer has been here inquiring about you and your prose. We are all interested. You've made the conquest of C. Graham, whom I treat worse than a dog, not having answered two of his letters.

Jessie's kindest regards. Borys talks about "nice man Jack." Forgive this familiarity.

To (Sir) Hugh Clifford

Pent Farm.
Monday, 9th Oct. 1899.

MY DEAR MR. CLIFFORD,

I received the book [2] three hours ago and—it is only too short! I've read it twice. I've also read the inscription, the wording of which I prize immensely, though I vow and protest that I never looked upon your critical notice in the light of an act requiring expiation. I am only too conscious of my ignorance, my audacity—and of all my other failings, which at your hands have received such a generous treatment.

Many thanks. I've lived for a few hours in your pages. Of the sketches I've not previously seen, "The Central Gaol" and the "Vigil of Pa' Tûa" are the two I like the best. [3] Of the others, "The Death March" [4] has been always my favourite; but indeed all are absorbing—to me at least. I would like to talk about them long—interminably; of the matter and of the manner too.

Of course, the matter is admirable—the knowledge, the feeling, the sympathy; it is sure to win perfect and full recognition. It is all sterling metal; a thing of absolute value. There can be no question of it, not only for those who know but even for those who approach the book with blank minds on the subject of the race you have, in more than one sense, made your own. And as to the manner—well! I know you are not a seeker after mere expression and I beg leave to offer only one remark.

You do not leave enough to the imagination. I do not mean as to facts—the facts cannot be too explicitly stated; I am alluding simply to the phrasing. True, a man who knows so much (without taking into account the manner in which his knowledge was acquired) may well

---

[1] *Lord Jim*. It was finished only in July, 1900.

[2] *In a Corner of Asia*, by Hugh Clifford, published by Fisher Unwin in October, 1899.

[3] "In the Central Gaol" and "The Vigil of Pa' Tûa, the Thief."

[4] The Death March of Kûlop-Sumbing.

spare himself the trouble of meditating over the words, only that words, groups of words, words standing alone, are symbols of life, have the power in their sound or their aspect to present the very thing you wish to hold up before the mental vision of your readers. The things "as they are" exist in words; therefore words should be handled with care lest the picture, the image of truth abiding in facts, should become distorted —or blurred.

These are the considerations for a mere craftsman—you may say; and you may also conceivably say that I have nothing else to trouble my head about. However, the *whole* of the truth lies in the presentation; therefore the expression should be studied in the interest of veracity. This is the only morality of *art* apart from *subject*.

I have travelled a good way from my original remark—not enough left to the imagination in the phrasing. I beg leave to illustrate my meaning from extracts on p. 261—not that I pose for an accomplished craftsman or fondly think I am free from that very fault and others much worse. No; it is only to explain what I mean.

. . ."When the whole horror of his position forced itself with an agony of realization upon his frightened mind, Pa' Tûa for a space lost his reason." . . . In this sentence the reader is borne down by the full expression. The words: *with an agony of realization* completely destroy the effect—therefore interfere with the truth of the statement. The word *frightened* is fatal. It seems as if it had been written without any thought at all. It takes away all sense of reality—for if you read the sentence *in its place on the page* you will see that the word *"frightened"* (or indeed any word of the sort) is inadequate to express the true state of that man's mind. No word is adequate. The imagination of the reader should be left free to arouse his feeling.

". . . When the whole horror of his position forced itself upon his mind, Pa' Tûa for a space lost his reason. . . ." This is truth; this it is which, thus stated, carries conviction because it is a *picture* of a mental state. And look how finely it goes on with a perfectly legitimate effect.

. . ."He screamed aloud, and the hollow of the rocks took up his cries" . . . It is magnificent! It is suggestive. It is truth effectively stated. But *"and hurled them back to him mockingly"* is nothing at all. It is a phrase anybody can write to fit any sort of situation; it is the sort of thing that writes itself; it is the sort of thing I write twenty times a day and (with the fear of overtaking fate behind me) spend half my nights in taking out of my work—upon which depends the daily bread of the house (literally—from day to day); not to mention (I dare hardly think of it) the future of my child, of those nearest and dearest to me, between whom and the bleakest want there is only my pen—as long as life lasts. And I can sell all I write—as much as I can write!

This is said to make it manifest that I practise the faith which I take the liberty to preach—if you allow me to say so—in a brotherly spirit. To return.

Please observe how strikingly the effect is carried on.

"When the whole horror of his position forced itself upon his mind, Pa' Tûa for a space lost his reason. He screamed aloud, and the hollow of the rocks took up his cries; the bats awoke in thousands and joined the band that rustled and squeaked above the man," etc., etc. In the last two lines the words hurrying—motiveless—already—defenceless—are not essential and therefore not true to the fact. The impression of *hurrying motiveless* has been given already in lines 2, 3, 4, at the top of the page. If they *joined*, it is because the others were *already* flying. *Already* is repetition. *Defenceless* is inadequate for a man held in the merciless grip of a rock.

And pray believe me that if I have selected this passage, it is because I am alive to its qualities and not because I have looked consciously for its defects.

For the same reason I do not apologize for my remarks. They are not an impertinence, they are a tribute to the work, that appeals so strongly to me by its subject, partly—but most by its humanity, its comprehension, by its spirit and by its expression too—which I have made a subject of critical analysis. If I have everlastingly bored you, you must forgive me. I trust you will find no other cause of offence.

Our meeting—your visit here—mark an epoch in my life. I wish my work would allow me to run up to town and see you before you return to the East; but I have been unwell, mentally powerless and physically unfit, my work has suffered a disastrous delay. I am a slave of mean preoccupations, alas!

"Friend" says the inscription—and I feel distinctly the richer for your friendship. Your and Mrs. Clifford's short apparition amongst us has left an abiding and valued memory. Jessie joins me in kindest regards to your wife and yourself.

Pardon this corrected and interlined letter. It's past midnight and I had a rough time with MS. all day.

To E. L. Sanderson

Pent Farm.
12 Oct. '99.

MY DEAR TED,

Were you to come with a horsewhip you would be still welcome. It's the only kind of visit I can imagine myself as deserving from you. Only

the other day Jessie asked me whether I had written to you and overwhelmed me with reproaches. Why wait another day? But I am incorrigible; I will always look to another day to bring something good,
something one would like to share with a friend,—something,—if only
a fortunate thought. But the days bring nothing at all,—and thus they
go by empty-handed,—till the last day of all.

I am always looking forward to some date, to some event, when I
finish this: before I begin that other thing,—and there never seems to
be any breathing time, not because I do much but because the toil is
great. I try at times to persuade myself that it is my honesty that makes
the burden so heavy, but, alas! the suspicion will force itself upon one
that, may be, it is only lack of strength, of power, of an uplifting
belief in oneself. Whatever the cause, the struggle is hard, and this may
be no more than justice.

I haven't been in town since last March, I haven't been to see you,
I have not gone to visit other people. My dear Ted, you have much
to forgive me: but try to imagine yourself trying your hardest to save
the School from downfall, annihilation, and disaster: and the thing
going on and on endlessly. That's exactly how I am situated: and the
worst is that the menace (in my case) does not seem to come from outside but from within: that the menace and danger or weakness are in
me, in myself alone. I fear I have not the capacity and the power to go
on,—to satisfy the just expectations of those who are dependent on my
exertions. I fear! I fear! And sometimes I hope. But it is the fear that
abides.

But even were I wrong in my fear the very fact that such a fear
exists would argue that everything is not right,—would in itself be a
danger and a menace. So I turn in this vicious circle and the work itself
becomes like the work in a treadmill,—a thing without joy,—a punish-
ing task.

You can see now why I am so often remiss in my correspondence.
There is nothing one would gladly write under that shadow. This is
the sort of thing that one writes, and the more one loves his friends, the
more belief one has in their affection, the less one is disposed to cast upon
them the gloom of one's intimate thoughts. My silence is seldom selfish
and never forgetful. It is often a kind of reserve, *pudor,* something
in the nature of instinctive decency. One expects to fall every instant
and one would like to fall with a covered face, with a decorous arrangement of draperies, with no more words than greatest men have used.
One would! And when one sits down, it is to write eight pages without
coming to the end of one's groans.

I am ashamed, bitterly ashamed, to make the same eternal answer, the
same eternal wail of incertitude, to your hospitable voice. I am now

trying to finish a story which began in the Oct. No. of *Blackwood.*[1] I am at it day after day, and I want all day, every minute of a day, to produce a beggarly tale of words or perhaps to produce nothing at all. And when that is finished (I thought it would be so on the first of this month,—but no fear!) I must go on, even go on at once and drag out of myself another 20,000 words, if the boy is to have his milk and I my beer (this is a figure of speech,—I don't drink beer, I drink weak tea, yearn after dry champagne) and if the world is not absolutely to come to an end. And after I have written and have been paid, I shall have the satisfaction of knowing that I can't allow myself the relaxation of being ill more than three days under the penalty of starvation: nor the luxury of going off the hooks altogether without playing the part of a thief regarding various confiding persons, whose desire to serve me was greater than their wisdom. Do you take me, sir? *Verb: sap:* that is, circumlocution is clear to the wise.

And yet,—one hopes, as I had the honour to remark above.

A book of mine (Joseph Conrad's last) is to come out in March. Three stories in one volume.[2] If only five thousand copies of that *could* be sold! If only! But why dream of the wealth of the Indies? I am not the man for whom Pactolus flows and the mines of Golconda distill priceless jewels (What an absurd style. Don't *you* think I am deteriorating?). Style or no style,—I am not the man. And oh! dear Ted, it is a fool's business to write fiction for a living. It is indeed.

It is strange. The unreality of it seems to enter one's real life, penetrate into the bones, make the very heartbeats pulsate illusions through the arteries. One's will becomes the slave of hallucinations, responds only to shadowy impulses, waits on imagination alone. A strange state, a trying experience, a kind of fiery trial of untruthfulness. And one goes through it with an exaltation as false as all the rest of it. One goes through it,—and there's nothing to show at the end. Nothing! Nothing! Nothing!

Let me remark with due solemnity that it is to-morrow morning already. For an apparently domesticated man to be "abroad" (in the 17th Century sense) with friends at 1.30 A.M. is (to say the least) reprehensible. Suffer me to leave you here at this turning that leads nowhere. That very turning is my way, my only way. You are going straight and, perchance, you know where,—and perchance, you are right! you are right! Upon the whole I shall suffer most from that separation. But I shall soon come out of my land of mist peopled by

---

[1] *Lord Jim.* It was published in *Blackwood's Magazine* from October, 1899, to November, 1900, inclusive.

[2] *Youth: A Narrative, and Two Other Stories* was published only in November, 1902.

shadows, and we shall meet again for another midnight communion,—as though we too also had been ghosts, shadows. I question however whether the most desolate shade that ever haunted this earth of ours carried in its misty form a heart as heavy as mine is,—sometimes.

I wanted to write you a sober, sensible letter: to explain, to make clear, to apologize—and before all to thank you for that fidelity which is for me one of the few real things in this world. Perhaps with the intuition of a heart not rebuked by appearances you will divine what I've not been able to set down,—for want of space,—yes, let us say, for want of space. Jessie sends her kind regards.

To R. B. Cunninghame Graham

Pent Farm.
14 Oct. '99.

TRÈS CHER AMI,

I was just wondering where you were when your dear letter arrived. I mean, dear,—precious. Well! *Vous me mettez du cœur au ventre:* and that's no small service, for I live in a perpetual state of intellectual funk. I only wish I knew how to thank you.

Shall I see you on your return from Madrid? The book that's gone to Heinemann is the History of the Jesuits [1] I suppose,—and I should think for next year. Now with this idiotic war [2] there will be a bad time for print. All that's art, thought, idea will have to step back and hide its head before the intolerable war inanities. *Grand bien leur fasse!* The whole business is inexpressibly stupid,—even on general principles: for, evidently a war should be a conclusive proceeding, while this noble enterprise (no matter what its first result) must be the beginning of an endless contest. It is always unwise to begin a war which, to be effective, must be a war of extermination: it is positively imbecile to start it without a clear notion of what it means and to force on questions for immediate solution which are eminently fit to be left to time. From time only one solution could be expected,—and that one favourable to this country. The war brings in an element of incertitude which will not be eliminated by military success. There is an appalling fatuity in this business. If I am to believe Kipling this is a war undertaken for the cause of democracy. *C'est à crever de rire!* However, now the fun has commenced, I trust British successes will be

---

[1] *A Vanished Arcadia, Being Some Account of the Jesuits in Paraguay* (*1607 to 1767*), by R. B. Cunninghame Graham, published by William Heinemann in 1901.

[2] The South African War.

crushing from the first,—on the same principle that if there's murder being done in the next room and you can't stop it, you wish the head of the victim to be bashed in forthwith and the whole thing over for the sake of your own feelings.

Assez de ces bêtises! Jessie's kind regards. We must be in town in November for your wife's play. *Rappelez-moi à son bienveillant souvenir.*

Drop me a line to say when you return.

To E. L. Sanderson

Pent Farm.
26 Oct. '99.

MY DEAREST TED,

I had no idea my wail had been so loud and so lamentable, and though I am sorry I have intruded with my miseries on your serious pre-occupations, I congratulate myself on my lack of restraint since it has drawn from you a fraternal answer. I never doubted the nature of your sentiments, but their inward certitude does not make their expression the less welcome. I am indeed a fortunate man. When the heart is full it is not full of words, whatever the proverb may say: and if you had come and shot a sack of diamonds at my feet, I could not have felt richer than when reading your letter: but as to answering it as it should be answered, it is vain for me to try. You must put the finishing touch by giving me the credit of such feelings, or make me worthy of it.

I've been especially thinking of you since I read the Proclamation. A sacrifice of that kind a man is always ready for, though in your case it must be, to say the least of it, a grave inconvenience. As to the war itself much might be said. I am a little out of touch with facts (though not totally ignorant of them), but one can apply general principles. Now it seems to me that, from the point of view of state-craft,—no war is justifiable which does not solve a question. A war should be a final act,—while this war is an initial act. This is the weak point. It will create a situation of which, unless I am much mis-taken, the country will get weary. The victory,—unless it is to be thrown away,—shall have to be followed by ruthless repression. The situation will become repugnant to the nation. The "reasonable Eng-lish ideals" (I am quoting Sir F. Milner's words) are not attained in that way. Their instruments are time and deep-seated convictions of the race,—the expansive force of its enterprise and its morality. We all know, we know instinctively, that the danger to the Empire is elsewhere,—that the conspiracy (to oust the Briton) of which we hear is ready to be hatched in other regions. It has peeped out at the time of the last Eastern crisis and is everlastingly skulking in the Far East. A war there or anywhere but in S. Africa would have been conclusive,—would have been worth the sacrifices. We have heard much of the sorrows of the Outlanders (which did not prevent them from growing fat), but now real sorrows have come in the last few days. May they be mitigated by a speedy and complete triumph, since the work is begun and the price is being daily paid.

I can't say that I shared in the hysterical transports of some public organs, for the simple reason that I expected to see displayed all the valour, perseverance, devotion which, in fact, have been displayed. Confound these papers. From the tone of some of them, one would have thought they expected the artillery to clear out at a gallop across hills and ravines and every regiment to bolt, throwing away arms and accoutrements. Those infernal scribblers are rank outsiders. No matter. It was very fine. Much finer than the generalship I can't help fancying. To have an intelligent idea of these matters one must have a good map and I do not possess anything that's worth a cent in that way. But it seems to me that if his "internal" lines were too short, the ground unfavourable or his force not sufficiently mobile to strike east or west with his whole strength, Sir. G. White would have been better in Ladysmith, for the presence of his force in an untrenched camp would have anyhow checked an invasion of Natal, while an assault on a chosen position decisively repulsed would have had all the consequences of a defeat upon the Boer army. Am I too imbecile for anything? The chamber criticism of strategy is generally imbecile. As far as I can see he clawed with one arm here and with the other there,—stretched pretty well too,—but in the end stopped nothing. However, we shall see. To a really great general these converging movements in his front would perhaps have given an opportunity. I revel in my imbecility.

I wonder how Buller will do it. I am glad he goes there and the papers shall have another general to talk about. I had Kitchener on the nerves. There was a correspondent who wrote of that extremely clever organizer in terms that would not have been unbecoming if applied to the Archangel of War himself. The men in India had done real military work without all that bell ringing and hornblowing. I daresay Buller is no Archangel either, but I pin my faith on him.

Tell your dear wife with our best love that Jess had some wretched trouble in her right wrist and it is still almost powerless. She can typewrite with her left hand but she "don't like" to write in type. This, I suppose, I ought to have written. I ought to! My fault, my great fault. I plead forgiveness, and if you stand my friend I doubt not I shall be forgiven.

It was good and sweet of her to ask us. Your Mother has been most kind. I simply dare not leave my table: I must go on and wait for more fortunate days.

You will drop me a line to tell me where you are stationed. Have you got your company?

My dearest Ted, your letter did me good. It is *great* to hear you talk like this of my work. I wish I could be sure the partiality of your affection does not mislead you. Ah! my dear fellow. If you knew how ambitious I am, how my ambition checks my pen at every turn. Doubts assail me from every side. The doubt of form,—the doubt of tendency,—a mistrust of my own conceptions,—and scruples of the moral order. Ridiculous,—isn't it? As if my soul mattered to the universe! But even as the ant bringing its grain of sand to the common edifice may justly think itself important, so I would like to think that I am doing my appointed work. With love.

To R. B. Cunninghame Graham

Pent Farm.
10th Dec. '99.

CHER ET EXCELLENT AMI,

I was so glad to hear from you. Borys got your card the day after. You are emphatically *a nice man*.

This country does not want any writers: it wants a general or two that aren't valorous frauds. I am so utterly and radically sick of this African business that if I could take a sleeping draught on the chance of not waking till it is all over, I would let *Jim* go and take the consequences.

As it is,—in the way of writing I am not much more good than if I were sleeping. It is silly of me to take a thing so much to heart, but as things go there's not a ray of comfort for a man of my complex way of thinking, or rather feeling.

It would do me good to hear you talk. I don't know why I feel so damnably lonely. My health is tolerable, but my brain is as though somebody had stirred it all with a stick.

Allah *is* careless. The loss of your MS. is a pretty bad instance: but look,—here's His very own chosen people (of assorted denominations) getting banged about and not a sign from the sky but a snowfall and a fiendish frost. Perhaps Kipling's "Recessional" (if He understood it,—which I doubt) had offended Him?

I should think Lord Salisbury's dying nation must be enjoying the fun.

I can't write sense and I disdain to write Xmas platitudes, so here I end. My wife and I send you unconventional greetings and as to Borys, he has said you are *a nice man;* what more can you want to be made happy for a whole year?

When do you return? Shall I see you here before you go North? I am vexed about the preface. Your prefaces are so good! It is quite an art by itself. Well. This time I am really done.

To Mme Angèle Zagórska [1]

Pent Farm, 25. 12. 1899.

MY DEAREST ANGÈLE,

Your letters, darling, are very interesting; they give me courage and are very precious to me; my ingratitude is all the blacker—but it is only in appearance that I am ungrateful. In reality I am not— I am only a man with a weak will—and full of good intentions, with which—as they say—hell is paved. What would you have, my dear? The Malays say: "The tiger cannot change his stripes"—and I—my ultra-slav nature.

Much might be said about the war. My feelings are very complex— as you may guess. That they—the Boers—are struggling in good faith for their independence cannot be doubted; but it is also a fact that they have no idea of liberty, which can only be found under the English flag all over the world. *C'est un peuple essentiellement despotique,* as all the Dutch. This war is not so much a war against the Transvaal as a struggle against the doings of German influence. It is the Germans who have compelled the issue. There can be no doubt about it.

You are mistaken in saying that it is the Government who sends soldiers. The English Government cannot make a single Englishman move, if he does not consent to it. The people's conscience has weighed the pros and cons and not only the conscience of the people but of the whole race. Canada and Australia are taking part in this war, which could not influence their material interests. Why? Europe rejoices and is moved because Europe is jealous and here in England there is more real sympathy and regard for the Boers than on the whole Continent, which calls out its compassion at the top of its voice. *Quelle bourde!*

---

[1] Original of this letter in Polish.

To E. L. Sanderson

Pent Farm.
28 Dec. '99.

DEAREST TED,

Thanks for your dear note. I didn't write, not knowing where you were, and we only sent a card to your wife addressed to Elstree. I had a notion she would be away, either with you or in Scotland.

All possible and imaginable good to you, my dear fellow. There's not a day I do not think of you. I was in hopes you would turn up in Shorncliffe, which would have been all the same to you (once away from home and school) but would have made a great difference to me.

I am upset by this war more than enough. From every point of view it is an unsatisfactory business. I say from every point, because the disclosure of our military weakness is not compensated by the manifestation of colonial loyalty. That was a thing one would have taken for granted. We who know how loosely the colonies were hanging to Mother's skirts are impressed and cheered,—but on the Continent they never understood the conditions and they take it as a matter of course. But the disclosure is a pleasant surprise to them, with nothing to counteract their satisfaction.

I hope you won't have to go: but I am very glad Roberts is going, —or gone. To Kitchener by himself I would not have liked to pin my faith. And may it all end speedily,—and well.

I am at work, but my mental state is very bad,—and is made worse by a constant gnawing anxiety. One incites the other and vice versa. It is a vicious circle in which the creature struggles.

Wife sends her best wishes and kind regards.

With love, my dear Ted.

To Edward Garnett

Pent Farm.
20 Jan. 1900.

DEAREST EDWARD,

You make my head whirl when you write like this. What a letter for a poor devil to get! You've knocked my evening's work on the head; I found it impossible to write any copy. You frighten me; because were I to let you take me up on these heights by your appreciation the fall before my own conscience's smile would be so heavy as to break every bone in my body. And yet what, oh! what would become of me if it were not for your brave words that warm like fire and feed like bread and make me drunk like wine!

No. I didn't know anything about *Jim;*[1] and all I know now is that it pleases you; and I declare, as true as there are blind, deaf-mute gods sitting above us (who are so clear-eyed, eloquent and sharp of hearing), I declare it is enough for me; for if you think that because I've not been sending you my MS. your opinion has ceased to be a living factor in my individual and artistic existence, you are lamentably mistaken. I was simply afraid. And I am afraid still. You see the work fragmentarily; and the blessed thing is so defective that even that far within it you cannot possibly (with all your penetration and sympathy), you cannot possibly know where I tend and how I shall conclude this most inconclusive attempt. You don't; and the truth is that it is not my depth but my shallowness which makes me so "inscrutable." Thus (I go cold to think) the surprise reserved for you will be in the nature of a chair withdrawn from under one; something like a bad joke—it will strike you no doubt. Bad and vile. Now had you taken the whole thing the fall would not have been so heavy, I imagine.

*   *   *

There has been a *John Kochanowski,* a 15th Century poet who wrote a threnody amongst other things, and really our literature dates from him. Of course his name is no more like mine than Brown is like Robinson. His name is derived from the word which in Polish means *love* while mine derives from the word *root.*

Then in the thirties of the 19th Century (or forties) there was a novelist of about, say, Trollope's rank (but not so good in his way) named *Joseph Korzeniowski.* That is also my name, but the family is different, my full name being Joseph Theodor Konrad <u>Nalecz</u> Korzeniowski, the underlined word being the appellation of our trade mark as thus: [Seal = Nalecz without which none are genuine. As a
                 Here]
matter of fact I and Alfred Borys Konrad Korzeniowski are the only two of that particular brand of Korzeniowski in existence. There are other families whose arms are like mine but whose names are altogether different. This is a distinct *bond*—though not a relationship in any sense. It may indicate a common origin lost in the mists of ages. It was always recognized as a title to good offices from a powerful family towards a humbler one—and so on.

My paternal grandfather, Theodor N. Korzeniowski, served in the cavalry. Decorated with the cross of "Virtuti Militari" (a plain white

[1] *Lord Jim.*

enamel with a green wreath of laurel and these words in the centre),
something in the nature of V. C. Attained the rank of captain in 1830
when the Russo-Polish War occurred, after which the so-called
Polish Army ceased to exist. Two wounds. Retired to a little hereditary
estate adjoining the extensive possessions of the family of *Sobanski*
(they are in the Almanach de Gotha), great friends and, I fancy,
distant relations. Administered the territorial fortune of Mme. Melanie
Sobanska. Wrote a tragedy in 5 Acts, verse, privately printed and
so extremely dull that no one was ever known to have read it through.
I know I couldn't, notwithstanding my family pride and the general
piety of my disposition.

My other grandfather, Joseph Bobrowski, landowner, man of wit,
owner of a famous stud of Steppe horses, lived and died on his estate
of Oratow: popular, greatly lamented. Never wrote but letters (and
very few of these) and a large number of promissory notes dedicated to
various Jews. Left a large family of sons and one daughter, Eva—my
mother. There was an extraordinary sister-cult in that family, from
which I profited when left an orphan at the age of ten. And my
mother certainly was no ordinary woman. Her correspondence with my
father and with her brothers which in the year 1890 I have read
and afterwards destroyed was a revelation to me; I shall never forget
my delight, admiration and unutterable regret at my loss (before I
could appreciate her), which only then I fully understood. One of her
brothers, Thaddeus, to whom I stand more in the relation of a son
than of a nephew, was a man of powerful intelligence and great force
of character and possessed an enormous influence in the Three
Provinces (Ukraine, Volhynia and Podolia). A most distinguished man.
Another, Stephen, was in 1862 chief of the Polish Revolutionary Committee in Warsaw, and died assassinated soon after the Polish outbreak of 1863.

None of the members of the many families to which these two are
related was a literary man; all made sacrifices of fortune, liberty and
life for the cause in which they believed; and very few had any illusions as to its success.

*   *   *

My father Apollonius N. Korzeniowski. Educated in the University
of St. Petersburg. Department of Oriental Studies and Philology. No
degree. Debts. Social successes and any amount of *"bonnes fortunes."*
Poet. Married 1855.[1] Came to Warsaw in 1860. Arrested in 1862 and

[1] In 1856.

after 10 months detention[1] in the Citadel condemned to deportation into Russia. First in Archangel,[2] then in Tchernikow. My mother died in exile. My father liberated in '67 on the representation of Prince Gallitzin that he was no longer dangerous. He was dying. Comedy in 5 Acts, in verse, of modern life (date about 1854). Trans: [lations] V. Hugo, *Légende des Siècles. Travailleurs de la mer; Hernani.* Alf. de Vigny, *Chatterton.* Drama (Verse) ; Shakespeare. *Much Ado About Nothing. As You Like It. Two Gentlemen of Verona. Comedy of Errors. Othello.* (These I remember seeing in proofs when sent for his correction. There may have been others. Some of these I read when I could have been no more than eight or nine years old.) After his liberation, in Cracow (Austrian Poland), one of the Editorial Committee of a Newspaper (*Kzas*) then founded, if I remember rightly, by Prince Leo Sapieha, but too ill to continue actively in the direction.

A man of great sensibilities; of exalted and dreamy temperament; with a terrible gift of irony and of gloomy disposition; withal, of strong religious feeling, degenerating after the loss of his wife into mysticism touched with despair. His aspect was distinguished; his conversation very fascinating; but his face, in repose sombre, lighted all over when he smiled. I remember him well. For the last two years of his life I lived alone with him—but why go on?

There were piles of MS. dramas, verse, prose, burnt after his death according to his last will. A friend of his, a Polish critic of distinction,[3] wrote a pamphlet entitled *A Little Known Poet* after his death. And so finis.

Have I written enough? I certainly did not mean to write so much, when I began. I always intended to write something of the kind for Borys, so as to save all this from the abyss a few years longer. And probably he wouldn't care. What's Hecuba to him or he to Hecuba? *Tempi passati,* brother! *Tempi passati.* Let them go.

To R. B. Cunninghame Graham

Pent Farm.
13 Febr. 1900.

CHER AMI,

Je me suis colleté avec la mort ou peu s'en faut. However not this

---

[1] Apollo Korzeniowski, arrested in October, 1862, was sent to Vologda, *four months* afterward, in January, 1863.
[2] Not in Archangel, but in Vologda.
[3] Stefan Buszczynski.

time yet, it seems. I've been ill since the 26th of Jan. and have only tottered downstairs yesterday.

Malaria, bronchitis and gout. In reality a breakdown. I am better, but I've no sense of *rebound,* don't you know: I remain under the shadow.

Ma pauvre femme est exténuée. Nursing me, looking after the child, doing the housework. She could not find a moment to drop you a line of thanks for Borys' purse. He was delighted with it and she wanted badly to write and tell you so. I suppose it isn't so much want of time but weariness that prevented her. I am afraid she'll break down next, and that would be the end of the world. I wish I could give her a change but,—*quelle misère!*

I think that to-morrow I'll be able to begin writing again. What sort of stuff it'll be, devil only knows. *Moi aussi je suis exténué. Il faut se raidir.* Pardon this jeremiad.

To R. B. Cunninghame Graham

The Pent.
3 March 1900.

TRÉS CHER AMI,

Just a word to thank you for your letter. *Vous me mettez du cœur au ventre,* though I can't possibly agree to your praises of *Jim.*[1] But as to *Buta* it is altogether and fundamentally *good:* good in matter,— that's of course,—but good, wonderfully good, in form and especially in expression.

I am sad we don't meet, but I couldn't come to town for the play [2] as I very much wished to do. No doubt managers are as stupid as the majority of publishers. I don't see the papers, only the *Standard.* It had a rigmarole but not even an attempt at any sort of appreciation, so I don't know how "Don Juan" went. Is it going to be printed?

I am trying to go on with my work. It is hard, but damn it all, if it is only *half* as good as you say, then why groan? Have you seen the last vol. of Mrs. Garnett's Turgeniev? There's a story there, "Three Portraits" really fine. Also "Enough", worth reading.

Mes devoirs très respectueux à Madame votre femme. Jessie sends her kindest regards. Borys is very fat and unruly, but wears the heart you've given him round his neck and thinks no end of it. Poor little devil, if he had a decent father he would come to something perhaps.

---

[1] *Lord Jim.* It was appearing serially in *Blackwood's Magazine.*
[2] A translation of José Echegaray's "Don Juan Tenorio," produced by Martin Harvey.

To Mrs. Sanderson

The Pent.
17th March 1900.

MY DEAR MRS. SANDERSON,

My wife thought I had written while I was under the impression she had done so days ago. I write to offer excuses for us both.

I doubly congratulate you on the recent victories. The sooner the war comes to its unavoidable conclusion, the better for the national conscience, which, in my view, is as much part of the Empire as the extent of the earth it holds: and of as great importance to its future and to its power. Nations, like men, often act first and reflect afterwards: the responsibility is with the leaders and the verdict with history, when the generations are gone and the truth of their sins and virtues alone remains.

But I don't know why I should inflict upon you my valueless meditations: and besides it is late. I had better refrain. You will share with me the first news of our dear Ted? Will you not? I am not anxious in any way, but every day he is in my thoughts,—he has his part in the silent life within, which goes on deep and steady under the noise, the exertions, the clashing thoughts of our daily existence.

Believe me, dear Mrs. Sanderson, always your most affectionate friend and servant.

To John Galsworthy

Pent Farm.
Thursday, May [7], 1900.

DEAREST JACK,

Impossible on Monday, but shall let you know soon the day of my liberation.

Went to see Crane yesterday at Dover. Been with him 20 minutes. Supported move from Brede pretty well. I was awfully shocked of course and had to put on jolly manners. He may yet escape.[1]

The Frewens (owners of Brede) pay *all his* transit to the Black Forest,—rather more than £100. A doctor friend goes with them.

---

[1] In a note dated May 5th, J. C. had written to J. G. to say that he was going the day after to stay with Stephen Crane.

"Ill himself Joseph Conrad dragged to Dover and watched the blue eyes rove to a sail that fled above grey water outside the window." (*Stephen Crane,* by Thomas Beer, p. 240.)

It is a long good-bye to England and Stephen seems to feel it very much. And it may be for ever! He is not *too* hopeful about himself. One lung quite intact at any rate.[1]

Do tell me about the McClure interview.

To John Galsworthy

Pent Farm
Friday [ab. 20th July 1900].

DEAREST JACK,

We are off in an hour—at last, and shall be back on the 16 or 17 Aug. to give their holidays to various children.

I've written to Blackwood mainly for the purpose of insinuating amongst other matters that a quick decision as to your story would be welcome. He has your address, but hurry of any sort is not in the tradition of the "House."

Meldrum professes great admiration for the *M. of D.*[2] It is evident to me he has been struck plumb-centre, and I am glad to find him discriminative. This does not settle the question of publication, but his opinion has a certain weight with Mr. B'wood.

The end of *L. J.*[3] has been pulled off with a steady drag of 21 hours. I sent wife and child out of the house (to London) and sat down at 9 A. M. with a desperate resolve to be done with it. Now and then I took a walk round the house, out at one door in at the other. Ten-minute meals. A great hush. Cigarette ends growing into a mound similar to a cairn over a dead hero. Moon rose over the barn, looked in at the window and climbed out of sight. Dawn broke, brightened. I put the lamp out and went on, with the morning breeze blowing the sheets of MS. all over the room. Sun rose. I wrote the last word and went into the dining-room. Six o'clock I shared a piece of cold chicken with Escamillo[4] (who was very miserable and in want of sympathy, having missed the child dreadfully all day). Felt very well, only sleepy: had a bath at seven and at 1.30 was on my way to London.

Same day we journeyed to Slough and saw the children. They are improved, very much liked, very happy. That's a success. From there we rushed straight on to the poor Hopes, where we slept two nights. Yesterday morning check from B'wood arrived and to-day we are off

[1] Stephen Crane died on the following 4th of June in Badenweiler.
[2] John Galsworthy's *Man of Devon*.
[3] *Lord Jim*. The writing of the novel had been finished on the 16th.
[4] His dog.

to join the disconsolate and much enduring Hueffer. Address: *4 rue Anglaise, Bruges.*

I am still well. Jessie too. Notwithstanding the heat. Borys in great form but exceedingly naughty except when actually travelling, when he is simply angelic.

This is all that will go on this piece of paper.

Our love.

To John Galsworthy

Grand Hôtel de la Plage
Knocke-sur-mer [1]
11 Aug. 1900

DEAREST JACK,

Pardon me not answering your letter. The boy has been very ill indeed, dysentery: and the danger of a fatal termination has not been over till yesterday. Jess showed lots of pluck. The poor little chap is a miserable object to behold. As soon as he has picked up a little strength we are coming back. I've had enough of this holiday.

Fortunately I had done with *Jim* before the boy fell ill. The corrected type went off five days ago and the very next day I had to devote all my energies to nursing, along with Jess, who, all the same, had to bear the brunt of it as you may imagine.

The whole hotel was in a commotion: Dutch, Belgians and French prowled about the corridor on the lookout for news. Women with babies of their own offered to sit up, and a painter of religious subjects, Paulus by name, rose up and declared himself ready to do likewise. Elsie Hueffer helped a bit, but poor H [2] did not get much collaboration out of me this time.

Well, it's over. We shall try to be home by the 20th. I've done nothing except, as I said, getting the end of *Jim* fit for print. There was a good deal to do to it, as a matter of fact.

The plan of your story is excellent. I can't enlarge just now, only this is certain, that such a story shall want an immense amount of execution. You must make the personal note very strong. Delighted to hear "Mte Carlo" finished. I can't get any news from Bl'wood as to the *M. of D.*[3] The delay is a good sign. They refused something of Hueffer's in four days. They were 3 weeks accepting "Karain." [4]

---

[1] In Belgium.
[2] Ford Madox Hueffer.
[3] John Galsworthy's *The Man of Devon.*
[4] It was published in November, 1897, in *Blackwood's Magazine.*

To Mrs. Reynolds

Pent Farm,
5th Sept. 1900

DEAR MRS. REYNOLDS,

The MS. heralded by your letter arrived this morning. I've had the time to read it. It is wonderfully well done: technically and in the clearness of the idea it is superior to the *Villa*.[1] Jack [2] is making giant strides; there is in his latest work,—notwithstanding the first person form,—a truly artistic aloofness even more pronounced than in the *Villa*. He is coming on! It is for me a wonderful example of what a determined singleness of purpose can achieve when there is a solid basis of a remarkable talent that I verily believe will go very far,—practically as far as he chooses to push it.

That I have detected the existence of that talent, when in the nature of things it could not be very obvious, I shall always remember with pride, but in all conscience I must disclaim the credit you give me of being of help to him. One needs to be a very exceptional person to be of real use to his fellow men. I've certainly talked, but had I never existed someone else would have found the same things to say,—though perhaps not with the same loving care for his promise. That much I may admit without self-deception.

Recognition shall come. Strictly speaking, what people think does not matter,—and yet everything is in that. I am afraid he can never look forward to other than limited appreciation. That he shall have it I feel certain,—and even the other kind is possible too. I say this deliberately, having my reasons for such a hope both of the artistic and also "human" order. But they are too many to be set down at length here.

With kindest regards to your husband and yourself, believe me, dear Mrs. Reynolds, your most obedient and faithful servant.

To John Galsworthy

Pent Farm,
7 Nov. 1900.

DEAREST JACK,

I was so touched by your letter.[3] Believe me I was, though I did not answer it at once. Indeed it is very difficult to answer such a

[1] *Villa Rubein,* by John Galsworthy.
[2] Mr. John Galsworthy. Mrs. Reynolds, to whom this letter is addressed, is the novelist's sister.
[3] About *Lord Jim.*

message from the very force of the emotions it awakens; I thought I was very fortunate to get such a response for my work. You've done so much for me and in so many ways that I have felt myself silenced a long time ago—but never have you done so much for me as when you wrote that letter.

I wanted to write to you about your book, that is really one of the reasons why I had not acknowledged your letter—which I could do, if I couldn't answer it with adequate expression. But, my dear Jack, I've been in such a state of wretchedness and worry that I could not find three words that would hang together. You know how paralyzed one is sometimes, and then we had talked,—I had tried to talk,—of the book so many times that it seemed to have become part of me—that part of belief and thought so intimate that it cannot be put into speech, as if it could not live apart from one's conscious self.

The preliminary note in the *Academy* was at least decent, "sense of style and eye for character." That is something,—and not a little thing to have come home to a casual review. Now what we want is to get the *A.* to get out a review which would have at least that amount of intelligence and discrimination.[1] Lucas [2] wrote to me that he no longer reviews for the *A.* unless books of verse. I am afraid they are awfully crowded: there is such a rush of fiction which had been held back by the Kruger-Chamberlain combination.

How are you? When are you coming? My flesh is weary and my spirit sinks. But I shan't treat you to any of that.

To Edward Garnett

Pent Farm,
12 Nov. 1900.

DEAREST E.,

You are great and good.

Yes! You've put your finger on the plague spot. The division of the book [3] into two parts, which is the basis of your criticism, demonstrates to me once more your amazing insight; and your analysis of the effect of the book puts into words precisely and suggestively the dumb thoughts of every reader—and my own.

Such is indeed the effect of the book; the effect which you can name and others can only feel. I admit I stood for a great triumph and I have only succeeded in giving myself utterly away. Nobody'll see it,

[1] *A.*, the *Athenæum.*
[2] E. V. Lucas.
[3] *Lord Jim.*

but you have detected me falling back into my lump of clay I had been lugging up from the bottom of the pit, with the idea of breathing big life into it. And all I have done was to let it fall with a silly crash.

For what is fundamentally wrong with the book—the cause and the effect—is want of power. I do not mean the "power" of reviewers' jargon. I mean the want of illuminating imagination. I wanted to obtain a sort of lurid light out [of] the very events. You know what I have done—alas! I haven't been strong enough to breathe the right sort of life into my clay—the *revealing* life.

I've been satanically ambitious, but there's nothing of a devil in me, worse luck. The *Outcast* is a heap of sand, the *Nigger* a splash of water, *Jim* a lump of clay. A stone, I suppose, will be my next gift to impatient mankind—before I get drowned in mud to which even my supreme struggles won't give a simulacrum of life. Poor mankind! Drop a tear for it—but look how infinitely more pathetic I am! This pathos is a kind of triumph no criticism can touch. Like the philosopher who crowed at the Universe, I shall know when I am utterly squashed. This time I am only very bruised, very sore, very humiliated.

This is the effect of the book upon me; the intimate and personal effect. Humiliation. Not extinction. Not yet. All of you stand by me so nobly that I must still exist. There is *You,* always, and never dismayed. I had an amazing note from Lucas. Amazing! This morning a letter came from Henry James. Ah! You rub in the balm till every sore smarts—therefore I exist. The time will come when you shall get tired of tending a true and most well-intentioned sham—and then the end'll come too.

But keep up! Keep up! Let me exhort you earnestly to keep up! as long as you can.

I send you the H. J. letter.[1] A draught from the Fountain of Eternal Youth. Wouldn't you think a boy had written it? Such enthusiasm! Wonderful old man, with his record of wonderful work! It is, I believe, seriously intended (the letter) as confidential. And to you alone I show it—keep *his* secret for us both. No more now. I've read *Petersburg Tales.*[2] Phew! That *is* something! That is many things—and the only thing—it is written! It is. That work is genuine, undeniable, constructed and inhabited. It has foundation and life. I hope the writer will deign to recognize my most fraternal welcome!

P. S. Pray send the James autograph back—registered. Our great love to you three. We *must* meet soon.

[1] In spite of research, it has not been possible to find that Henry James letter among J. C.'s papers.
[2] *Petersburg Tales,* by Olive Garnett. Heinemann, 1900.

To (Sir) Edmund Gosse

Pent Farm,
18 Jan. 1901.

DEAR MR. GOSSE,

Very many thanks for the names, which are lovely; and for all the additional information.[1]

It is indeed very kind of you to write in such terms—and thus I am exceedingly rewarded for my cheek in setting Pawling on you.

Nevertheless I am very much ashamed. If I were to make an inroad upon your time I wish it had been on some more promising occasion. This story promises to turn out a deplorable pot-boiler; unless, before it is too late, the gods wake up and are good to me. I don't see why they should. However the way of the gods (as those of Chinamen, *pace* Bret Harte), are dark, and there may be salvation, somewhere, before the last line is written.

To John Galsworthy

The Bungalow,
Winchelsea Nr Rye
Sussex.
20th June 1901.

MY DEAR JACK,

Jess sent me on your letter. Yes, next Sunday week will do excellently well. I've been longing to see you and, like Antæus in touching the earth, draw some strength from the contact of your friendship.

I've finished "Falk"[2] and I've written another story since. Now I am here working at *Seraphina*. There are 10,000 words which I am going to write in *manu propriæ*. I reckon to be done on Sunday sometime. On Monday we go to the Pent: and on Wednesday perhaps I may run up to London with the MS. of *S.* to see Pinker, Meldrum[3] and Watson, my banker. It is a weary life. But I am cheered to hear from you. I *am most* anxious to see the play—also the verses. The story of *The Outlook*,[4] Ford sent me some time ago. We enjoyed it!

[1] Some information used in *Falk*.

[2] "Falk" had been finished in May: the other story J. C. had written at that time was "Amy Foster." *Seraphina* is the first version of *Romance*.

[3] Of Blackwood's.

[4] "A Reversion to Type," by John Sinjohn. *The Outlook*, May 18, 1901.

To John Galsworthy

11 Nov. 1901.

DEAREST JACK,

I did not write about the book[1] before, first because Jess had it,—and she reads slowly,—and then I had at last some proofs of mine, a whole batch which it took me several days to correct. Nevertheless I've read the book twice—watching the effect of it impersonally during the second reading—trying to ponder upon its reception by the public and discover the grounds of *general* success,—or the reverse.

There is a certain caution of touch which will militate against popularity. After all, to please the public (if one isn't a sugary imbecile or an inflated fraud) one must handle one's subject intimately. Mere intimacy with the subject won't do. And conviction is found for others, —not for the author, only in certain contradictions and irrelevancies to the general conception of character (or characters) and of the subject. Say what you like, man lives in his eccentricities (so called) alone. They give a vigour to his personality which mere consistency can never do. One must explore deep and believe the incredible to find the few particles of truth floating in an ocean of insignificance. And before all one must divest oneself of every particle of respect for one's character. You are really most profound and attain the greatest art in handling the people you do not respect. For instance the minor characters in *V. R.*[2] And in this volume I am bound to recognize that Forsyte is the best. I recognize this with a certain reluctance because indubitably there is more beauty (and more felicity of style too) in the *M. of D.* The story of the mine shows best your strength and your weakness. There is hardly a word I would have changed; there are things in it that I would give a pound of my flesh to have written. Honestly,—there are. And your mine-manager remains unconvincing because he is too confoundedly perfect in his very imperfections. The fact is you want more scepticism at the very foundation of your work. Scepticism, the tonic of minds, the tonic of life, the agent of truth,—the way of art and salvation. In a book you should love the idea and be scrupulously faithful to your conception of life. There lies the honour of the writer, not in the fidelity to his personages. You must never allow them to decoy you out of yourself. As against your people you must preserve an attitude of perfect indifference, the part of creative power. A creator must be indifferent; because directly the "Fiat!" has issued from his

[1] *The Man of Devon and Other Stories.*
[2] *Villa Rubein.*

lips, there are the creatures made in his image that'll try to drag him down from his eminence,—and belittle him by their worship. Your attitude to them should be purely intellectual, more independent, freer, less rigorous than it is. You seem, for their sake, to hug your conceptions of right and wrong too closely. There is exquisite atmosphere in your tales. What they want now is more air.

You may wonder why I write you these generalities. But first of all, in the matter of technique, where your advance has been phenomenal and which has almost (if not quite) reached the point of crystallization, we have talked so much and so variously that I could tell you nothing that you have not heard already. And secondly these considerations are not so general as they look. They are even particular, inasmuch that they have been inspired by the examination of your work as a whole. I have looked into all the volumes, and this—put briefly, imperfectly and obscurely,—is what they suggested to me.

That the man who has written once the *Four Winds* [1] has written now the *M [an] of D [evon]* volume is a source of infinite gratification to me. It vindicates my insight, my opinion, my judgment, and it satisfies my affection for you,—in whom I believed and am believing. Because this *is* the point: I *am* believing. You've gone now beyond the point where I could be of any use to you, otherwise than just by my belief. It is if anything firmer than ever before, whether my remarks above find their way to your conviction or not. You may disagree with what I said here but in our main convictions we are at one.

To Arnold Bennett

Pent Farm,
10 Mch 1902.

MY DEAR SIR,

The reading of the *Man from the North* has inspired me with the greatest respect for your artistic conscience. I am profoundly impressed with the achievement of style. The root of the matter—which is expression—is there, and the sacred fire too. I hope you will give me the credit for understanding what you have tried for there. My dear Sir, I do envy you the power of coming so near to your desire.

The thing as written is undeniable. To read it was to me quite a

[1] *From the Four Winds,* by John Sinjohn, John Galsworthy's first book; published in 1898.

new experience of the language; and the delight was great enough to make me completely disregard the subject.

This at first; but as you may suppose I've read the book more than once. Unfortunately, I don't know how to criticize; to discuss, however, I am ready. Now the book (as a novel, not as a piece of writing) *is* disputable.

Generally, however, I may say that the die has not been struck hard enough. Here's a piece of pure metal scrupulously shaped, with a true —and more—a beautiful ring: but the die has not been struck hard enough. I admit that the outlines of the design are sharp enough. What it wants is a more emphatic modelling; more relief. And one could even quarrel with the design itself.

Nothing would give me greater pleasure than to have it out with you, the book there on the table, to be thumped and caressed. I would quarrel not with the truth of your conception but with the realism thereof. You stop just short of being absolutely real because you are faithful to your dogmas of realism. Now realism in art will never approach reality. And your art, your gift, should be put to the service of a larger and freer faith.

P. S. Of course I may have misunderstood your standpoint utterly. I want to hear what you have to say, if you think it worth while to say anything to me. Only let it be *viva voce*. Come when you can spare a day. I won't be likely to have forgotten the book. We shall be back at home after next Monday.[1] We can put you up and next day I could deliver you safe at H. G.'s [2] palatial residence.

To Miss M. Harriet M. Capes [3]

Pent Farm.
22nd March 1902.

DEAR MISS CAPES,

Your fancy is most kind but I fear it is a far cry from Prospero's Island to Patusan.

I have been greatly moved by your letter, by the kindness of your thought, by the generosity of your appreciation; and my wife, a person of simple feelings guided by the intelligence of the heart, has begged me for it to put into her own copy of the book. As it is only just that she should have her share of whatever's best in the hazard of

[1] From Winchelsea.
[2] H. G. Wells.
[3] To whom Joseph Conrad dedicated *A Set of Six* later on.

our indifferent fortunes, I have presented it to her for that purpose.

It is very late; it is very still; I have pushed my work aside to take up this sheet: and I only wish I had some part of your gift of convincing expression in which to clothe adequately the truth of my gratitude.

I have just re-read your gracious message. I cannot believe that I deserve so high a commendation. That you should give it to me is not my merit but yours alone—for the reader collaborates with the author. What I am most grateful for is the *artistic* sympathy and the delicate intelligence of your praise. But how to thank you I do not know, with my weary hand ministering to my jaded thought. I find my mind lame and outdistanced, and all I can say is that if you have found me worthy of your praise you have made me feel that your praise is eminently worth having: for to confer upon my unworthiness the greatest favour an author may receive you have found the just word and the penetrating phrase.

As soon as my next volume comes out I promise to myself the happiness of sending you a copy. Meantime pray let me assure you that your letter is not a small part of my reward for these anxious and perplexed hours which fall to the lot of us who write.

I am, dear Miss Capes, with a very sincere gratitude, your most obedient servant.

To John Galsworthy

Pent Farm.
25 June 1902.

DEAREST JACK,

Imagine that with "The End of Tether" [1] lying on the table ready (or all but) the lamp exploded and the whole thing is consumed! That was on Monday evening. On Tuesday by noon I had a comforting message from *B'woods* about it. If I can rewrite 4,000 words by the 2nd next or so the situation is saved as far as "Maga's" concerned. But what a setback! *Enfin!*

Heaven's unkind to Kings and to authors this year. [2]

My dear fellow, you did put new heart into me with your letter about the "Tether." But Edward is not very far wrong.

[1] The last tale of the *Youth and Other Stories* volume. The first instalment of "The End of the Tether" was published in the July issue of *Blackwood's Magazine,* and the others, monthly, to December inclusive.

[2] This was the year of King Edward VII's illness.

To John Galsworthy

Pent Farm.
5 Oct. 1902.

DEAREST JACK,

They are beasts. I've just received a note from H. M.[1] declining with many complimentary expressions.

I am sending you the MS. by this same post registered.

After all we must expect this sort of thing. No work is judged on its artistic merits: and there's no doubt that the book must rub many susceptibilities the wrong way. If you remember what tempest of anger *Madame Bovary* has raised by the sheer sincerity of its method alone you will understand perhaps that your sincerity,—extending further than mere method,—must prepare itself for a struggle. Upon my word, the book is worth the sweat and the dust of it.[2]

The temper of the present time is against it a little. You must not forget that when I (without a little of the value you display here) have got myself accepted with the *Folly,* it was during a boom in fiction, such as this century is not likely to see for a few years yet. I do not mean to say that you should wait. Of course not! I only point out another difficulty in addition to the book's excellence which stands in its way.

I don't know what you'll resolve on doing at once. I should suggest a certain expenditure of work on it on the lines we have discussed.

After all it is a short work. It will stand expanding.

Next thing I would suggest is a certain compromise,—a concession to the need of popularity. Something must be done to the end. I will expound my meaning when you come down, and you must come down on the book's business on the first convenient day after the 15th inst. Why after the 15th inst. and not before I'll explain when we meet. That I shall by then be free of the "Tether" is not the only reason.

Let me know what you feel and think and undergo.

P. S. For God's sake *don't, don't* get disgusted.

To Arnold Bennett

Pent Farm.
6th Nov. 1902.

MY DEAR BENNETT,

I wonder what you think of me? Well, I have deserved some hard thoughts, but only in a certain measure. Obviously I might have sent a

[1] H. Meldrum.
[2] Refers to *The Island Pharisees,* early draft.

civil line to acknowledge the book;[1] but obviously too one does not like to send a civil line in acknowledgment of E. A. Bennett's book. The gift is on another footing of welcome.

Of one thing you may be sure, that my silence, my unconscionable delay, had not for cause indifference. The word looms monstrous as I write. Neither was I made lazy by an excess of happiness, or busy with riotous living. The reason was worry, the terrible worry of having to re-write a story (completed and then burnt by a fatal accident),[2] with the next instalment of "Maga" and the impossibility of concocting a reasonable sentence confronting me at every turn. It was like a nightmare.

But if I could not write to you, I had found time to read your book. I read it once, twice, and then kept it upstairs for dipping into when I came up to bed, jaded with my unavailing efforts to express myself in the absence of any sort of mood; and your firm grip, the firm grip of style and the mastery of the subject, have more than once refreshed my weariness.

I doubt if hitherto my mind had been fresh enough to appreciate your work—intellectually as it deserves to be. Its appeal had been to me emotional, a matter of art purely as apart from underlying thought. Of course, you understand that my emotion is awakened by the *skill* of your work first—and I may almost say: first and last—this word in my mind embracing everything; from the first coördination of your inspiration, through the effective processes of your thought, down to the last small touches of expression, delightful to trace along the pages and which resume to me the whole extent of the remarkable gifts which you display in the freshness and the cadence of your sentences.

It is indeed a thing *done:* good to see and friendly to live with for a space. This is the final impression—the whole feeling freed from that quarrelsomeness of one craftsman appreciating another—if you do me the honour to take me for a fellow craftsman. That I could drag up points for discussion you may be pretty sure; I have no other way of showing my love of the *work* when I meet the *man* face to face; but to criticize in detail (even if to laud)—that I cannot do on paper; and if you, by chance, should care to receive my argumentative tribute to your excellence you must choose any day after the 16th inst: for a rush into Kent. We can put you up, you know, in a sort of haphazard way and when you get tired of my inanities you may fly to Wells[3] for refuge. It's

[1] *Anna of the Five Towns*, with the Dedication: *"'To Joseph Conrad from E. A. Bennett, Trinity Hall Farm, Hockliffe, Beds., 11 Sept., 1902."*
[2] "The End of the Tether."
[3] H. G. Wells.

only seven miles. I would be most truly delighted to receive a warning note from you.

That the advance upon the *Man from the North* is great is undeniable. Just in what that advance consists it's not so easy to say without losing one's way amongst mere superficialities—for there too the advance is very marked. The other, the deeper change, the essential progress, is felt right through but not so easy to hold up. The excellence (in its place) of the first par. of Chap. XII is easy to point out, or the mastery —the obvious mastery—of pp. 164, 165. My dear fellow, it is fine, very fine; I am thankful to see it written. But there are other passages, other pages and the whole spirit of the book informed by a less apparent excellence.

There is too the whole conception of the story, whence, of course, flows the characterization. On this one could say much. I am afraid of falling into twaddle without the stimulus of your presence and your voice. I will only then say that the conception seems to me too logical. It's a cryptic saying and does not make my criticism clear in the least— not even to myself.

But on that I end with a congratulatory and hearty handshake. It *is* good, my dear Bennett: and you *know* it is good: and I know that you shall do even better.

Kindest regards.

P. S. I perceive I haven't after all thanked you for sending me the book. The letter however is written with that object, as you may have guessed. I shall send a vol. of my rot when it appears—or have a copy for you when you come.

To (Major) E. Dawson

Pent Farm.
12th December 1902.
Thursday.

MY DEAR DAWSON,

I snatch the first piece of MS. paper to hand, for I have delayed too long my answer to you.

With many thanks for your hospitable scheme, I am afraid that it cannot be carried out this month. However, next year is near enough and your plan is too seductive not to be seriously considered. Don't forget however that (with all my qualities[?]) I am reduced to write for dear life literally; and that when I put forward the claims of my work, it is no conventional excuse, but iron necessity that speaks.

Ceci posé, you may trust my very sincere desire to see you again and to make your brother's acquaintance; but as to a definite answer at this moment, I must beg your indulgence. It all depends how I get on with the story begun some six years ago and which *must* be finished in March, *"Faudra voir,"* as our neighbours say. I shall drop you a line early in January. This care apart, I think that's a magnificent occasion for me to go wrong, to fling my pen,—so to say,—*"par dessus les moulins"* and cease to be a respectable (and bored) workman for two or three days.

I had the *Spectator* from Clifford a day or two before your letter. Many thanks. As to Clifford, I think his reservations (and they are too few, in all conscience) are perfectly just and proper, as far as they go. As to his commendation, I am not sure; the personal element enters into that; we are on very friendly terms and he is very human.

In regard to what you say of greatness, I doubt if greatness can be attained now in imaginative prose work. When it comes, it will be in a new form; in a form for which we are not ripe as yet. Till the hour strikes and the man appears, we must plod in the beaten track, we must externally *"rabacher"* the old formula of expression. There is no help and no hope; there is only the duty to try, to try everlastingly, with no regard for success. Kindest regards.

To John Galsworthy

Thursday
Pent Farm [early 1903].

DEAREST JACK,

I shall turn up at Holld P[ark] Av[enue] some time between 11 and 12. I can't be more precise, because the trains are not trustworthy.

Up to last Monday I had slight sciatica and a slightly lame foot; these slight infirmities (which had no charm of novelty) have departed now without medicamentations—on the cheap—and no harm done. Only with my head full of a story, I have not been able to write a single word—except the title, which shall be, I think: *Nostromo:* the story belonging to the "Karain" class of tales ("K" class for short—as you classify the cruisers).

Will you leave whatever MS. is ready in the flat for me? Going back there from H. P. A. about 3 or 4, I shall have time to begin reading it at once. I couldn't wait—I really could not. Don't forget this request of mine, my dear Jack.

Your "program' is simply lovely and accepted with enthusiasm.

To (Sir) Hugh Clifford

Pent Farm.
26th February 1903.

MY DEAR CLIFFORD,

I ought to have thanked you before but I preferred to read the book [1] first. I've read it twice, with casts back here and there.

The book is remarkable—and that it will be very much remarked I have no doubt. For myself I've been immensely interested by that in the book which you alone could have told us. And you have told it excellently well, with vivacity, with admirable touches, with an ease I quite envy you. I should not be in the least surprised if the book did turn out a popular success—which as usual would be given to it for what is least valuable, for the mere "novel" side of it. Well! and that is an achievement too deserving a word of congratulation. Of course for me *Since the Beginning* is a much more significant work, of greater feeling, of greater intrinsic value, less of a "novel," more of a creation, better worth presenting. Here on the other hand we have more skill in presentation. A distinct advance.

The fault I would find is a certain immaturity or rather superficialness in Maurice's character. That sort of romantic and adventurous impulse argues a certain depth of character, a certain firmness of fibre, a resolution that will stand more than a shock or two—whereas that young man seems as nervous as a cat in his disappointment, in his disenchantment, in his horror. He is terribly unscrupulous and too emotional to be quite convincing in his emotion. It looks a little as though he were not quite responsible for his actions and his feelings. When one thinks of a Christian, and presumably a gentleman, already disillusioned (for you do strike that note almost at once) for nothing as it were, for a half-faded whim, carefully shooting at the Dutch officers and then directly afterwards beside himself with horror at the mutilation of the dead bodies, one mistrusts the genuineness of both manifestations. In short, it seems to me that you make him too savage and too squeamish, in particular instances, and too unthinking in general.

Of course, I may have misunderstood your intention. The most intelligent amongst us are very stupid and I don't lay claim to an exceptional dose of intelligence. Moreover you know my opinion—that criticism is a vain thing against a man's conceptions as to life, character, morality and whatever else goes to make up the only truth that matters. Criticism can be only applied usefully to facts—which don't matter. Thus I've offered

[1] *A Free-Lance of To-day,* by Hugh Clifford. Methuen & Co.

these remarks upon Maurice Curzon (Maurice not Nathaniel) who is a creation (whereas Nathaniel is only a Viceroy) in no cavilling spirit of fault-finding but simply for your consideration as one friend speaks to another, in the belief that in the most imbecile remark there may be found a particle of truth—else we had much better have been all born dumb.

There's much to say yet—if only to talk of the pleasure of reading whatever you write. And that's a truth too, if rather stupidly put. But it is late (to-morrow in fact) and I am made stupid by ten hours of steady trying to write something that by no effort of vanity I can imagine as giving pleasure in the reading to anybody on earth.

Kindest regards.

To H. G. Wells

Pent Farm.
Thursday, 1903.

DEAREST H. G.,

An excellent volume.[1] Last time I saw you you spoke of it slightingly—and this only adds to my envy of your astounding gift—for if this is the sort of thing you throw off while you whistle!—Well!

Your power of realization of whatever you choose to imagine is astounding. The *force* of your imagination is even more surprising than its extent. The usual aspects in the Accelerator, the absolutely convincing effects in the *spiders*, fill me with admiration. You know what I mean exactly.

Filmer strengthens my conviction (derived from *Wheels of Chance* and *Love and Mr. Lewisham*) that, at bottom, you are an uncompromising realist. There is a cold jocular ferocity about the handling of that mankind in which you believe, that gives me the shudders sometimes. However, as you do believe in them, it is right and proper and excellent that you should get some fun in making their bones rattle. And can't you do it too! Well, more power to you—I'll do the sighing and slobbering and lamenting and sneezing—or whatever it is I am trying to do—and never getting done; which last is the only irony I've been able to achieve.

The ghost story is very good. As a matter of fact *in execution* you never falter. Of conceptions, of course, in the mass and variety of your work, some must be slighter than others. The fat man is good fooling,

---

[1] *Twelve Stories and a Dream,* by H. G. Wells.

dam' good—and quite sufficiently ferocious. The Rome business is by no means bad—but I understand *that* being thrown off. However, in some strange way it does not read like Wells at all. The fairy story is the weakest, I fancy. The last thing is in the tone of the *Sleeper*—absolutely—with all the high qualities—and that something subtly wanting that one felt in the big book.

Your wife looked delightfully well. Is the baby better? Has he got reconciled to his milk?

I, my dear Wells, am absolutely out of my mind with the worry and apprehension of my work.[1] I go on as one would cycle over a precipice along a 14-inch plank. If I falter I am lost.

To R. B. Cunninghame Graham

Pent Farm.
19 Mch. 1903.

TRÈS CHER AMI,

I hope you've forgiven my long silence. It is not, on reflection, a very great transgression; seeing that the best of us have but a few thoughts and that of these the best worth saying have a trick of being unutterable—not because of their profundity but because there is a devil that tangles the tongue or hangs to the penholder, making its use odious and the sound of words foolish like the banging of tin cans.

With this exordium—*c'est le mot, n'est-ce pas?*—I approach you with the offering of my book whose title page proof[2] I've just sent back to the Yahudi. It is to appear on the 22nd of April (not on the 1st as the War Office Army Corps do) and the exordium above is a sort of explanatory note upon the brevity of its dedication.

I have been reading again the *Vanished Arcadia*—from the dedication[3] so full of charm, to the last paragraph with its ironic aside about the writers of books "proposing something and concluding nothing" and its exquisite last lines bringing out the all-resuming image of travellers "who, wandering in the Tarumensian woods, come on a clump of orange-trees run wild amongst the urundays.'"

A fit beginning and a fit note to end a book for which I have the greatest admiration, wherein profound feeling and the poor judgment of such reason as Allah deigned to give me are in perfect accord. Not

---

[1] *Nostromo.*

[2] *Typhoon and Other Stories,* which was dedicated to R. B. Cunninghame Graham.

[3] To the Author of *Santa Teresa, Her Life and Times,* etc.

for me are such beginnings and such endings. I should like to draw your attention therefore to the austere simplicity of the "To R. B. Cunninghame Graham" and nothing more—if my conscience didn't whisper, what you will see without any pointing out, that this is not austerity, but barrenness and nothing else—the awful lack of words that overcomes the thought struggling eagerly towards the lips.

Et voilà! It is poor, poor: the dedication saying nothing and the book proposing something, wherefrom no power on earth could extract any kind of conclusion: but such as they are, and more worthless than one single solitary leaf in the wilderness of the Tarumensian woods, they are yours.

Je vous serre la main.

To Ford Madox Hueffer

Pent Farm,
Tuesday. [1903]

MY DEAR FORD,

This is what I've done.

I've sent parts I, II, & IV of *Seraphina* [1] to Pinker with instructions to send on to Edinburgh as soon as clean typed. The second copy goes to the States. Our copy of pts. II & IV to come here. Pt. I does not want any tinkering any more. Part II I've worked at a little—reducing and bringing into line in matters of detail which we have overlooked here and there.

Then to give the story a fair chance I have given up the idea of presenting the *Rescue* to B'wood. This was McClure's wish and intention. However, without my consent he can't do that. I had reserved B. to myself.

Meldrum seems to think the acceptance of *Seraphina* a fairly certain thing. M. goes North next week and will help W. B'wood to read the parts I, II, & IV. I write an epitome of p. III and shall send it to Scotland in a day or two.

I've studied p. III as a whole very earnestly. It is most important and it wants doing over. It must be given hard *reality*. The treatment as it stands is too much in the air—in places. I don't want to bother you now by going into the argument. I shall do the thing myself, but of course I would want to speak to you about it. Don't let this interrupt your work on the dear old Harry. I hear you've been gathering

---

[1] It refers to *Romance*.

the pollen and the sweetness of the B'sh Museum and assume you are fabricating now the specimen combs.

I've made no combs—I've been (like Soame) [1] ill—very ill—but if my arrangements come off, I won't "stop the confounded presses and spoof old Hueffer."

On the other hand, pray don't curse me in your heart. I am surprised I've preserved my sanity all these days—but never mind.

There's no doubt that Heinemann means to work up *The Inheritors*. In Pawling's opinions there is nothing against the book's success but the general slump in the trade. Of the slump, alas, there can be no doubt. I had heard of it from Meldrum, who has no conceivable reason to mislead me.

Otherwise P. would be *certain* of success. I've never before heard such talk of anything with my name to it. So hopeful, I mean. There shall be a campaign. Different plans are under consideration. One of them is to start a general discussion on Methods of Collaboration. Have you noticed in the last *Academy* a sort of preliminary whisper? That's it. The other hare, it seems, is to be a philosophical hare. That's what Nietzsche's philosophy leads to—here's your over-man—I said. I kept my gravity in the big armchair and with extreme sobriety made suggestions: the authors by the introduction of the *4th D[imension]* tried to remove their work from the sphere of mere personalities. They attack not individuals, but the spirit of the age—the immoral tendencies arising from a purely materialistic view of life which even reach the lower classes (Slingsby, I suppose).

I had hard work to keep my countenance with the photo of the great Callan, on the mantelpiece, looking at me. Pawling wanted to know who Fox was. I smiled enigmatically. P. *has* read the book. He talked glibly of the D. de Mersh, of your aunt (she's no aunt of mine) in Paris, of Churchill, of Gurnard, (he called him Chamberlain half the time), of Polehampton (he winked and I winked), of Callan—"that's Crockett." My lower jaw fell. (I swear that this is exactly and verbatim what happened.) He looked me hard in the eye.

"Of course it's Crockett. There's no man who had worked that kind of business more."

I asked him not to let it out; and he said: "Oh, no. Of course not." By the immortal Jove, it was like a chapter out of the very book itself.[2]

Anyway, that's what's in the wind. When you good people come along, I shall tell you more. Burn this letter for fear the German girl should

[1] Soame Forsyte in John Galsworthy's books.
[2] *The Inheritors.*

sell it to a Belgian newspaper and we should stand revealed as 4th dimensionists ourselves.

I am much better for the rush to town. Otherwise all goes badly with me. But never fear. I shall get the thing written before very long.

Let us know when you good people are coming.

Love from us all.

To R. B. Cunninghame Graham

Pent Farm
2 May, 1903

TRÈS CHER AMI,

Thanks for your good letter. I am glad you like the shorter stories, but *je me berce dans l'illusion* that "Falk" is *le clou* of that little show.

Of course: Gambusino. I ought to have corrected my proofs carefully.

The book (*Maison du Péché*) [1] has arrived and is now half read. Without going further, my verdict is that it is good, but is not *fort*. For that sort of thing *no matter how good,* I always feel a secret contempt, for the reason that it is just *what I can do* myself, *essentiellement*.

Fundamentally I believe that sort of fiction (I *don't* mean the *subject,* of course) is somehow wrong. Too easy. *Trop inventé:* never *assez vécu*. There is a curse on the descriptive analysis of that sort.

Kindest regards from us both.

To R. B. Cunninghame Graham

Pent Farm
1903
9 May.

TRÈS CHER AMI,

Don't let your dedicatory obligation interfere with your peace of mind. Frankly, I am more than repaid by the satisfaction of seeing your name at the head of my book.[2] It is a public declaration of our communion in more, perhaps, than mere letters and I don't mind owning to my pride in it.

And if you will *mettre le comble à vos bontés* you may render me a service by coming to see me here. (I speak not of heartfelt pleasure— *cela va sans dire*), I want to talk to you of the work I am engaged on

---

[1] A novel by the French authoress, Marcelle Tinayre.
[2] *Typhoon and Other Stories* (William Heinemann, London, 1903.)

now.[1] I hardly dare avow my audacity—but I am placing it in Sth America, in a Republic I call Costaguana. It is however concerned mostly with Italians. But you must hear the *sujet* and this I can't set down on a small piece of paper.

Shall I send your copy of *Typhoon* to the club at once or may I keep it here till you find time to run down to my wretched ranch in the wilderness?

Tout à vous.

To R. B. Cunninghame Graham

Pent Farm
8 July 1903

TRÈS CHER AMI,

Your delightful enthusiasm for *les trois contes*[2] positively refreshed my mind, jaded with a sort of hopeless overwork.

I forward you the effigy (executed by Jacob, *artiste photographe*) of your humble friend and servant. You are not however expected to compromise yourself by keeping it in a prominent place.

Trêve de plaisanteries! I am dying over that cursed *Nostromo* thing. All my memories of Central America seem to slip away. I just had a glimpse 25 years ago,—a short glance. That is not enough *pour bâtir un roman dessus*. And yet one must live.

When it's done I'll never dare look you in the face again. Meantime (and always)

Tout à vous.

Présentez mes devoirs à Madame votre femme. What of the novel? When is it coming out? I admit I've been struck and excited by your mere hint of its subject.

To J. B. Pinker

Pent Farm.
22nd August 1903
Saturday.

MY DEAR PINKER,

This is half of the book, about 42,000 or so.[3] I send it as forming only one part, the First, entitled: "The Silver of the Mine."

[1] *Nostromo.*
[2] *Typhoon and Other Stories.*
[3] *Nostromo.*

I suppose we will have to divide it in two, somewhere, to balance the other half planned in two parts, IInd "The Isabels" and IIIrd "The Lighthouse." Which then would become respectively IIIrd and IVth. But where to divide and what title to give I don't know. It must first be typed clear and then we will consider. *Don't* let the typist *number* the chapters, on that account.

I have never worked so hard before—with so much anxiety. But the result is good. You know I take no credit to myself for what I do—and so I may judge my own performance. There is no mistake about this. You may take up a strong position when you offer it here. It is a very genuine Conrad. At the same time it is more of a Novel pure and simple than anything I've done since *Almayer's Folly*.

Of the other half of the book a lot is done, written actually on paper; though not fit to be shown even to you. In fact it is not typed yet. My wife had bad neuralgia (we suppose) in the right hand and it has delayed the completion of even this part: for as you know I work a lot upon the type.

If people want to begin printing (serial) say in Sept^{er} you may let them safely—for you know that, at the very worst, M. stands in the background (quite confidentially you understand). But there's no reason to anticipate anything of the kind. If I am to break down, it will be after this infernal thing is finished.

But it's a miserable life anyhow. Have you sent anything to Watson [1] this month? I daren't draw a check. But I felt too sick of everything to write you before. Moreover, my salvation is to shut eyes and ears to everything—or else I couldn't write a line. And yet sometimes I can't forget—I remember the tradesmen, and all the horrors descend upon me. Damn! Try to help me out to the end of this and then we will see how we stand. And then there will be nothing for it but to start at once on the Mediterranean story which is contracted for.[2] What will become of the *Rescue* then, devil only knows! Enough! My head bursts with these silly worries. If you call on Wells, do come and see me too.

P. S. Do you know anything of the date for *Romance?* The proofs hang fire a good deal. And yet—who knows—the story seems very promising. It may do the trick.

[1] His banker.
[2] Probably "The *Tremolino*" (*Mirror of the Sea*)

To John Galsworthy

Pent Farm
22 August 1903

DEAREST JACK,

The book is, this moment, half done [1] and I feel half dead and wholly imbecile.

If you want to do your part by a man, for whom you have done so much already, then do not fail to come down here the first day you can spare.

To work in the conditions which are, I suppose, the outcome of my character mainly, is belittling, it is demoralizing. I fight against demoralization, of which fight I bear the brunt and my friends bear the cost. All this is very beautiful and inspiring to think about,—and elevating and encouraging and, I can't think of any more pretty words.

Pawling, if he's in London, shall get my letter to him inquiring about *The Pharisees* [2] on Monday next—I wondered too what was going on.

I didn't write to you because, upon my word, I am ashamed to write to anybody. I feel myself strangely growing into a sort of outcast. A mental and moral outcast. I hear nothing—think of nothing—I reflect upon nothing—I cut myself off—and with all that I can just only keep going, or rather keep on lagging from one wretched story to another—and always deeper in the mire.

We are so glad to hear your father is really better. Remember us all round, pray, as kindly as you know.

And do come. The prospect of your going abroad fills me with dread. Why? Nerves?

Don't you think I ought to apologize for this silly letter? I do!

To the Hon. Mrs. Bontine

Pent Farm
26 August 1903

DEAR MRS. BONTINE,

I venture to send you this copy of the book [3] dedicated to your

[1] *Nostromo.*

[2] John Galsworthy's novel, *The Island Pharisees.*

[3] The copy of the book alluded to bears this inscription: *Avec les hommages respectueux de l'Auteur, 1903.*

son, as a tribute,—very inadequate alas!—to his great gifts which I am proud of being able to understand and appreciate.

Pray accept it as a sign of my affectionate admiration for him and of my profound respect and my gratitude for the interest you have been good enough to manifest in my work.

> I am, dear Mrs. Bontine
> your most faithful and obedient servant.

To Ford Madox Hueffer

September 1903.

MY DEAR FORD,

Here's the end of *Romance*. I beg to recommend to you earnestly the alterations and additions suggested in my set of proofs.

From about half of p. 460 I have written on embodying my conception of the end, which, you'll see, is exactly yours with some alterations.

Jack [1] (who leaves to-night) has read with enthusiasm the whole (uncorrected) part. He absolutely admires the whole of the prison scenes and especially the trial. I am of his opinion. He has said several quite intelligent things in appreciation.

I won't bother you with my reasons for what I have done; I have done nothing hastily—and the intention is obvious in every case. Jessie suggested that the reunion with S. [2] should be made plain—and (as for the temper of average readers) her opinion may be allowed some weight. As she has volunteered it I must suppose that she had felt the necessity very strongly. Upon the whole I urge upon you to accept my version or rather some version to that effect.

Jack begs that the opening of parph. *"It was rather tremendous"* should be eliminated. His very words are: that the Judge's speech *per se,* coming at the end of the admirable trial scene, has a tremendousness which is diminished by being pointed out. I propose, in case you would consider that change, that the par: should begin straight away with—*"My dignity,"* etc. However, that is not an important point. I don't know quite how I feel. I am sure your feeling will be right. Be careful. The thing is too emphatically good to be pulled to pieces casually.

I repeat: I've only written the final scene because it would have

[1] John Galsworthy.
[2] Seraphina.

not been quite fair simply to write you that something had to be done. This is a suggestion—the shadow of a suggestion. *You* must do the thing yourself.

My love to you all.

P. S. Be assured that I've done nothing casually. I've kept this two days. There's no use delaying any longer. I am sure you will not think that I've been wantonly interfering with quite a remarkable piece of work. Quite remarkable in execution, in conception, and still more distinguished in its suggestiveness. I congratulate you.

To H. G. Wells

Pent Farm.
2nd Oct. 1903.

MY DEAR WELLS,

I have neither appeared nor written because I have been gouty for the last week. The attack is not very severe, but I have felt startlingly ill with it. Absolutely knocked over. Why? I don't know. It used not to be so.

Drop me a line and tell me how you are. Jessie made a cheering report as to your wife's appearance; at the same time she says she has heard the ominous name of thick [?] pronounced in reference to something you must not do—or must do. This makes me wonder whether you did not bring from your holiday some beastly cold or some beastly little ache—as so often happens.

I would like to know that you are in your best form, whether you are working or not.

Now I've lived with your book for some days, I like it more. What surprises me is to find you so strangely conservative at bottom. In the end I don't discover more points where we are in contact, I felt all these as I went along on my first reading. The divergences which arise from the dissimilar sides of our natures become more definite in the process of thinking as was to be expected, because one does not profoundly examine where one cordially agrees. Generally the impression of *soundness* is strong all through. I must stop. If I were not so depressed generally, I would try and write on, but I am afraid, in my present state, to say something too stupid while meaning something tolerably reasonable. There are really one or two points I would like to talk over with you seriously. One of them would be on a matter of tact, or rather discretion, in the attitude you take up, which to me seems incomprehensible on *your* part and generally disadvantageous to you.

But enough. Most affectionately yours.

To Arnold Bennett

Pent Farm.
19th Nov. 1903.

MY DEAR BENNETT,

You must think me a brute. I don't even attempt to palliate an inexcusable delay in thanking you for *Leonora*. Still when I tell you that I am some four months behind with a wretched novel I am writing for Harpers you'll understand the state of my mind.

Yes. You *can* do things; you present them with a skill and in a language for which I wish here to thank you as distinctly as possible, and with all the respect due to such a remarkable talent.

Remains the question of conception; the only one in which discussion as between you and me is possible. And here the first criticism that occurs is that there is not enough of Leonora herself. The pedestal is, as it were, too large for the statue. And that's about the only objection that can be made to the book as a *work*. With the sheer pleasure of reading it, that—say—defect does not interfere. It is only in thinking it over that the objection arises. And it is impossible to read *Leonora* without afterwards thinking it all over—with great satisfaction, undoubtedly, and yet with some regret also.

You see I am frank with you; and I am frank because I have a great regard for your high ideal of workmanship, and for the ways of your thought. But one would need to talk it over with you to make one's meaning clear. Discussion alone could do that; for you must not imagine that I am trying to pick holes; I am too much fascinated by your expression, by the ease of your realization, the force and the delicacy of your phrases. Whether you obtain them by hard toil or by an amazing inborn ability does not matter; these qualities are there. That you can also go to the bottom of your subject *Anna*[1] proves sufficiently well; though even in that book, perhaps? . . .

However, don't mind me. It is very possible that I am too romantic and don't seize quite your true intention.

I trust that when you come over here we may meet. You really ought

---

[1] *Anna of the Five Towns.*

to spare me an evening and we can put you up for the night—after a rough and ready fashion.

To H. G. Wells

Pent Farm.
30 Nov. '03.

MY DEAR H. G.,

Indeed I did not expect you in this awful weather, especially as Jessie reported you with a cold.

I was laid by the knee (this time) the day after we travelled up together. I did not feel particularly bright even then, or else I would have succumbed to your blandishments and stayed for a dinner and a chat in town.

Things are bad with me—there's no disguising the fact. Not only is the scribbling awfully in arrears but there's no "spring" in me to grapple with it effectually. Formerly in my sea life, a difficulty nerved me to the effort; now I perceive it is not so. However, don't imagine I've given up, but there is an uncomfortable sense of losing my footing in deep waters.

Romance 's gone into 2nd ed: I hear. That, no doubt, does not mean much, but still it is better than any of my other books did do. Is *Men in the Moon* doing well for you—I mean *really* well? After all, my dear boy, for all our faith in our good intentions and even in our achievements, a paper-success (as I call it) is not a strong enough tonic. I say so because for me, writing—*the only possible writing*—is just simply the conversion of nervous force into phrases. With you too, I am sure, tho' in your case it is the disciplined intelligence which gives the signal—the impulse. For me it is a matter of chance, stupid chance. But the fact remains that when the nervous force is exhausted the phrases don't come—and no tension of will can help.

Don't imagine I am grumbling. I had ten times the luck I deserved. All this talk is very stupid but it comforts me to worry you a little.

Our love to all your house. I am touched by Archer's Repentance (Would do as title for short story). It strikes me, my dear Wells, that, in your quiet, almost stealthy way, you are doing a lot for me; if it were not for you a lot of people would not know of my existence, anything palpable, and still less of my involved form of narrative. I will be delighted to meet Prof. York Powell. Don't forget to send me Metchnikov's book. I am really curious to see that.

To John Galsworthy

Pent Farm.
30 Nov. 1903.

MY DEAREST JACK,

I have been ill again. Just got down, shaky, weak, dispirited.

No work done. No spring left to grapple with it. Everything looks black, but I suppose that will wear off, and anyhow, I am trying to keep despair under. Nevertheless I feel myself losing my footing in deep waters. They are lapping about my hips.

My dear fellow, it is not so much the frequency of these gout attacks, but I feel so beastly ill between, ill in body and mind. It has never been so before. Impossible to write,—while the brain riots in incoherent images. It is sometimes quite alarming.

I've just written refusing Mrs. Hoare's invitation for an evening function on the eighth, and also a dinner of Smith's for the 10th. I got a card the other day and meantime advert[isement]s are appearing of the first edition being exhausted just one month after publication.[1] That is better than anything of mine has ever done. *Et voilà!* What a Romance!

I've been trying (lying on my back in bed with one knee and one ankle swollen) to think of a title. But I've been unable to think of anything better than the *Phylacteries*.[2] In fact, if *Pharisees* is impossible, then the other is the right title, it seems to me. Does P. object to it on popularity grounds? or what? Why don't you let them try their hand themselves at a name, if they are so mighty difficult to please? There was some bother of that sort about the *Nigger of the N.*[3] I remember. But whatever the name, that book, my dearest Jack, shall lay solid ground under your feet. With the next you shall begin to climb,—and build. I am glad I've lived long enough to see and with wit enough left to perceive you've found yourself.

Do come, my dear Jack, as soon as you can and help me through a day or two. Bring what you've written to the very last word. I *want* to see it all.

[1] Referring to *Romance*.

[2] It refers to *The Island Pharisees*.

[3] As a matter of fact, I remember the late William Heinemann showing me a letter by J. C. suggesting *thirteen different titles* for *The Nigger of the "Narcissus."* Unfortunately, that letter, which was seen for the last time in 1920, has been mislaid and has evaded every search.—G. J. A.

To H. G. Wells

Monday [1903].

DEAR H. G.,

The lecture is splendid. It is striking in its *expression* and as nearly perfect as things of to-day can be in its tone, and of a sort most attractive to me. I call it scientific eloquence—that is, eloquence appealing not to the passions, like the eloquence of the orator, but to the reason. That in this case it is calculated for the smaller capacity of the general public makes it no less scientific; for it is calculated perfectly for the understandings you have had to address, and *there* is the best of a successful achievement whether in art, in letters or in politics.

Its sheer *pronouncement* is difficult to criticize because of its extremely skilful moderation. Indeed that skill is extremely striking. You make a case. All the criticisms I've seen (now, after reading the lecture) strike me as extremely unfair—I would say uncandid, did I not know how honest a total misapprehension of the plainest meaning can be.

When I try to analyze to myself the merits of its *substance,* I find the difficulty of weighing the imponderable. Do not suspect that I have in my mind the uselessness of such an inquiry. I am, I flatter myself, too intelligent to take such a stand. But with my rooted idea of the whole value of the future (whatever we wish to make it or find it) consisting in what we do endure and shape *to-day* I can't help wishing you had emphasized that view—which surely is not foreign to your conviction? Is it? The future is of our own making—and (for me) the most striking characteristic of the century is just that development, that maturing of our consciousness which should open our eyes to that truth—or that illusion. Anything that would help our intelligences towards a clearer view of the consequences of our social action is of the very greatest value—and, as such, a guide. I salute you.

I shall try to descend on you for a talk very soon.

To (Major) E. Dawson

Pent Farm,
21st. Dec. 1903

MY DEAR DAWSON,

Perfectly correct. The chief mate on the forecastle head takes charge of all the operations connected with the raising and securing of the anchor; and generally when getting under weigh the chief officer takes charge forward and the second mate aft, where he is under the eye of the captain (or rather Master) who is in command of the whole thing.

This is the absolute practice in sailing ships and steamers of the Merchant Service. There may be a special routine and different "stations" in large mail-boats, perhaps. But I doubt it; and, in any case, it cannot be very different. The chief officer even there is, I am pretty sure, responsible for the efficiency and correct handling of what is called "ground tackle," chains, anchors, fish and cat davits and all purchases appertaining thereto, windlass, etc., etc. When a steam windlass is used, the carpenter is driving it. This is his work even in steamers. The boatswain is with the mate to carry out orders.

I think I have answered fully your question.

I was glad to hear from you. Yes, my dear fellow, we shall meet before you leave. I shall make it my pleasurable business to see you directly the thing is practicable. My wife sends her kind regards and joins me in most cordial wishes for your happiness and prosperity.

I am delighted to hear *B'wood's* is hospitable to your stuff.[1] Don't talk of pot-boilers. We are all writing pot-boilers. The best work of the best man has gone into pot-boilers. I had an awful year of it. Never mind.

To R. B. Cunninghame Graham

Pent Farm.
26th Dec. 1903.

CHER AMI,

I snatch this piece of MS. paper first of all to thank you for remembering the boy at this festive (?) season. Next to tell you that *H. de Soto*[2] is most exquisitely excellent; your very mark and spirit upon a subject that only *you* can do justice to,—with your wonderful English and your sympathetic insight into the souls of the Conquistadores. The glamour, the pathos and the romance of that time and of those men are only adequately, truthfully conveyed to us by your pen: the sadness, the glory and the romance of the endeavour, together with the vanity of vanities of the monstrous achievement, are reflected in

---

[1] About that time *Blackwood's Magazine* published several essays, sketches or reminiscences by E. Dawson: "A Reconnaissance," "A River of Cathay," "The Affair at the Green-River Mine," "The Prisoner," etc.

[2] *Hernando de Soto, Together with an Account of One of His Captains, Gonçalo Silvestre,* by R. B. Cunninghame Graham. London, W. Heinemann, 1903.

your unique style as though you had been writing of men with whom you had slept by the camp fire, after tethering your horses on the threshold of the unknown.

You have an eye for buried jewels! Pizarro going about mournfully with his hat pulled down on his ears after the death of Atahualpa is new to me. He is made unforgettable at last. *"C'est énorme d'humanité,"* as the great Flaubert would have yelled to the four winds of heaven. What a touch! Behold in this Conquistador my long lost brother together with those others: the *Indio gentile hombre* shouting insults, underneath his tree, and the thirty lances riding on to the sea, some of them already with death sitting on the pillion behind, to be received with the question: "Have you seen any signs of gold in the country?" One seems to hear the very voice. *C'est la vérité même!* It's the most amazingly natural thing I've ever read: it gives me a furious desire to learn Spanish and bury myself in the pages of the incomparable Garcilaso—if only to forget our modern Conquistadores.

Their achievement is monstrous enough in all conscience,—but not as a great human force let loose, but rather like that of a gigantic and obscene beast. Leopold is their Pizarro, Thys [1] their Cortez, and their "lances" are recruited amongst the *"souteneurs, sous-offs, maquereaux, fruits-secs"* of all sorts on the pavements of Brussels and Antwerp. I send two letters I had from a man called Casement,[2] premising that I knew him first in the Congo just 12 years ago. Perhaps you've heard or seen in print his name. He's a Protestant Irishman, pious too. But so was Pizarro. For the rest I can assure you that he is a limpid personality. There is a touch of the conquistador in him too; for I've seen him start off into an unspeakable wilderness swinging a crookhandled stick for all weapons, with two bulldogs, Paddy (white) and Biddy (brindle), at his heels and a Loanda boy carrying a bundle for all company. A few months afterwards it so happened that I saw him come out again, a little leaner, a little browner, with his stick, dogs and Loanda boy, and quietly serene as though he had been for a stroll in a park. Then we lost sight of each other. He was, I believe, B[riti]sh Consul in Beira, and lately seems to have been sent to the Congo again, on some sort of mission, by the Br. Govt. I have always thought that some particle of Las Casas' soul had found refuge in his indefatigable body. The letters will tell you the rest. I would help him, but it is not in me. I am only a wretched novelist inventing wretched stories and not even up to that miserable game; but your good pen, keen, flexible and straight, and sure like a good Toledo blade, would

[1] See Chap. VII.
[2] Roger Casement, see the chapter entitled "In the Heart of Darkness."

tell in the fray if you felt disposed to give a slash or two. He could tell you things! Things I've tried to forget: things I never did know. He has had as many years of Africa as I had months—almost.[1]

Another small matter. S. Perez Triana [2] heard from Pawling of my longing to get away south (when possible) and has written me the kindest letter imaginable, offering information and even introductions. I am quite touched. But pray tell me whether he is Colombian Minister in Spain and if it behoves me to *lui donner de l'Excellence* on the envelope. I don't want *faire une bévue* and, after all, I know him very little. And *à propos,* what do you think of the Yankee Conquistadores in Panama? Pretty, isn't it? *Enfin!*

Veuillez présenter mes devoirs les plus respectueux à Madame votre Femme.

Borys instructed me to send his love to you. Jessie's kind regards.

Tout à vous.

To H. G. Wells

7th Feb. 1904.
17 Gordon Place,
Kensington.
London, W.

MY DEAREST H. G.,

I am a kickable person for not letting out a squeak about myself for you. But we've been in a sort of tempest ever since our arrival here.

Jessie fell in the street and wrenched both her knees. No joke to her and an awful anxiety to me. However, she gets on very well but no doubt expensively. Watson & Co.[3] failed and I've lost a good friend, for he did back me up through all these years. Of course, I shall be bothered now about my overdraft and so on. No matter. I've been working at *Nostromo,* besides writing a play in one act (based on my "To-morrow" story) on the suggestion of S. Colvin,[4] who has been very friendly. Another acquaintance which I owe to you, my dear fellow, in the long list of your good offices.

I've started a series of sea sketches [5] and have sent out P.[inker] on

---

[1] Joseph Conrad, as has been stated, spent six months in Africa, in 1890.

[2] Santiago Perez Triana, diplomat and author, then the Colombian Minister in London and Madrid.

[3] J. C.'s bankers.

[4] Sir Sidney Colvin.

[5] The first chapters of *The Mirror of the Sea.*

the hunt to place them. This must save me. I've discovered that I can dictate that sort of bosh without effort at the rate of 3,000 words in four hours. Fact. The only thing now is to sell it to a paper and then make a book of the rubbish. Hang!

So in the day *Nostromo* and, from 11 to 1 A. M., dictation. No more just now. We trust that you both and chicks are well. Our dear love.

To Arnold Bennett

Pent Farm.
Feb. 1904.

MY DEAR BENNETT,

Excuse typing. I haven't got into the way of writing after a bout of gout yet. As it happens I have dramatized "To-morrow" myself and I leave to your unbiased judgment to say which version—the English or French—is the more individual and artistic. Both MSS. go by book post.

Tree [1] has my play to look at through the agency of Sidney Colvin. Frankly, in my opinion, the French dramatization has for its only merit the evidently good knowledge of the English language. It is too long in exposition (and so is mine, I fear), and for the rest lacks force in dialogue. I think I could write something much more striking in French myself; but if, on reflection, you think it feasible to show my rendering to your friend, and he would like to translate it, accepting the spirit of my conception and letting me see the MS., I would of course agree to his terms, he working the French end of the business while I shall try to do something with it here, if no more but to secure a performance by the Dramatic Society. Colvin takes a great interest in the thing.

We have had a rough time of it generally, serious misfortunes hindering my work and destroying the peace of my soul, but I shall say nothing of them just now.

Many thanks for the trouble you have taken and apologies for suggesting more.

Believe me, my dear Bennett,
With great regard.

You will notice my play has full stage directions.
It makes it long in reading, rather.
Tree has a slightly shortened version and therefore an improved

[1] Sir Herbert Beerbohm Tree.

one—but there was only one copy of it. The fisherman is cut down considerably, also old Carvil at the very beginning. A situation or rather action which repeats itself is eliminated in one place. That one would be the version to translate. But in essentials *this is* the play.

To H. G. Wells

Pent Farm.
Wednesday to Friday. [1904]

DEAREST WELLS,

It is not likely to occur to a daily reviewer, who would be more concerned with the text and not critical as to the attitude of the writer. Moreover it is absurd to suppose that the best of daily reviewers could possibly feel the interest I have in the book,[1] a jealous care, as it were, that its appeal should not appear narrowed by any chance phrase.

Practically, for the moment, the thing is without importance. People are concerned with your views and your suggestions—to approve or to combat. I however (with my man in view) have looked at the *tactics* of what seems to me the opening of a campaign on your part. For this is what in the last and most general pronouncement the book amounts to. It is—and as a matter of fact the whole tone of it implies that—it is a *move*. Where the move to my apprehension seems un-sound is in this, that it seems to presuppose—or even to establish—a sort of select circle to which you address yourself, leaving the rest of the world outside the pale. It seems as if they had to *come in* into a rigid system, whereas I submit that Wells should *go forth,* not dropping fishing lines for particular trout but casting a wide and generous net, where there would be room for everybody; where indeed every sort of fish would be welcome, appreciated and made use of. Your first few pages proclaim an intellectual exclusiveness—and also an exclusiveness of feeling which (legitimate as it may be) can also serve your sincerity at the expense of truth. However this [is] a larger consideration which I do not wish now to pursue. But practically from the point of view of efficiency an exclusive attitude is always a disadvantage; and in social work especially, since it leads straight to clique'ism, to the formation of a select circle of disciples, to a fatal limiting of influence.

Why should you say that you write only for people who think this or that: Who feel this or the other thing? And if you even think so—and so intend—there is no necessity to *say* so. That's what I mean by saying that such a declaration serves your sincerity at the

[1] Probably *A Modern Utopia.*

expense of the truth—which is in you to expand and propagate. After all, why should you preach to people already convinced? That sort of thing leads only to a sort of high priesthood in a clique and it should be left to people who seek simply the satisfaction of their vanity. It is just to the unbelievers that you should preach; and believe me that no one is so benighted (emotionally or rationally) not to be spoken to with some effect by *him* who can speak. And that you *can* speak is a fact that cannot be questioned. No one's position is too absurd to be argued with. An enlightened egoism is as valid as an enlightened altruism—neither more nor less. The principle of absolutism did not fail to maintain itself because there is anything absurd in absolutism, but because autocrats had made themselves unbearable through a sheer want of intelligence. And that is the danger. However I am going off the line here. The immediate practical danger of which I am thinking is lest it should suddenly be said, "Ah yes, The New Republicans— these are the people who look at the world as a breeding place." Each system runs that sort of danger, and my idea is that it should be mini- mized by an initial reticence. Generally the fault I find with you is that you do not take sufficient account of human imbecility which is cunning and perfidious.

You see this is not criticism; indeed it has nothing to do with the book. This view occurred to me and I put it before you, rather obscurely, because upon my word I am not well enough to think in an orderly way.

So here I end, trusting that your feeling won't be that I had better mind my own business.

I would dearly love a talk with you. If you come (as I hope you will) on Monday or Tuesday, come to lunch. If you want to be met, say so by postcard or wire. And I would like the sight of a few repre- sentative cuttings, if you don't mind bringing them in your pocket. Jess sends her love to your wife, whom she could not visit because she has been nursing me ever since her last call.

Affectionately.

To R. B. Cunninghame Graham

Pent Farm.
18th May 1904.

TRÈS CHER AMI,
It is only from Pawling's letter to-day that I learn you are here. And first, my thanks for the brass censer-cup (I call it) which I

received some time ago. It is a thing I like—first with affection as coming from you and next from taste because it is brass for which I have a fondness. The form is good too. Is it meant for embers to light one's pipe? Or is it for burning perfumes? Anyway, it contains cigarettes now and stands at my elbow as I write or read.

Pawling's proposal of a joint article is fascinating. Whether it is practicable, that is another affair. I desire it to come off. The question hangs on your inclination and leisure. It would be jolly to have a day's sail, and a talk between sky and water: say starting from Deal in one of their galleys through the Downs and round Nth Foreland to Margate Roads. But I am afraid it would bore you to death. And in such promenades there is always too much sun,—or not enough; too little wind,—or else a confounded, unnecessary blast: and yet, now and then, one falls upon a perfect day. Is your luck good? I mean that propitious fortune of which Sylla, the dictator, was the spoilt child. As to my luck, I prefer to say nothing of it. I am absolutely ashamed to mention it because if "Fortune favours the brave," I must be about the poorest sort on earth. *Enfin!*

Do let me know how you are. I presume you've been in Morocco. Rothenstein could not tell me—only the other day. *Il est artiste celui-là —et pas bête. N'est-ce pas?*

Kindest regards from us all.
Tout à vous.

To William Rothenstein

Pent Farm,
27th June 1904.

MY DEAR ROTHENSTEIN,

I work desperately but slow—much too slow for the situation. I am unable to say whether moving from home would put me off or not. I fear it would. I don't know. I dare do nothing. Either my soul or my liver is very sick. If it is the liver then the cold shall make it worse. Even here I go about shuddering when a cloud passes over the sun. And I am tired, tired as if I had lived a hundred years.

It is late,—and to-morrow is another dread day. C. Graham has been here for the Sunday and we talked much of you. He was in very good form and very friendly, but the episode of his visit has not refreshed me as much as I expected. I am not myself and shall not be myself till I am born again after *Nostromo* is finished.

Our dear love to you four people. *Je tombe de fatigue.*

To R. B. Cunninghame Graham

Pent Farm.
2 July 1904.

TRÈS CHER AMI,

Cigarettes came first and the two books followed. You are very good. Your too short visit has been a God-send. You've left me believing once more in the reality of things.

Hudson's *Sparrow* is really first rate and just in the tone I expected. *C'est une belle nature,* which never falls short in its domain. One can depend upon him.

The other volume I've been reading with a surprised admiration. It shall be an abiding delight—I see that much. But I don't pretend to have seen *everything* as yet. The sheer interest in themes and workmanship stand as yet in the way of deeper appreciation. One must read oneself into the true quality of the book.

And so poor Watts [1] is coming to the end of his august career. What a full and rounded life. And yet it seems poor in stress and passion, which are the true elixirs against the majestic overpowering tediousness of an existence full of allegoric visions. *Dieu nous préserve de cette grandeur!* Better be born a lord,—a king,—better die archpriest of an incredible religion.

My wife sends her kind regards and Borys his love. The cricket set is a great and big success.

Tout à vous.

Veuillez me rappeler au gracieux souvenir de Madame votre Mère dont je n'oublierai jamais le bienveillant accueil.

To (Sir) Edmund Gosse

Pent Farm.
19th Aug. 1904.

MY DEAR MR. GOSSE,

It has come to my isolated ears that it is given out at large, that it is said,—in what exact words I don't know, but said in effect, that: "Pinker deals harshly with Conrad." Such a statement injurious to Pinker, becomes by implication an aspersion upon Conrad in a way which I need not point out to your insight. I suppose that anything may be said (and even believed) of a man who has not a large balance at his bankers. The only thing worth consideration is: who says and who believes.

---

[1] G. F. Watts, the artist.

Without troubling to trace what is said to its source, I am extremely anxious that you should not believe it. Therefore were it to reach you (as it well may, since it has reached even me) *je vous prie de n'en rien croire. Cela n'est pas!*

I have no taint in my character either of vice, indolence or subserviency which could ever make me the victim of such a situation as is implied in that piece of baseless gossip. And on the other hand, my good friend Pinker—tho' he does not advertise himself by a volume of adulation from "men of letters"!—is neither stupid nor a man without a conscience: as that same gossip would imply also. For it would be a very stupid move to "deal harshly with Conrad." His conscience I'll leave in his hands, where I think it is in good keeping.

He has known me for six years. He has stepped gallantly into the breach left open by the collapse of my bank: and not only gallantly, but successfully as well. He has treated not only my moods but even my fancies with the greatest consideration. I would not dream of wearying you with details and figures: but his action, distinctly, has not been of a mercenary character. He cannot take away the weariness of mind which at the end of ten years of strain has come upon me; but he has done his utmost to help me to overcome it by relieving the immediate material pressure,—and the even more disabling pressure of human stupidity. But let that pass! How much can he expect in return for these services? I don't know. But I fear I am not a "profitable" man for anybody's speculation.

I venture to write thus openly, because the world is aware of the benevolent interest you take in my work. As to my personality, I am quite conscious of its insignificance but very little concerned as to what it is. But I may say this much for it: that any sort of underhand dealing is utterly revolting to it by tradition, by training and by nature.

I ought to apologize for troubling you with my handwriting: but as it is a question of sentiment turning on loyalty to a man and on fidelity to the truth of facts, I am sure not only of your indulgence but of your approval.

Believe me, my dear Mr. Gosse, with many feelings of which the note is sincerity, very faithfully yours.

To John Galsworthy

Pent Farm,
1st Sept 1904

DEAREST JACK!

Finished![1] finished! on the 30th in Hope's[2] house in Stanford in Essex, where I had to take off my brain that seemed to turn to water.

---

[1] *Nostromo.*   [2] G. F. W. Hope.

hung brighter than a
man of silver in the
moonlight, in that cry
of a longing heart
sending its never ceasing
vibration into a sky
empty of stars, the
genius of the magnificent
Capataz de Cargadores
dominated the place.

The End

30th Aug. 1904

J. Conrad-le-Hope

The last page of the first draft of "Nostromo".

For a solid fortnight I've been sitting up. And all the time horrible toothache. On the 27th had to wire for dentist (couldn't leave the work) who came at 2 and dragged at the infernal thing which seemed rooted in my very soul. The horror came away at last, leaving however one root in the gum. Then he grubbed for *that* till I leapt out of the chair. Thereupon old Walton said: "I don't think your nerves will stand any more of this."

I went back to my MS. at six P.M. At 11.30 something happened— what it is, I don't know. I was writing, and raised my eyes to look at the clock. The next thing I know I was sitting (not lying) on the concrete outside the door. When I crawled in I found it was nearly one. I managed to get upstairs and said to Jessie: "We must be off to-morrow." I took 30 drops of chlorodyne,—and slept till 7. Sydney went off on his bike to Ashford at 8.30, and at 10 the motor car was in the yard: a 12 h. p. Darracq. I sat by the man's side like a corpse. Between Canterbury and Faversham he said to me. "You look ill, sir, shall I stop?" Sittingbourne I remember as a brandy and soda. Good road. Steady 24 miles an hour. In Chatham, street crowded, packed. Going dead slow knocked down a man,—old chap, apparently a bricklayer. Crowd around cursing and howling. Helped him to my front seat and I standing on step got him to the hospital in 10 minutes. No harm. Only shaken. Saw him all comfy in bed for the rest of the day.

In Rochester, Hope waiting for us. Had something to eat,—and *tasted it too,* for the first time in 10 days. On crossing the river, began to revive on the ferry. Jessie very good and Borys quite a man watching over Mama's "poor leg" and warning off porters with luggage. At five, in sight of Stanford-le-Hope Railway station, petrol gave out. Man ran on and ran back with two gallon tin.

That night I slept. Worked all day. In the evening dear Mrs. Hope (who is not used to that sort of thing) gave me four candles and I went on. I finished at 3. Took me another half-hour to check the numbering of the pages, write a letter to P. and so on.

I had not the heart to write to you that same night nor yet the next day. Wasn't sure I would survive. But I have survived extremely well. I feel no elation. The strain has been too great for that. But I am quite recovered and ready for work again. There can be no stoppage till end of November when the Sketches'll be finished.[1] And then, I fancy, something will have to be done to get away.

I was with Pinker yesterday talking matters over. If I had known your Hampstead address I would have wired you. There is wanting

---

[1] The Sea Sketches: viz: *The Mirror of the Sea.*

to the finish of this undertaking the sanction of your presence and voice.

Drop me a line. Come down if you can! But I hardly dare to suggest that.

I don't know how you are, how everybody is.

I'll write to you soon. Love from all.

To Edward Garnett

Pent Farm,
3 Sept. 1904.

MY DEAR EDWARD,

I drop you these lines just to say that *Nostromo* is finished; a fact upon which my friends may congratulate me as upon a recovery from a dangerous illness. Therefore I am writing to dear Jack Galsworthy, to you and . . . but there do not seem to be many more friends whose congratulations would be enlightened enough for such an occasion.

Your article in the *Spectator* [1] in which you beat a dummy called Benson with a stick called Rutherford [2] is, as an exercise in whacking, simply admirable. It is something more too, since it has made me take down from the shelf the *Revolution in Tanner's Lane*. Your stick, my dear boy, has a queer aspect of a mediæval staff already. But it's good and more than good. It's precious wood of straight fibre and with a faint, delicate scent. But I regret the dissipation of your energy, the waste of vigour, and the sound of divine blows lost in an unresonant medium. No dust is seen to fly. There is no dust, even, in the dummy. Not so much truth as there would be in a handful of dust. Nothing! For I have looked on the dummy too with a malicious pleasure and a melancholy curiosity. Alas! This is what we are all coming to—at least what I am coming to. A few days later I saw (and read) in the *Standard* a warm and gentlemanly appreciation of the dumminess of your dummy. Amen! And I beheld the bald summit of my ambition. Some day I shall write a thing that'll be reviewed thus and not otherwise. Then in the dead of night, in the woods about the Cearne, wearing the cope and the pointed mitre of a High Priest, in the secrecy of a persecuted faith, by the light of a torch held by David clad in the white vestments—you shall bury my tame and impotent soul. You'll

[1] *The Speaker* is meant: which a little while before, in July, had published Conrad's article on Anatole France.
[2] Mark Rutherford.

bury it alive—by God!—and go home smiling ironically, and sleep no more that night.

Meantime, what do you think of the subject on the enclosed piece of paper?[1] Will the public stand it? Can my tact and sense of the proprieties be trusted on that classical theme?

My love to you all.

P. S. Send me back the scrap, please—with a word of how you are.

To William Rothenstein

Pent Farm
3rd Sept. 1904

MY DEAR ROTHENSTEIN,

The book is finished:[2] it has been finished for a couple of days now, but I have been too tired, to flat to write to you at once. The last month I worked practically night and day, going to bed at three and sitting down again at nine. All the time at it, with the tenacity of despair.

What the book is like, I don't know. I don't suppose it'll damage me: but I know that it is open to much intelligent criticism. For the other sort I don't care. Personally I am not satisfied. It is something,—but not *the* thing I tried for. There is no exultation, none of that temporary sense of achievement which is so soothing. Even the mere feeling of relief at having done with it is wanting. The strain has been too great, has lasted too long.

But I am ready for more. I don't feel empty, exhausted. I am simply joyless,—like most men of little faith. To see you would do me good. I count the days. I must take Jessie to London to see Watson Hood. I am sorry to say that her heart seems to be troubling her again of late. She is very cheery however. Your dear wife's letter has brightened her up.

Plans of work with ideas of getting away for the winter jostle in my head. I won't say anything more now. Only, our dear love to you four people with the hope of meeting you soon for a day or so.

To R. B. Cunninghame Graham

Pent Farm.
7th Oct. 1904.

TRÈS CHER AMI,

I forgive you (generously) the treacherous act of looking at a frag-

---

[1] This was a sketch of a Napoleonic subject. (Edward Garnett's note.)
[2] *Nostromo*.

ment of *Nostromo*.[1] On your side you must (generously) forgive me for stealing and making use in the books of your excellent *"y dentista"* anecdote. The story comes out on Thursday next. Don't buy it. I'll send you a copy, of—and in due,—course. I expect as by right and in virtue of our friendship an abusive letter from you upon it: but I stipulate a profound and unbroken secrecy of your opinion as before everybody else. I feel a great humbug.

I am glad to hear you are in possession of your new house. I wondered where you were. Hudson [2] imagined you in Morocco. I met him the other day: dear as ever but a little depressed.

I notice there is no date yet to the advertisement of your next (Duckworth) volume.[3]

I don't suppose you'll remain very long now in the "black North." We are contemplating a flight somewhere for the winter. Capri perhaps? *Quien sabe!* Don Pietro Canonico Ferraro, I hear, lets half his house and terrace with a south exposure above a grove of orange trees,—and so on. It may be worth trying.

Our kindest regards. I am on the point of taking Jessie to London to the doctors. *C'est triste.*

To R. B. Cunninghame Graham

99b, Addison Rd. London, W.
31st Oct. 1904.

TRÈS CHER ET BON AMI,

Your letter was indeed worth having and I blush deeply as I re-read it both with pleasure and shame. For in regard to that book I feel a great fraud.[4]

What is done cannot be mended. I know that you have made the most of my audacious effort: but still it is to me a comfort and a delight that you have found so much to say in commendation. Your friendship and good nature, great as they are where my person and scribbling are concerned, would not have induced you to accept anything utterly contemptible,—that I know. It is a great load off my chest. Now as to an explanation or two.

---

[1] *Nostromo* appeared in serial form in *T. P.'s Weekly;* it ran from January 29, 1904, to the very day of the above letter, Oct. 7th, and was published in book form by Harper & Brothers in November of the same year.

[2] W. H. Hudson.

[3] *Progress,* which was published during the next year.

[4] It refers to *Nostromo.*

I don't defend Nostromo himself. Fact is he does not take my fancy either. As to his conduct generally and with women in particular, I only wish to say that he is not a Spaniard or S. American. I tried to differentiate him even to the point of mounting him upon a mare, which I believe is not or *was not* the proper thing to do in Argentine: though in Chile there was never much of that nonsense. But truly N is nothing at all,—a fiction, embodied vanity of the sailor kind,—a romantic mouthpiece of the "people" which (I mean "the people") frequently experience the very feelings to which he gives utterance. I do not defend him as a creation.

Costaguana is meant for a S. American state in general; thence the mixture of customs and expressions. *C'est voulu.* I remembered but little and rejected nothing.

"Mi alma" is a more serious mistake. I've heard a little girl so address a pet small dog as they swung in a hammock together. What missed me was this, that in Polish that very term of endearment, "My soul," has not the passionate significance you point out. I am crestfallen and so sorry.

Pasotrote I've heard somehow, somewhere, from someone,—devil knows where.[1] But the mistake is in the word canter which I wrote persistently, while I really meant *amble,* I believe. I am appalled simply.

I am compunctious as to the use I've made of the impression produced upon me by the Ex. Sr Don Perez Triana's personality. Do you think I have committed an unforgivable fault there? He'll never see or hear of the book probably.

I end with a general apology for ever attempting a tale of this kind; and with the renewed assurance of the great pleasure your good long letter has given me. It is a very magnificent sign of forgiveness on your part. *Tout à vous de cœur.*

P. S. My wife sends her kind regards. She is not at all well and I am very anxious. Borys too has been in bed a week now. Tonsillitis. The temperature went up to 103 on two nights. But he is mending, I am glad to say. Rothenstein likes the book. He got hold of the inwards with an amazing intelligence. E. Garnett likewise wrote me a most appreciative letter. As to the public, it will turn its back on it no doubt.

Ce sera un four complet. I don't care.

---

[1] It ought to be "pasitrote."

To Mrs. John Galsworthy

[Undated] 1904.

MY DEAR MRS. GALSWORTHY,

This preface [1] is not worthy the excellence of your translation. Really it is not. I am quite miserable about it. However, I've expanded a couple of paragraphs, whether for better or worse, I don't know. I was struck with dismay at the horrid bareness of the thing. I don't suppose D'th [Duckworth] will object. After all it makes no difference to him if I drivel for a few lines more,—and the very first paragraph may be taken out if that's any help towards squeezing the thing into the allotted space. Pray tell them that, and I trust you will do me a comrade's favour by seeing the revise for punctuation and grammar and sense. I never thanked you for your letter, but Heaven's my witness I was ashamed to take it unto myself.

I am always your most faithful friend and servant.

[1] "Preface" means the Preface written by Conrad for a volume of translations of Maupassant stories, *Yvette and Other Stories,* by Mrs. John Galsworthy.

END OF VOLUME I